CALVIN LITTLEJOHN

PORTRAIT OF A COMMUNITY IN BLACK AND WHITE

CALVIN LITTLEJOHN

PORTRAIT OF A COMMUNITY IN BLACK AND WHITE

BOB RAY SANDERS

FOREWORD BY DON CARLETON

A joint project of TCU Press • Fort Worth, Texas
and The Dolph Briscoe Center for American History • Austin, Texas

Library of Congress Cataloging-in-Publication Data

Littlejohn, Calvin, 1909-1993.
Calvin Littlejohn : portrait of a community in black and white /
foreword by Don Carleton ; Bob Ray Sanders.

p. cm.

ISBN 978-0-87565-381-5 (cloth : alk. paper)
1. African Americans--Texas--Fort Worth--History--20th century--Pictorial works.
2. African Americans--Texas--Fort Worth--Social conditions--20th century--Pictorial works.
3. Littlejohn, Calvin, 1909-1993.
I. Carleton, Don, 1947- II. Sanders, Bob Ray. III. Title.

F394.F7L88 2009

976.4'531500496073--dc22 2009002351

TCU Press
P.O. Box 298300
Fort Worth, Texas 76129
817.257.7822
http://www.prs.tcu.edu
To order books: 800.826.8911

Designed by Whittington & Co., Austin, Texas

Printed in China

First edition

DEDICATION

For his tireless effort in helping to preserve his grandfather's remarkable collection of photographs and negatives, and for his commitment to make those images accessible to the larger public, we dedicate this book to Ron Abram, his sister, Michelle Abram-Hogan and his twelve-year-old daughter, Kristen, who undoubtedly would make her great-granddad proud.

We also publish this work in honor of Ron's father, W. B. Abram, and in memory of his mother, the late Bobbie Jean Abram, who was Mr. Littlejohn's daughter and a longtime educator in the Fort Worth School District.

And, because Calvin Littlejohn loved his adopted home and its people so much, we especially dedicate this publication of his work to the black community of Fort Worth who absolutely cherished the man with the camera.

CONTENTS

ACKNOWLEDGMENTS

While consulting on this project has been a labor of love for me, this book would not exist had it not been for the foresight, passion, and commitment of the people at the TCU Press, namely director Judy Alter, editor Susan R. Petty, and production manager Melinda Esco. Their determination—and Judy's steady, guiding hand throughout—kept all of us motivated and on task.

Special thanks also go to the folk at the Dolph Briscoe Center for American History at The University of Texas at Austin where the tens of thousands of images created by Calvin Littlejohn are archived. The meticulous cataloguing and identification of the photographs, the pinpointing of dates and the magnificent job of overseeing the reproduction of the photos will be forever cherished. My deepest gratitude is extended to all of you, but especially Dr. Don Carleton, executive director; Erin Purdy, associate director of communications; and Dr. Holly Taylor, editor and head of publications.

Mr. Littlejohn's visual work speaks for itself, but thanks to two special men, we were able to include the photographer's voice in this book. I'm most grateful to my friend and longtime colleague Alan Govenar, director of Documentary Arts, Inc., and co-founder of the Texas African American Photography Archives in Dallas, and to John Wheat, another of those remarkable individuals at the Dolph Briscoe Center for American History, where he is archives translator. Their interview of Mr. Littlejohn, recorded just two years before his death, was an invaluable source about the man, the place, and the times. Alan, author of Portraits of Community: African American Photography in Texas *(1996), for years has been a collector and documentarian of black photography in Texas and folk art throughout the country.*

The book certainly would not have been as complete without the extraordinary and loving efforts of some native and/or longtime Fort Worth residents who spent hours helping to identify many of the faces pictured in Mr. Littlejohn's work. So, a very special thanks to Sarah Walker, Opal Lee, Revodia Johnson, Marjorie Crenshaw, Lonnell Cooper, and Beverly Brown Washington. Of course, I must acknowledge my wife, Dorothy, and son, Chandon, who understood how important this project was to me, and were most patient as I spent more and more time trying to produce it.

FOREWORD

The mission of the Dolph Briscoe Center for American History at the University of Texas at Austin is to collect, preserve, and make available documentary and material culture evidence encompassing key themes in Texas and U.S. history. Among its many historical treasures, the Briscoe Center holds more than 5 million photographic images from the late 1840s to the present, including the archives of leading photojournalists.

In 1994 the Briscoe Center and the Texas State Historical Association collaborated on the book *Behold the People: R. C. Hickman's Photographs of Black Dallas, 1949–1961*, which featured images from the Center's R. C. Hickman Photographic Archive. The success of that book and widespread interest in the collection led me to look for similar photographers in other cities in the hopes of adding to the Center's photography collections. About that same time, the family of Fort Worth photographer Calvin Littlejohn contacted me about the collection and the possibility of preserving it at the Center. After a few meetings, the Littlejohn family generously decided to donate to the Center the thousands of photographs he took over almost half a century. They had seen the Hickman book and hoped that one day the Littlejohn photographs would be showcased to make others aware of his extraordinary career.

The Calvin Littlejohn Photographic Archive consists of Littlejohn's professional work done primarily in the Fort Worth area, including studio portraits, group portraits at social gatherings, church services, school events, birthday parties, and other images documenting the African American experience in North Texas. The collection includes approximately 70,000 film negatives and 55,000 prints.

Like his contemporary, R. C. Hickman, Calvin Littlejohn photographed a racially segregated Texas community during an era of rapid change. He recorded the events, large and small, that marked the lives of ordinary people. For almost fifty years he photographed weddings, funerals, church services, high school football games, and everything in between, sometimes pictures of people at work, or at sporting events. He took children's school pictures every year. He took family portraits for Christmas cards. He recorded sorority meetings, birthday parties, and children hula-hooping.

If African American celebrities were in town to sing (such

as Ruth Brown), play ball (Jackie Robinson), or box (Joe Louis), he photographed them at hotels and people's homes. He photographed politicians and community activists too, from Harry Truman, Thurgood Marshall, and Martin Luther King to Jimmy Carter, Jesse Jackson, Hillary Clinton, and George W. Bush.

Calvin Littlejohn died in 1993, leaving an estate of thousands of photographs. Happily for historians and others interested in this community either Calvin Littlejohn or his wife, Lucretia ("Lou"), wrote notes about the negatives and prints on the envelopes they were stored in, which more often than not listed the name of the purchaser of the photographs, not necessarily the subject. After Littlejohn's death, his family added descriptive comments to some of the images, but most had very little information about the people and places in them.

Enter Bob Ray Sanders of the *Fort Worth Star-Telegram*. He was already on board with TCU Press to write the introduction for the book, but he also provided immeasurable help with the captions for the photographs. He met with and talked to people in the African American community in Fort Worth, people who had known Calvin Littlejohn and, more importantly, who recognized the people in the pictures. A note on the envelope of negatives said "Mrs. Cary's funeral." Thanks to Bob Ray and his sources, we now know her first name, her husband's and son's names, what church held the funeral, and that her son was the first black school board member in Fort Worth.

I hope that as people read this book they will be able to identify more of the people in it. Even unidentified, however, they still are known—the children who scowled at the photographer, the child who grinned by his birthday cake, the bride tossing a bouquet. It is this visual social history that brings these people and the world they lived in out of the shadows of the past and memory. The Briscoe Center houses many photography collections, and all of them have stories to tell.

I am pleased to have TCU Press as our partner on this book. Judy Alter and her highly skilled staff have worked hard and they have produced a wonderful book. I also want to thank Bob Ray Sanders for his invaluable contributions. And, of course, a special thank you to the Littlejohn family for their donation of the photographs and for their cooperation on this project to make the images available to a wider audience.

John Wheat, the Briscoe Center's sound archivist, conducted an oral history interview with Calvin Littlejohn a few years prior to the photographer's death. This interview, which is housed in the Center's Oral History Collection, allowed Calvin Littlejohn's voice to shine through and enabled him to contribute to this book.

Several Briscoe Center staff members worked on the Littlejohn project, and their efforts are deeply appreciated. Archivist Zach Vowell catalogued the collection, scanned many of the images and worked on the online exhibit. Lynn Bell curated an exhibit of Littlejohn photographs that was on display at the George Washington Carver Museum and Cultural Center in Austin during the summer of 2008. Holly Taylor, head of publications, selected the photos for publication and worked with Erin Purdy, associate director for communications, to coordinate the project with TCU Press. Photographic archivists Linda Peterson and Hal Richardson facilitated access to the collection and scanned many of the images. I convey a sincere thank you to all.

Don Carleton
Executive Director
Dolph Briscoe Center for American History
The University of Texas at Austin

"So one day I'd been to the store, and there I was on the way back. And a guy was up on one of them great big boards—the guy that changed the sign board—placing the sign up there. They'd gotten to the point, just about finished. And they laid that last lap down; it was the face of a black boy, with a big tooth out in front and his mouth wide open, eating a slice of watermelon... And I said, 'I'm gonna learn this, so I can—whenever I have a chance—I'm gonna show the best side of these people that's being rejected so.' And that was my mission. That's why I stayed with it, trying to learn something about it."

—*Calvin Littlejohn*

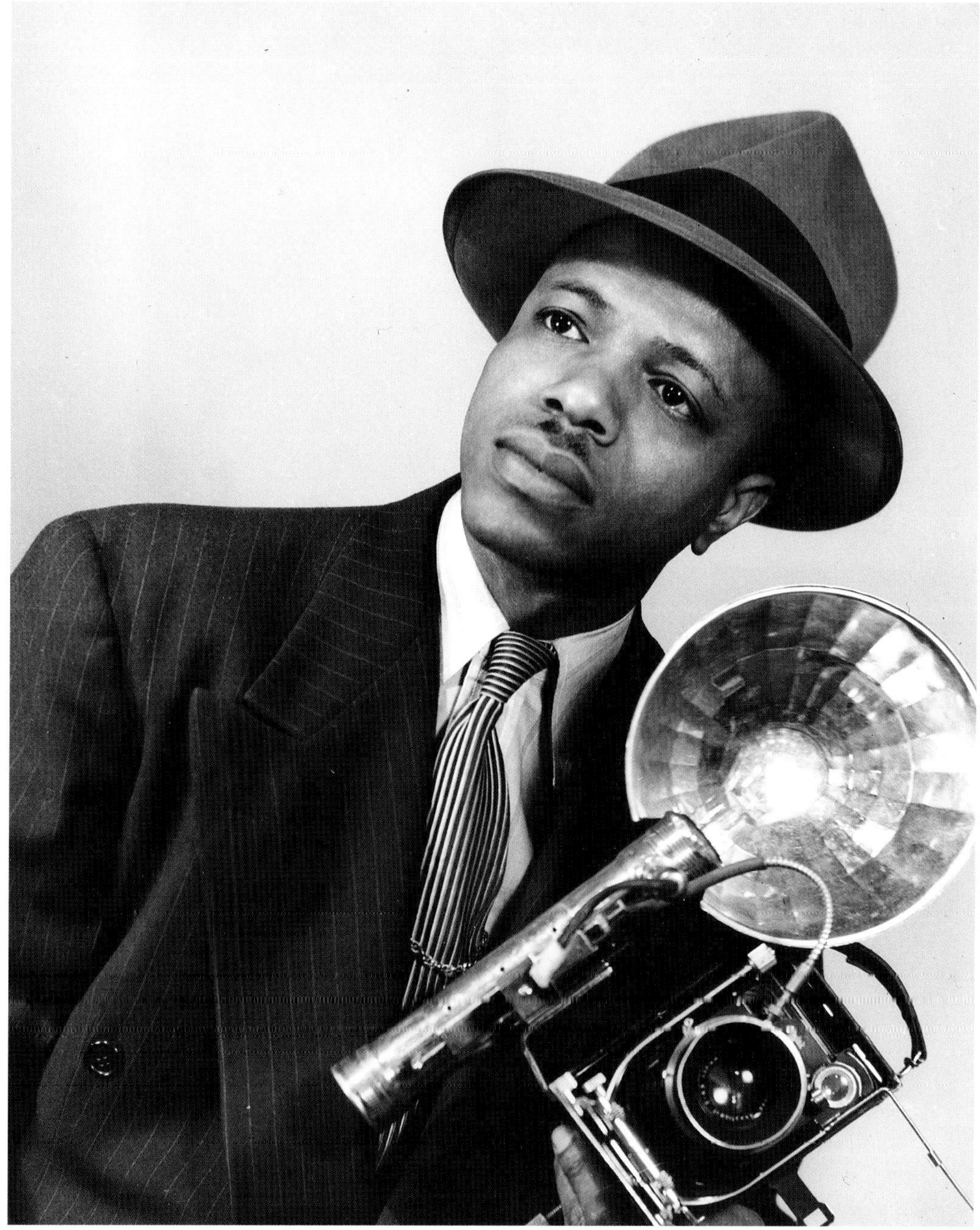

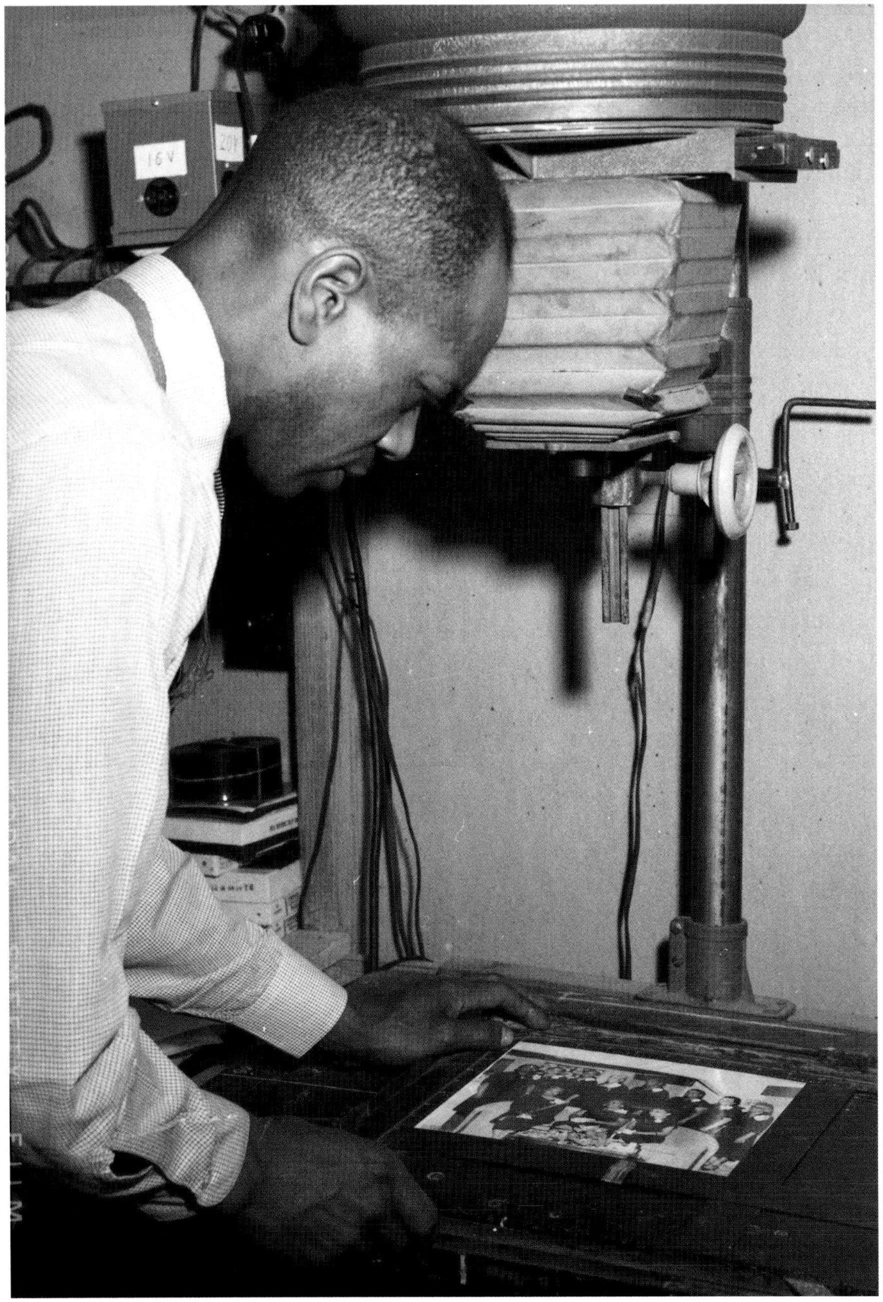

INTRODUCTION

The year 1934 would be memorable for many reasons. It was the year tyranny was on the rise in the world, with Adolf Hitler naming himself the Führer in Germany and Benito Mussolini firmly entrenched as dictator of Italy. In the United States, people found themselves gripped in the vice of the Great Depression, with many out of work and struggling by any means to feed their families. Well-known criminals were on the decline that year with the apprehensions or deaths of the notorious Baby Face Nelson, Pretty Boy Floyd, and John Dillinger and, of course, the violent ambush of admired bank robbers, Bonnie and Clyde.

Despite the turmoil around the world and tensions in America, a radio show—with white actors who later performed in black face—still had the country laughing at the antics of *Amos 'n' Andy*. Even those folk who were born with black faces, during times of segregation and discrimination and bad economies, had reasons to be happy and thankful: for family, opportunity (although limited) and well-connected,

Left: Calvin Littlejohn in his studio working with photographic enlarger.

though struggling, communities.

Fort Worth, Texas, was a sleepy little "big" city of just over 167,000 population in 1934, the year Calvin Littlejohn, a slender young black man from Arkansas, came to town as a servant for a white family. Almost immediately he began what would become a lifelong career of serving the black community. And there would be nothing remotely related to the depictions of *Amos 'n' Andy* or black kids grinning over a slice of watermelon in Littlejohn's portrayal of his adopted home and the people he came to appreciate and love.

The city in Texas was quite different from his rural upbringing in Arkansas where he had been raised mostly by a grandfather, a former slave who proved to be a shrewd and industrious businessman, but who also would fall victim to the times, the economy, and a fateful accident that would force the young Littlejohn to assume adult responsibilities before becoming a teenager.

Littlejohn, who perhaps always felt a connection to Texas because of his grandfather's history, was born in Cotton Plant, Arkansas, in 1909. His grandparents had been born slaves in Kentucky, but during and after the Civil War slave owners tried to hold on to their human property by moving them south into Louisiana and southeast Texas.

As a teenager, Littlejohn said, his grandfather had a great interest in the cowboys he had met in Texas and wanted to know more about horses and cows, and eventually "made his way up the east coast of Texas as a horse trader." After arriving in Texarkana, the grandfather, who could not read nor write, learned that homesteads were available where an individual could buy a "section of land" (640 acres) for $3,000. He purchased acreage in the Cash River Bottom area of northeastern Arkansas.

Because it was bottom land, most of it would flood each year, but the high ground was abundant with a variety of timber, fruit trees, grapes, and berries. He made a good living off of the 150 or so cleared acres and would later sell 490 acres at a great profit. In rural Arkansas, he was considered a wealthy black man who was respected for his keen business sense and accomplishments.

Grandpa took care of his children until they were adults, and then he expected them to make it on their own, Littlejohn told an interviewer once. When he "came along," Littlejohn said his father disowned him and his mother died when he was nine, leaving him to be cared for by his grandparents. He was a "bright-eyed" curious youngster who was obedient and ran errands for his granddad such as fetching and shining his shoes. Those chores, he said, naturally fell on him because the granddad's youngest son was fourteen years older than his grandson, Calvin.

Young Calvin was able to remember a few of the good days, recalling especially that his grandfather had the "Cadillac" of the day, "a surrey with a fringe on top." But it didn't take long before the worst would come. "I was there [the] year when he met an accident," Littlejohn told oral history interviewers. "He was a 32nd Degree Mason; he went to make some men—you know how they make men—on a Saturday night. On his way back, about one or two o'clock, his mule fell with him. And he rammed, and rammed that horn of the saddle right in his gut and tore him up. He became a semi-invalid.

"When they brought him home he couldn't do too much, you know, on the farm at that time. I had to increase my responsibility at nine: feed and tend the horses and all that kind of thing. So, he decided, living seven miles from town, that he needed to move closer to town to have some place to stay where he could go to the doctor and all that kind of thing. So he opted to buy a twenty-acre piece of land in town with a little house. He remodeled it into a bungalow."

Shortly after getting the small house in order, Littlejohn said there was a mysterious happening. "The bank bust," he said. "And the story—you know the story from there on. Lost every cock-eyed dime he had, 'cause he had all of his money in the bank."

At age fourteen Littlejohn said he had become responsible for the welfare of the entire family because all of his grandfather's children were gone and "they ain't thinking about coming back." On one hand, that experience would be beneficial, but it also would be detrimental. "That's where I got my business experience," he said proudly. "I had to go and sell a little cotton, I had to go along and make the deal for borrowing the money, and putting the hay up and everything." He was in the ninth grade at the time and, unfortunately, his education suffered. Every spring in the month of March he had to quit school to start preparing the land for farming.

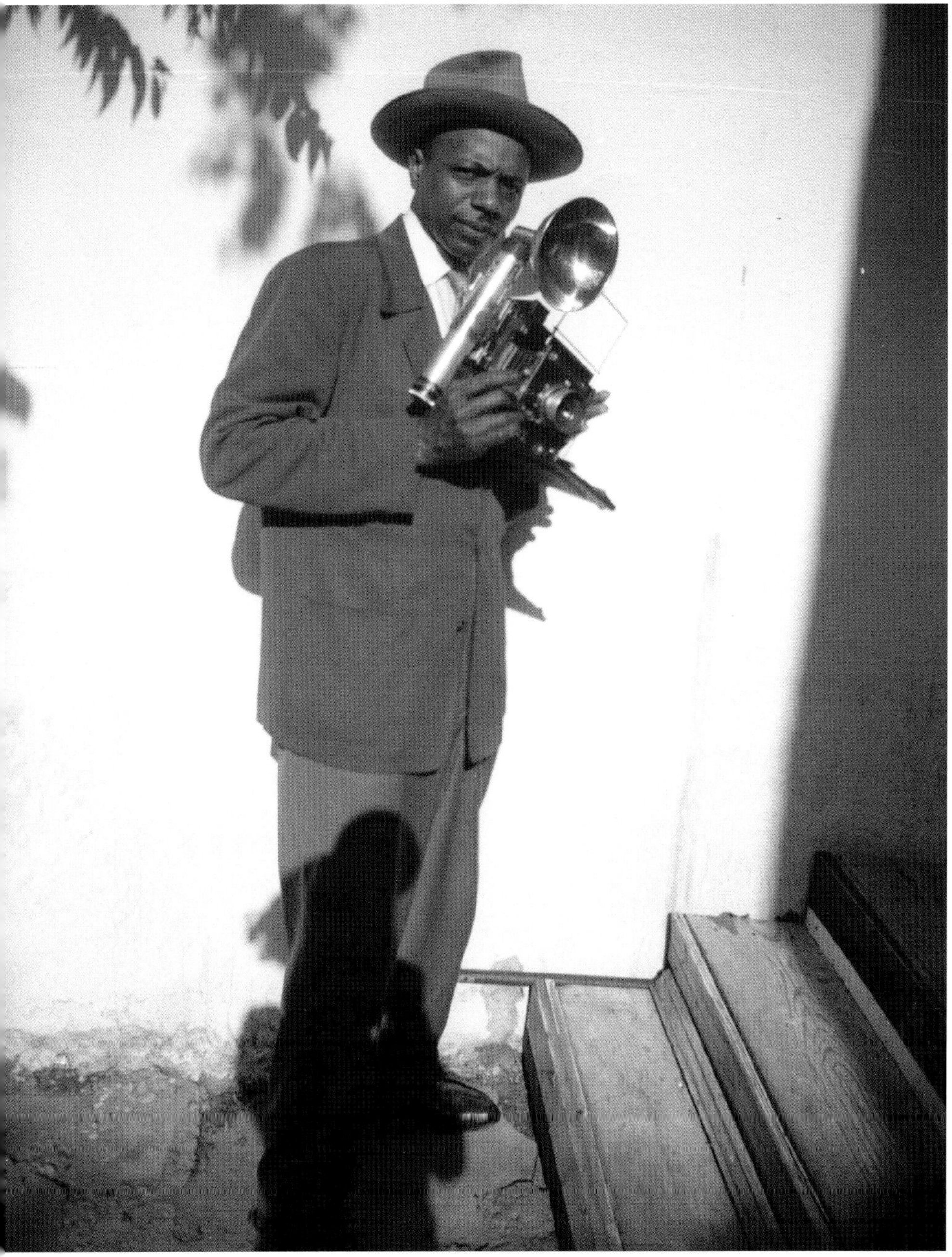

"Consequently, I could never—never could finish the school year," he said. "I stayed in the ninth grade for four years."

It was in that fourth year of the ninth grade that the grandfather, still seeing the potential in his grandson, encouraged the eighteen-year-old Calvin to get a job, make enough money for school and to go to college. Littlejohn got a $5-a-week domestic job (including room and board) with a local white family and made enough to pay for tuition at Philander Smith College in Little Rock where he would study commercial art. After all, he had a talent for drawing and he had taken a correspondence course in graphic art.

He also had been cunning and privileged enough to make his way into the domain of two local theaters where union craftsmen often were busy making sets for the proscenium stages. The curious young man began by asking simply to watch them work, but noticing his interest, the union workers—against union rules—gave him odd jobs to do.

"In 1933 there was no chance for me to join the union, see," Littlejohn recalled. "But they figured it out. They went

Left: Calvin Littlejohn holding his camera on the job. Photo by his wife, Lucretia Littlejohn.

down and complained to the boss they needed more money, they just had to have more money. And then they just—when they got the money they would cash it and they'd throw a little off to me and that's the way I got paid."

To and from his job with the union guys every day, he passed a photography studio which did enlargements. Littlejohn's natural curiosity and artistic interest led him into that photo shop where he got a job inscribing names and titles for the photos. As he asked questions about the difference in photography and graphic arts he was learning, the owner of the shop answered patiently and gave him lessons in the camera, lighting, and the use of shadows.

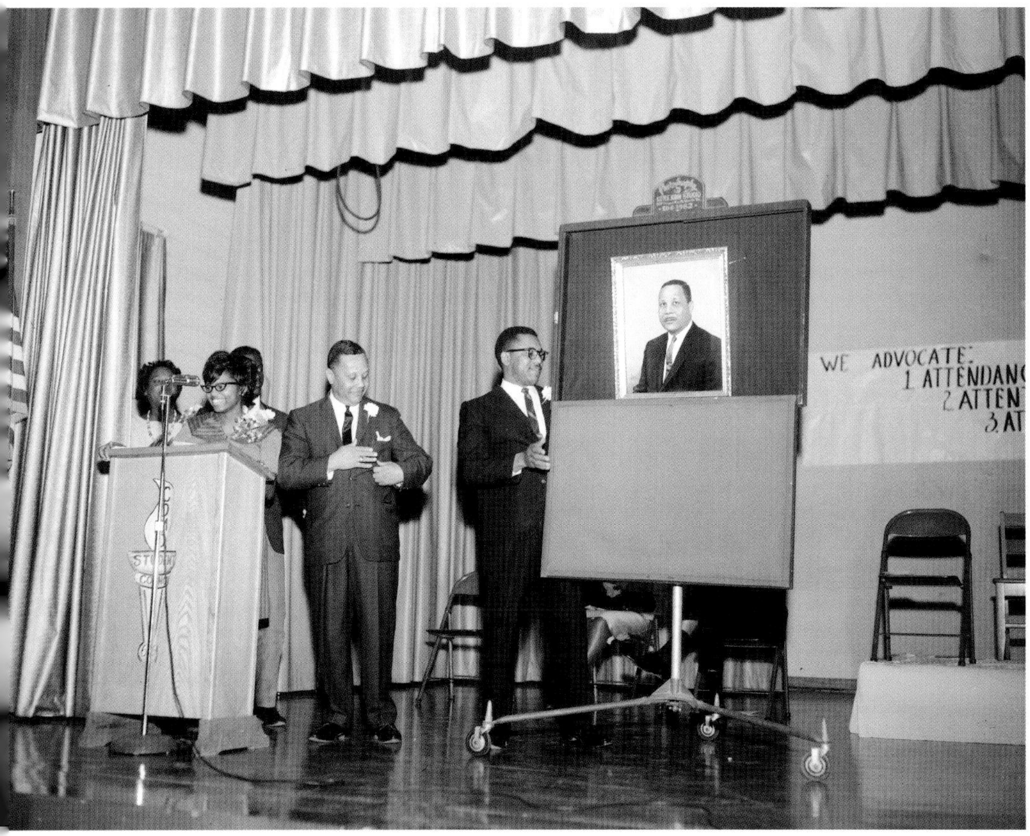

Still, these were tough times, and his domestic job played out when his employers decided to move to Texas. He couldn't find any other work in the small Arkansas town, so he persuaded his former employers to let him ride with them to Fort Worth where he would be able to look for work and, he said, "that's how I hoboed here with them."

Littlejohn continued to live with the family for a while and was so regarded by them that he was often referred to by the mother as her "fourth" child, surprising those who knew that she only had three children—two boys and a girl: Meyers, Richard, and Elizabeth. Visitors to the home would laugh when the mistress, while looking over the top of her cards during a bridge game, would point to young Calvin entering the house and say, "There's the fourth one."

Left: Como High School, unveiling of Calvin Littlejohn's portrait of Principal Oscar M. Williams, Jr., January 31, 1964. Principal Williams is on the left.

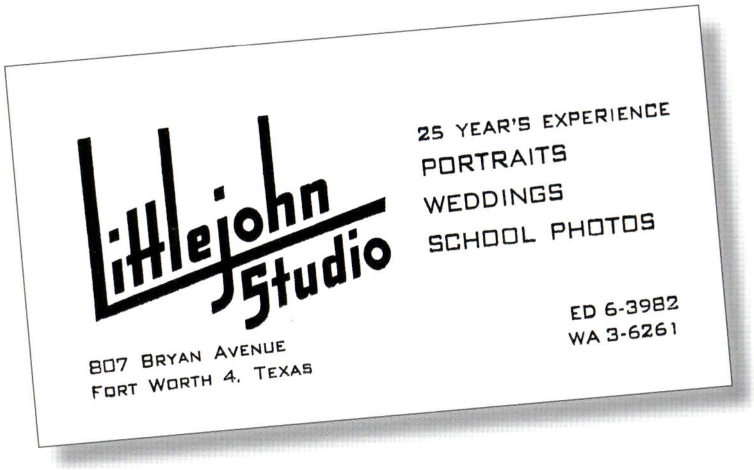

Left: Calvin Littlejohn's business card.

Littlejohn considered it a good life, being treated like another son in the family even though years later he would scoff at the "horrendous salary" he received: $3.50 a week, plus room and board. Actually, it was not bad money; in those days it was *good* money.

"Three fifty? Shoot, I paid my tuition at the college," he said with laughter in his voice. "And I bought me a suit—for $21. Paid a dollar a week on it."

A well-fitting suit complete with starched white shirt and tie, and short-brimmed hat would become his trademark, along with the camera and its detachable flash. He would become such an iconic figure in Fort Worth that he could be identified by simply looking at his shadow or silhouette.

Littlejohn even went to a cooking school in the Lake Como area of the city after the lady of the house bluntly told him he needed to be a better cook. There weren't many cooking jobs in hotels or restaurants at the time, so he went to work for another prominent Fort Worth family who had two young boys. "I was a nurse and a cook and a chauffeur, at $8 a week, and stayed in the servants' quarters, you see."

One Saturday while cleaning the house, he discovered in a closet a portrait of the woman's grandfather. As he gazed at the painting with an obvious look of intrigue, the woman came in and asked what he was doing. When he explained that he was a painter and simply was admiring the work, the woman said, "You're too ambitious." He quickly put everything back in its place and finished cleaning the house.

"Two weeks after that I was fired—out on the street," he said.

That may have been one of the best things to happen to him, and to black Fort Worth. Shortly afterward, Littlejohn rented space in the basement of a house and began painting landscapes which the landlord's son helped him sell.

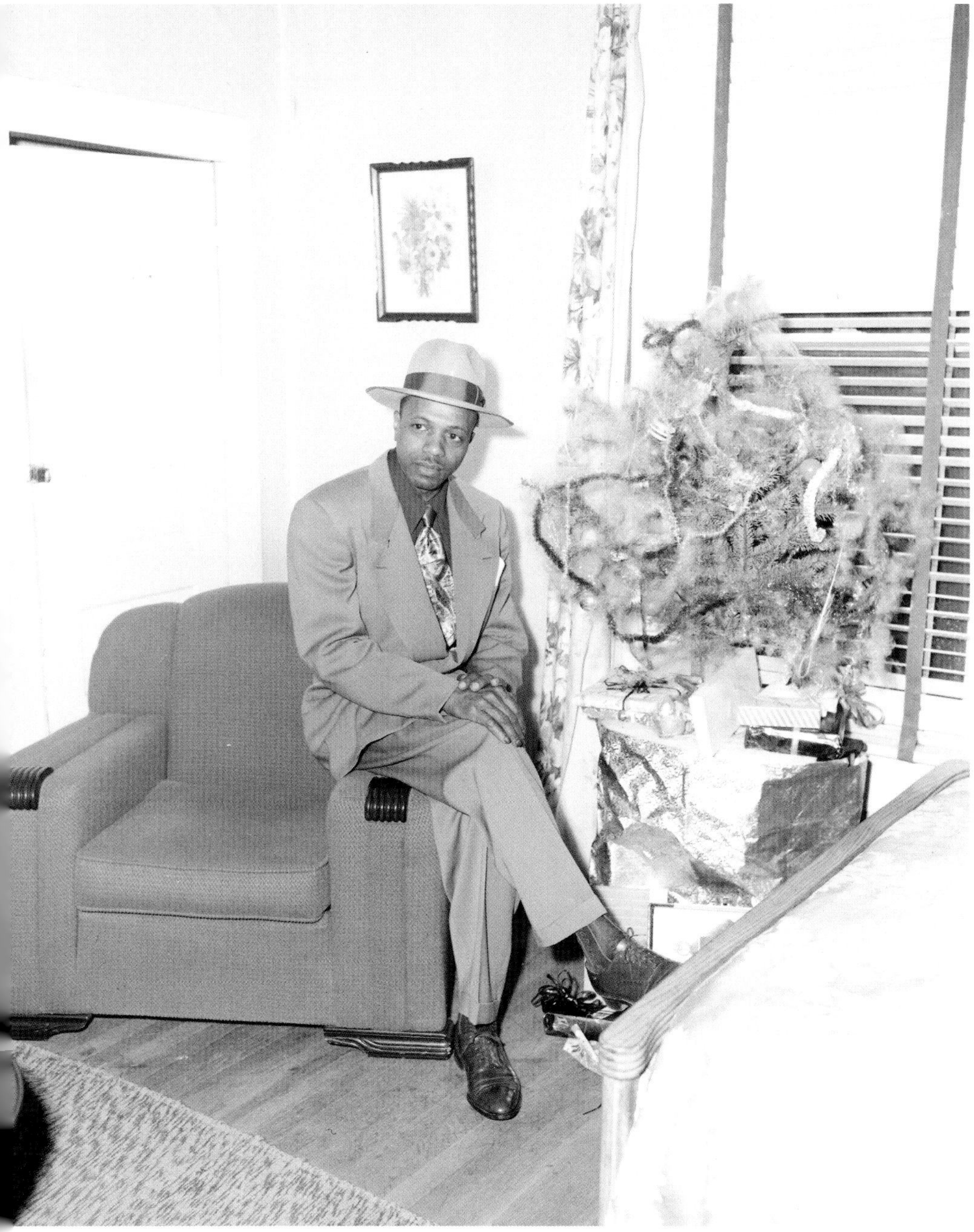

His work was being noticed, and he got a big break when an art teacher hired him to help prepare her students for an annual contest. That eventually led to a job with the school district, teaching in the industrial arts department.

Because the district only had one photographer, the only black high school in town, I. M. Terrell, was being neglected. Littlejohn was assigned to be its official photographer, including taking pictures for the yearbook and school newspaper. His professional career was launched, and he would soon open his first studio, located in his home.

"My first location was in my little quarters where I lived on Ninth Street," he said. "I lived in the same place, upstairs, on Ninth Street, when I opened my first professional studio. I lived there, I made the pictures there, and I had my little cot." He barely made enough money to pay the rent and the notes on his cameras, he said, because "for the simple reason I was the only professional black photographer that had been in Fort Worth, that they could remember." His clients simply were not accustomed to paying much money for photos.

Left: The photographer relaxing at home, Christmas 1950.

"I was hard beat to get them to understand, you know, that you could pay more than 50 cents for a picture."

During this time Fort Worth was like most other southern and Texas towns: segregated. But unlike many cities rooted in segregation, in which blacks lived only in one section, often across the railroad tracks, blacks in Cowtown lived in every quadrant of the city—north, south, east and west—and a few pockets in between like the Riverside neighborhood.

The city also had a thriving black downtown business district (much of it around Ninth Street where Littlejohn had set up shop), complete with hotels, restaurants, a movie theater, a bank, and a major hospital, pharmacy and nursing school. In addition, in each of the neighborhoods, there was some form of commerce to serve those black residents. And, of course, there were schools and churches. All would eventually be seen through Littlejohn's lens.

Segregation was just a fact of life, with African Americans relegated to separate schools, swimming pools, and parks; forced to ride in the back of buses and drink from water fountains marked "Colored"; and, if permitted in a theater for a special show, were directed to sit in the balcony or a special "Negro Section."

In spite of the Jim Crow laws and the unequal treatment that accompanied them, Fort Worth was regarded as having a benevolent brand of racism, generally leaving the black community alone with little of the harassment or abject violence demonstrated in other cities. There were incidents in the first half of the twentieth century, including a lynching in

Below: Littlejohn family, Christmas 1950.

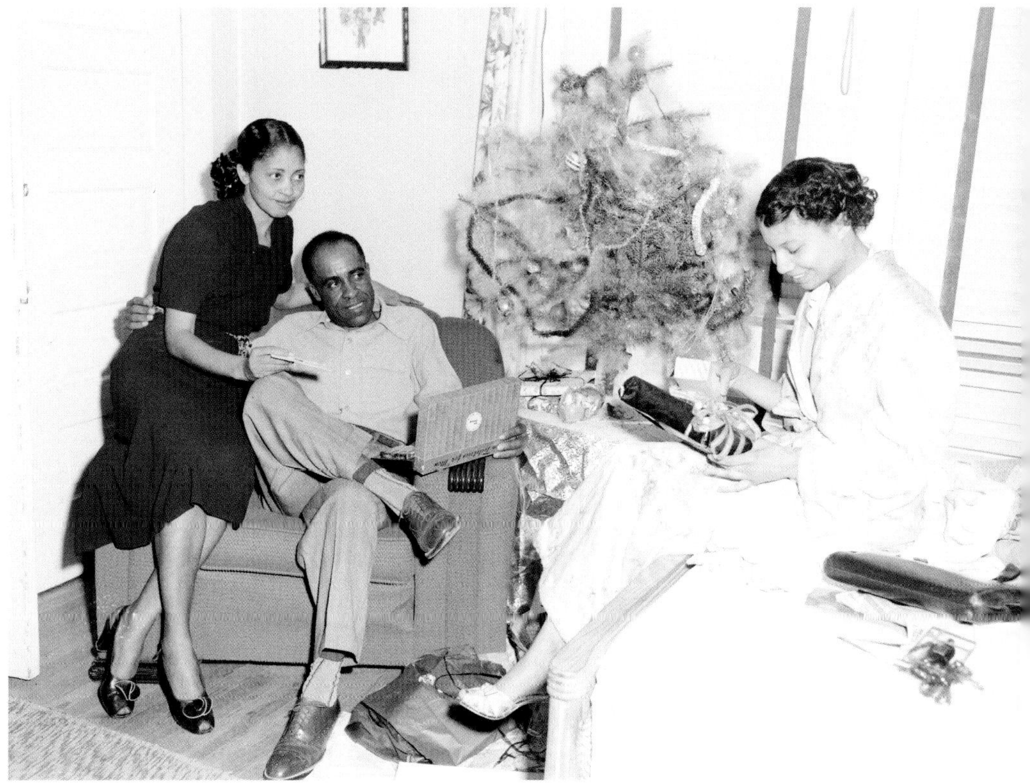

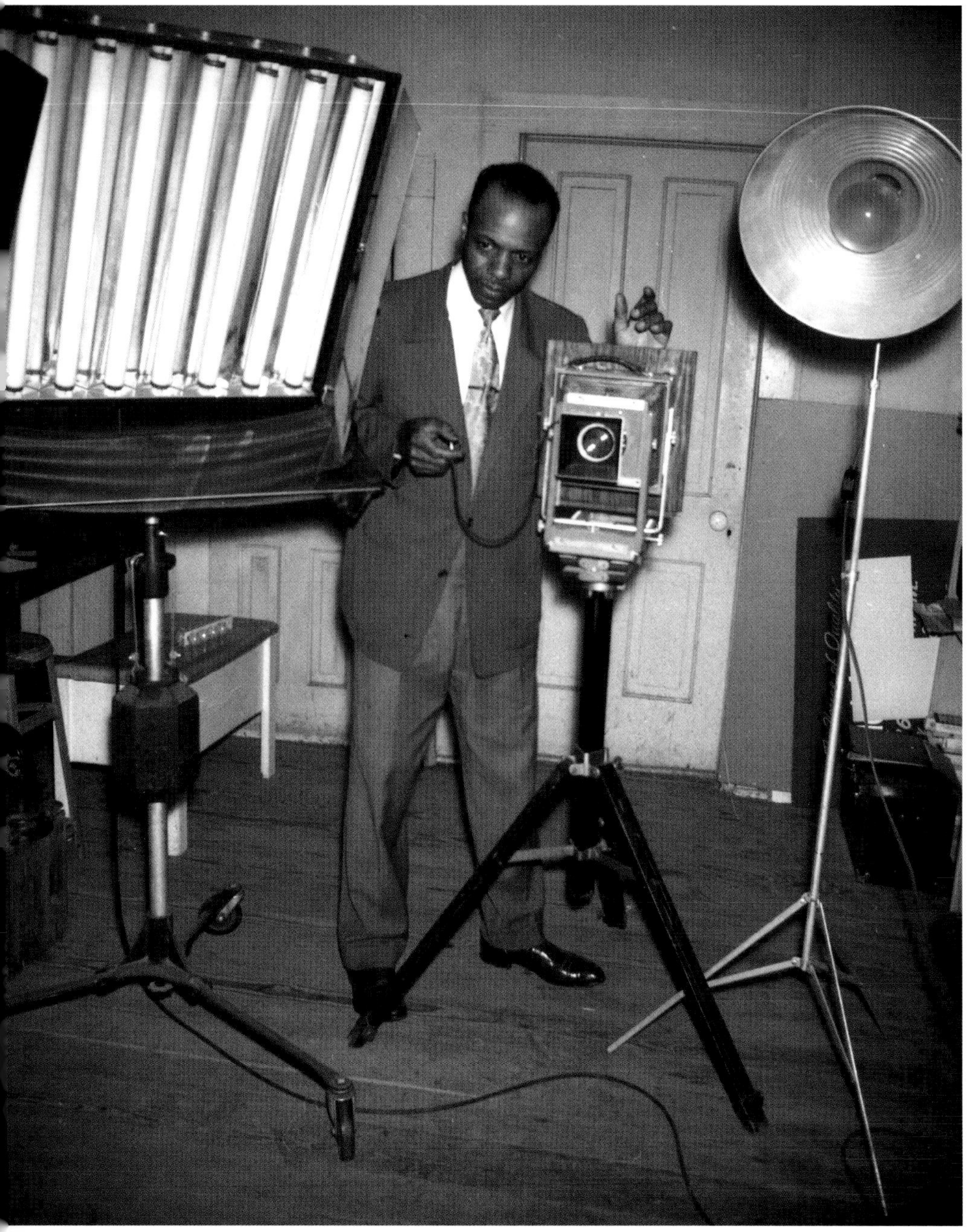

1921, which were ugly indeed. But, for the most part, whites and blacks got along as long as each kept their place.

Many looking back on segregation today might conclude that black people in those days were in constant misery. How could they not be, considering that they were treated as second-class citizens, you might ask. Actually, most people would tell you that they were quite happy, putting their energy into their families and those close-knit communities. While most publicly owned venues were closed to them, except on some special occasions, the black community had its own "public" spaces, including the Masonic Lodge, where major social and entertainment events were held.

There were black nightclubs in the city, and when black entertainers came to town, often to play for all-white audiences, they would find their way to the black community. Many of them stayed in the Jim Hotel or in the homes of well-known African American leaders on the city's South Side.

Littlejohn was ubiquitous—he had to be. He had many people wondering how he could be in so many places,

Left: Calvin Littlejohn behind the studio camera and lights.
Photo by Lucretia Littlejohn.

seemingly at the same time. In addition to all of his school, community, business and church photography, when anyone famous (black or white) came to town, Littlejohn photographed them. He was often at the airport when they arrived, at the speaking or performance event, in the home where they stayed, and even showed up when they went to dinner.

This was a time when the local daily newspapers didn't cover the black community. About the only time a black man got his picture in the paper was if he had been accused of killing a white man or raping a white woman. There were black newspapers in town, including one that Littlejohn helped start, the *Como Monitor*, and his photos were often published in those.

Littlejohn's life in Texas was interrupted for a while during World War II, but he used that army experience to continue to develop his photographic skills. While stationed at Fort Leonard Wood, Missouri, he took pictures of training exercises and other activities on the base.

Although Littlejohn was seen as being a one-man band, during most of those tough years he had his devoted wife, Lucretia, working alongside him, setting his appointment schedule, accompanying him on photo shoots and even assisting in the darkroom. Lucretia was his second wife.

"Married six years for the first time; "thirteen years a bachelor and then married again," he said, explaining laughingly. "I courted thirteen years before I married [her] because she was my secretary."

Right: Lucretia Littlejohn presenting a gift to Jackie Robinson with Roy Campanella at the table, November 11, 1949.

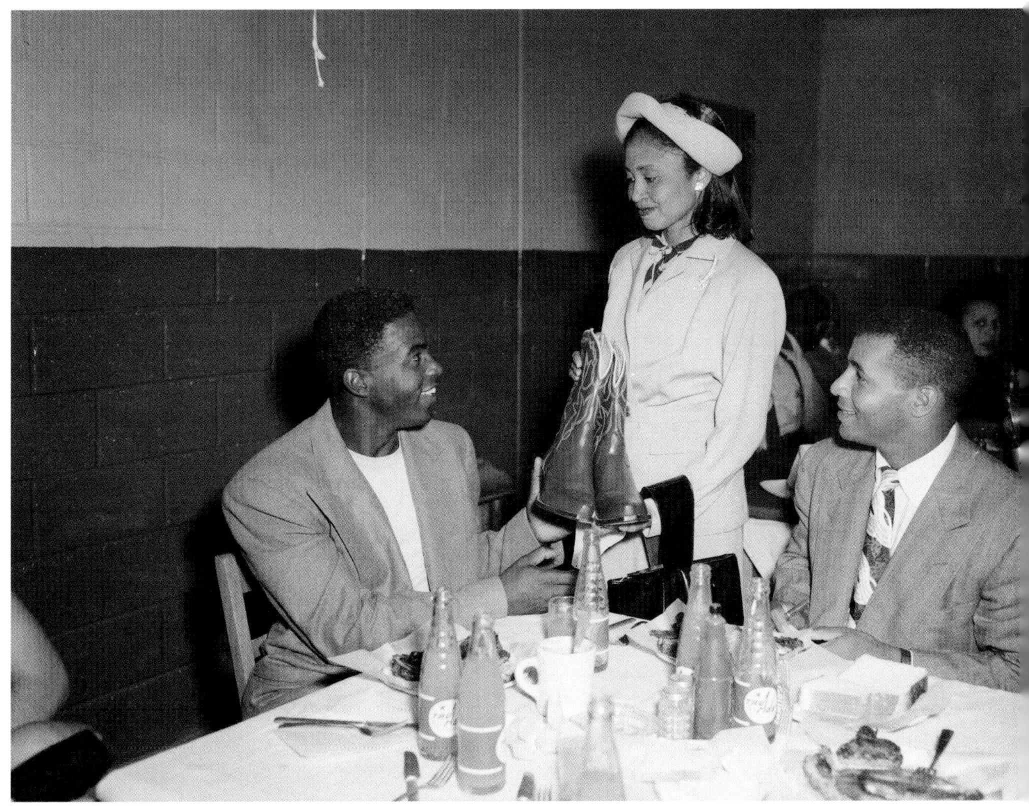

The pair was a dynamic duo, but in order to keep up with all of his contracts and orders, especially the school photo shoots and the massive printing jobs, the photographer had to invent ways to meet the demand. He made his own enlarger that would produce different sized prints, and he fashioned a camera that would take a hundred feet of film and produce up to 320 exposures.

"So there again I invented something else, known as the Plantation Printer, which I don't even show. It's a great big thing," he said. "And with that, when I expose that 46 millimeter [film]...and I can put five frames at one time, and expose five frames at one time. Each frame is scientifically balanced for light, according to the density of its negative. I invented that."

Littlejohn, however, said flatly that he never set out to be the documentarian of the Fort Worth black community. He was simply trying to earn a living using the talent he had in the profession he loved.

An unassuming and relatively quiet man, Littlejohn was definitely in command when he got behind the camera and began positioning people for poses. He had no problem giving orders to the great and famous just as he did to first-graders at an elementary school.

Many people in Fort Worth who were photographed by this giant of a man at the time of their birth were still having their pictures taken by Calvin Littlejohn almost literally until the day he died in 1993 at the age of eighty-four.

He left his mark on a city that he watched change through the lens of a camera. He did what he originally set out to do: to capture the best of a community, focusing on its good times and leaving the negative issues to be recorded by others. Because he was so prolific, he left behind thousands of prints and negatives which help capture a time and place—a dynamic community—that might simply have been forgotten had the slender young man from Arkansas not hitched a ride to Texas in 1934.

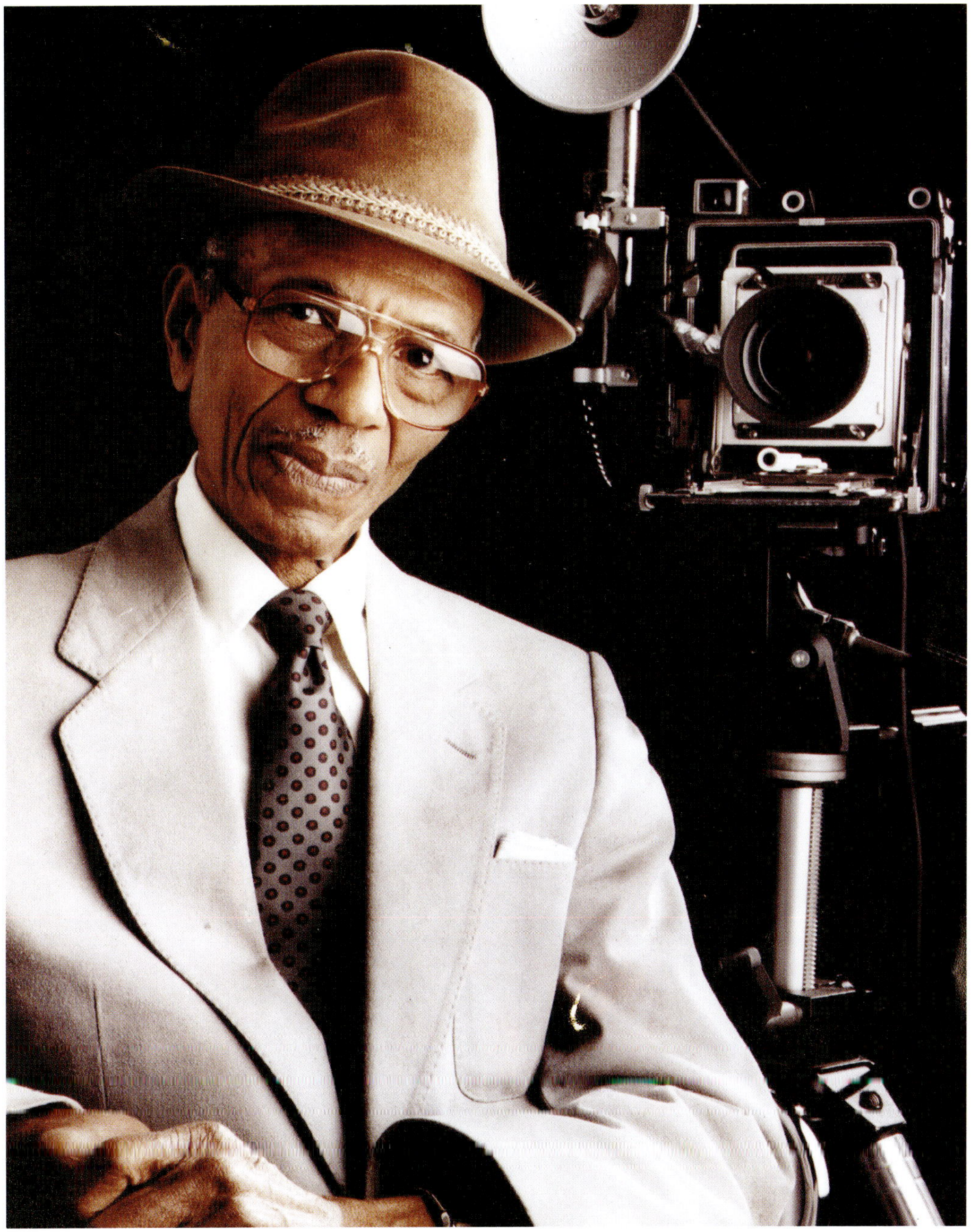

Left: Calvin Littlejohn, self-portrait, 1991.

PART 1 SCHOOLS

"... and then I saw a need for photography because I. M. Terrell [High School] was having trouble getting photography to make the yearbooks and things because the city of Fort Worth had one photographer on payroll. And he was trying to make all [the events] and naturally he just couldn't make 'em all, you know. I. M. Terrell was being neglected ... And I started there and adopted that school and they adopted me. That's how I got in photography."

—Calvin Littlejohn

I. M. Terrell High School had evolved from the very first public school established for African Americans in Fort Worth in 1882. It was originally called East Ninth Street Colored School, and its first principal was Isaiah Milligan Terrell, for whom the school was officially named in 1921.

By the time Calvin Littlejohn got to town, Terrell was in its final location on East 18th Street and was serving not only the black students in Fort Worth but those who lived in surrounding communities. By the late 1950s, when three additional black high schools had been added to the district, African Americans from seventeen towns — from as far away as Weatherford, Grapevine and Roanoke — were bused to the school.

The building boom of new schools came as Fort Worth officials tried desperately to circumvent the impending school desegregation decision from the U.S. Supreme Court, *Brown v. the Board of Education of Topeka*, in order to prove that the school district, while separate, was equal in its treatment of black students. Three existing black junior high schools were chosen to become high schools with one advanced grade added each year until each had 12th grade classes.

By 1960, there were three additional high schools serving the black communities on the East Side (Paul Lawrence Dunbar), West Side (Como) and North Side (Milton L. Kirkpatrick). All of them had newspapers and yearbooks and would need the help of a professional photographer. Littlejohn, who had begun his contract work photographing students and events at Terrell, later served each of those schools as well as elementary and junior highs throughout the area.

In order to keep up with all the work, the photographer would have to develop a technique of taking hundreds of exposures without changing film, and he "invented" a method of making multiple prints at the same time.

Ironically, just as the threat of integration had helped create three new black schools in the city, by 1973 desegregation had forced the closing of three of the four high schools in Fort Worth, including the historic I. M. Terrell. Only Dunbar would remain.

Littlejohn then found himself in competition with larger and better staffed photo studios that were eager to get all the school contracts they could, including the predominantly black ones. He simply saw it as another challenge in life and accepted it.

Right: I. M. Terrell High School drum major, Joseph Wells, and majorette, Carlene Phillips, 1948.

Far Right: I. M. Terrell High School Homecoming, November 18, 1949.

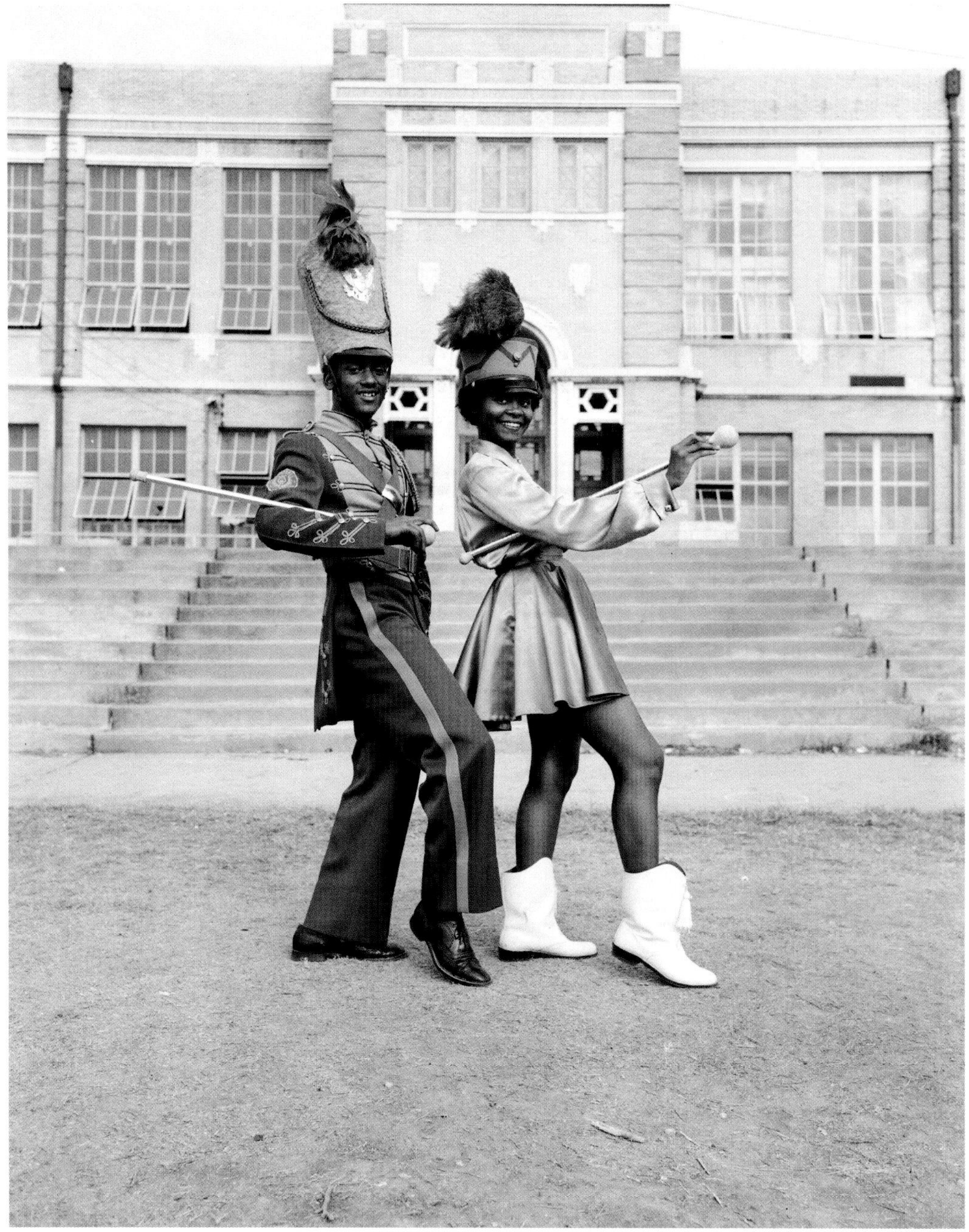

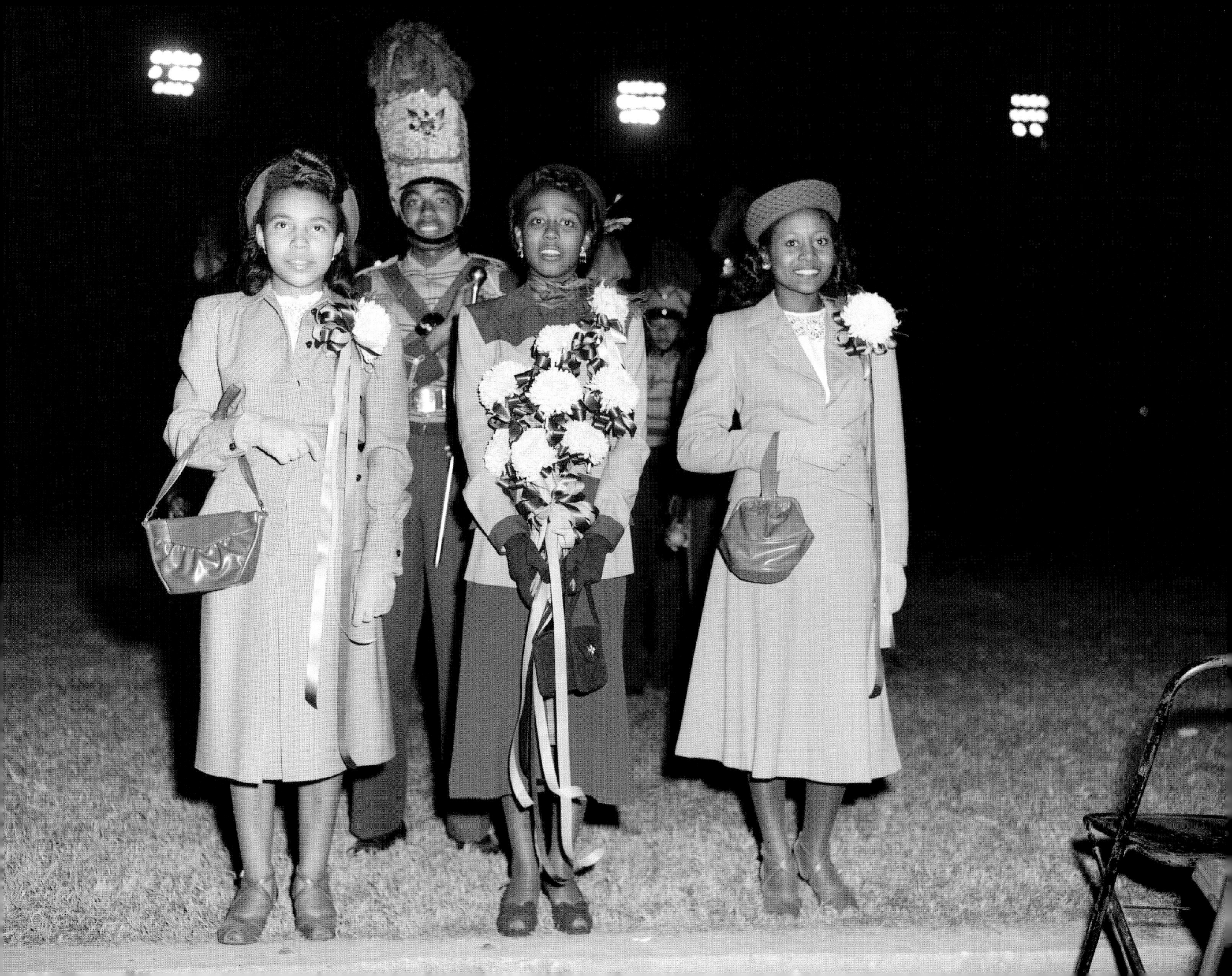

Right: I. M. Terrell High School Homecoming, unidentified band member, November 18, 1949.

Far Right: I. M. Terrell High School football players, November 8, 1949.

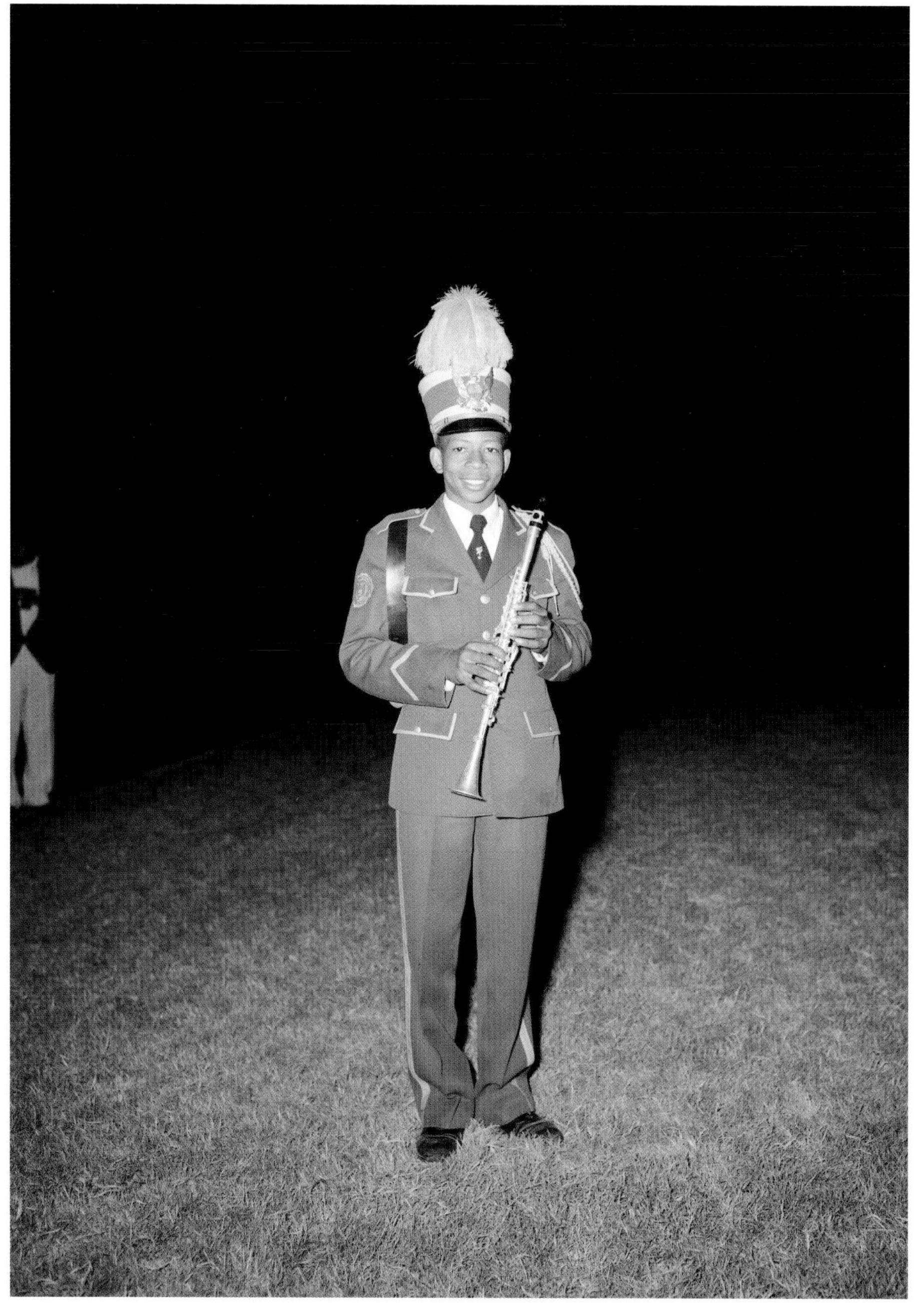

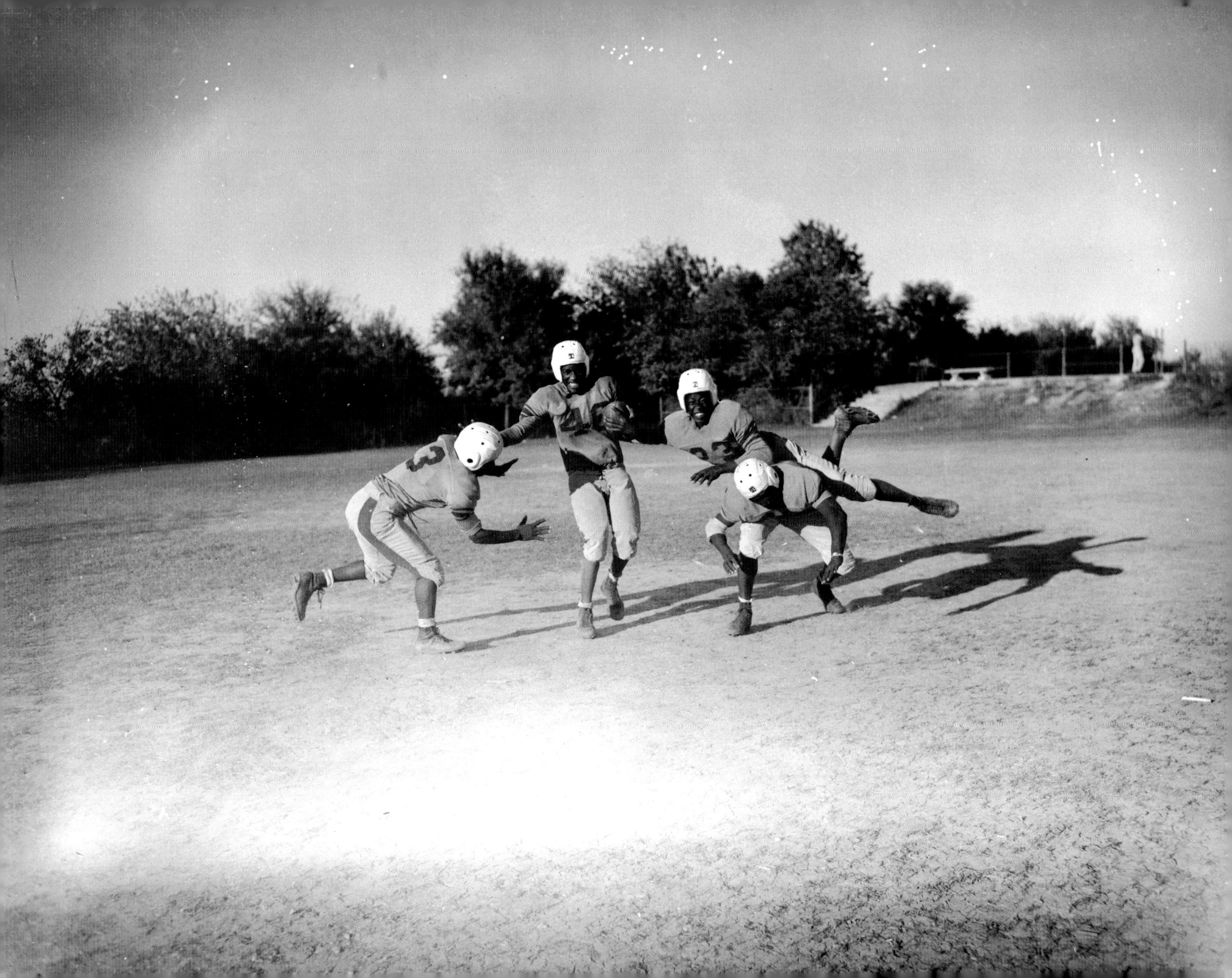

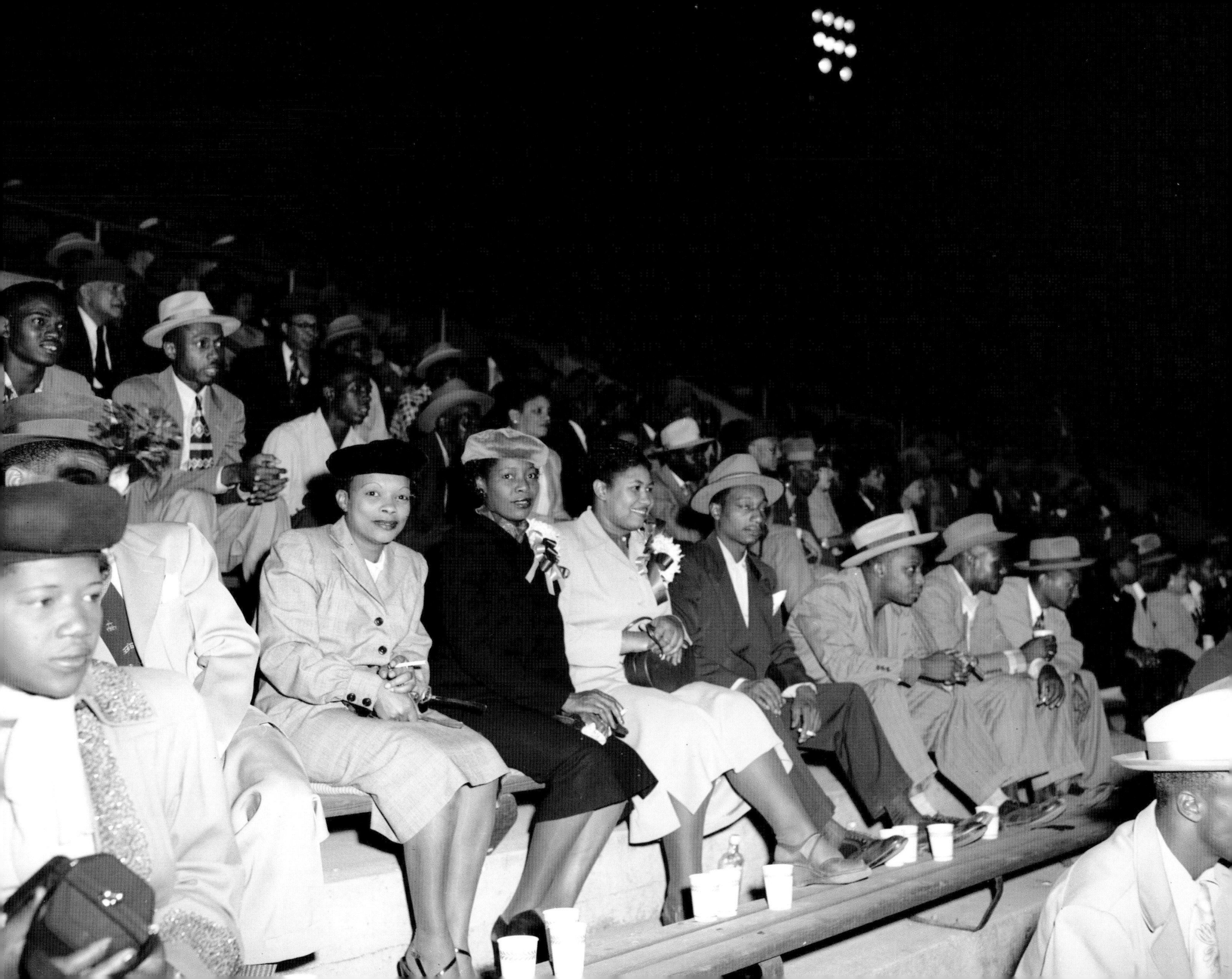

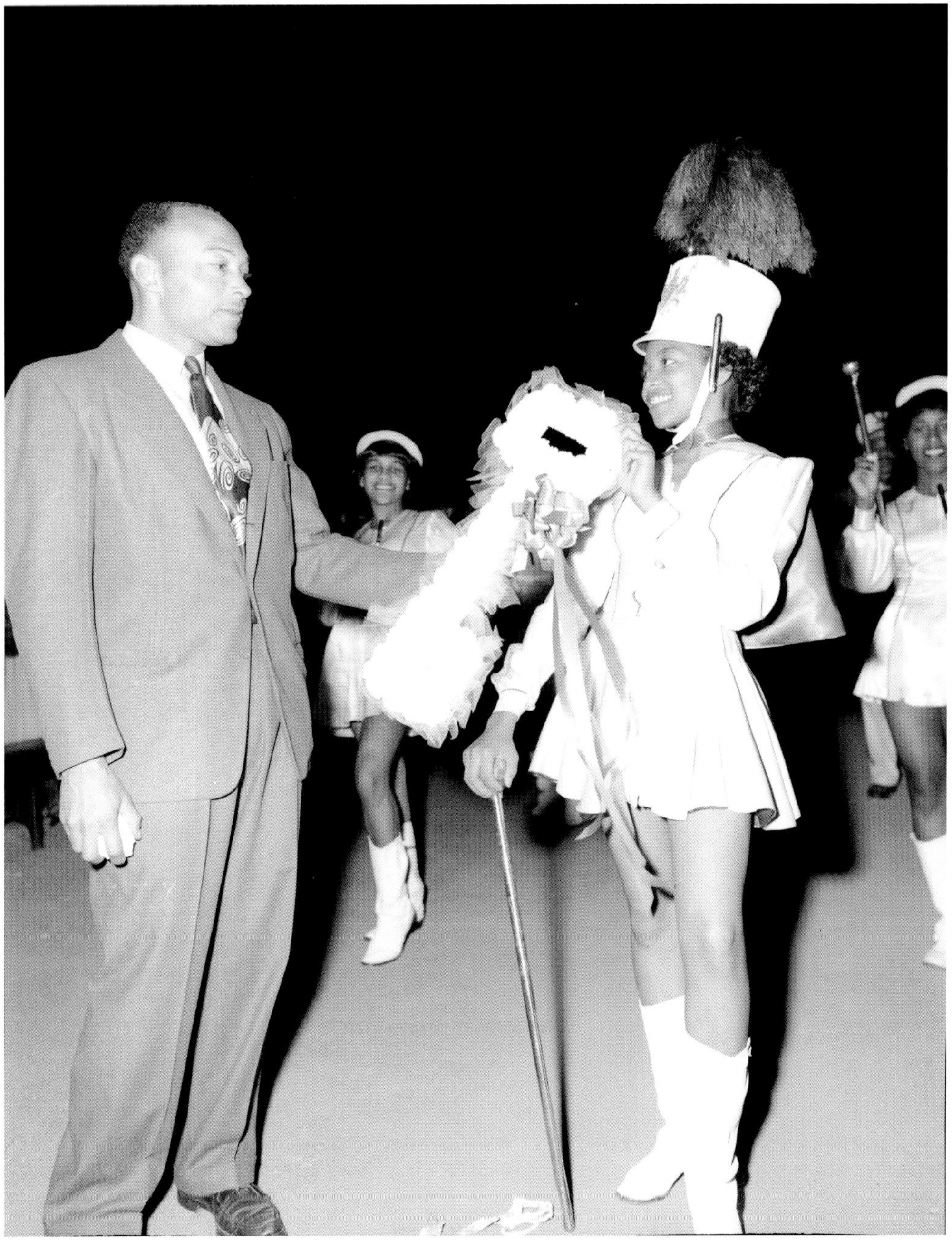

Far Left: Crowd watching I. M. Terrell High School football game, November 8, 1949.

Left: I. M. Terrell math teacher Douglas Sutton presenting the ceremonial key to the drum majorette.

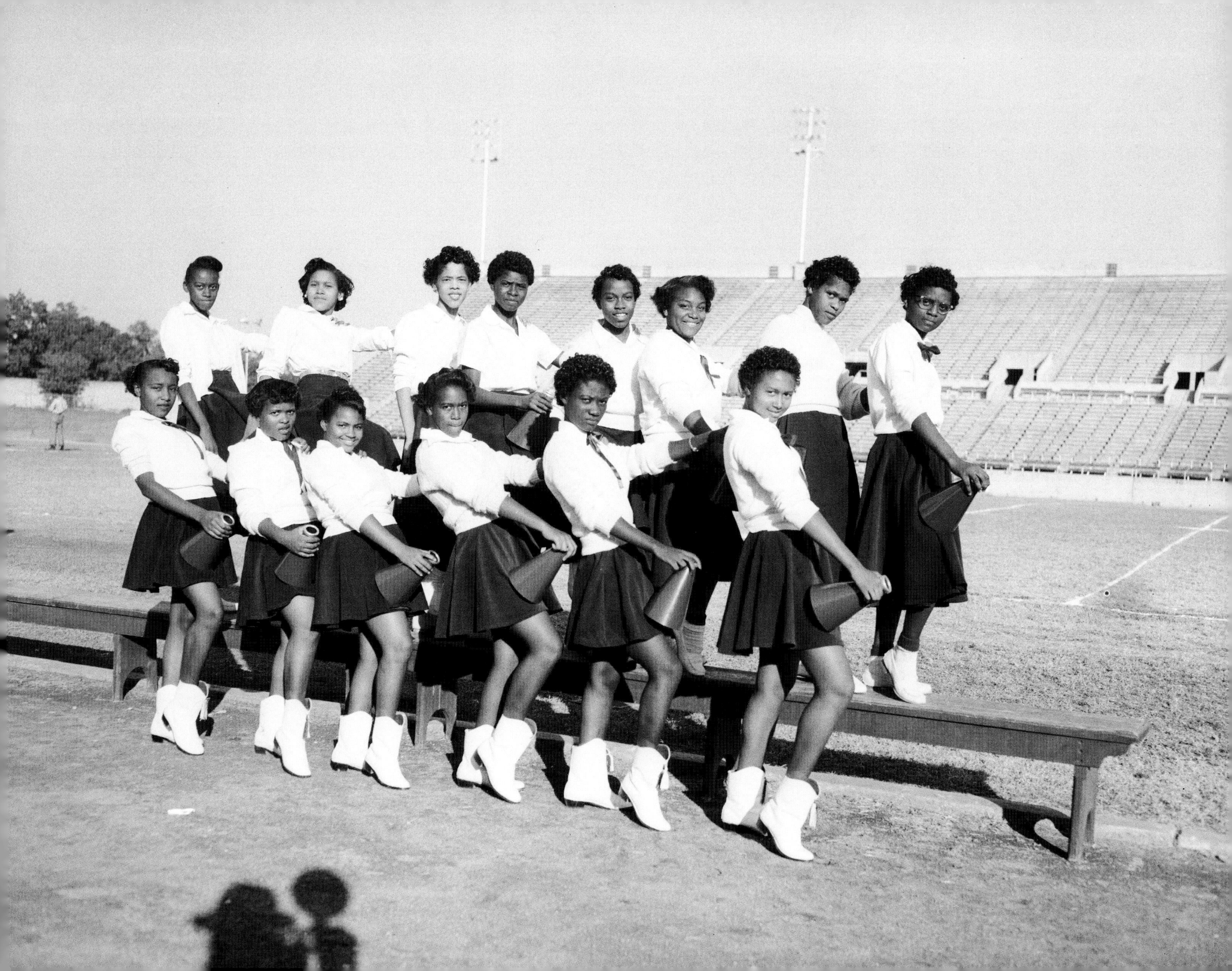

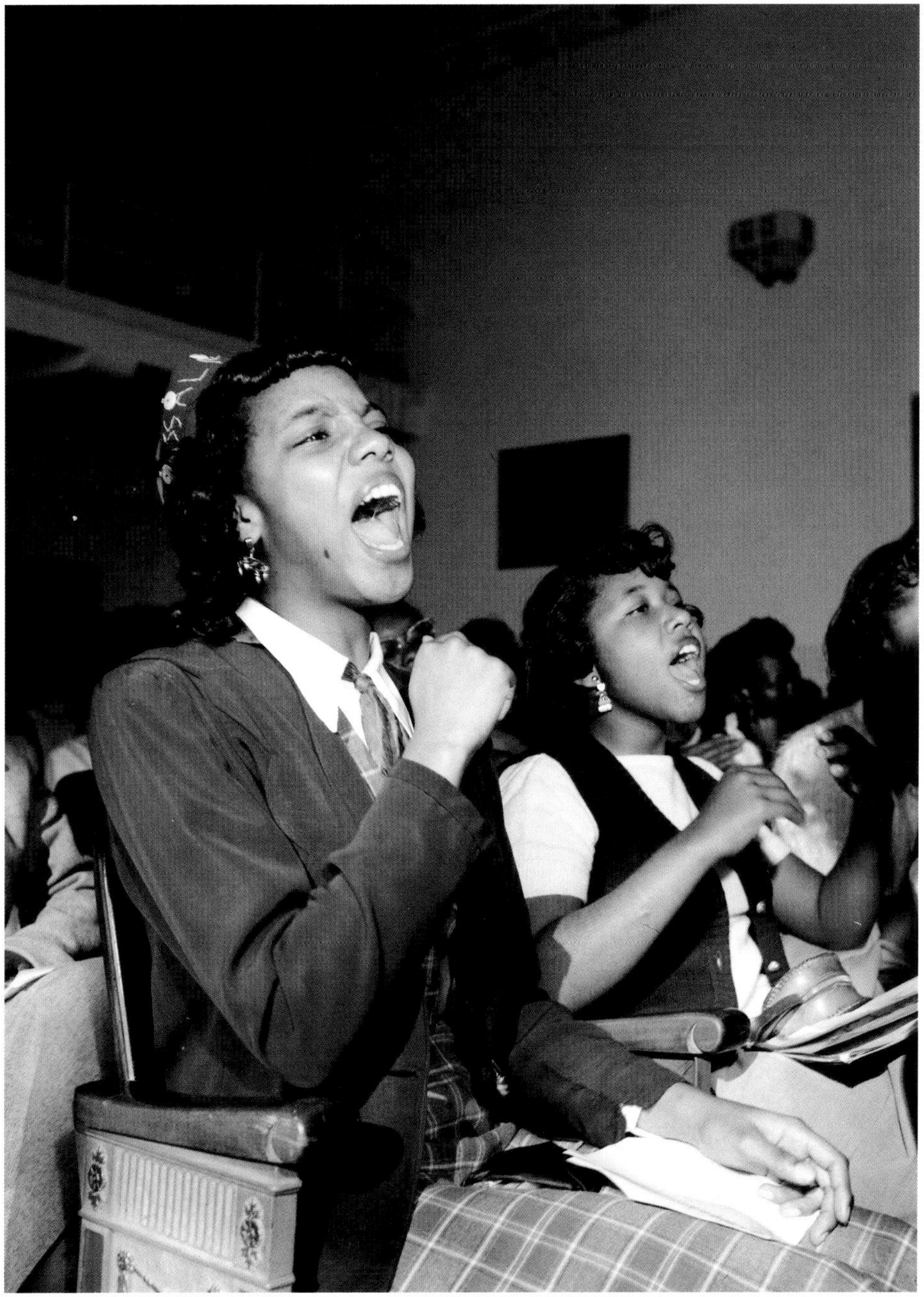

Far Left: G. W. Carver Junior High School pep squad, 1954. Note photographer's shadow in foreground.

Left: I. M. Terrell High School Homecoming pep rally, 1954.

Next Page, Left: Como High School, Senior Prom, May 7, 1959.

Next Page, Right: I. M. Terrell High School football players, Joseph Breedlove, #60, captain; Theron James, #88, co-captain; and quarterback Sidney Nichols, #11, 1958.

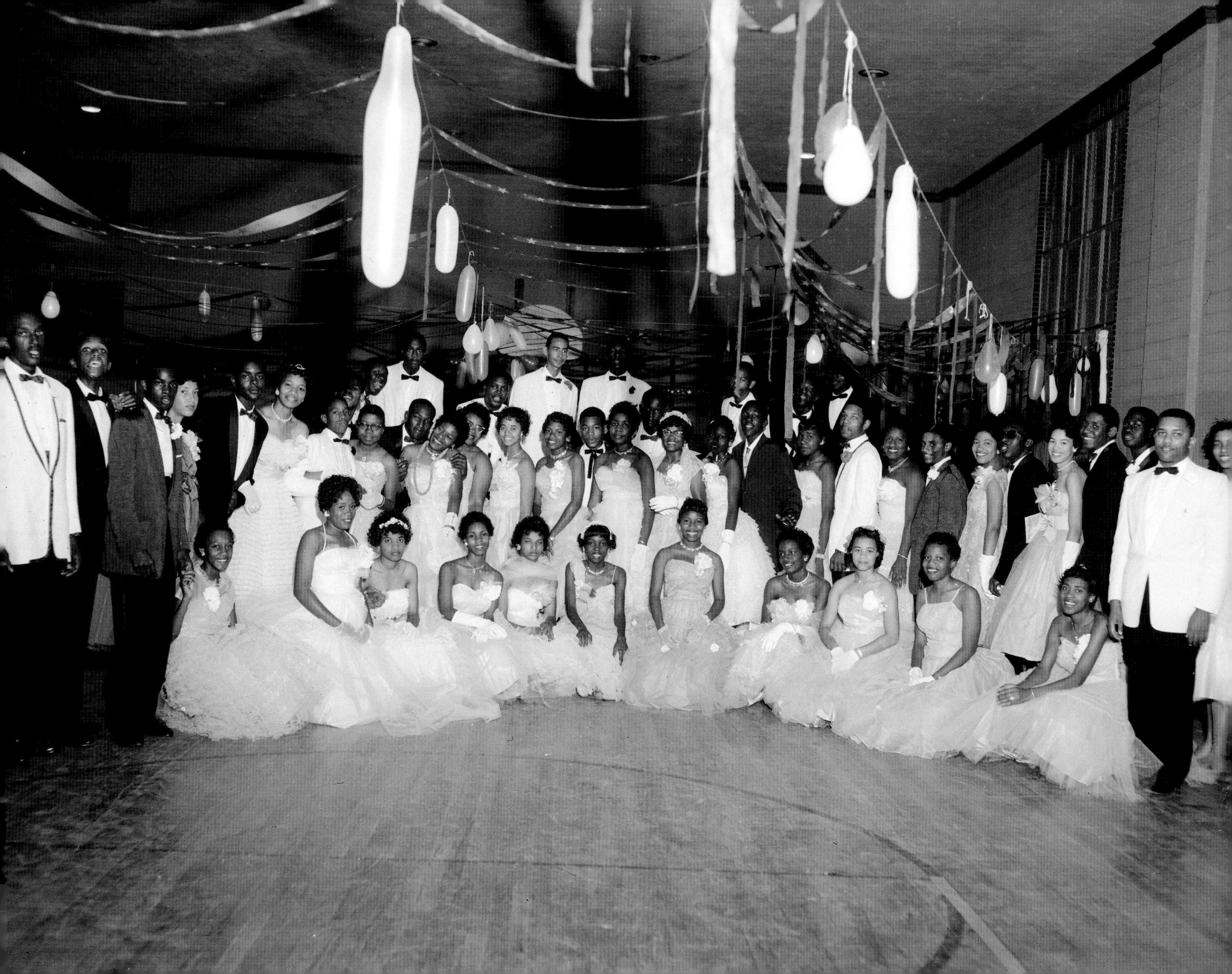

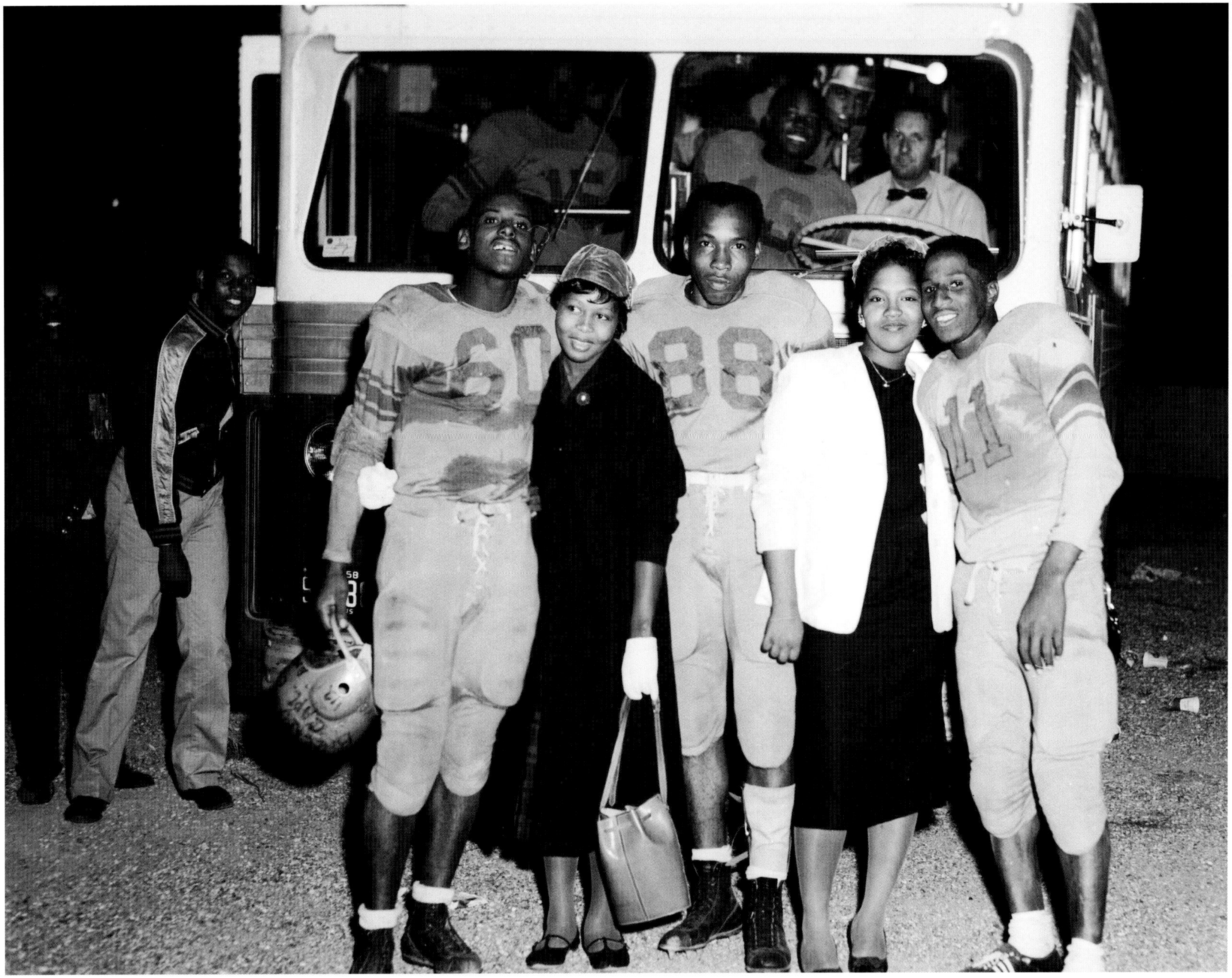
60
88
11

Right: Calvin Crosby and May Lois Hughes, Como High School Prom, 1963.

Far Right: Como High School Homecoming Court, Nov. 12, 1960. From left: Robert McAfee, Ruth Hall, Enard Baxter, Jane Marshall, Robert McKentosh and Connie Willaims.

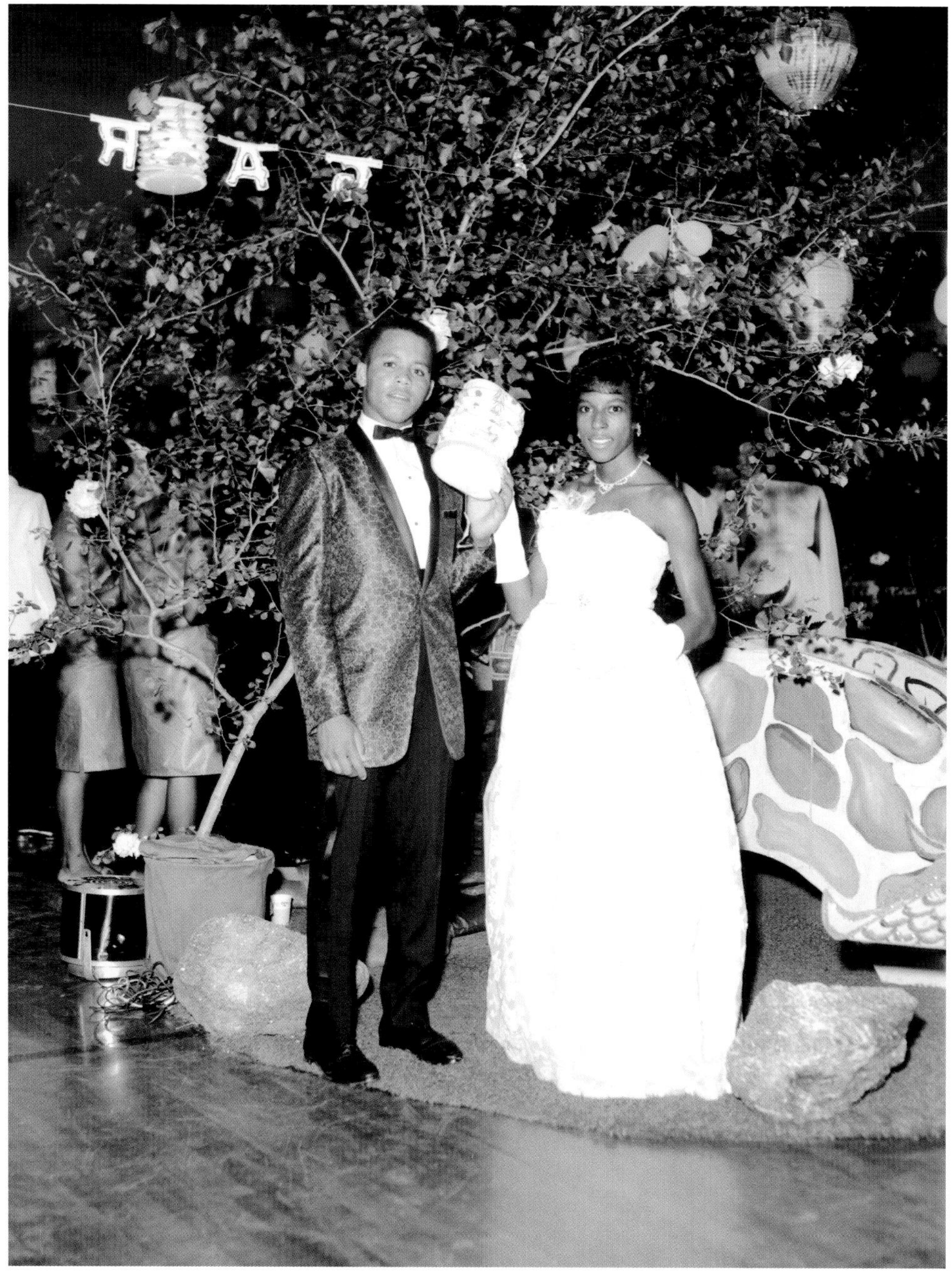

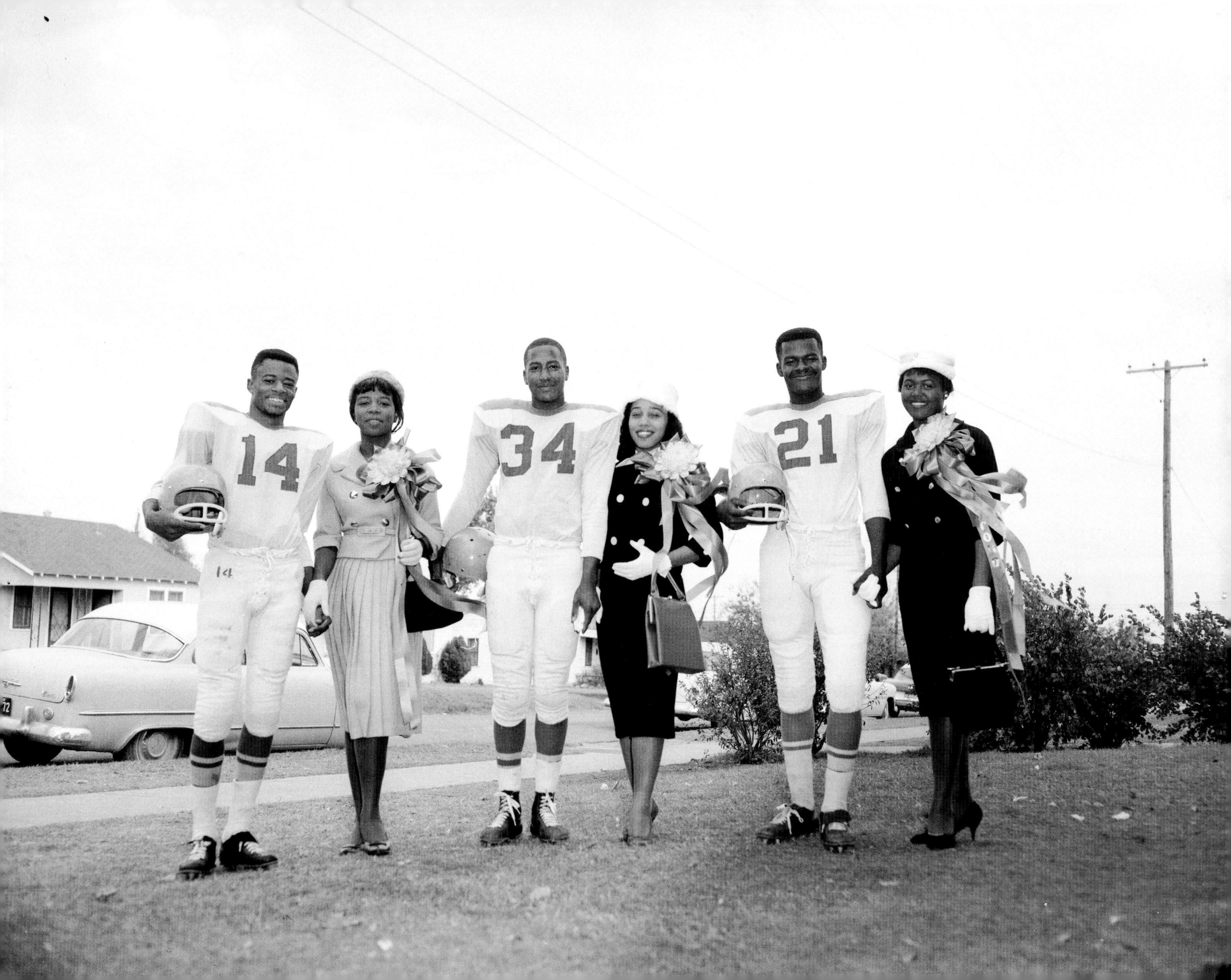
14
34
21

Right: Leaner Liggins, senior at I. M. Terrell High School (midterm), 1950.

Far Right: I. M. Terrell High School home economics class, October 1960.

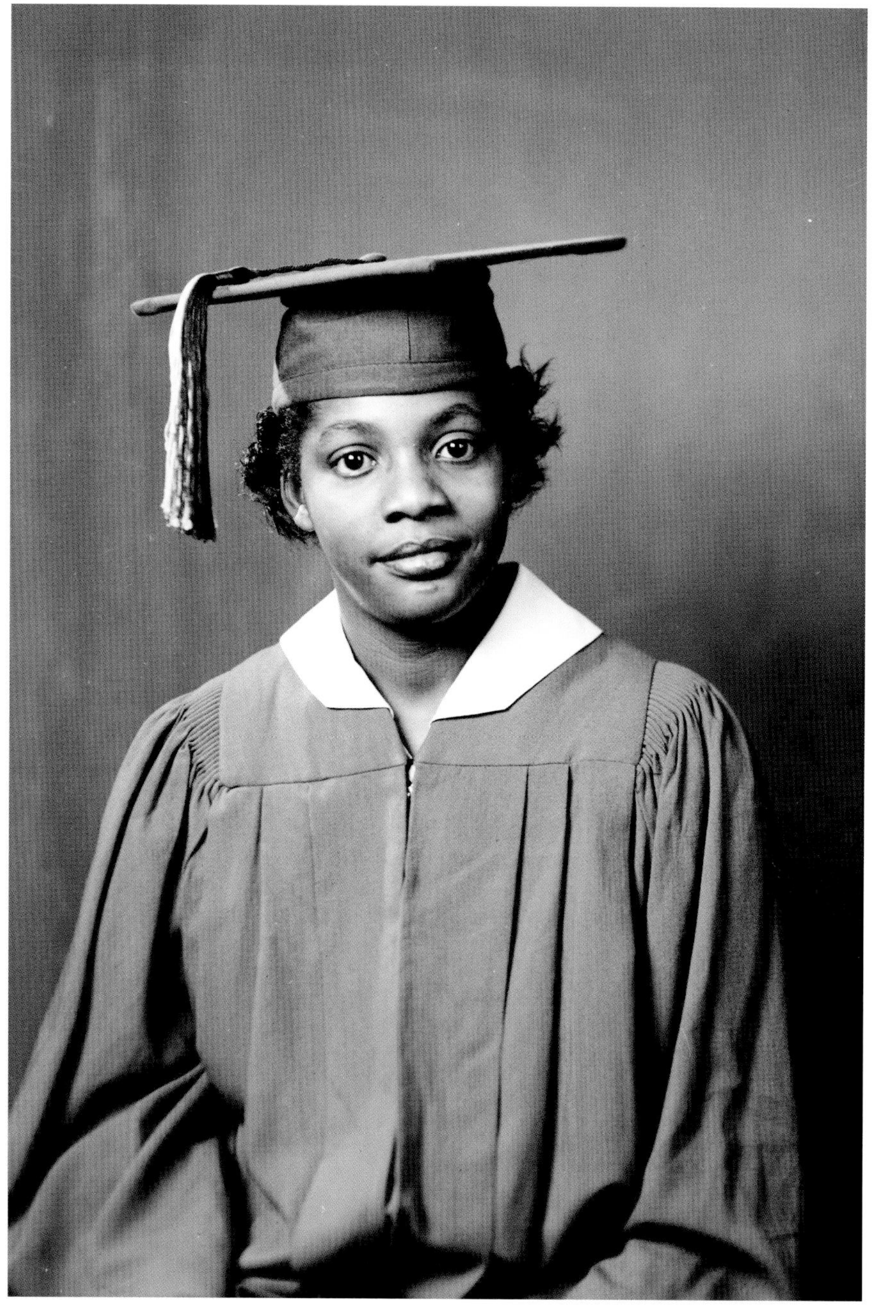

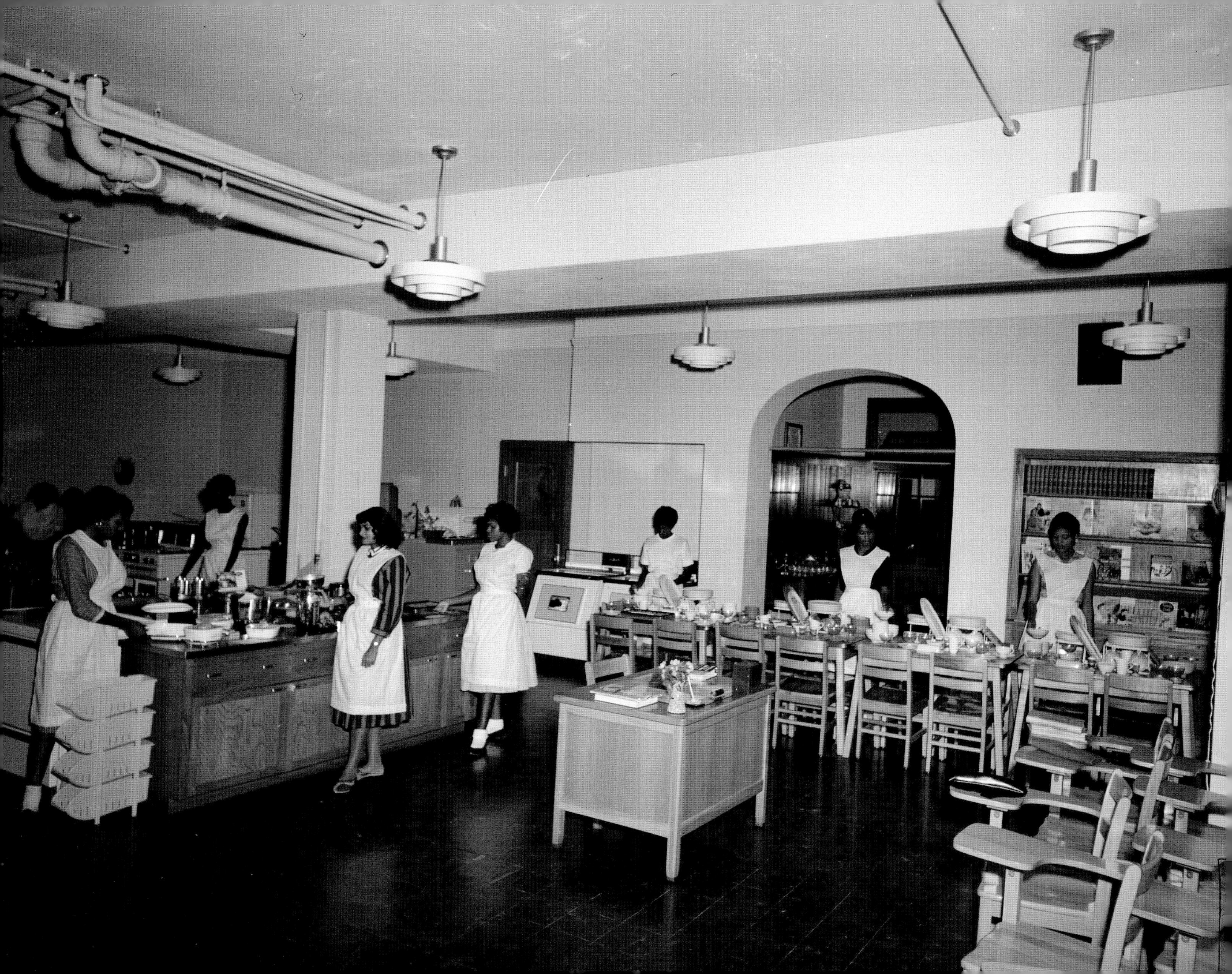

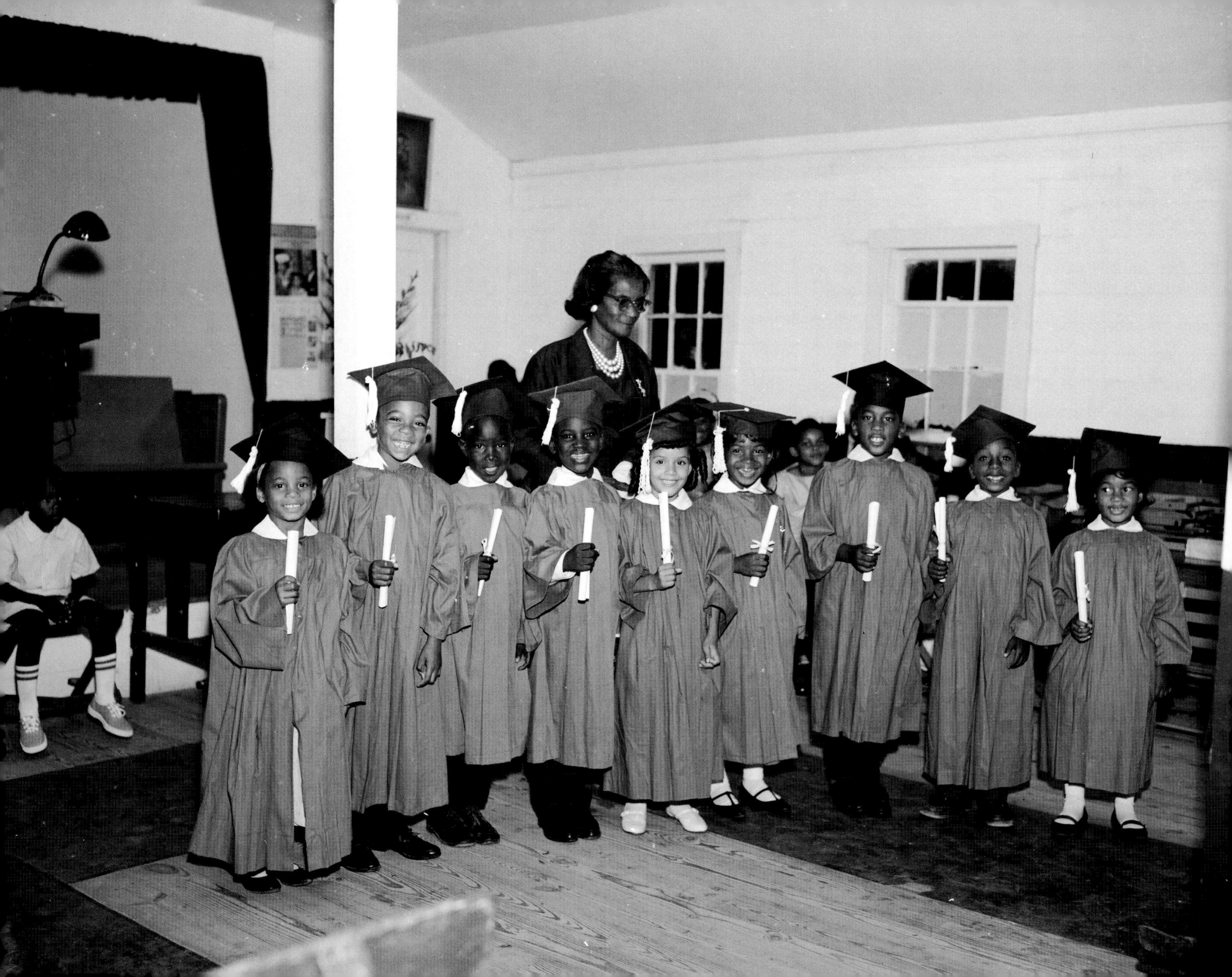

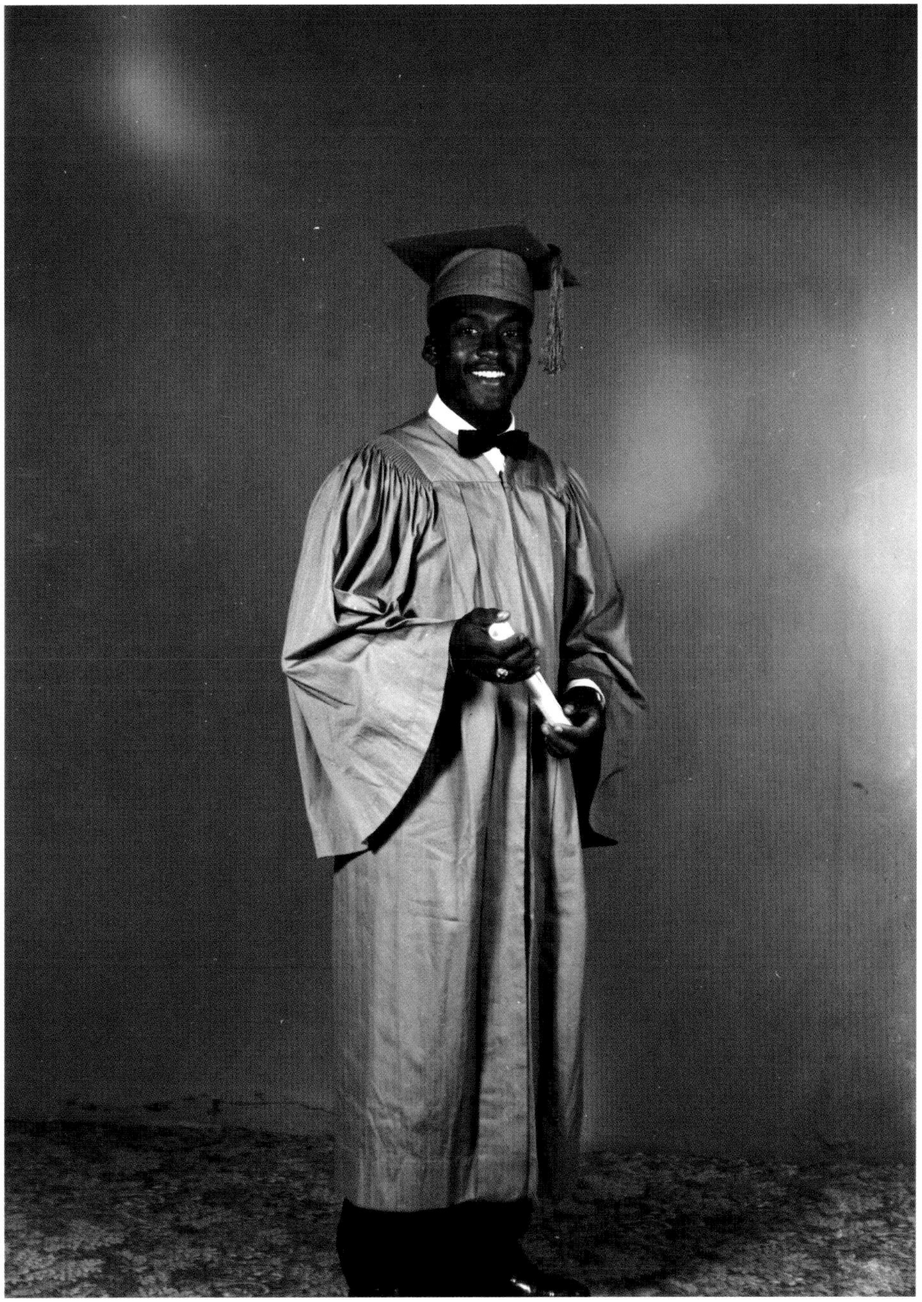

Far Left: Kindergarten graduation, June 5, 1964.

Left: McKinley Wright, youngest son of the Reverend Clay Wright, I. M. Terrell High School senior portrait, May 11, 1953.

Right: Dunbar High School basketball player Charles "Stilt" Williams being interviewed by student journalist, Flossie Lee. 1966.

Far Right: Dunbar High School track team, 1966. From left: Luther McGowan, Melvin Hill, Edgar Rice, Melvin Baker, and Spencer Harris. Harris was one of the first black athletes at TCU and is now a retired public school coach and administrator.

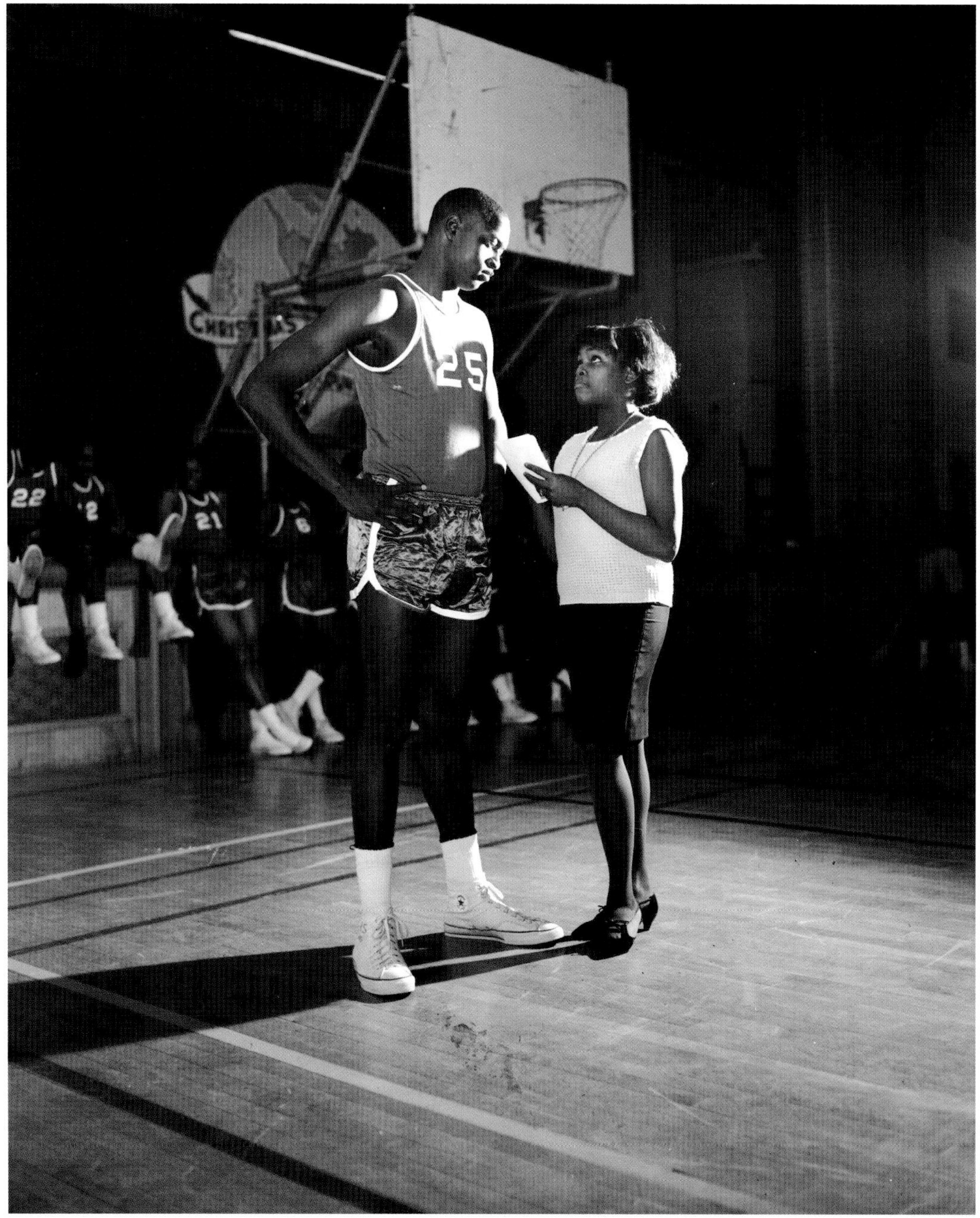

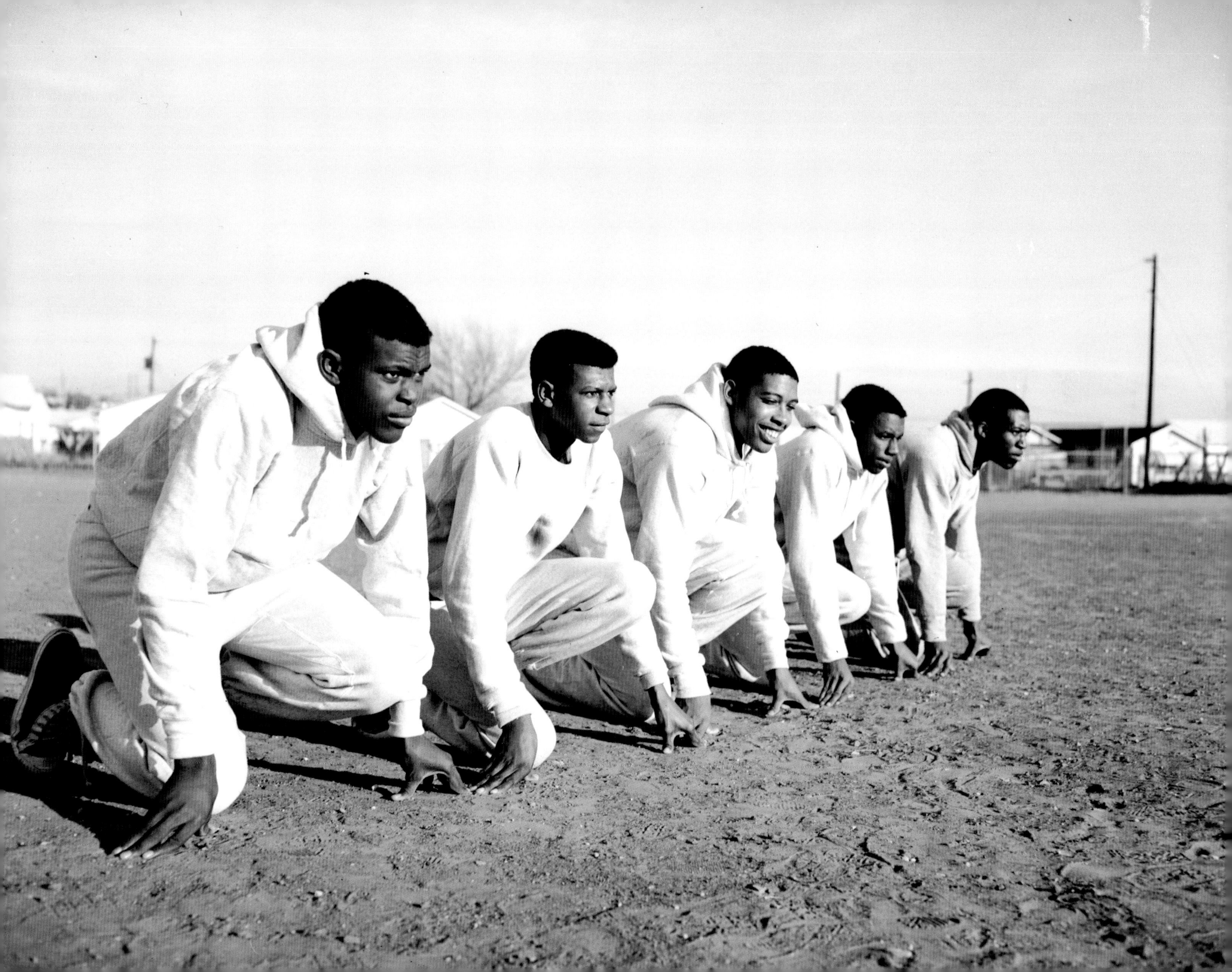

Right: I. M. Terrell High School Homecoming, 1971.

Far Right: Dunbar High School music students practicing in the gym, c. 1965. Charles Scott, director, is at the piano.

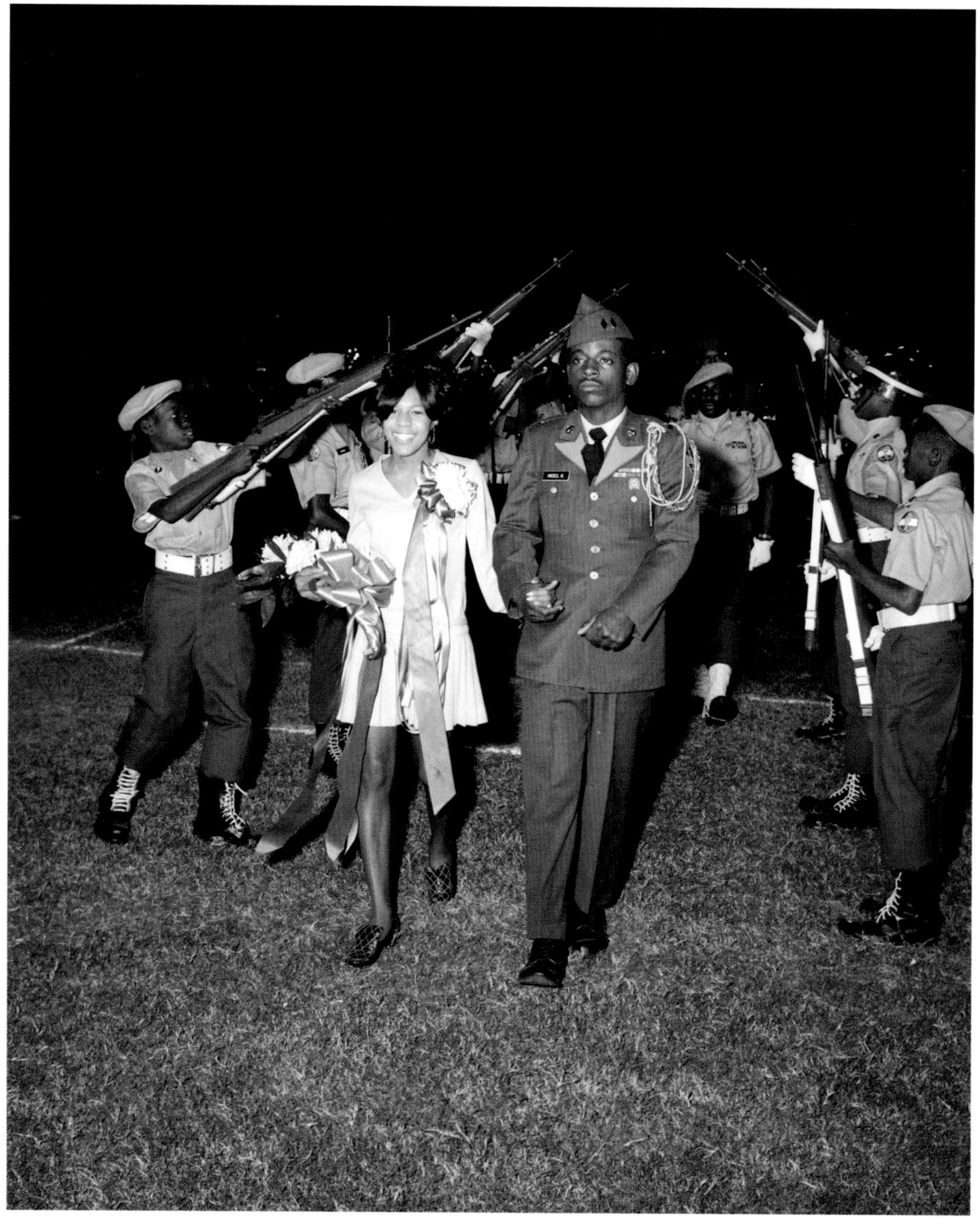

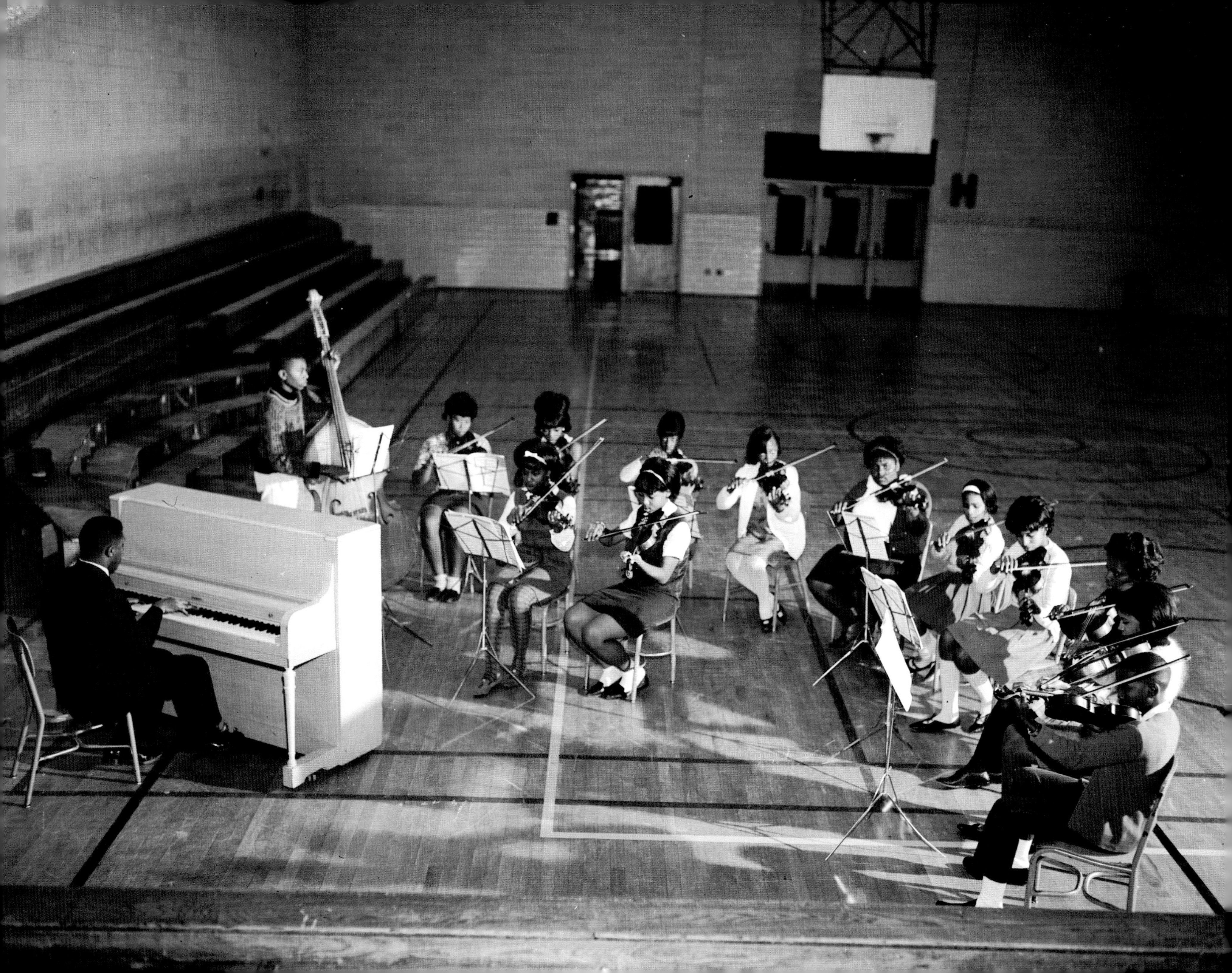

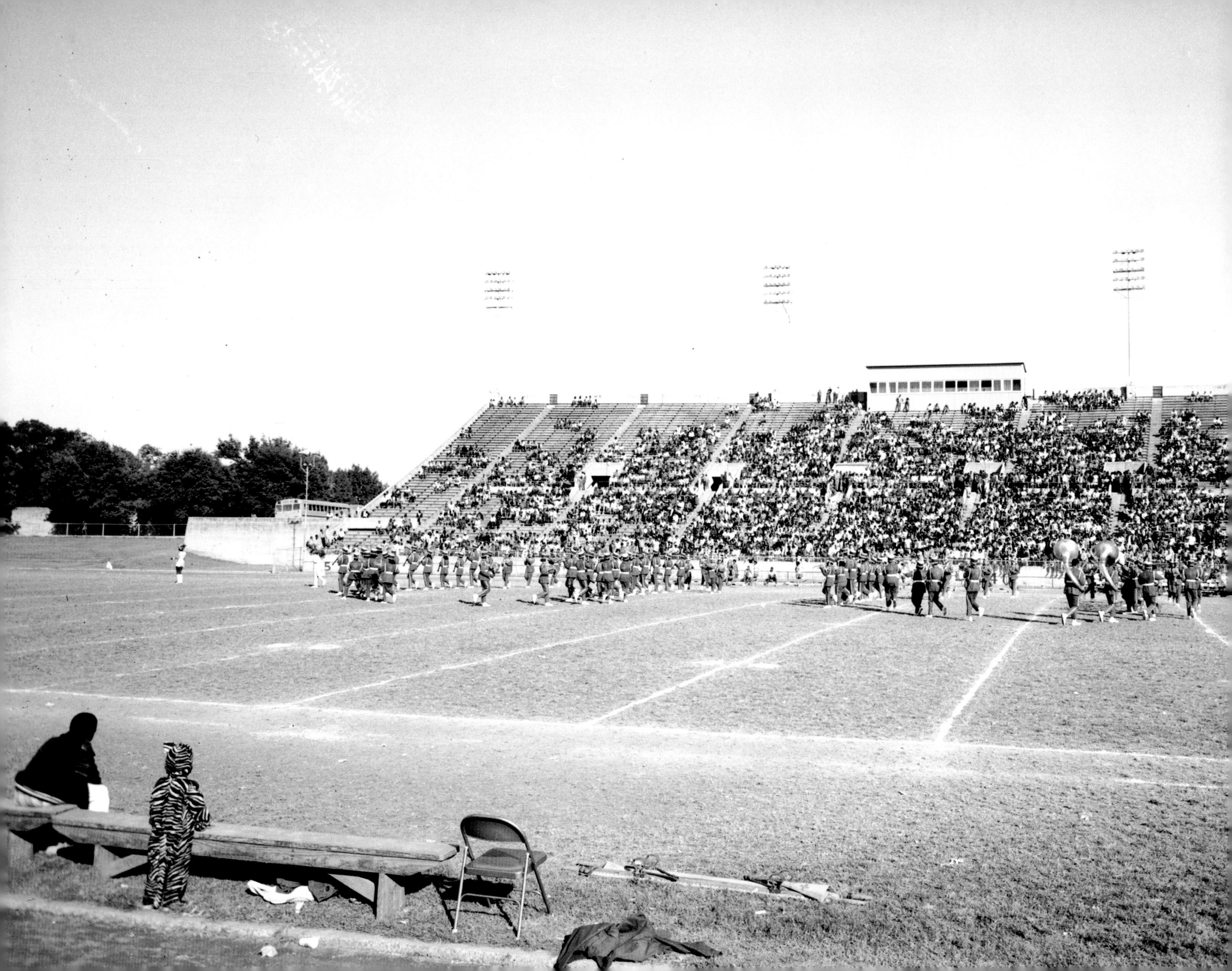

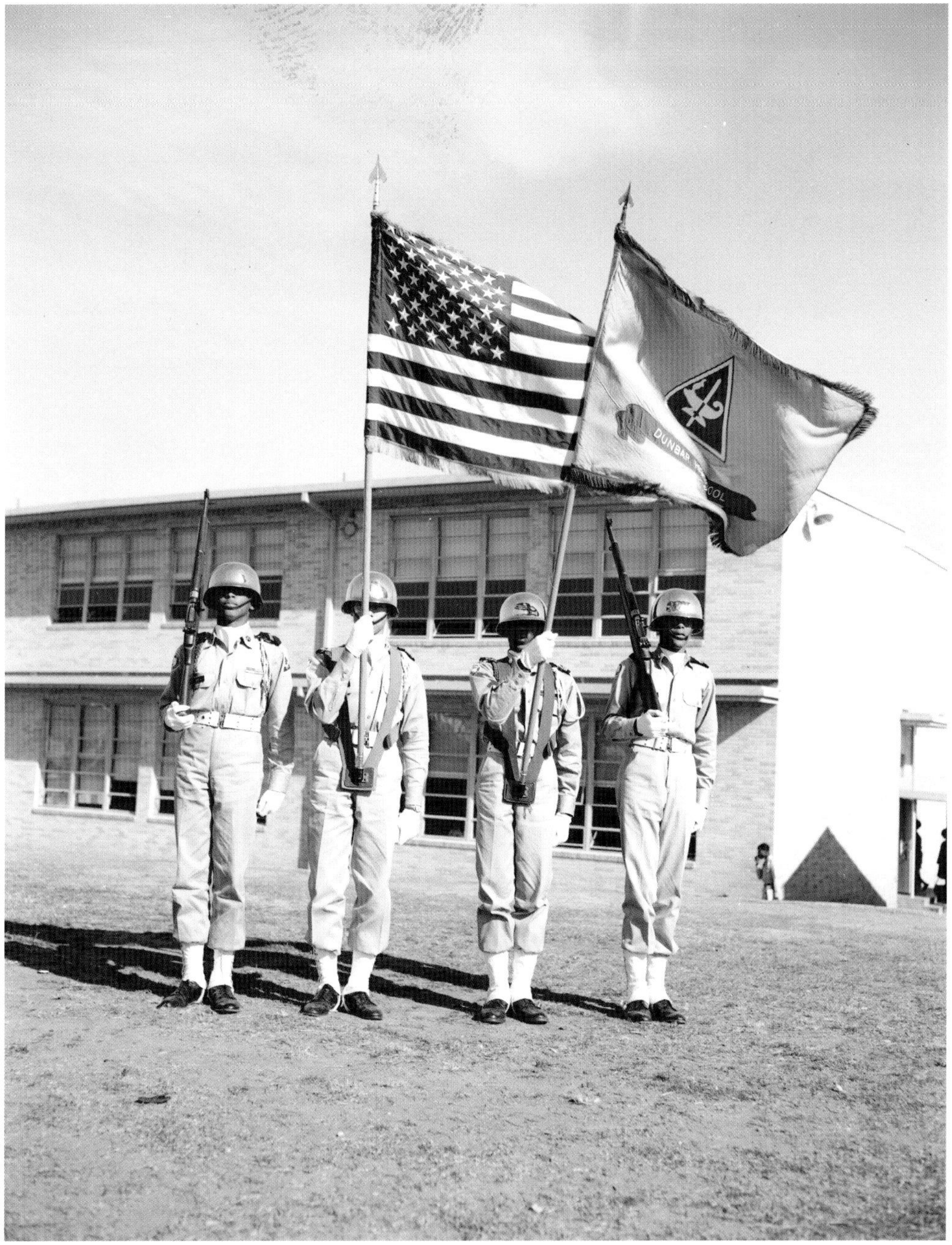

Far Left: I. M. Terrell High School marching band performs on field while opposing team's mascot looks on, 1969, probably the homecoming game, usually played on Thanksgiving Day against Dunbar, whose mascot is the "Wildcats."

Left: Dunbar High School ROTC Color Guard, 1966.

Right: Miss Billie Barbers, honor student and Kirkpatrick High May Day Queen, May 9, 1958.

Far Right: I. M. Terrell High School students at work in science lab, 1969. The girl in the center of the picture (dark dress with white color and cuffs) is Hattie Faye Calloway Allen, who later became a music teacher in the FWISD.

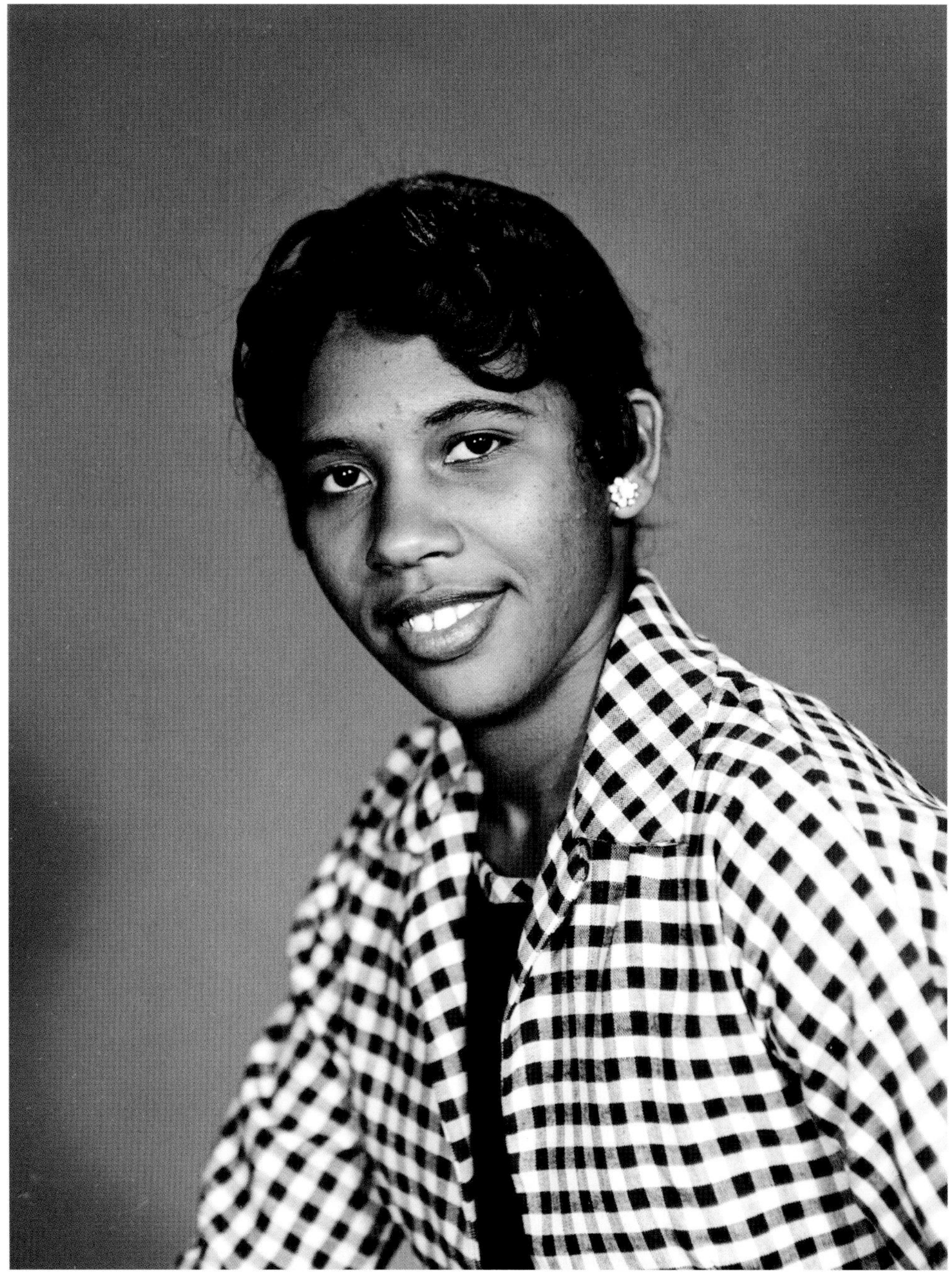

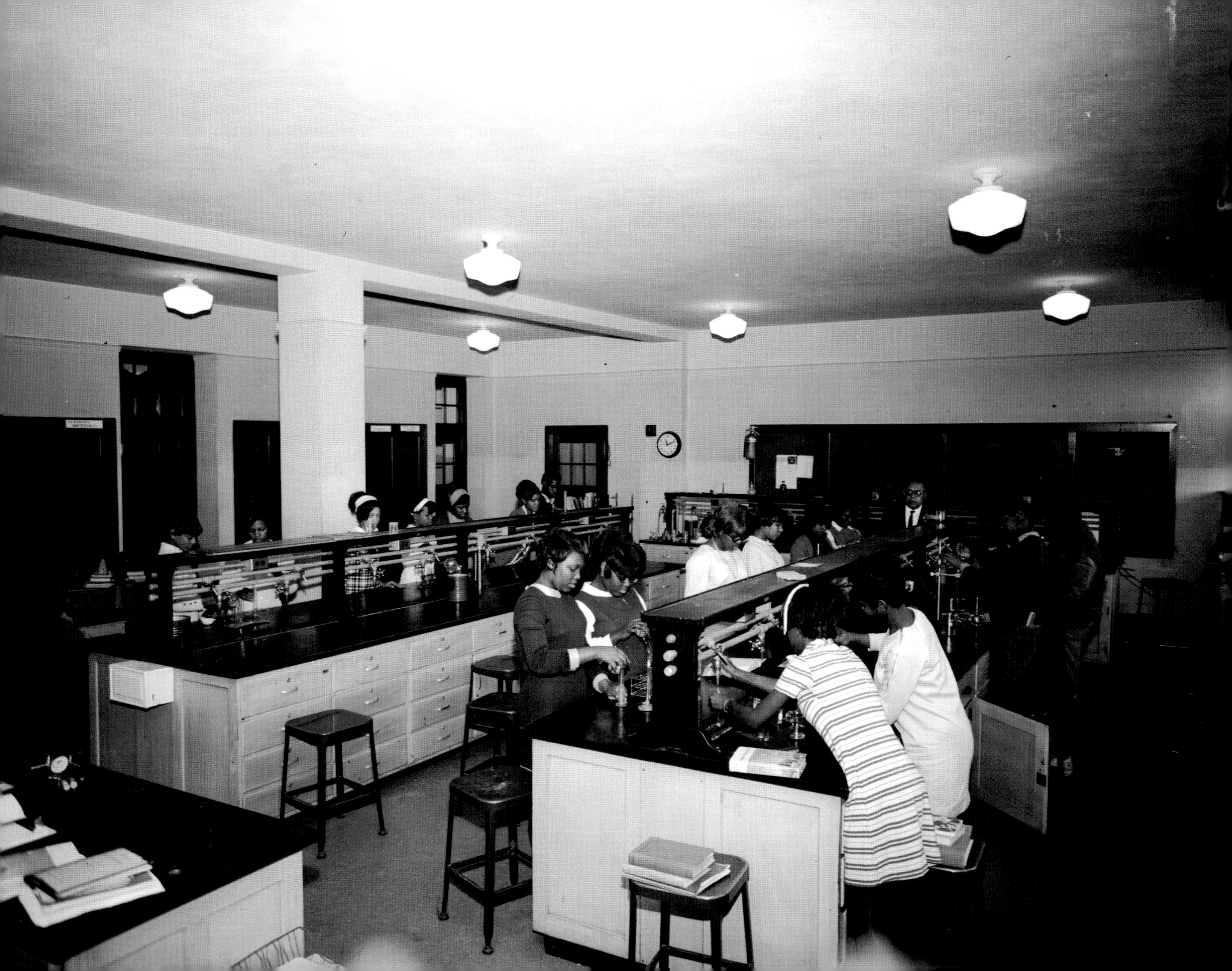

PART 2 BUSINESSES

"I was out—you might laugh about this—but I had a topic on streetcar cards. And I was supposed to make a poster for Muncie Underwear, for streetcar cards. In the country I had never seen a streetcar; I didn't know what they were."

—Calvin Littlejohn

Although he may have been from a small country town in Arkansas, the photographer quickly came to understand that he had to manage his own business and that other black businesses in the city could be a significant customer base.

In Fort Worth there was a major black business district in downtown as well as others in basically every section of the city. It was not just barbershops and beauty shops; not just hamburger stands and barbecue joints, although those were among his early and supportive clients.

Hotels and restaurants. Movie theaters and nightclubs. A major black bank and taxi cab companies. Hospitals and pharmacies. Lawyers, medical doctors and dentists. The Fort Worth African American business community was a vibrant one, thanks in part to segregation. Black entrepreneurs, with their vision and ambition, sought to fill the void that white businesses either wouldn't serve or would not serve with even a modicum of respect.

Those businesses thrived, and as they did those businessmen and women wanted their stories documented. They needed photographs for advertising on flyers, placards, and in the black newspapers. Calvin Littlejohn was there to oblige.

Of course, some of those same business people wanted Littlejohn also to be around for their special family or social occasions. Somehow, he found a way to do it all.

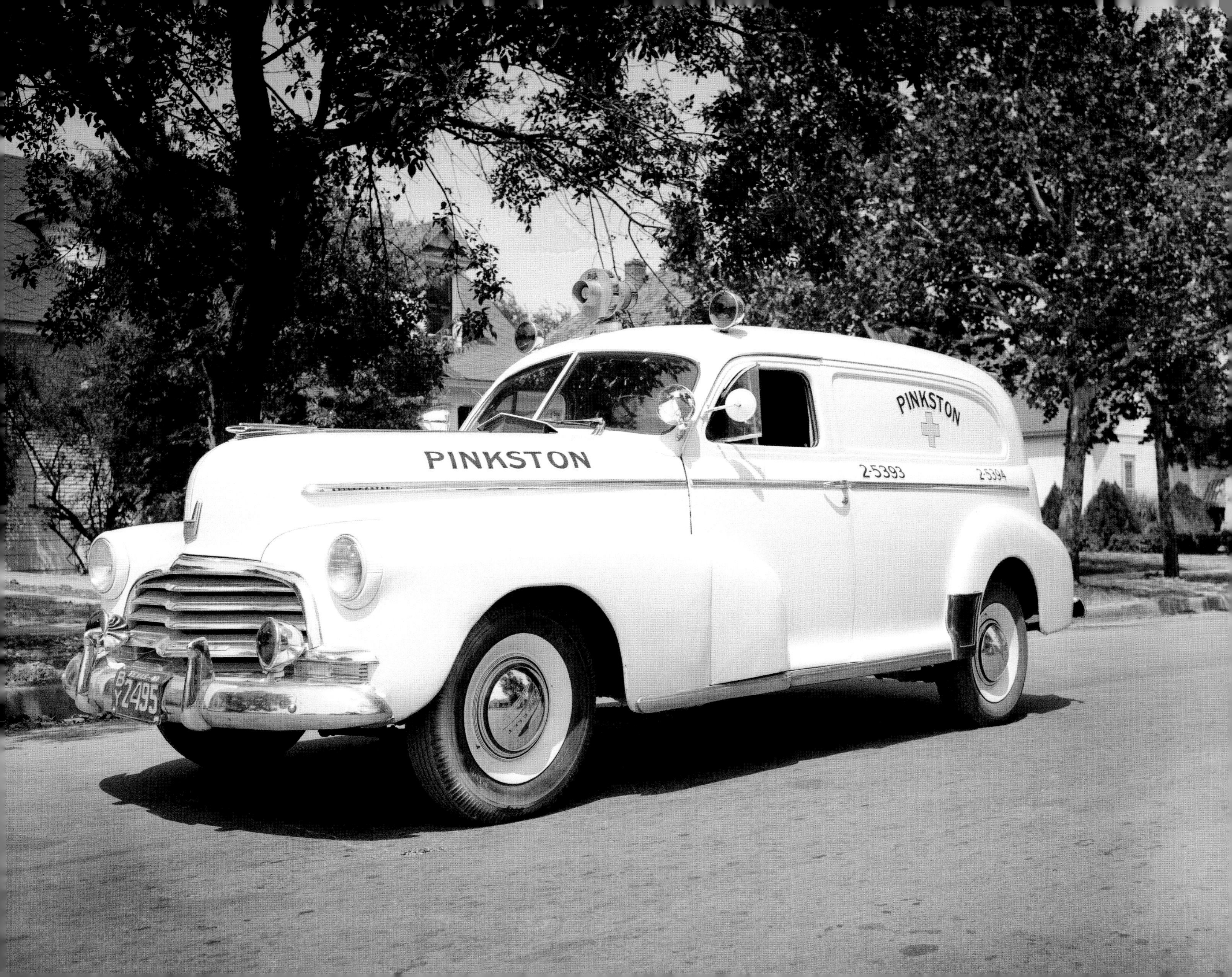
PINKSTON
PINKSTON
2-5393
2-5394

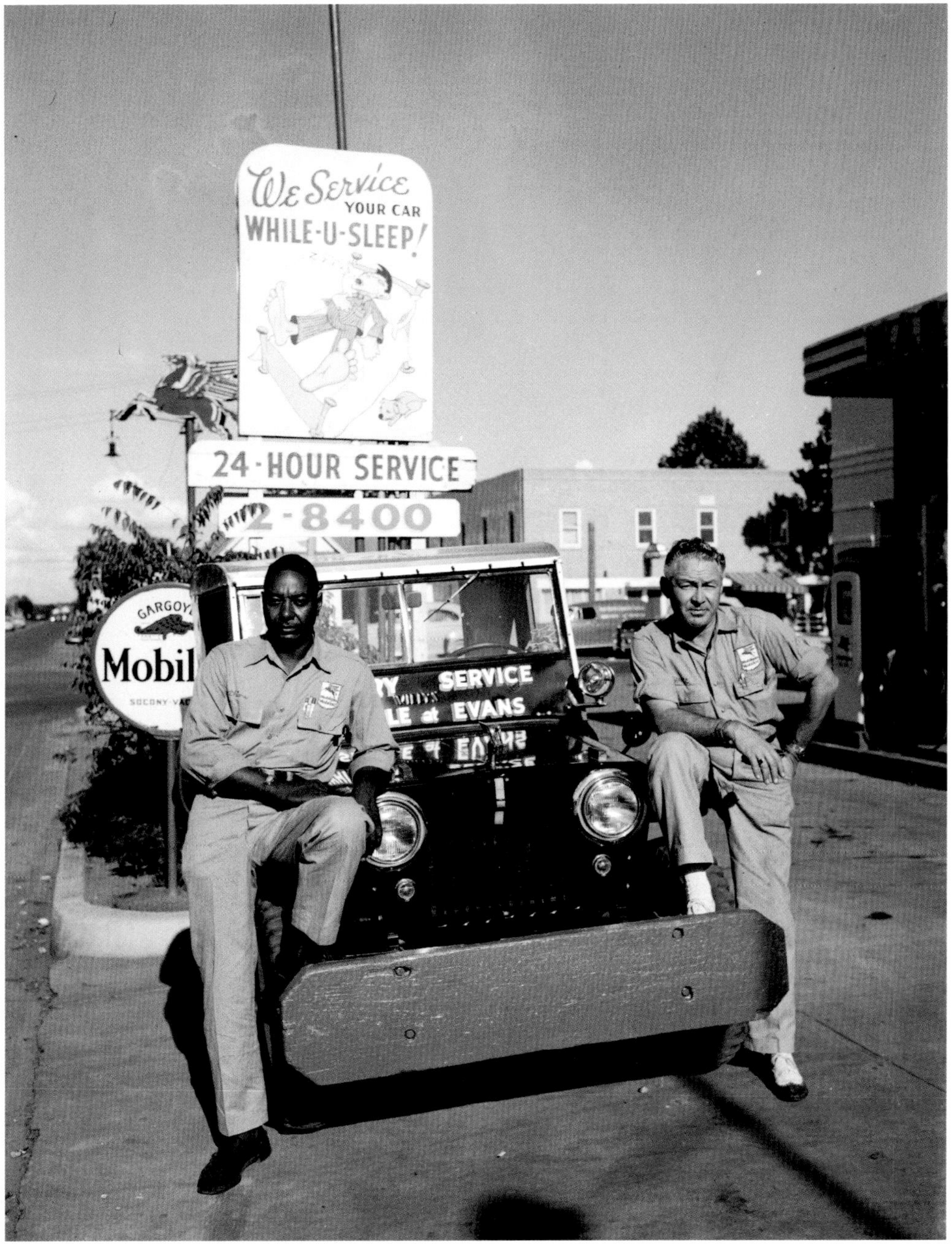

Far Left: Pinkston Funeral Home ambulance, 1948.

Left: Whit Fry Filling Station, 1949.

Next Page, Left: Mr. John Lillie, Little John's Bar-B-Q, 1966.

Next Page, Right: Funeral procession at Mount Gilead Baptist Church conducted by Brown-Hardee Funeral Home, August 20, 1950.

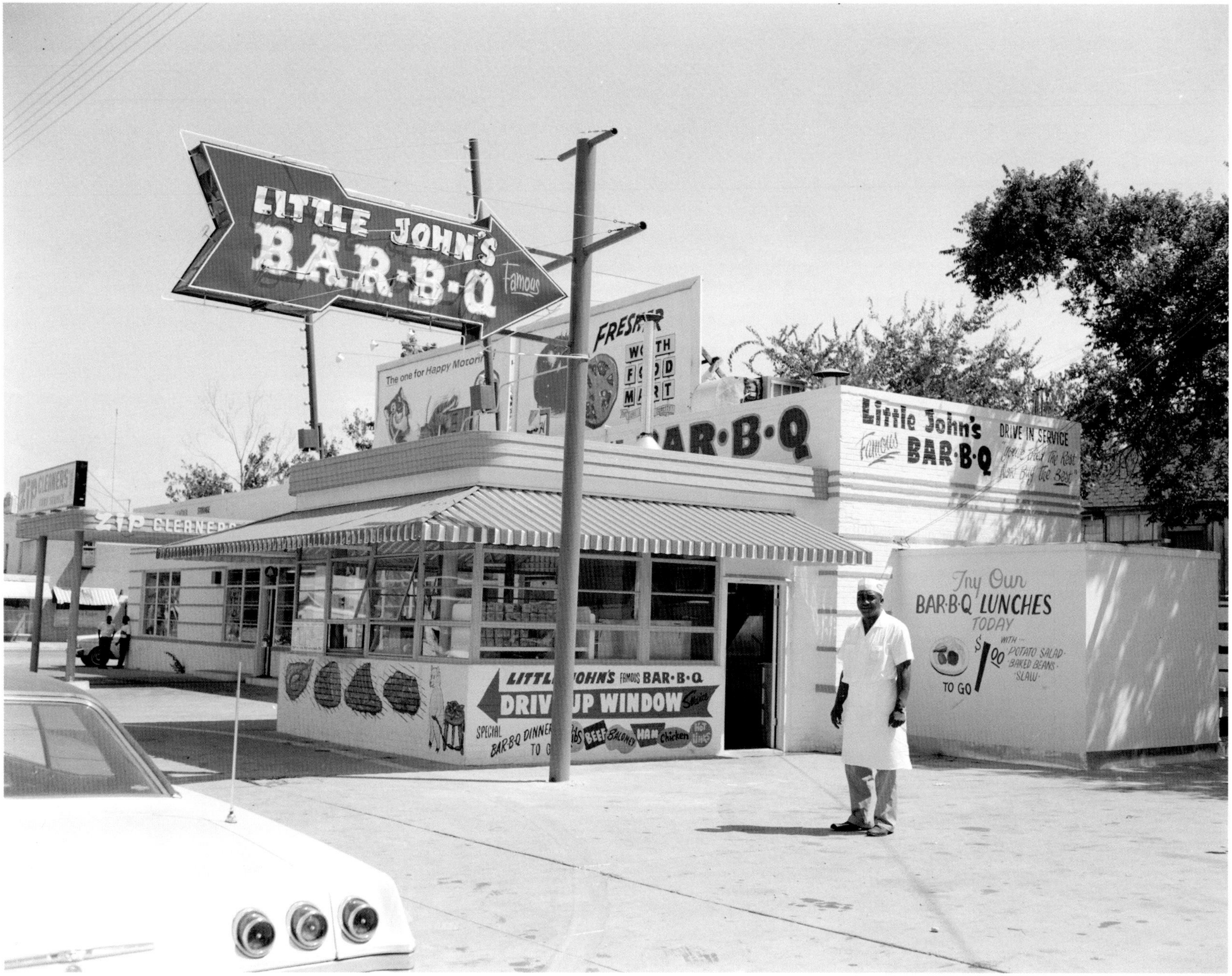
LITTLE JOHN'S
BAR-B-Q
Famous
BAR-B-Q
Little John's
Famous BAR-B-Q
DRIVE IN SERVICE
ZIP CLEANERS
DRIVE UP WINDOW
Try Our
BAR-B-Q LUNCHES
TODAY
$1.00
WITH
POTATO SALAD
BAKED BEANS
SLAW
TO GO

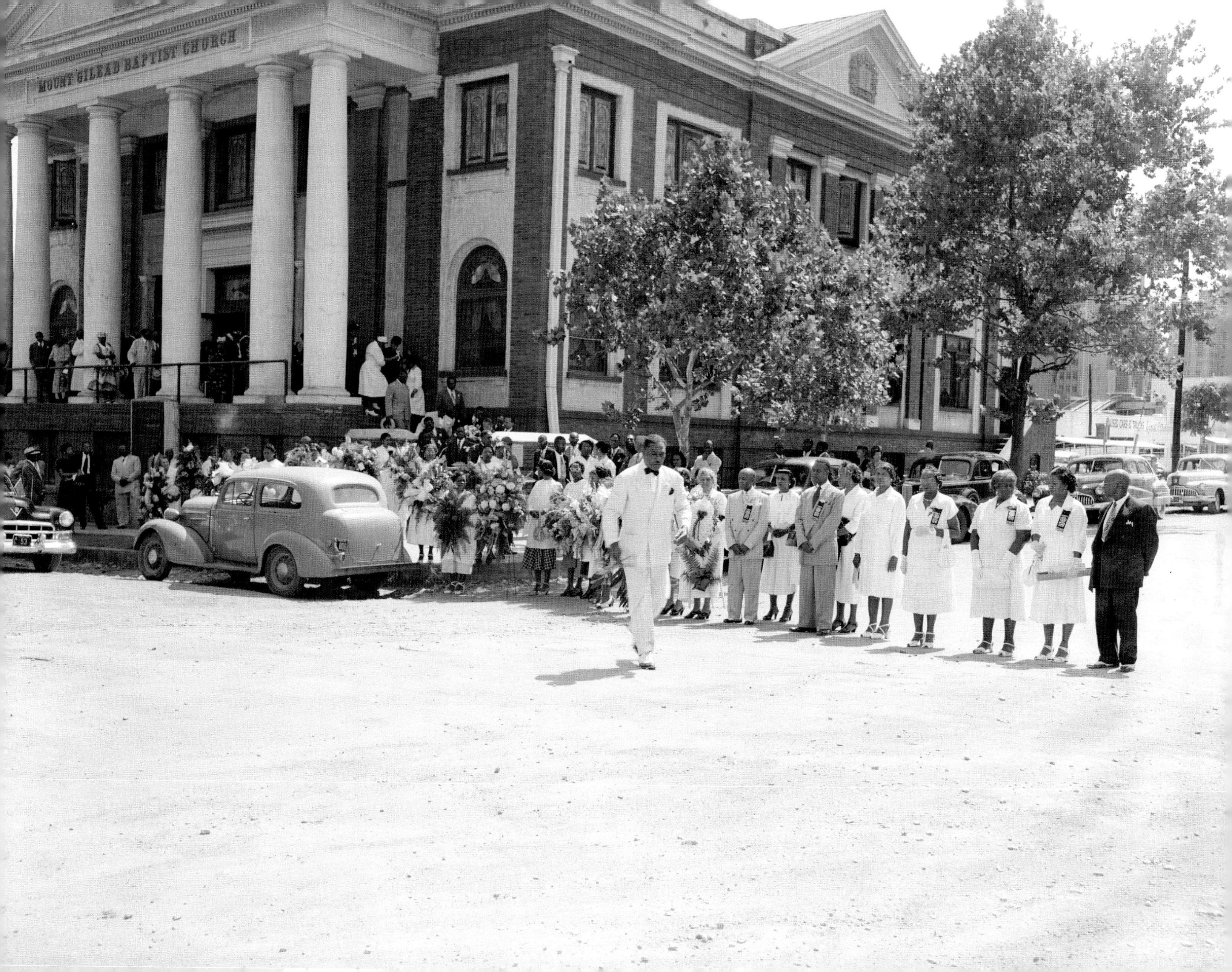
MOUNT GILEAD BAPTIST CHURCH

Right: Jazz saxophonist Illinois Jacquet (left) at the Flint Hotel, with C. W. Flint, Jr.

Far Right: A soldier's funeral at Baker Funeral Home, April 6, 1949.

Next Page, Left: Rodger Payne, pharmacist, at work at Payne's Drug Store, c. 1949.

Next Page, Right: Ethel Ransom Memorial Hospital, c. 1940.

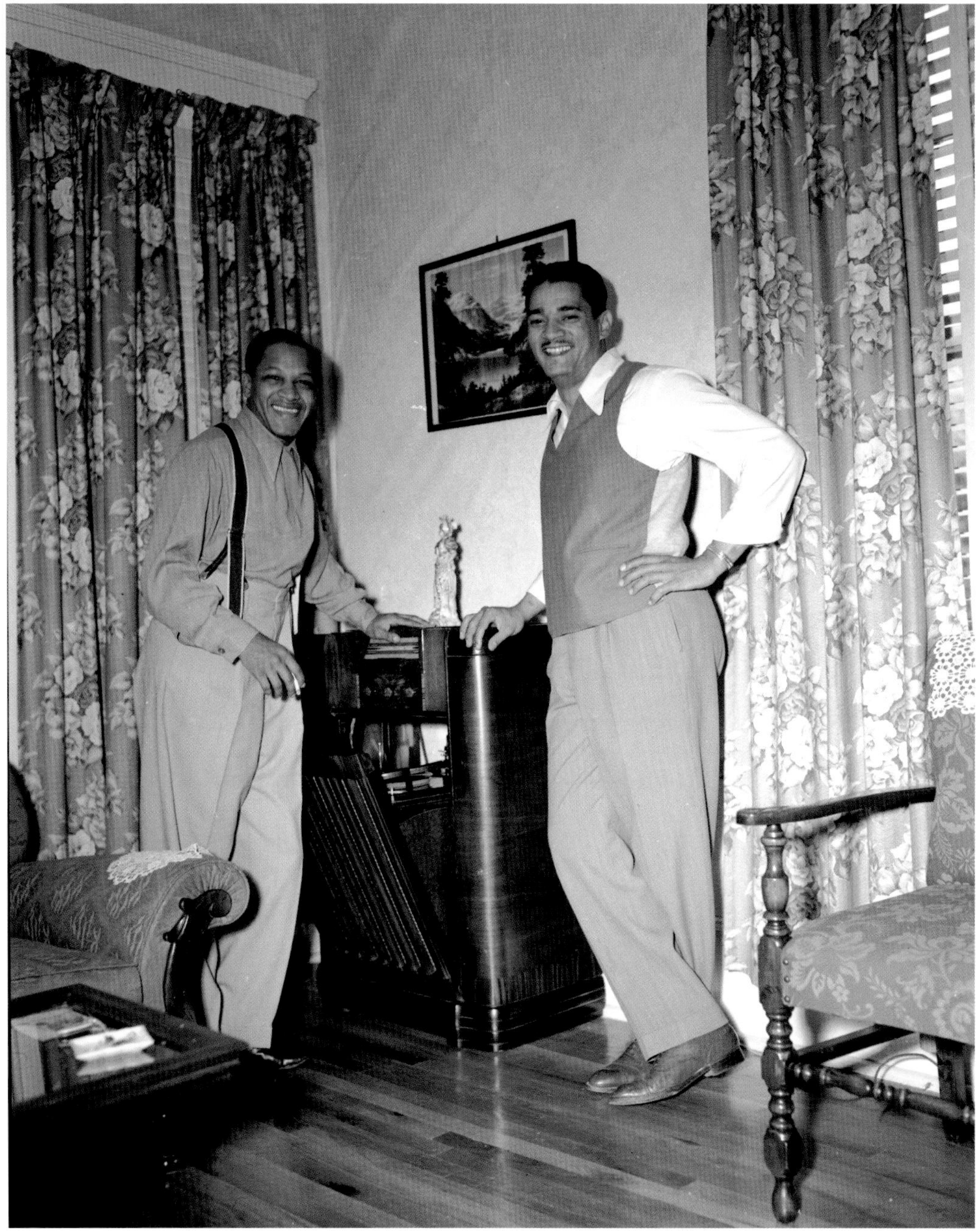

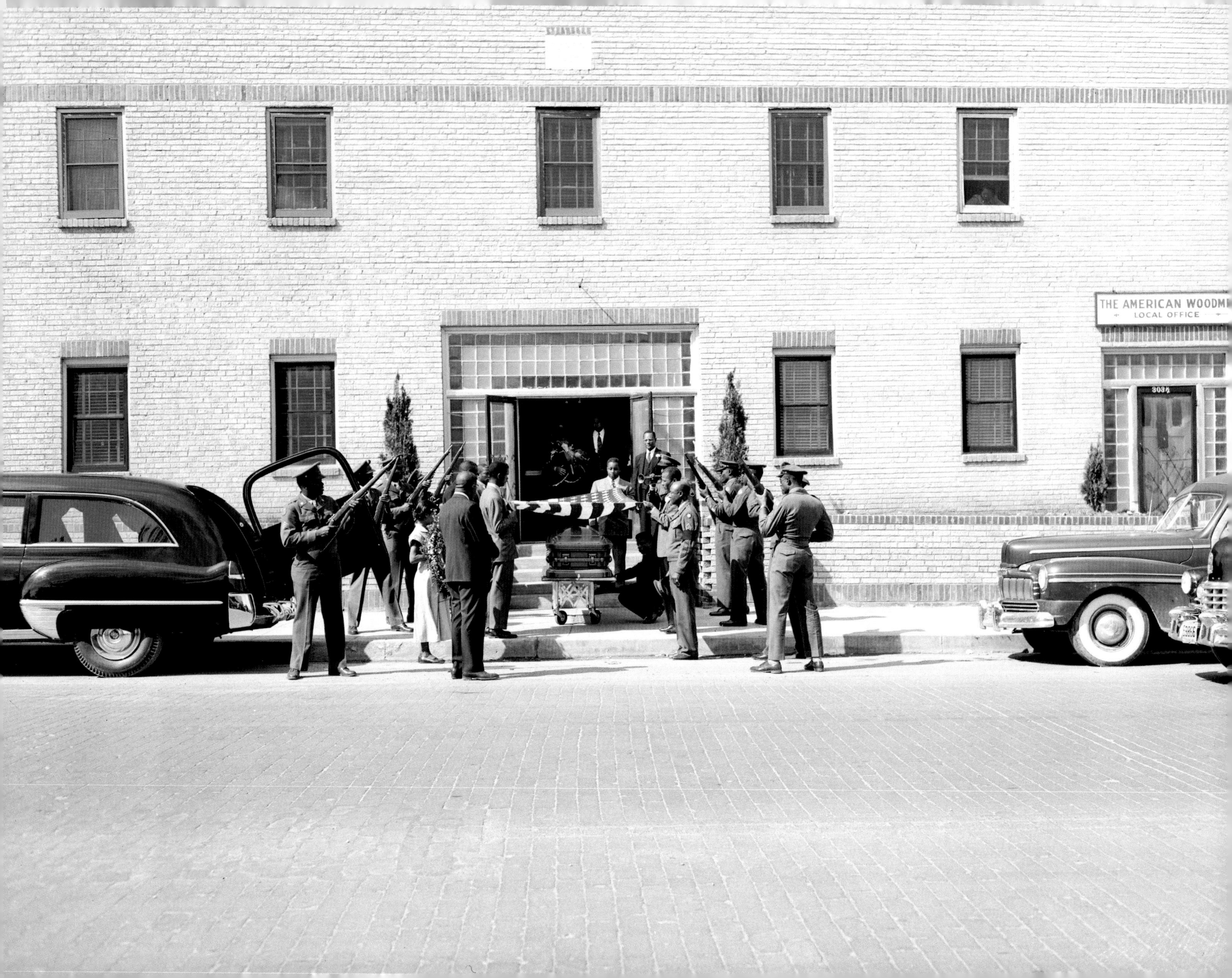
THE AMERICAN WOODM
LOCAL OFFICE
3034

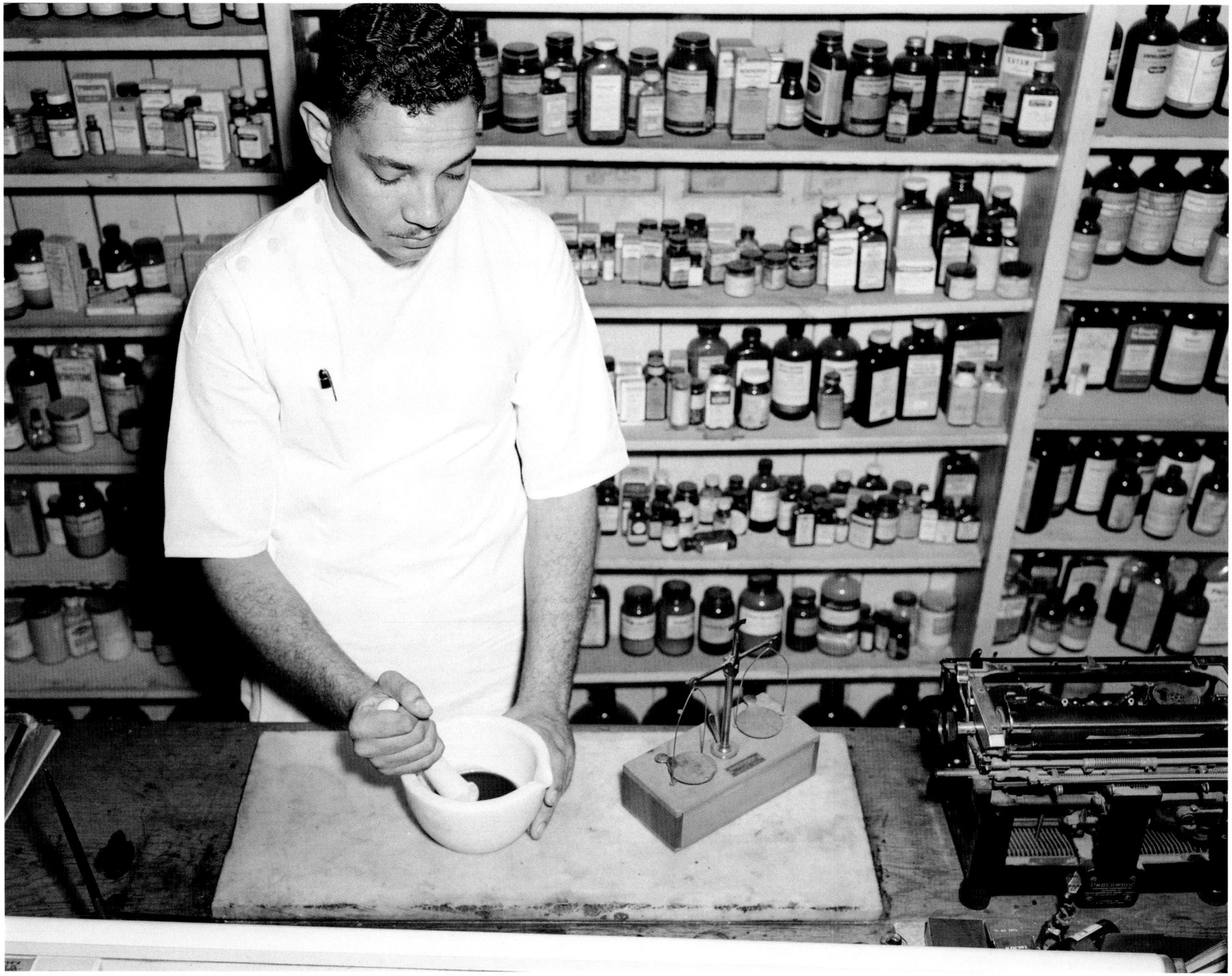

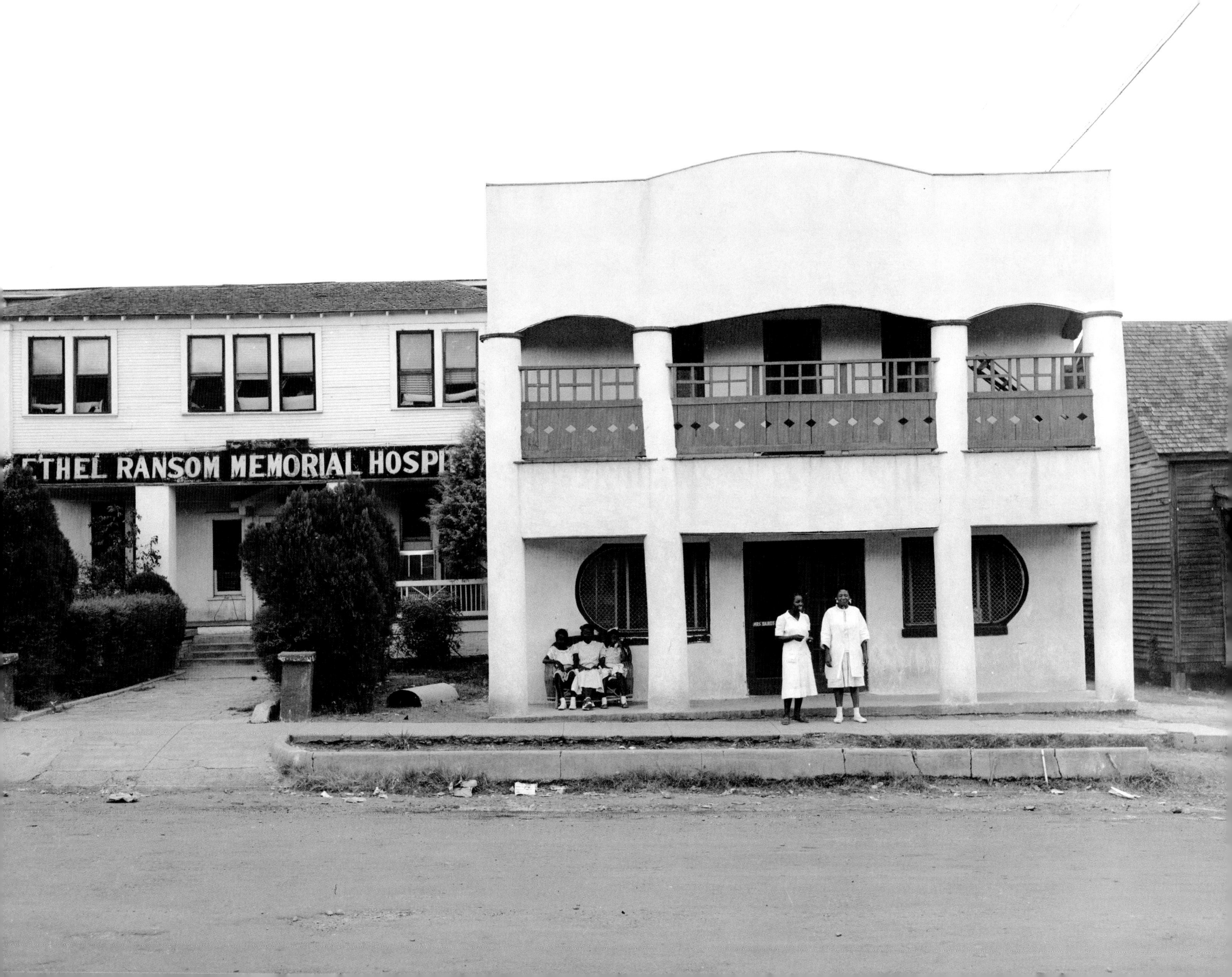
ETHEL RANSOM MEMORIAL HOSP

Right: Mrs. Lucille Smith demonstrating Lucille's Hot Roll Mix, Dallas grocery store, March 18, 1950.

Far Right: U. S. Smith's Famous Bar-B-Q building and parking lot, located on the city's North Side.

Next Page, Left: Customers in the main lobby of Fraternal Bank and Trust, 1950.

Next Page, Right: Two women seated in the school room of Dickerson's Beauty School, located on Rosedale Street and Illinois Avenue.

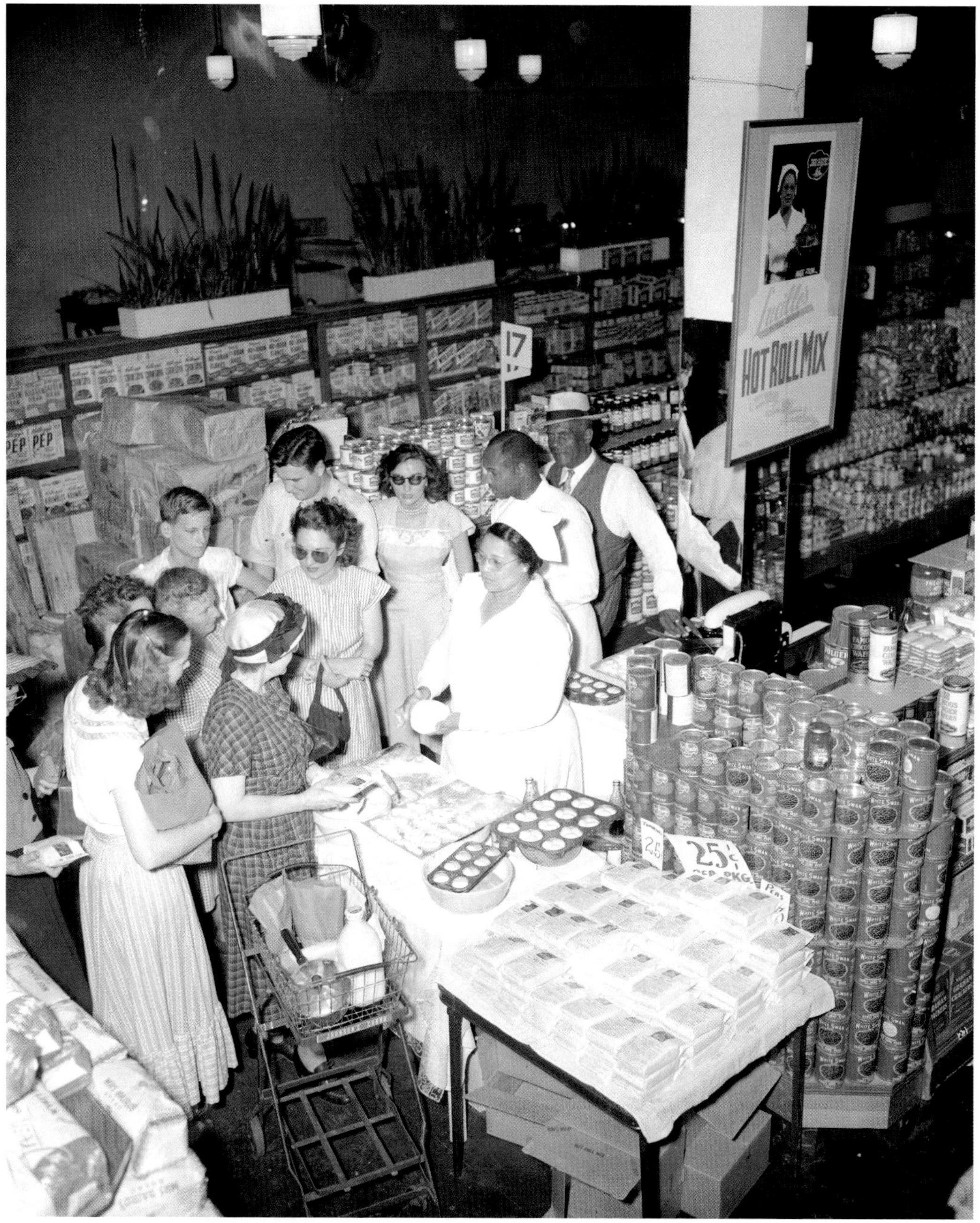

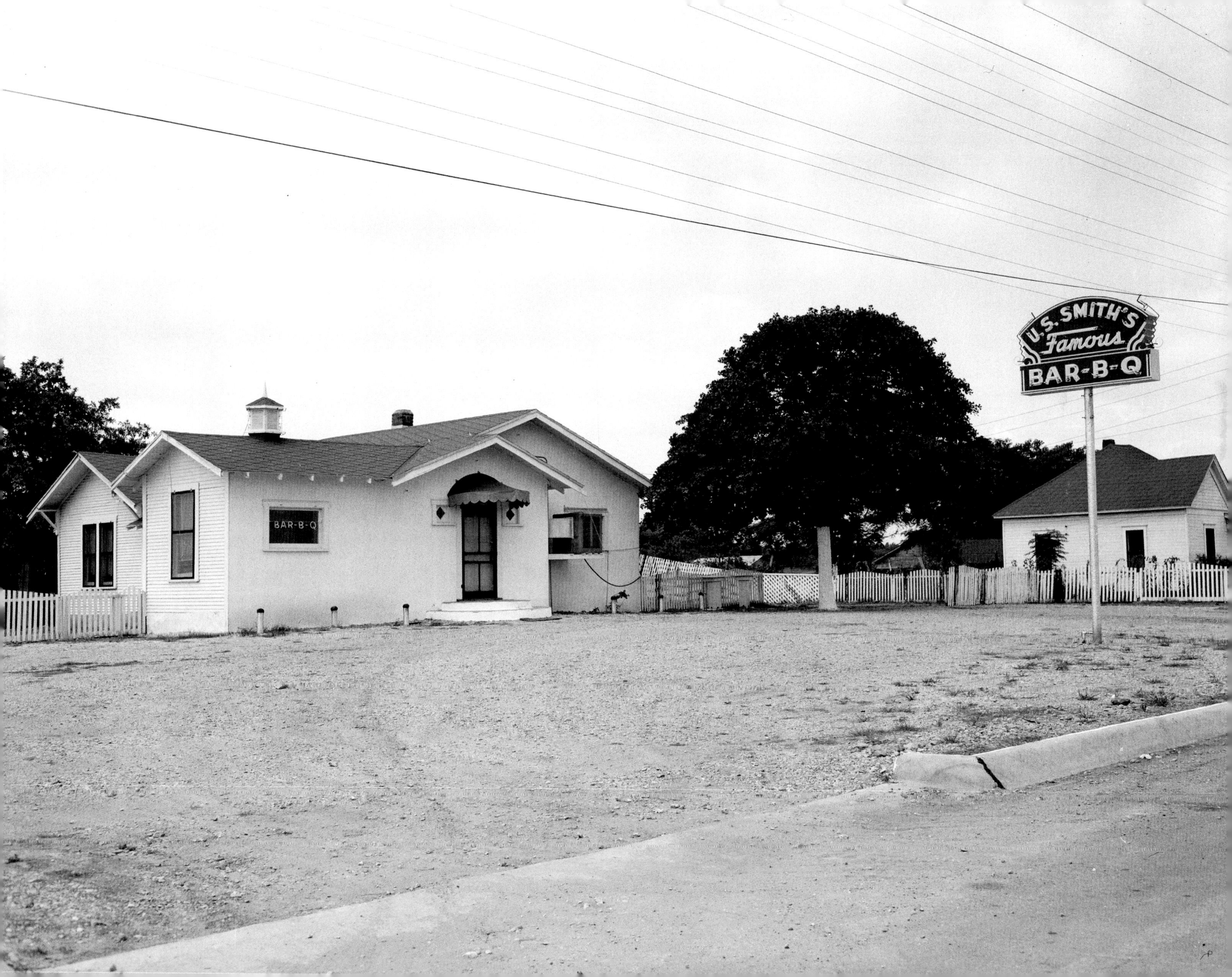
BAR-B-Q
U.S. SMITH'S
Famous
BAR-B-Q

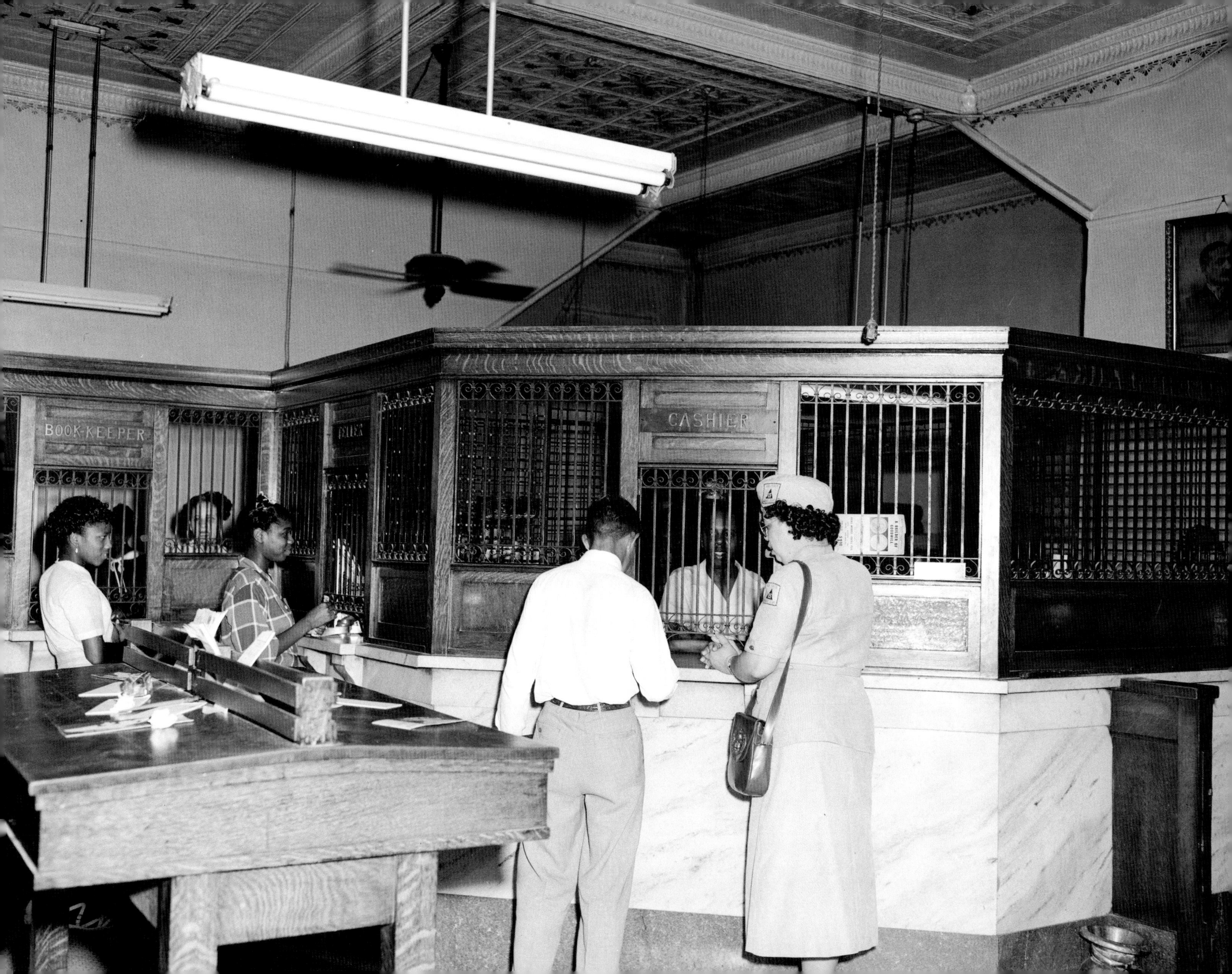
BOOK-KEEPER
CASHIER

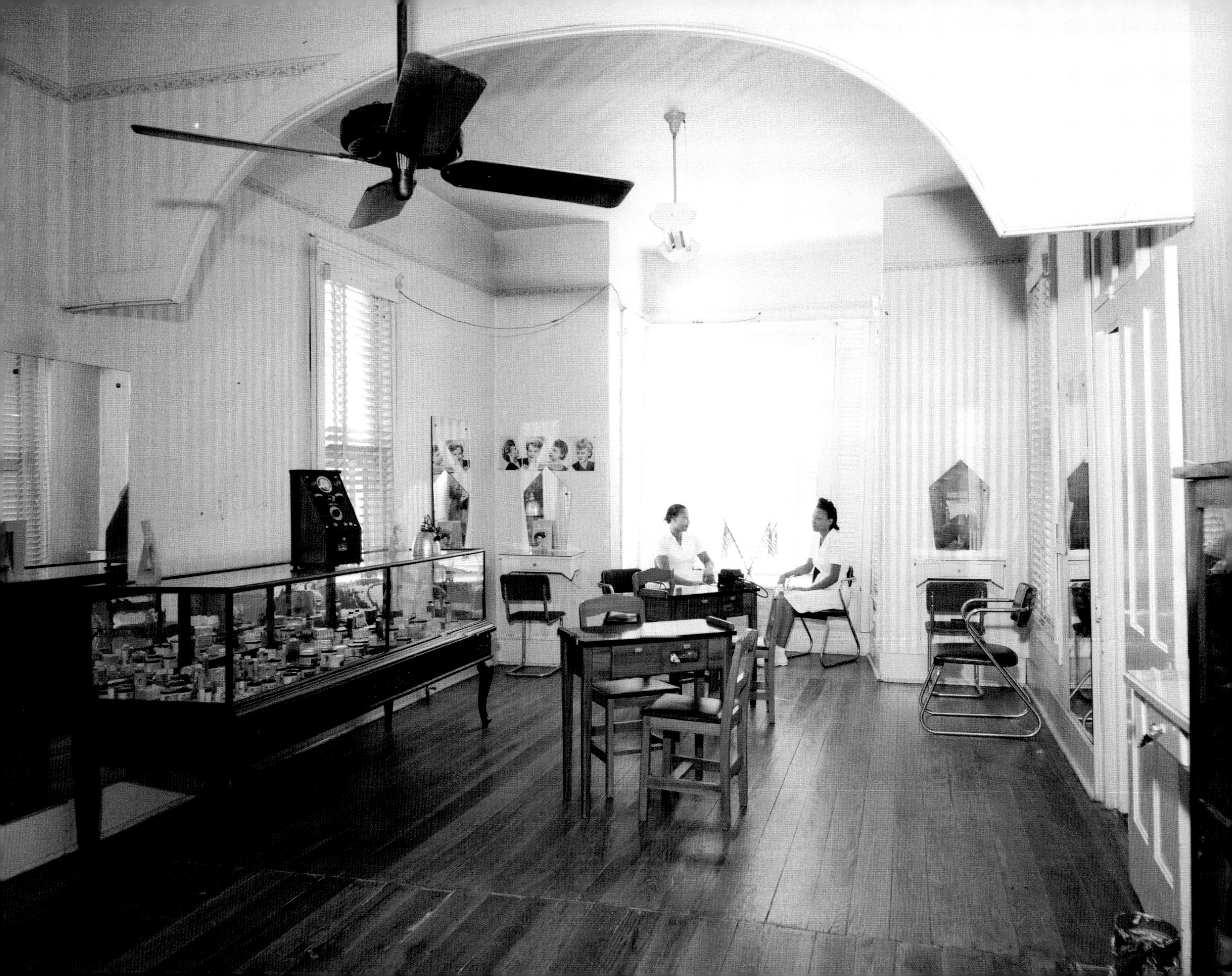

Right: Fashion Dress Shop—Mrs. Bertha Mitchell, proprietor, is on the right. March 9, 1951.

Far Right: A "George Washington Tea" at Dickerson's Beauty School.

Next Page, Left: Dickerson's Beauty School, February 22, 1949.

Next Page, Right: Barbershop owner Homer Williams at work, 1951.

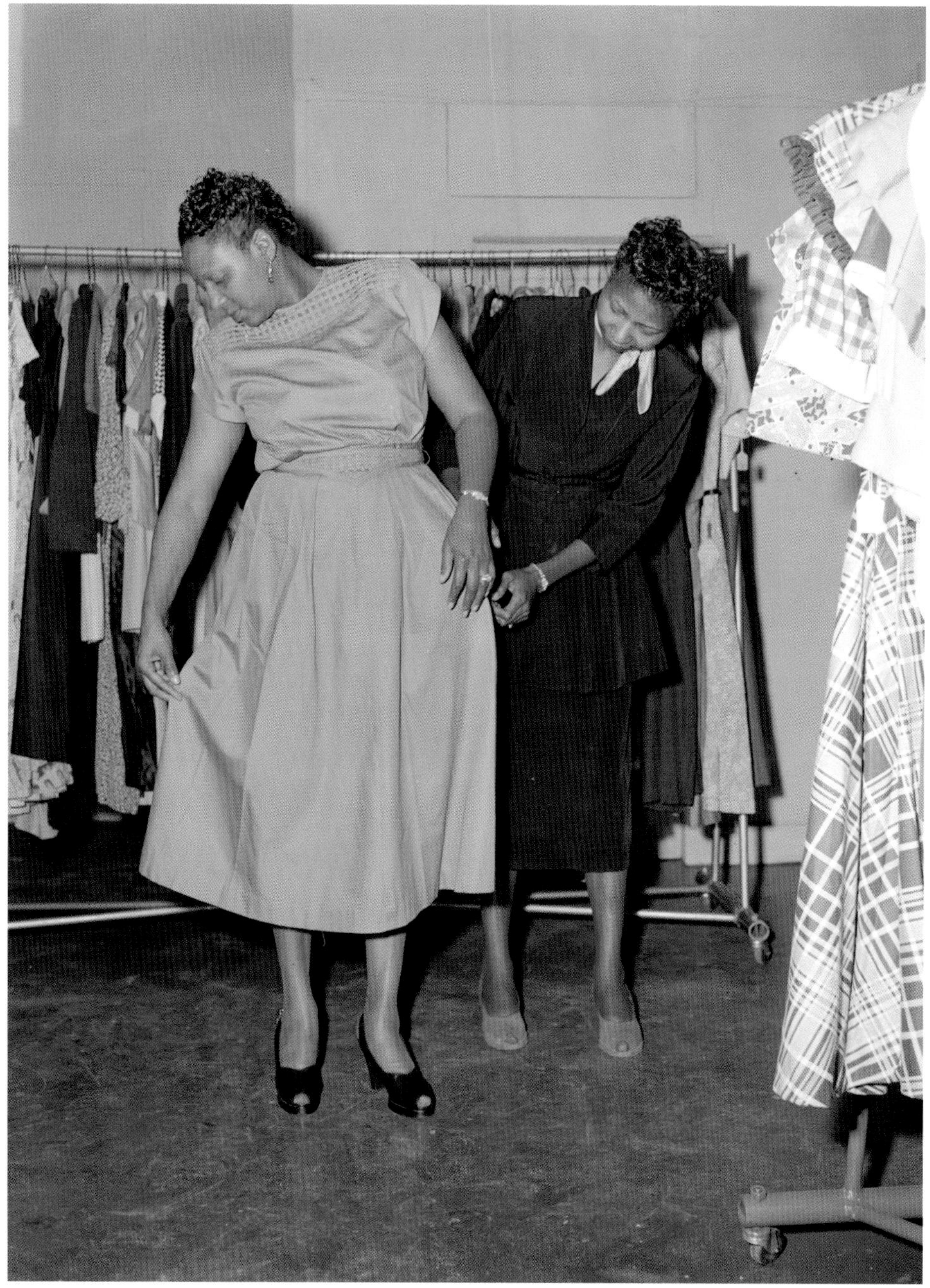

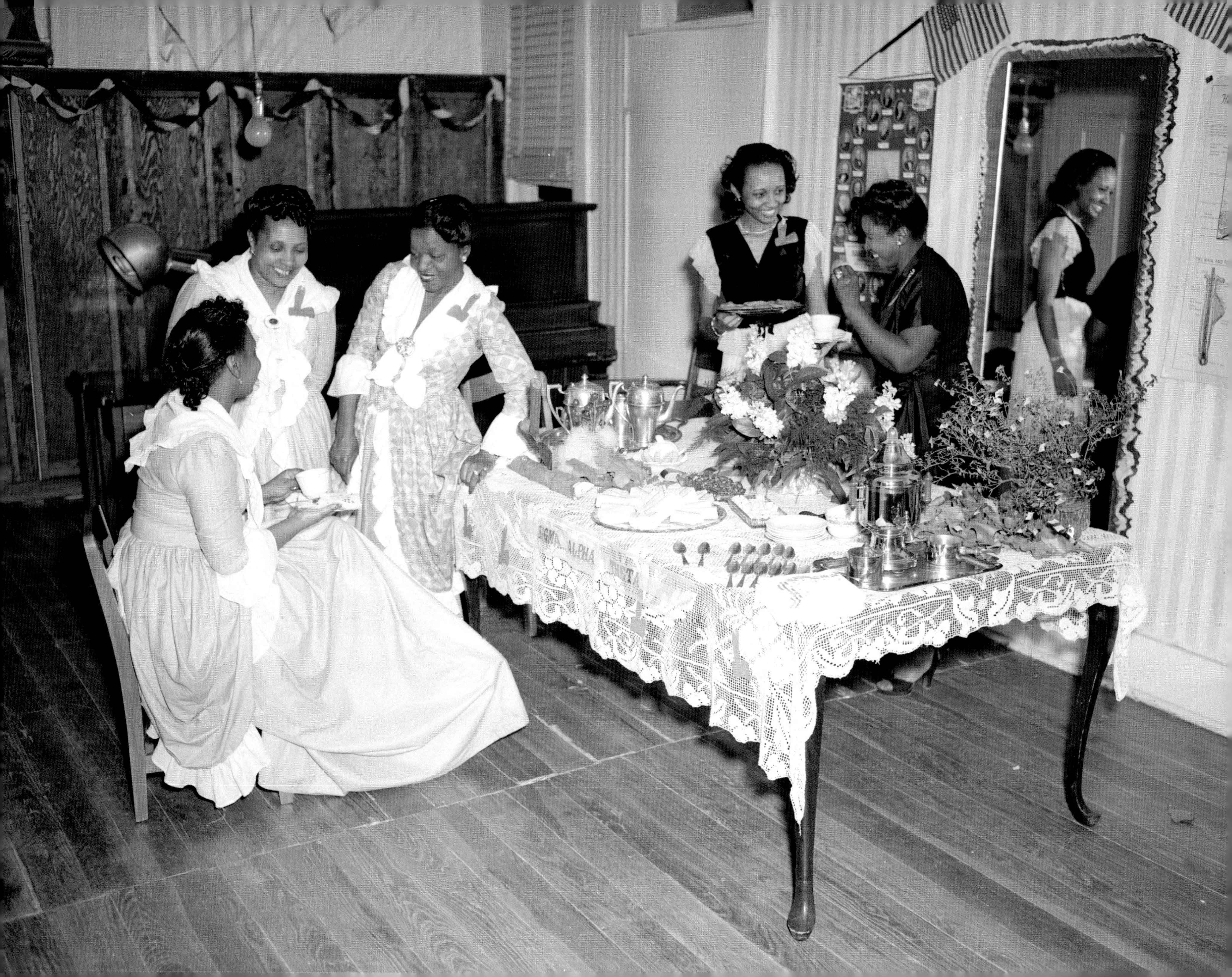

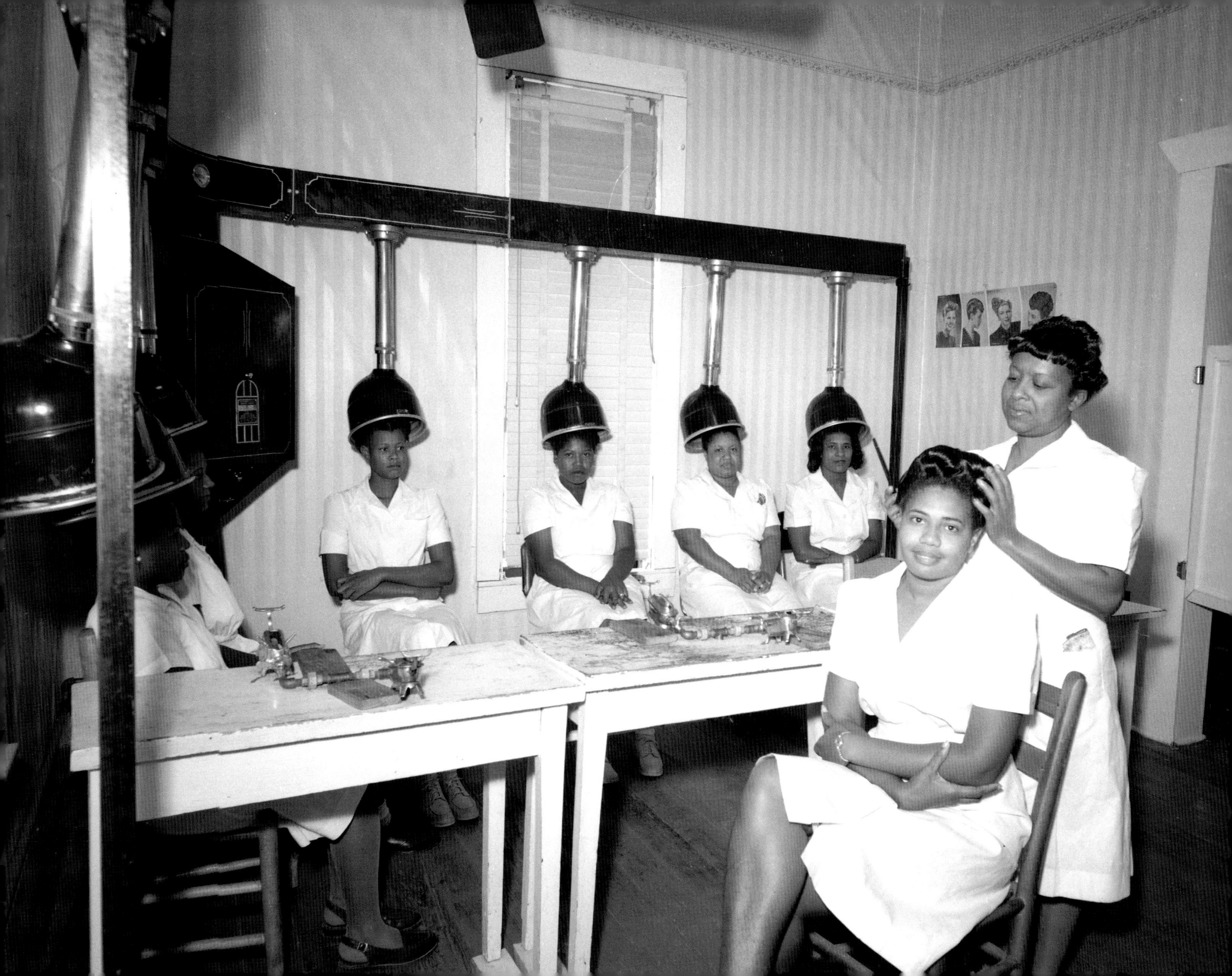

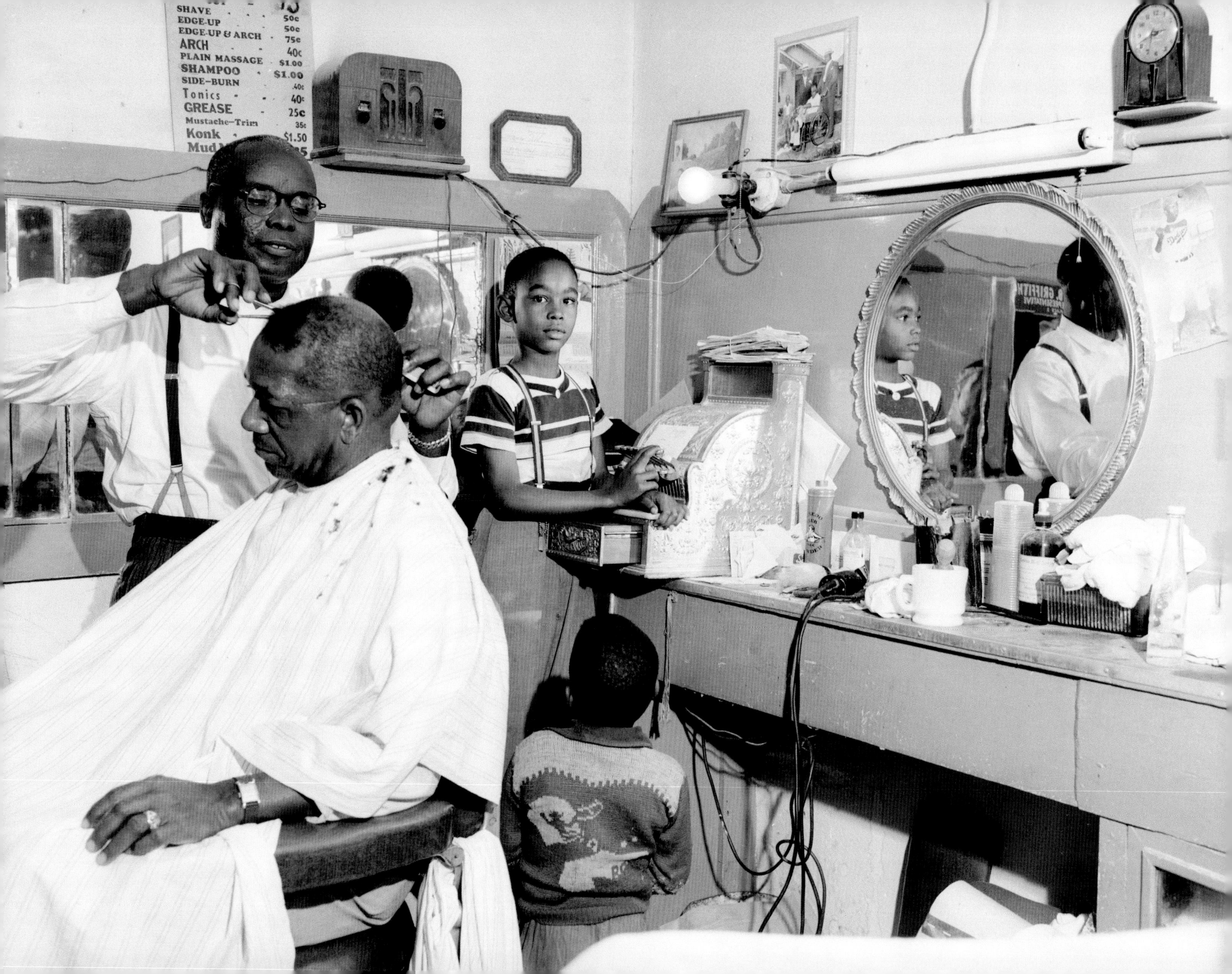
SHAVE
EDGE-UP 50c
EDGE-UP & ARCH 75c
ARCH 40c
PLAIN MASSAGE $1.00
SHAMPOO $1.00
SIDE-BURN .40c
Tonics 40c
GREASE 25c
Mustache-Trim 35c
Konk $1.50

Right: Mrs. Robinson's grandson, studio portrait, December 10, 1950.

Far Right: Pee Wee's Shoe Shop on Terrell Avenue, December 29, 1959.

Next Page, Left: Milbane Grocery on New York Avenue, 1954.

Next Page, Right: Fresh Air Taxi Stand on Magnolia Avenue.

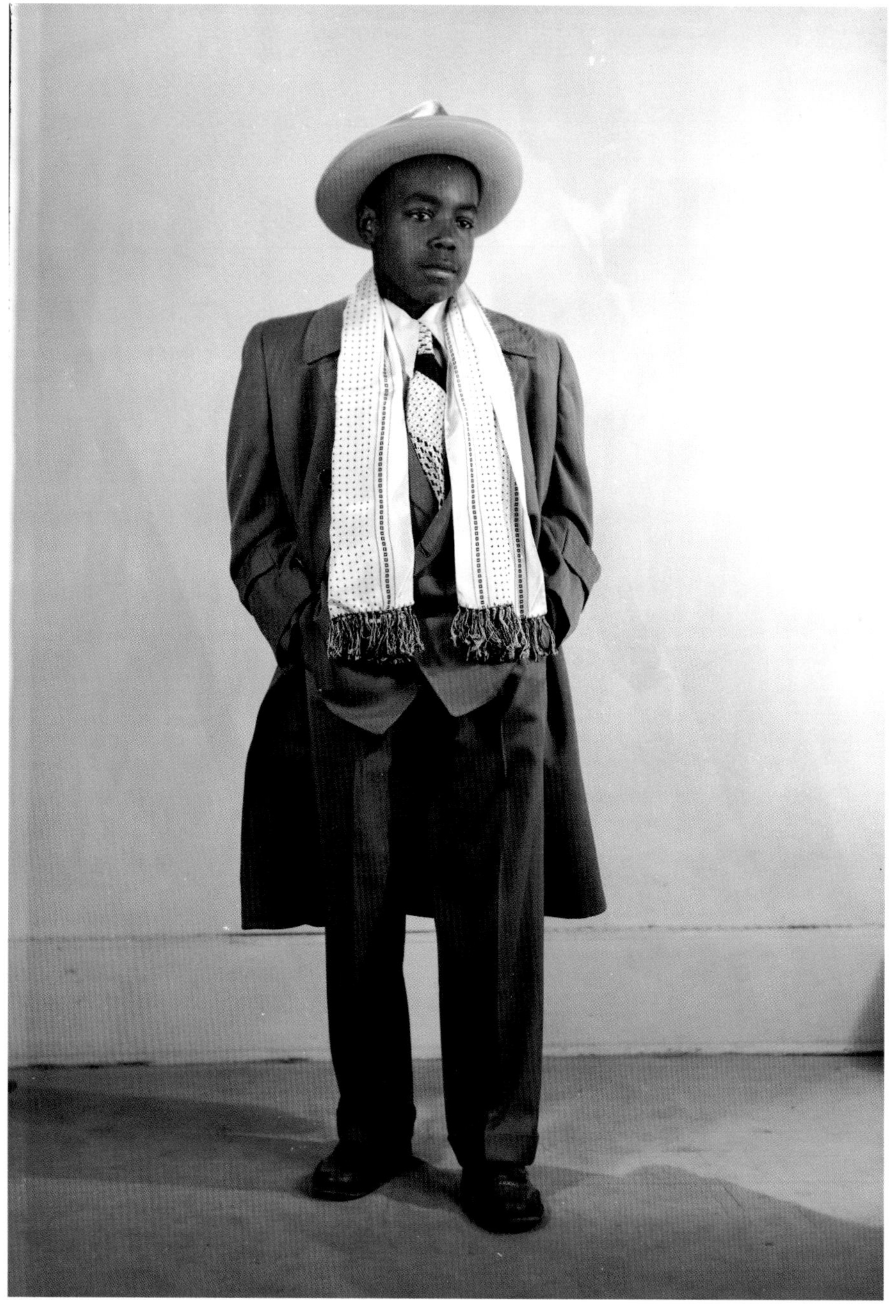

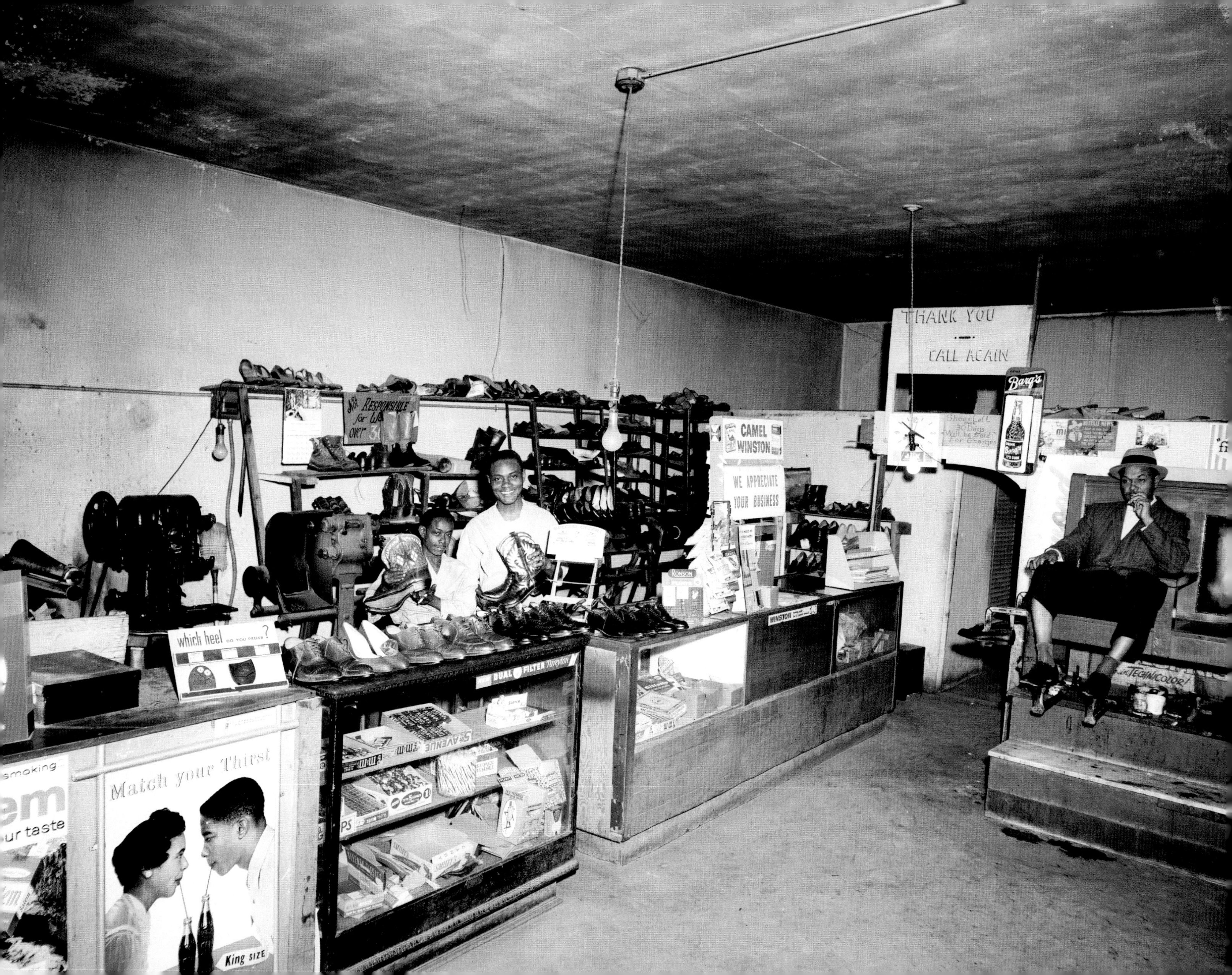

THANK YOU
CALL AGAIN
CAMEL
WINSTON
WE APPRECIATE YOUR BUSINESS
Barq's
Shoes Left over 30 Days Will be Sold For Charges
which heel
DUAL FILTER Tareyton
WINSTON
RONSON
5th AVENUE
Match your Thirst
King SIZE
smoking...
your taste

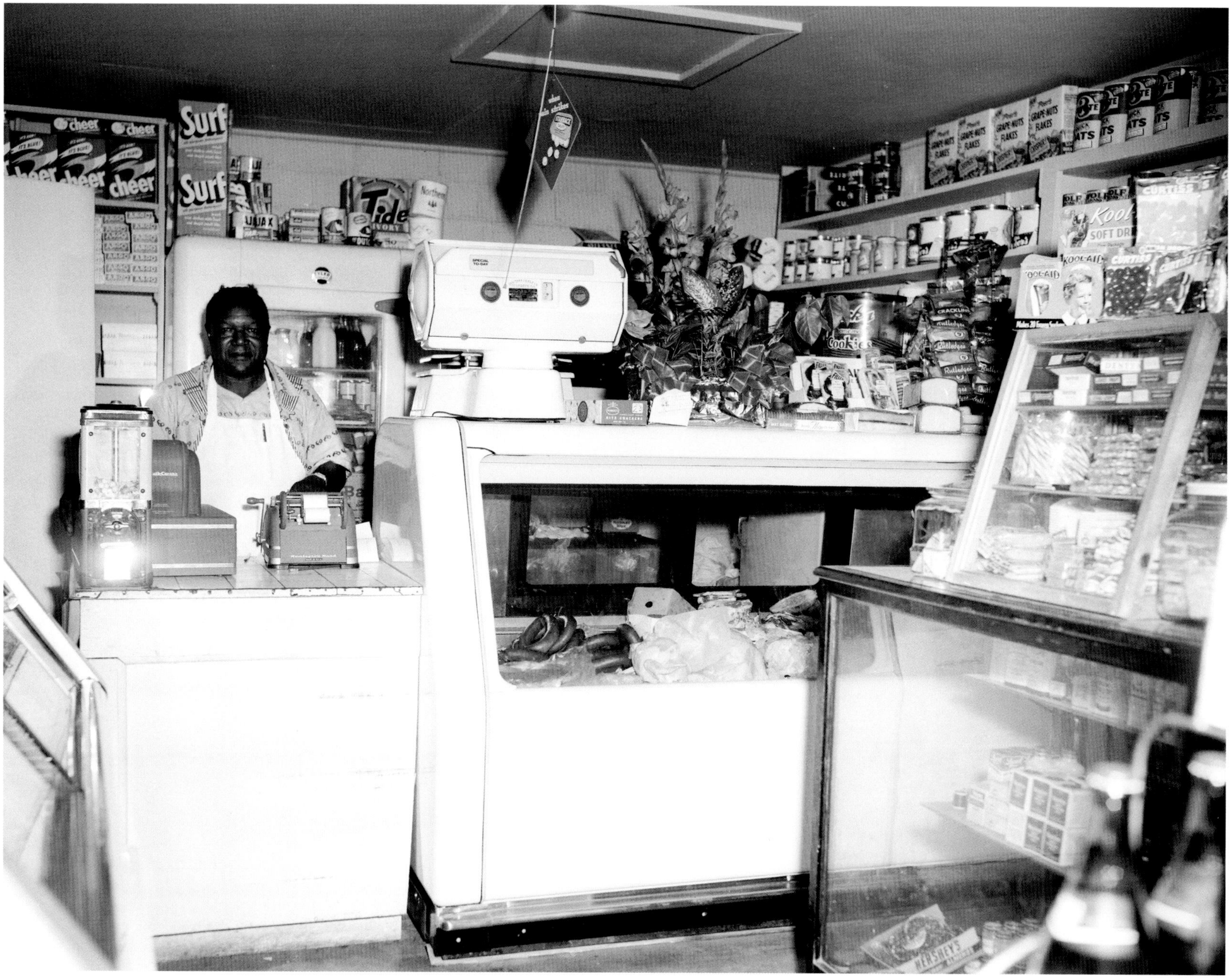
cheer
Surf
Tide
GRAPE-NUTS FLAKES
CURTISS
Cookies
HERSHEY'S

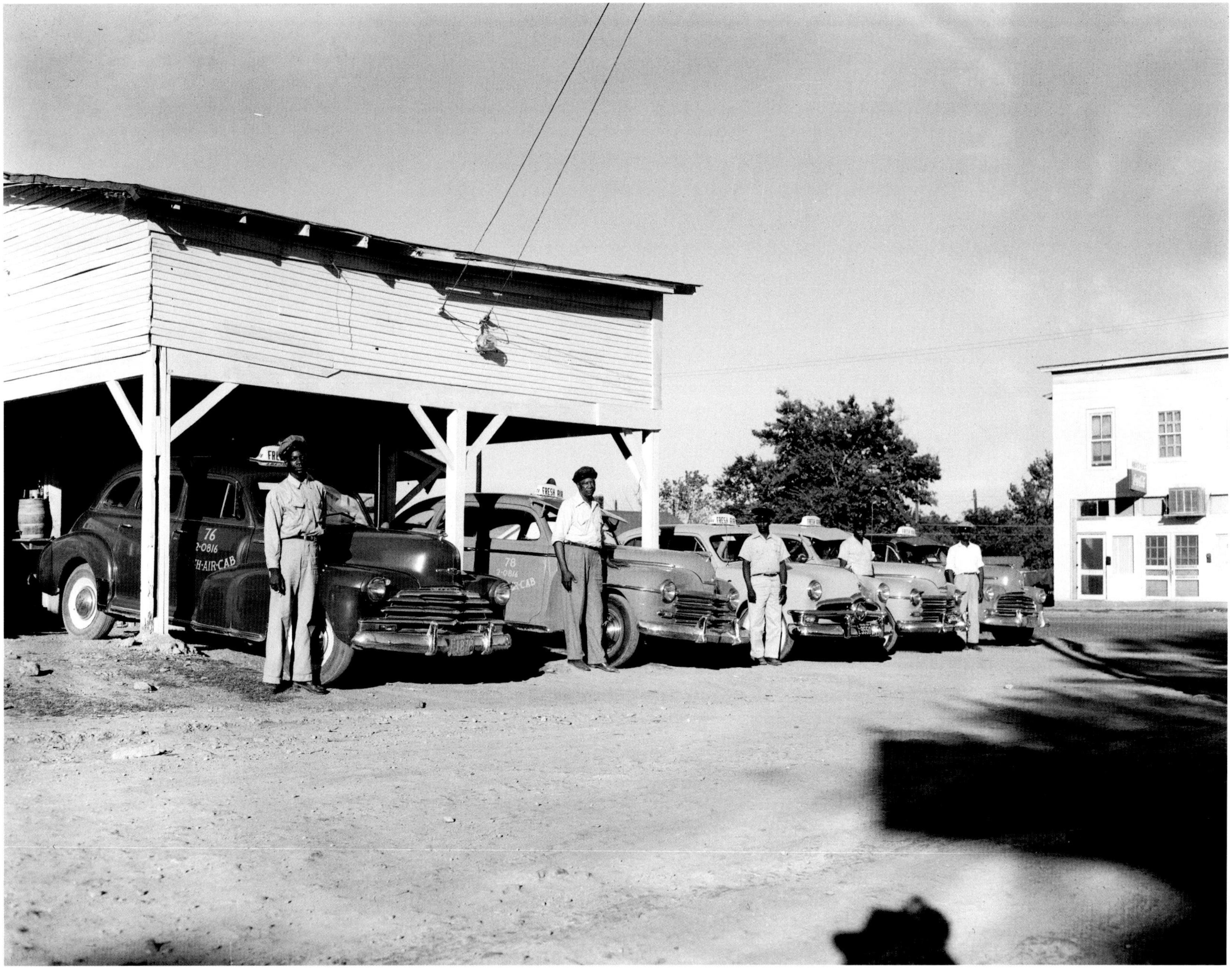
FRESH AIR
76
2-0816
78
2-0816

Right: Mr. U. S. Smith, studio portrait in chef's uniform, March 23, 1949.

Far Right: Bill "Gooseneck" McDonald, founder and president of Fraternal Bank and Trust, seated at the desk in his office, 1950.

Next Page, Left: Brothers Oscar Cooper, Jr., (left) and Lonnell Cooper (center) with friend Hugh Talton at the main bar of the Jim Hotel in downtown Fort Worth, 1947. Lonnell Cooper became one of the first black police officers hired by the city of Fort Worth in the 1950s. The hotel was owned by brothers Oscar Cooper, Sr., and Levi Cooper.

Next Page, Right: Flint Hotel, 1400 Jones Street, 1949.

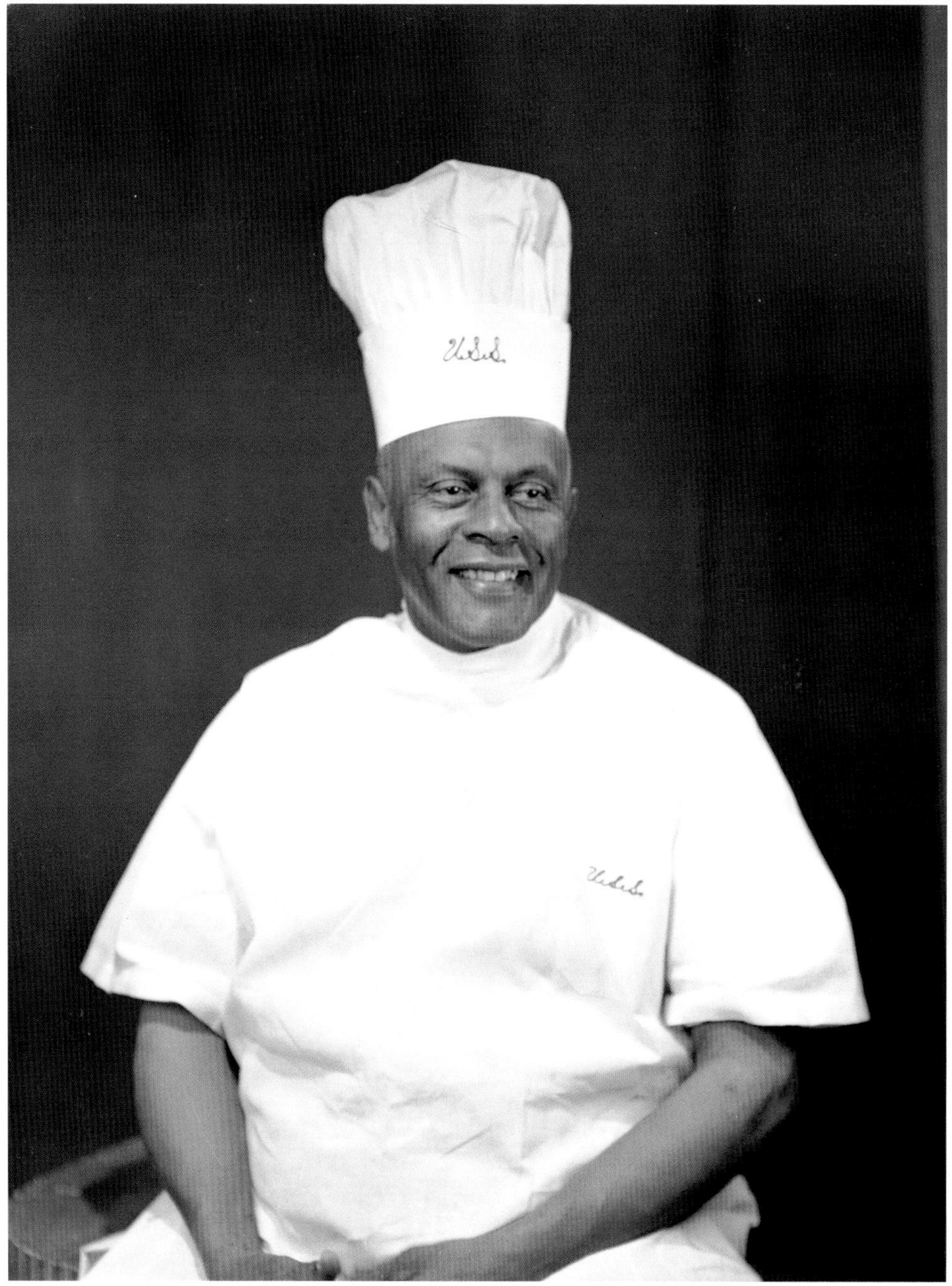

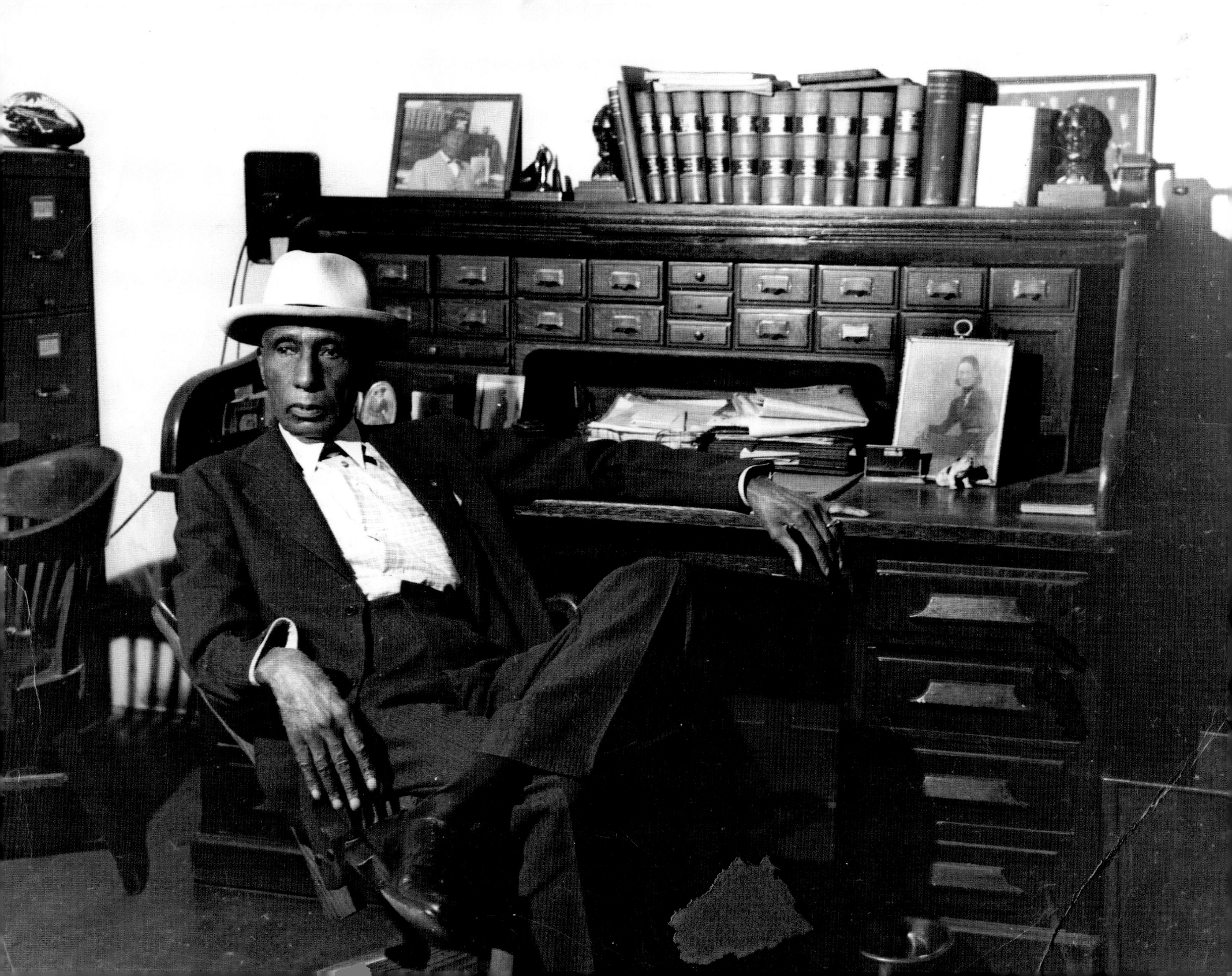

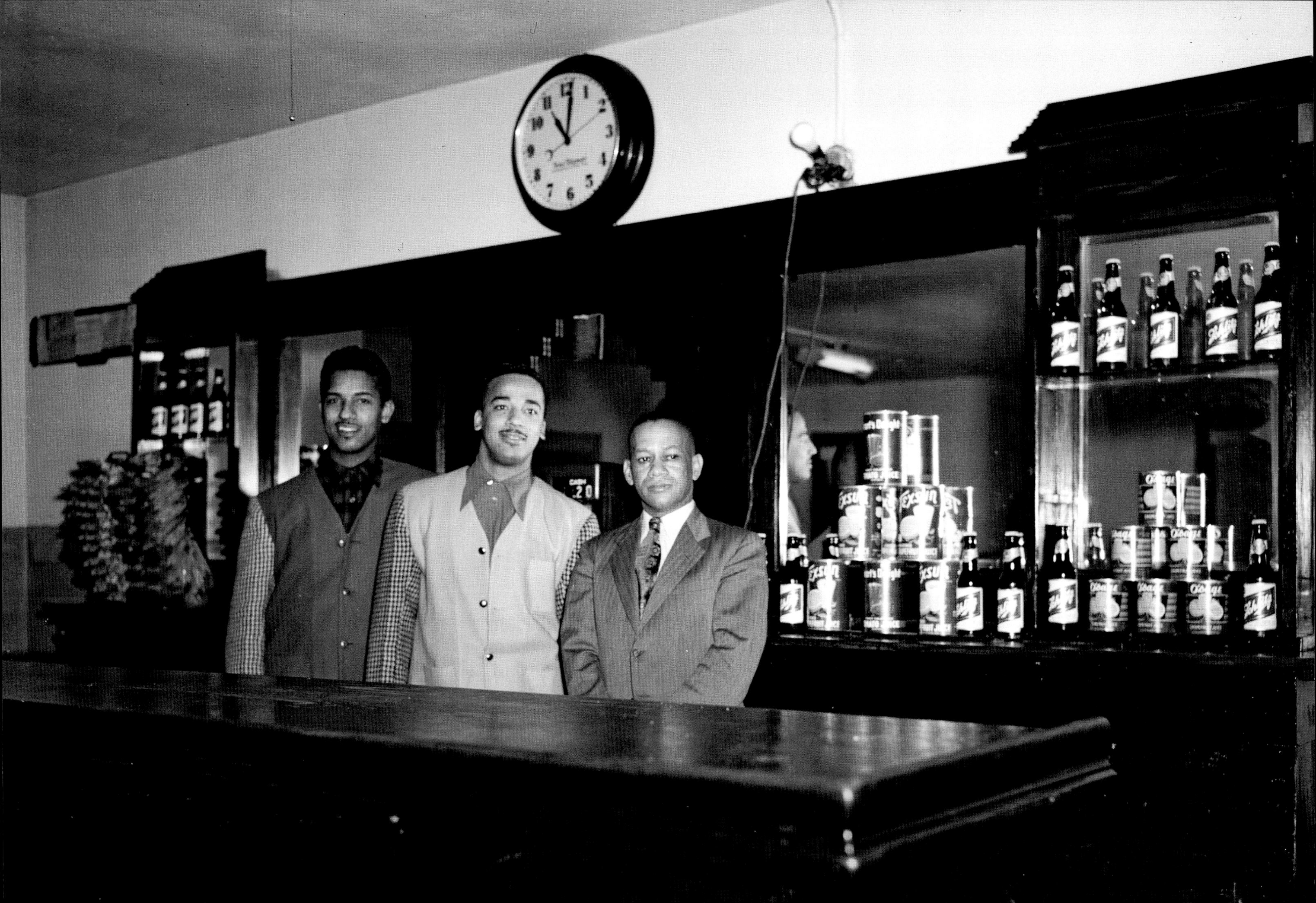
Texsun
Schlitz
Osage

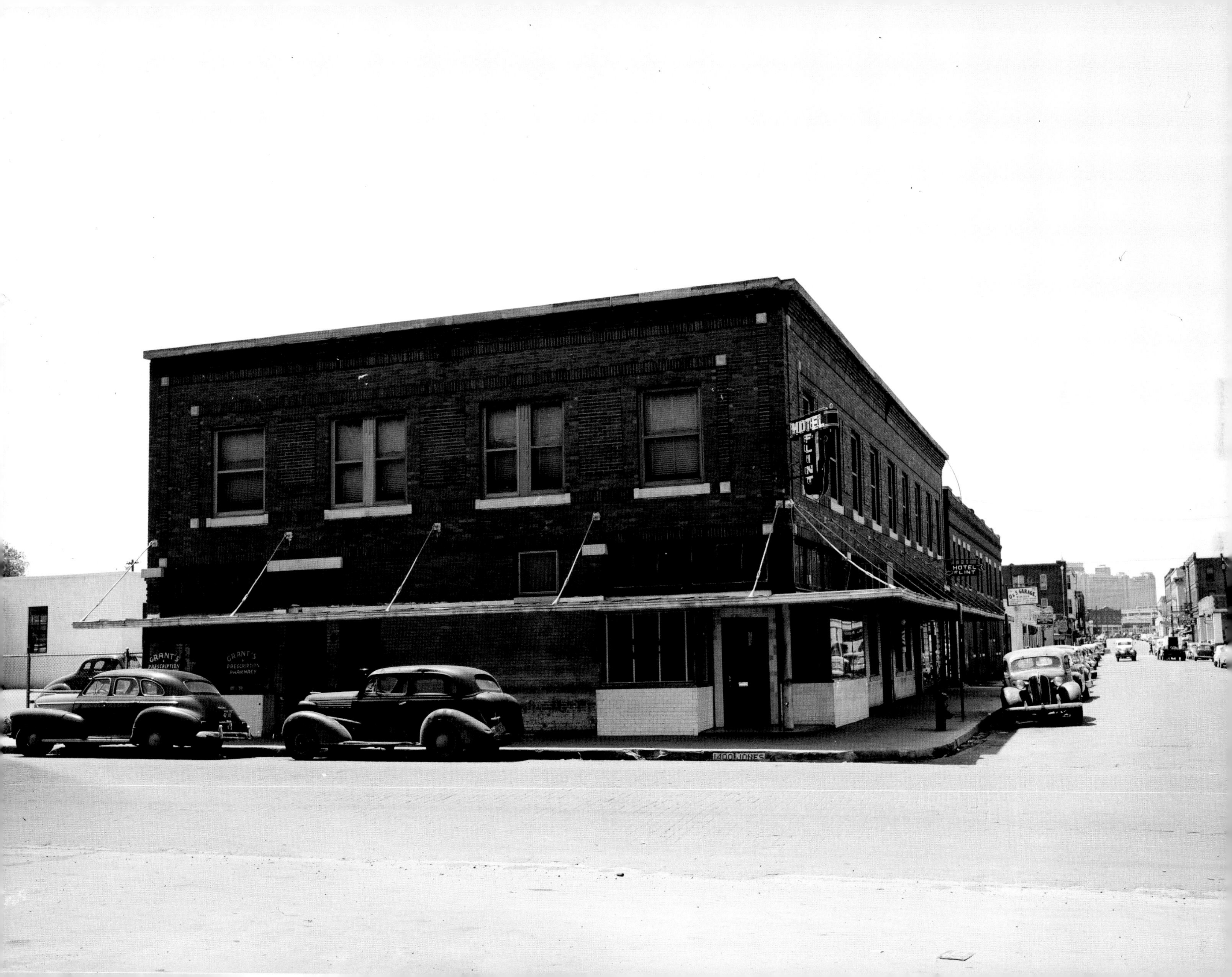
HOTEL
FLINT
HOTEL FLINT
GRANT'S PRESCRIPTION
GRANT'S PRESCRIPTION PHARMACY
1400 JONES

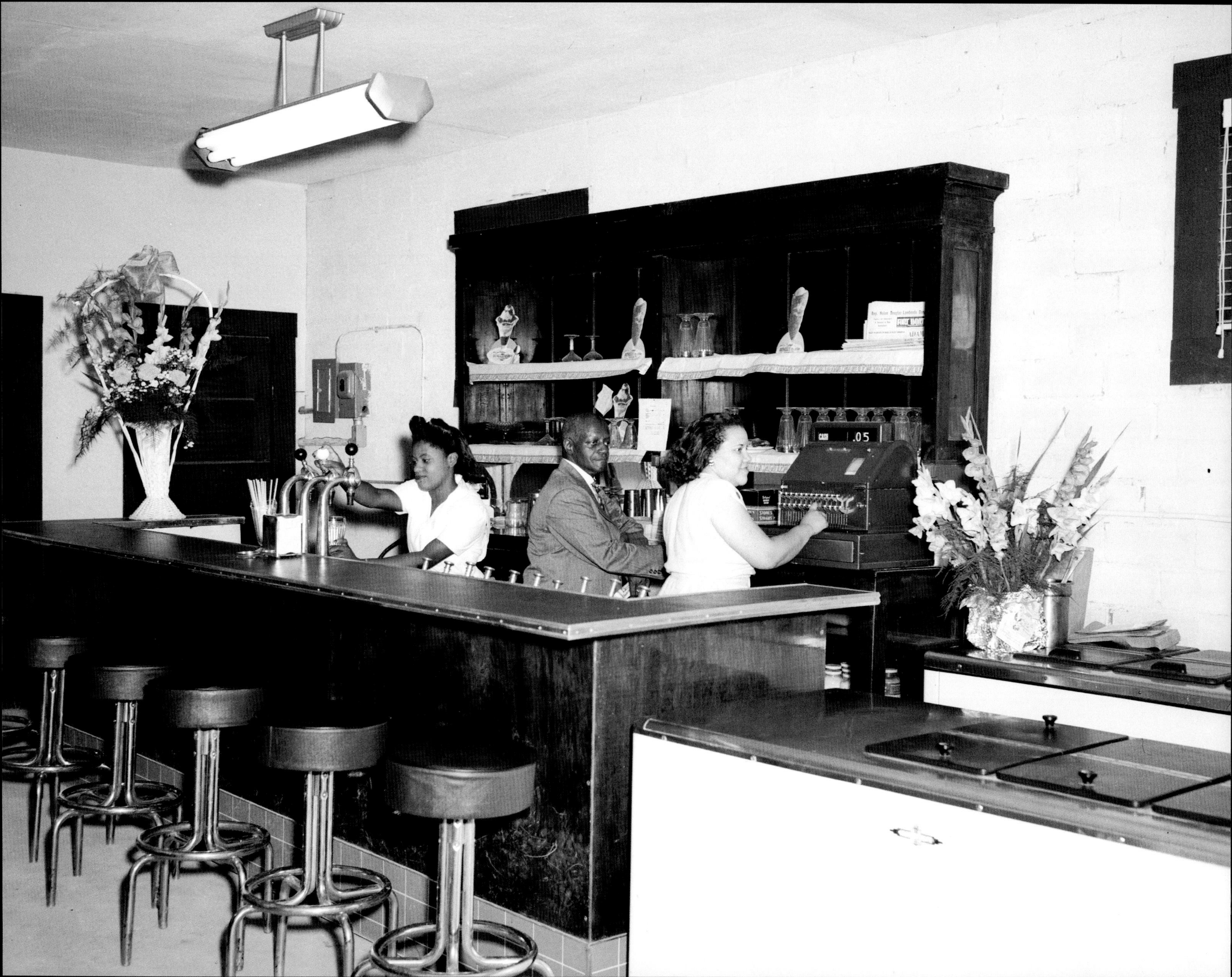
CASH
.05

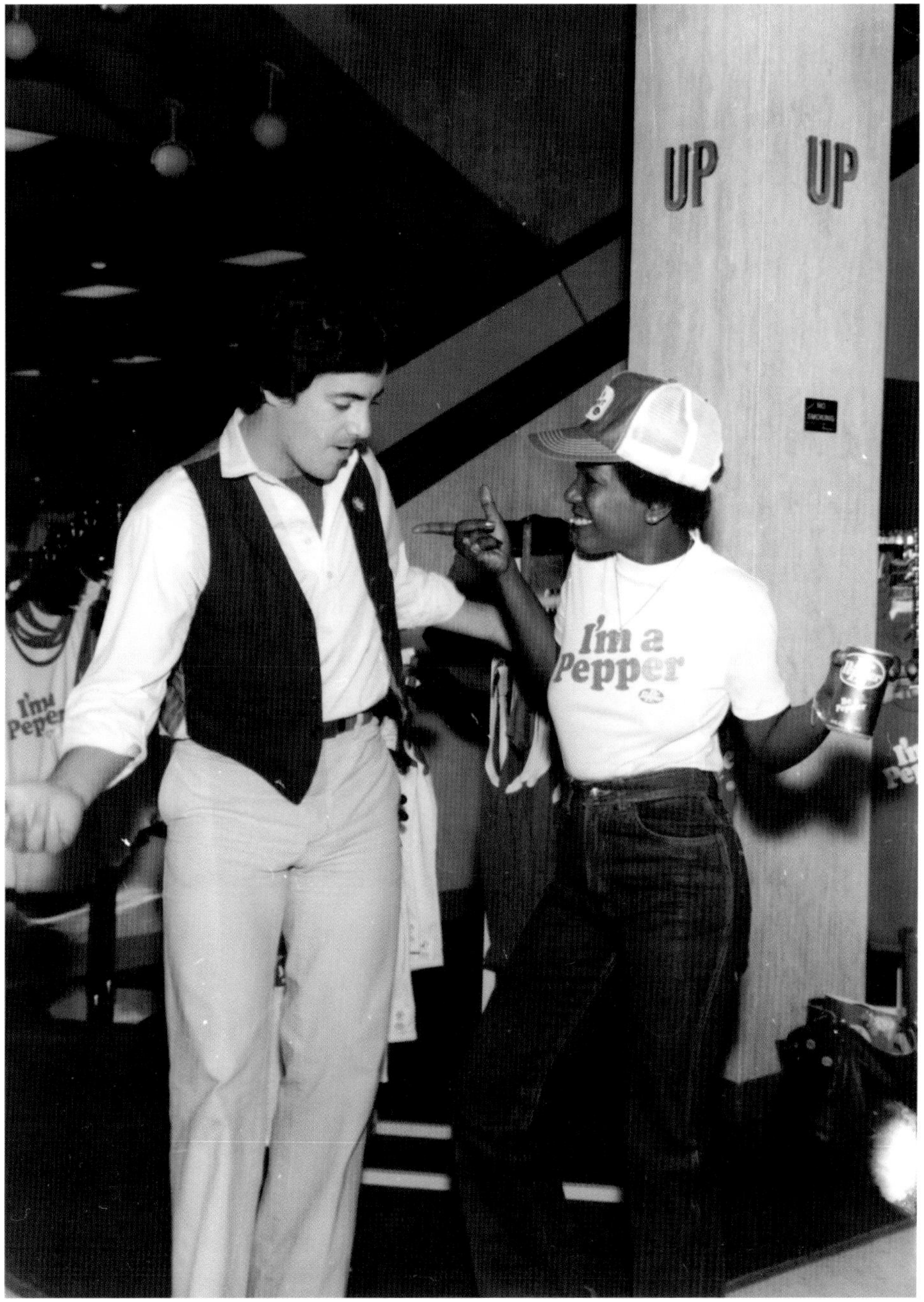

Far Left: The soda fountain counter at Dr. Ransom's Drug Store. The man in the photo is Dr. R.A. Ransom, Sr. The woman on his right is his wife Davila.

Left: Dr Pepper commercial, May 1980.

Next Page, Left: High Hat Beauty Salon demonstration, October 18, 1965.

Next Page, Right: Children at Randel Howard's Laundromat, 1989.

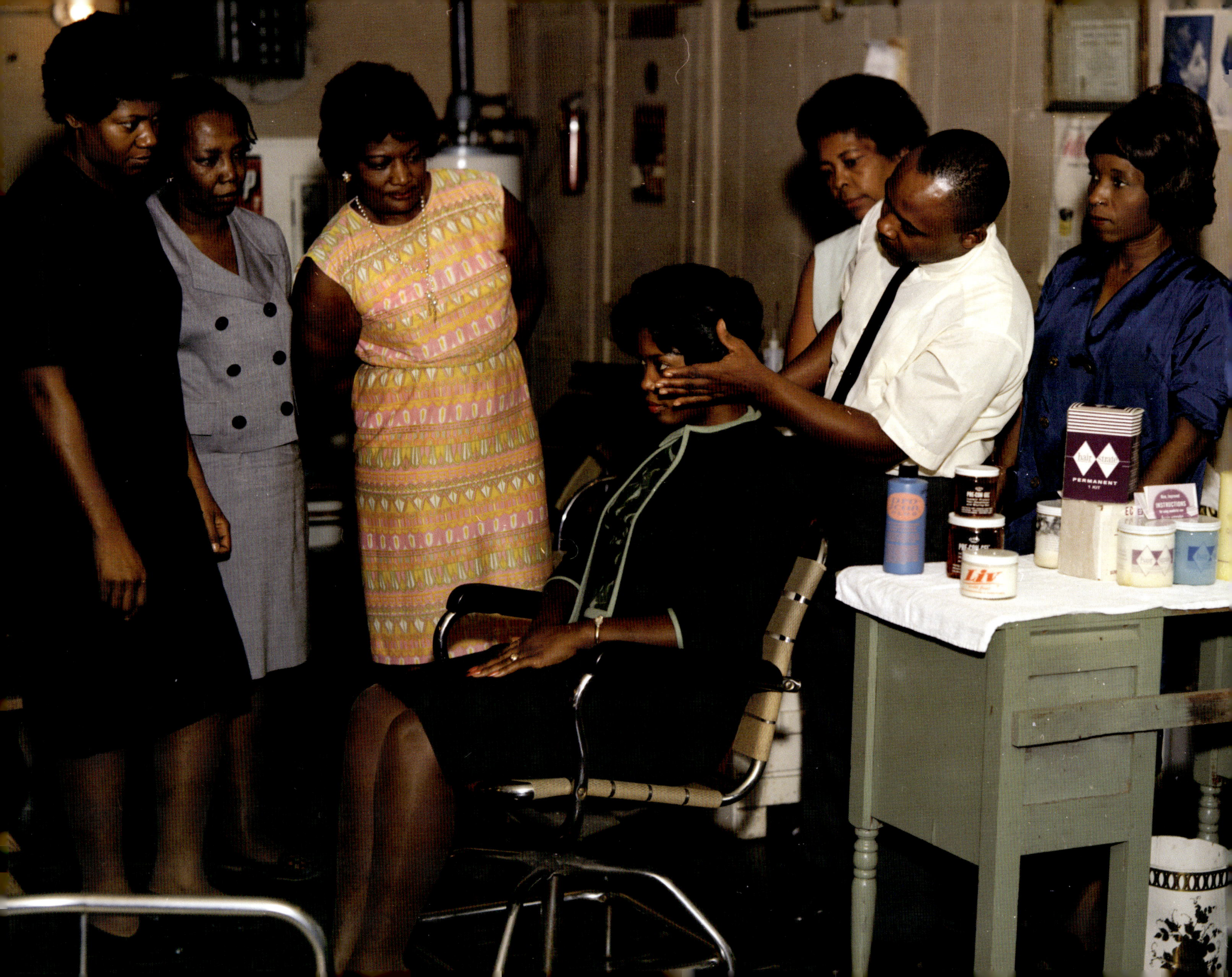
PERMANENT
INSTRUCTIONS
Liv

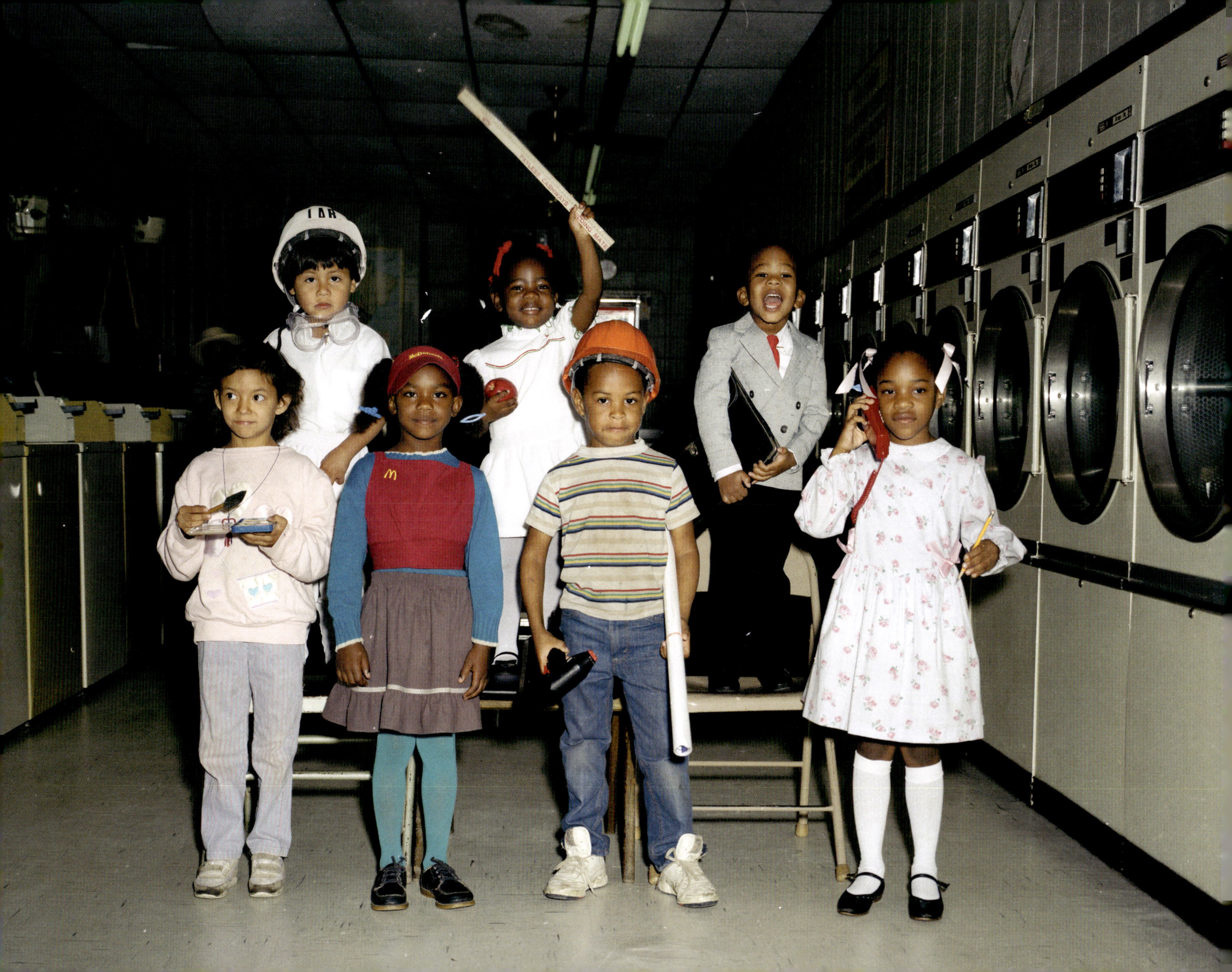

PART 3

COMMUNITY & SOCIAL EVENTS

"And then, I found out it was hard even for me to make enough money to pay the rent there and pay the notes on my cameras, and support myself on what I was making, for the simple reason I was the only professional black photographer that had been in Fort Worth—that they could remember...I was hard beat to get them to understand, you know, that you could pay more than 50 cents for a picture."

—Calvin Littlejohn

Although the black community was relegated to its segregated boundaries, social life flourished for a hard-working people who looked forward to those events and activities which allowed them to forget, for a little while, the hardships brought on by Jim Crow and the pressures of everyday living.

In many respects, blacks had the same kinds of organizations and societies as whites—they were sometimes smaller in scope and certainly limited as to where they could convene but in no way limited in enthusiasm or in professional or intellectual excellence.

There were proud sororities and fraternities, orders of the Masons and Eastern Star, literary clubs that brought famous writers to town, a bevy of nightclubs that attracted local and national musicians and, of course, youth organizations designed to motivate and challenge young people whom they felt would one day live in a different world, one in which they would never have to confront "Whites Only" or "Colored" signs.

Other than churches, there were not many venues for major events, although the Masonic Lodge played host to conventions as well as one-night stands by famous entertainers. And in several neighborhoods there were smaller community spaces, which accommodated readings, receptions, and parties.

Unlike the white world, where blacks rarely were permitted to enter except as servants, black people often saw whites come into their segregated world to be exposed to their culture.

Except for family albums, much of the evidence of that black life would have been lost had not Calvin Littlejohn been around with his trusted camera and keen eye. He took great care in recording the activities—small and large—of a community he proudly called his own.

Right: Herman Milton, studio portrait, December 22, 1948.

Far Right: Mechanics, c. 1941.

Next Page, Left: Mr. Paris Holmes, car wreck, January 10, 1956.

Next Page, Right: The first black graduates of Fort Worth's Police School, January 1951. From left: Charles Wright, Jack Gray, Benny Griffin, and Travis Bell.

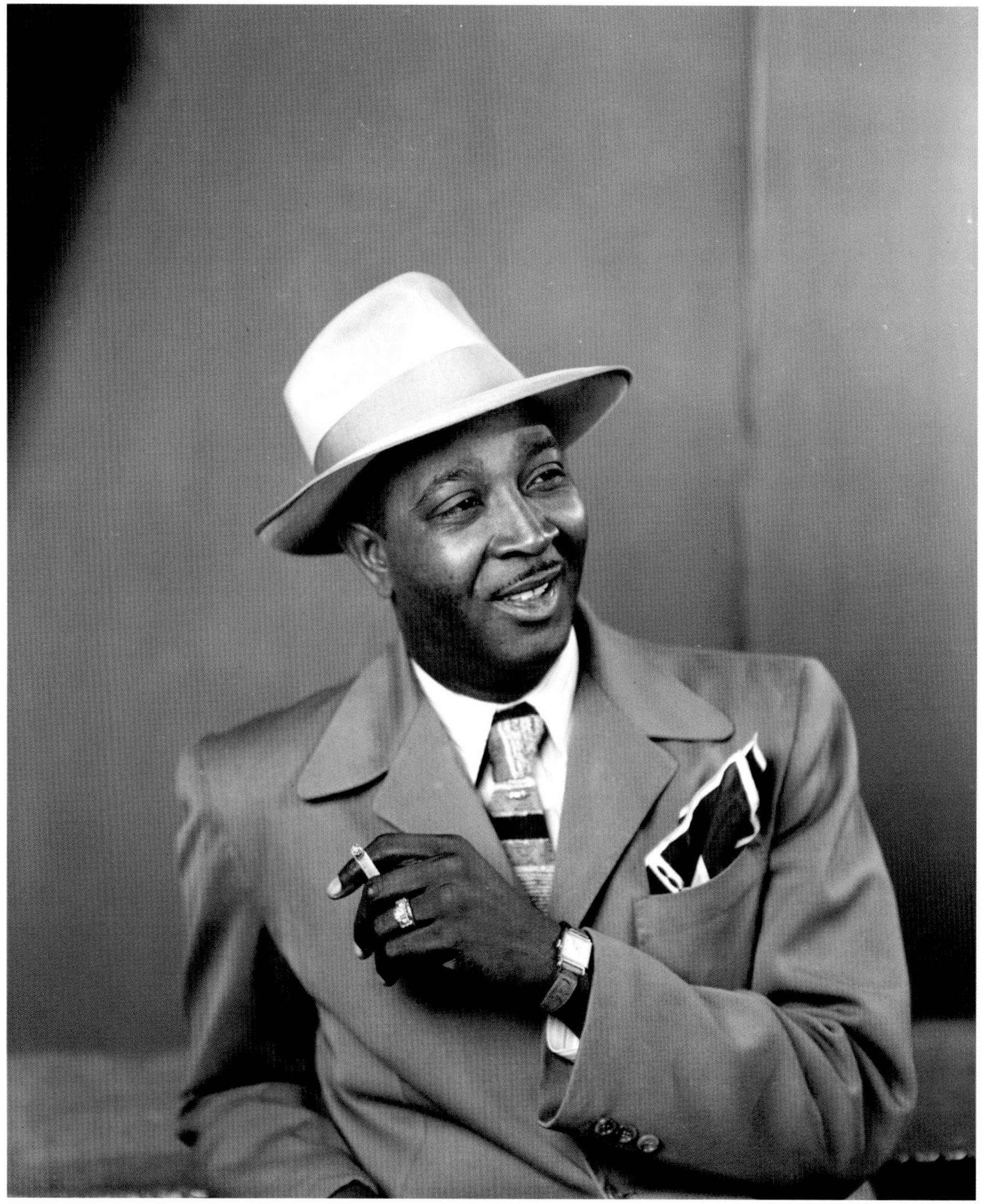

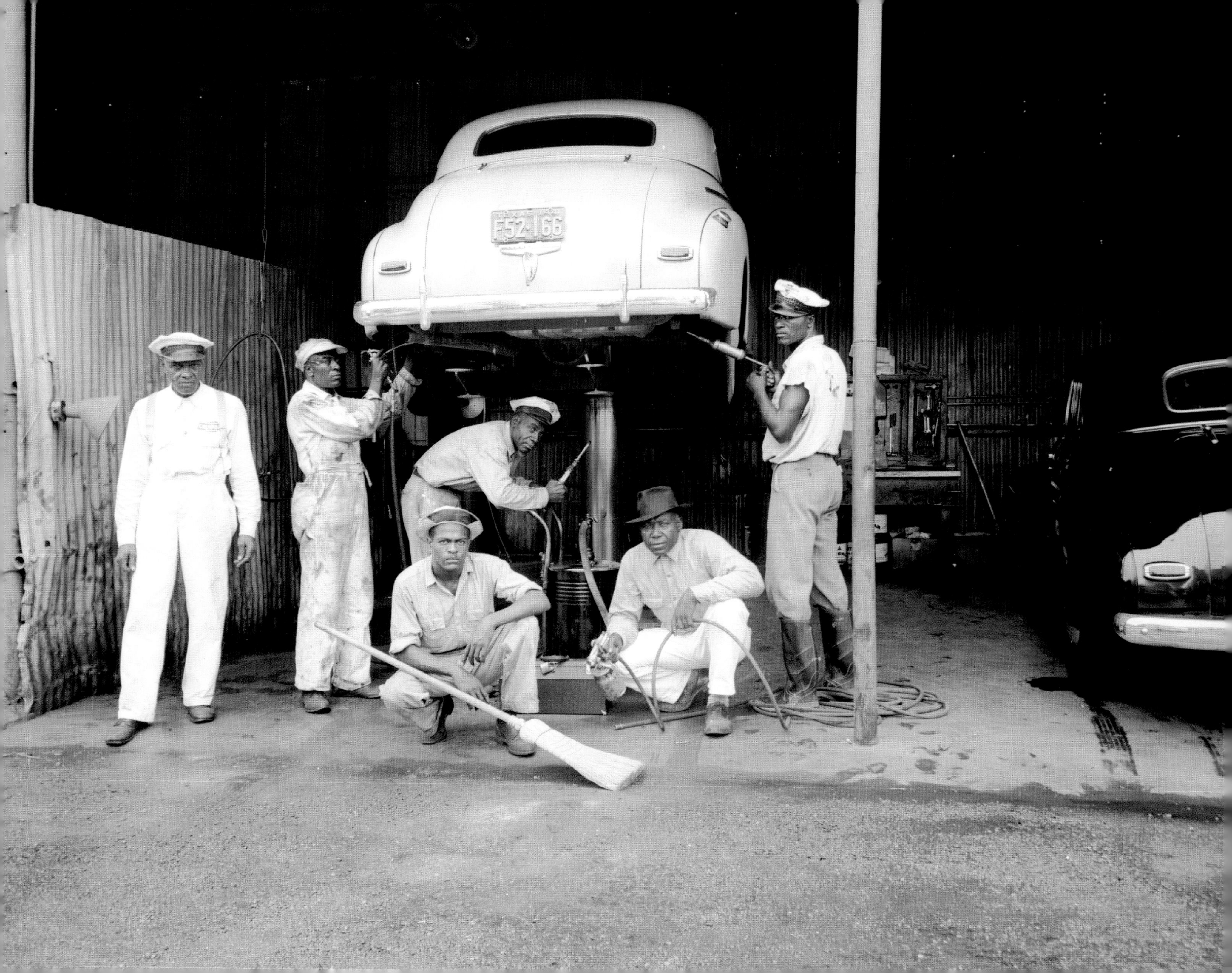
TEXAS
F52-166

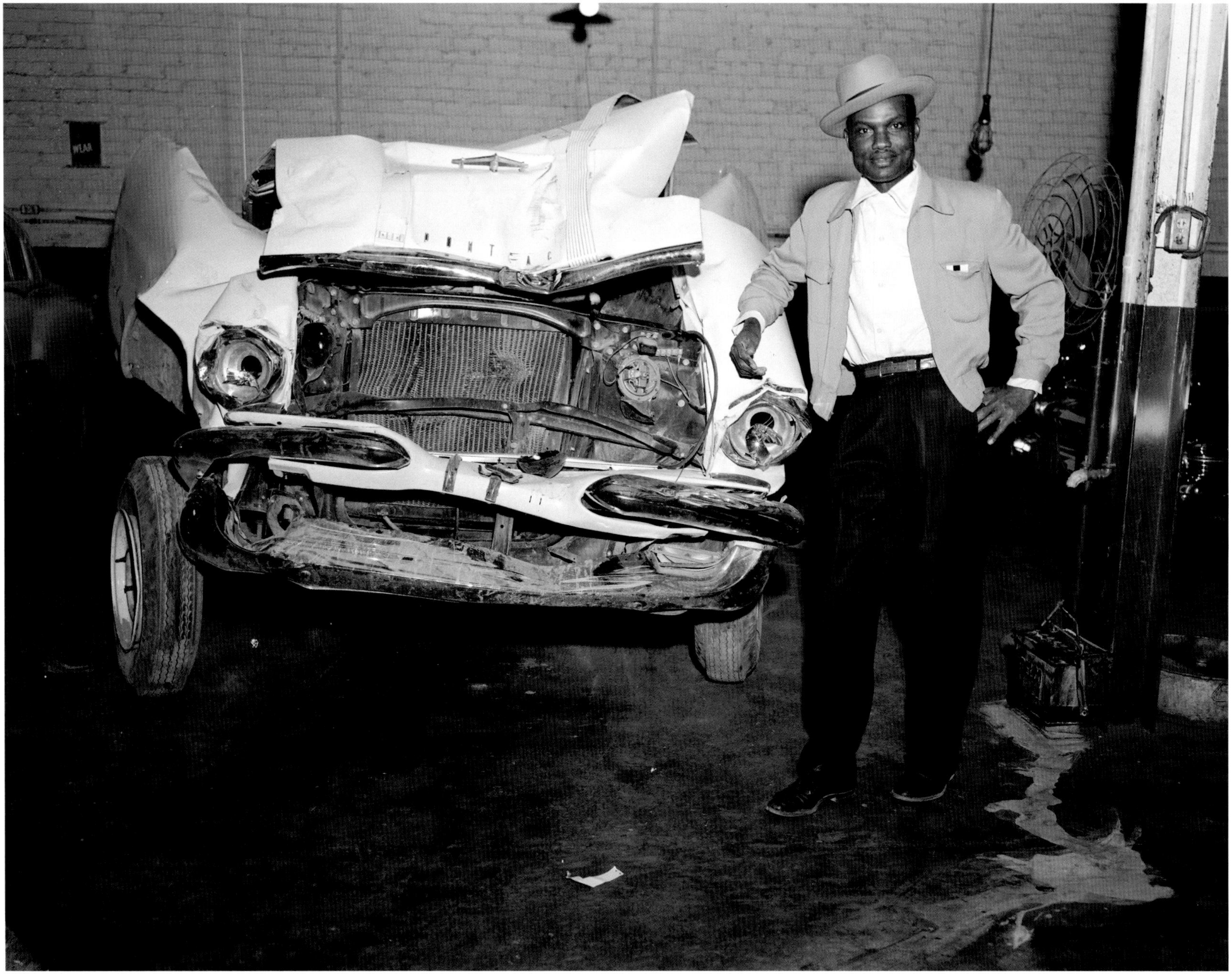

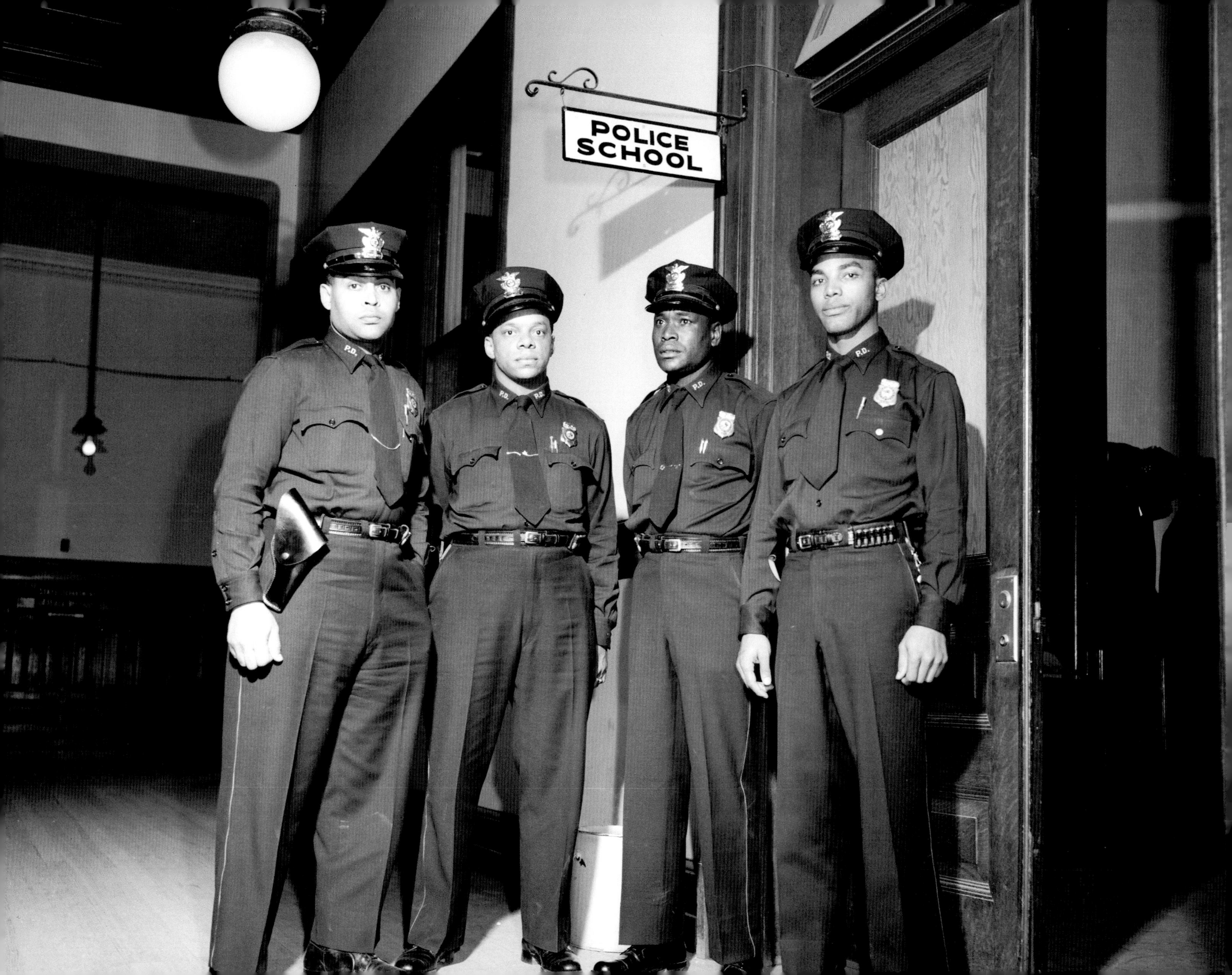
POLICE
SCHOOL

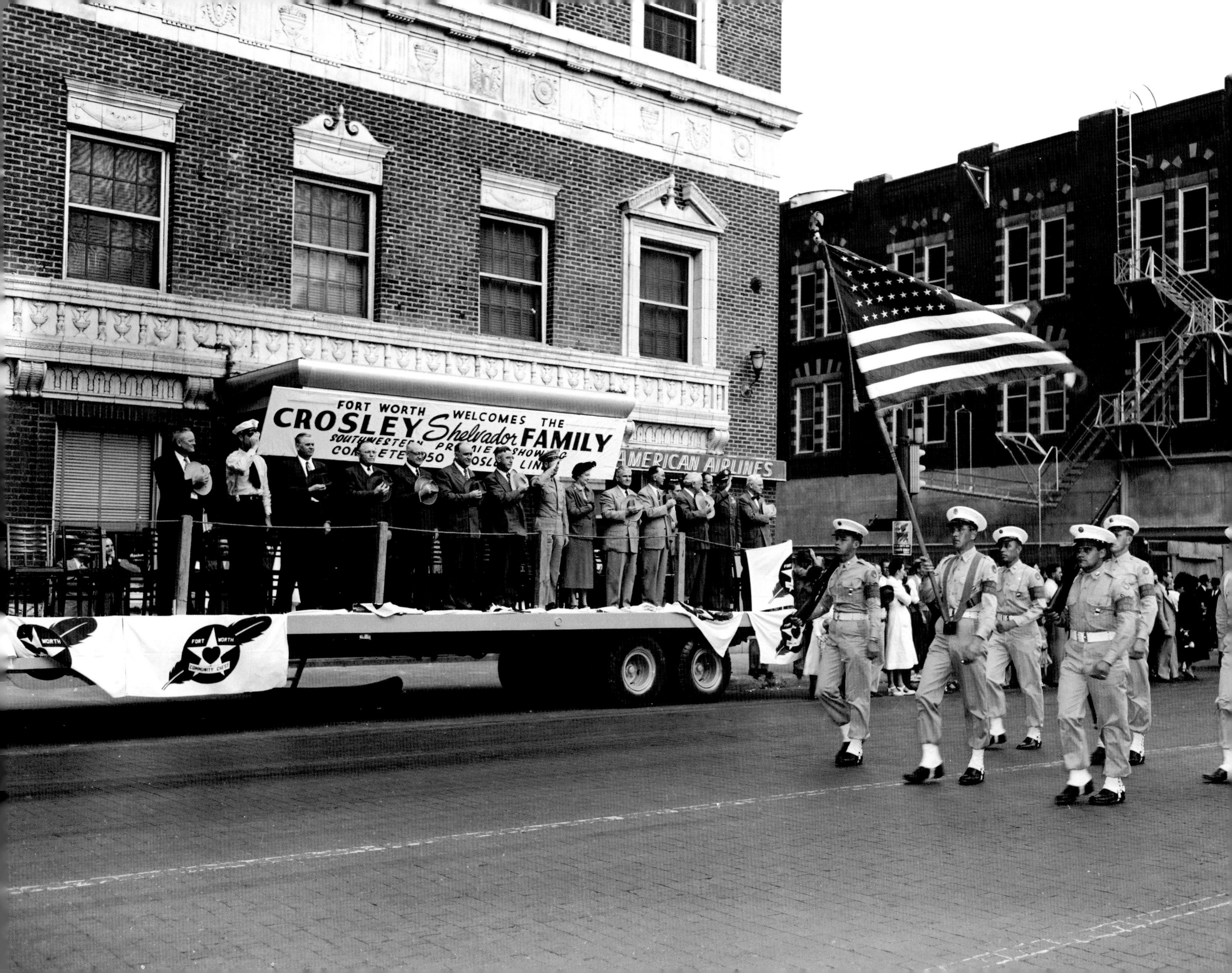
FORT WORTH
WELCOMES THE
CROSLEY Shelvador FAMILY
AMERICAN AIRLINES
FORT WORTH
COMMUNITY CHEST

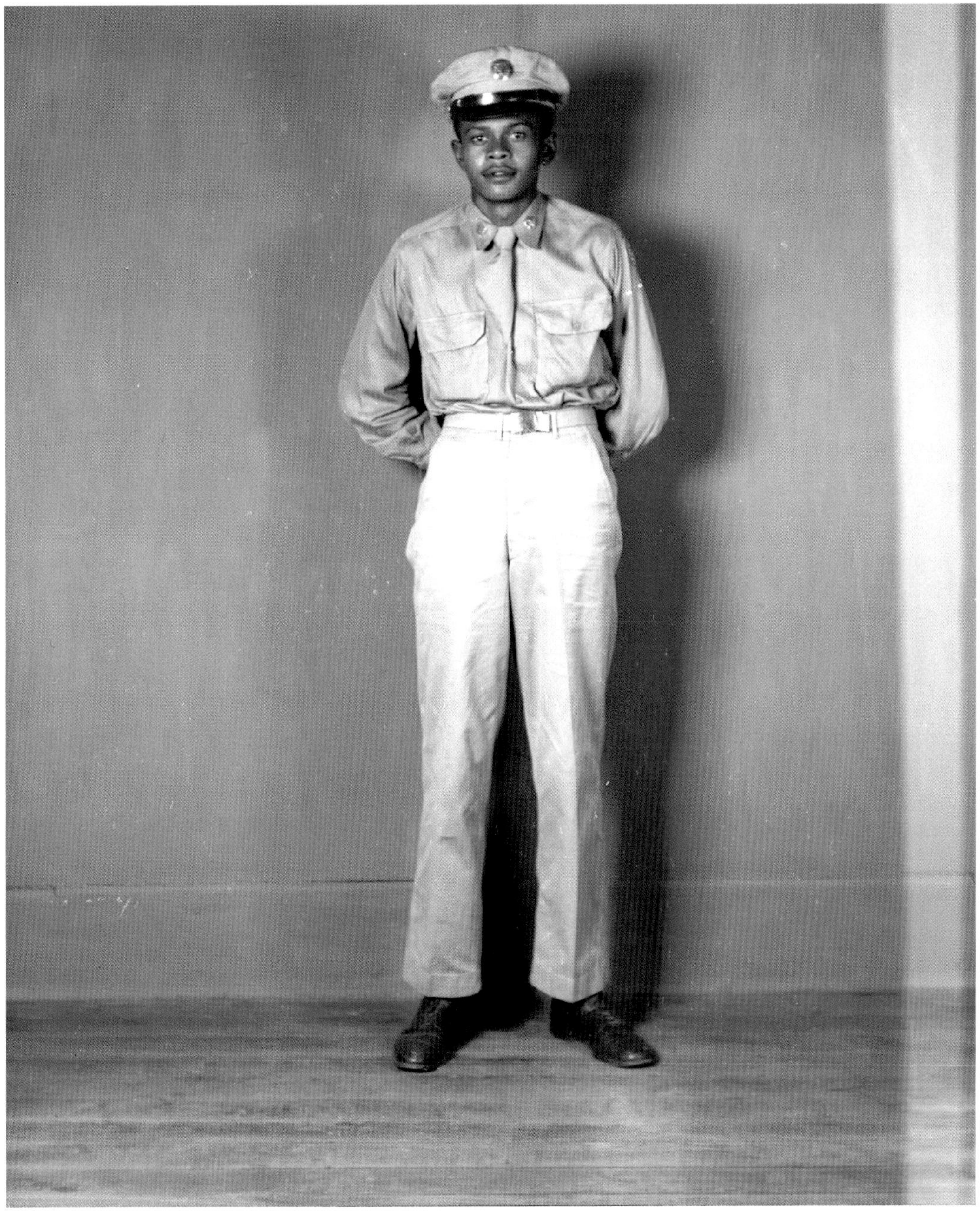

Far Left: Fort Worth Urban League's Red Feather Parade, October 15, 1949.

Left: Soldier, studio portrait, September 3, 1948.

Next Page, Left: Masons' Party—Harold Baker (of Baker Funeral Home family) is at left; Lonnie "Fat" Dixon is center, December 4, 1948.

Next Page, Right: Black Masons in Fort Worth prepare to distribute boxes at Christmas time, 1965.

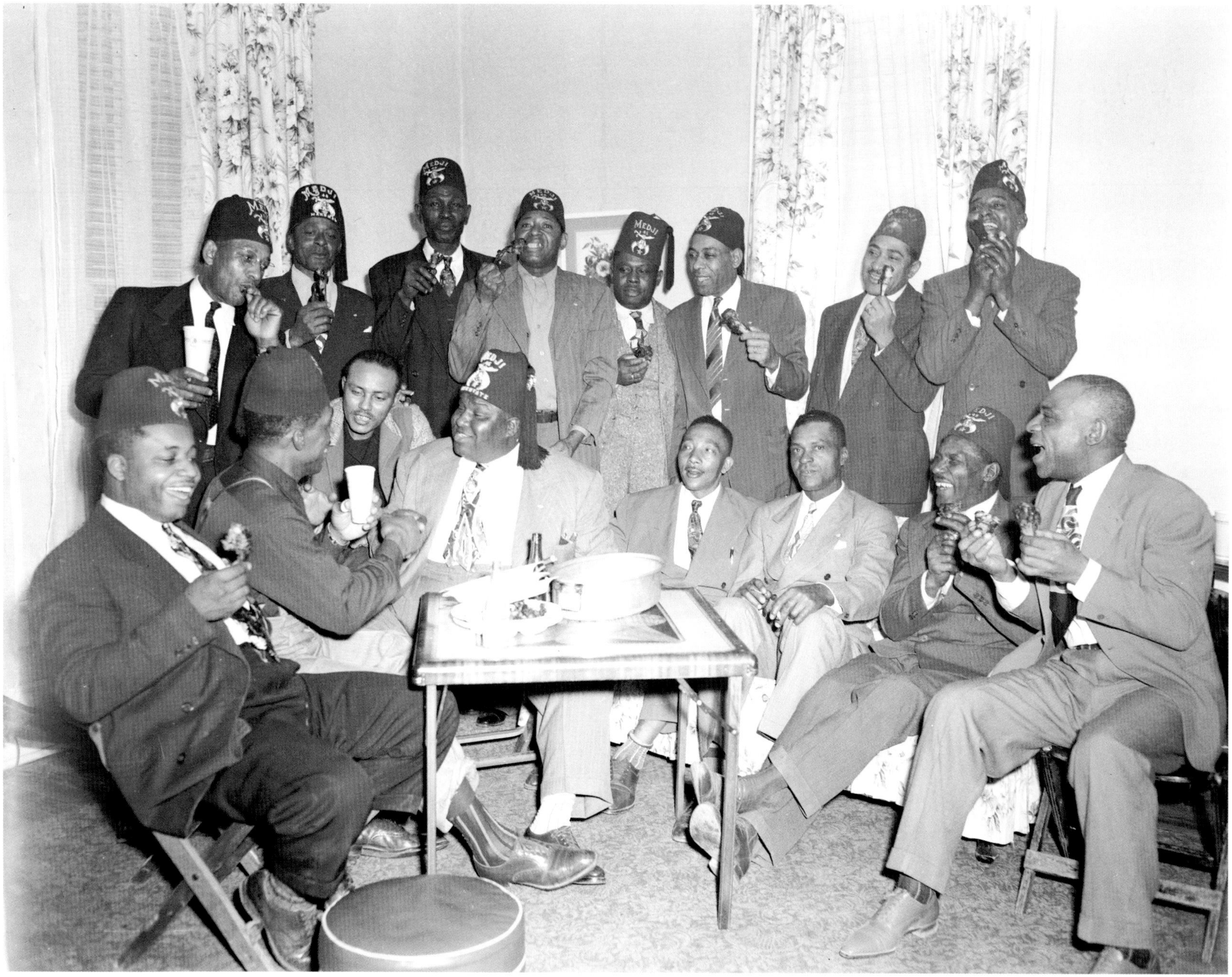
MEDJI
MEDJI
MEDJI
MEDJI

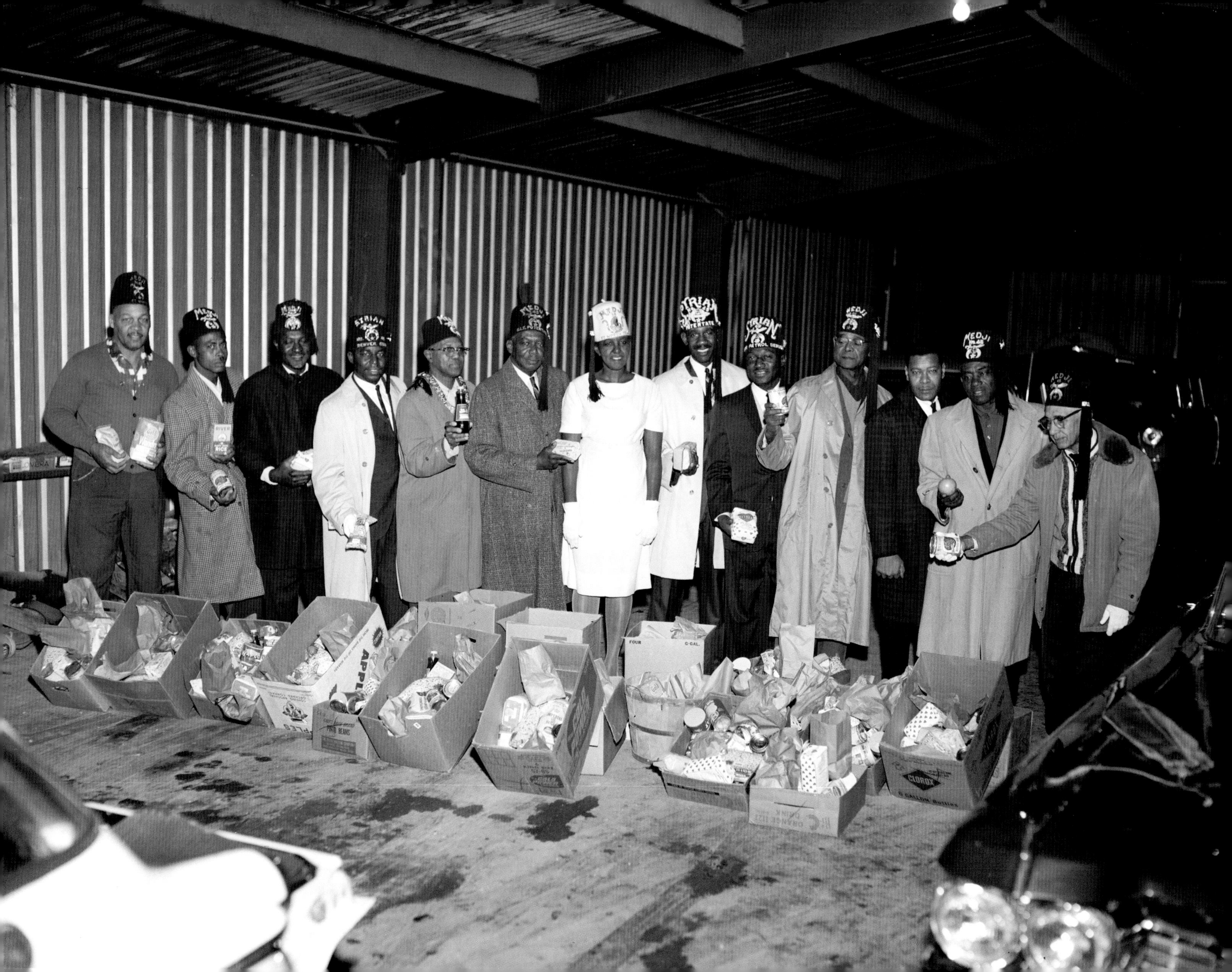
MEDJI
SIRIAN
RIVER
RICE
FOUR
CLOROX

Right: Homer Williams, a barber, is the man in the wheelchair. He is pictured in other photos.

Far Right: The Fort Worth Urban League's Red Feather Parade, October 15, 1949. In the center is C. R. "Coot" Wise, one of the owners of The Fort Worth Mind, *a black weekly newspaper.*

Next Page, Left: Two men sitting on dry land near flooded street and houses in the Rock Island Bottom neighborhood.

Next Page, Right: Man with two horses riding through a flooded street in front of homes in the Rock Island Bottom neighborhood, Fort Worth, May 17, 1949.

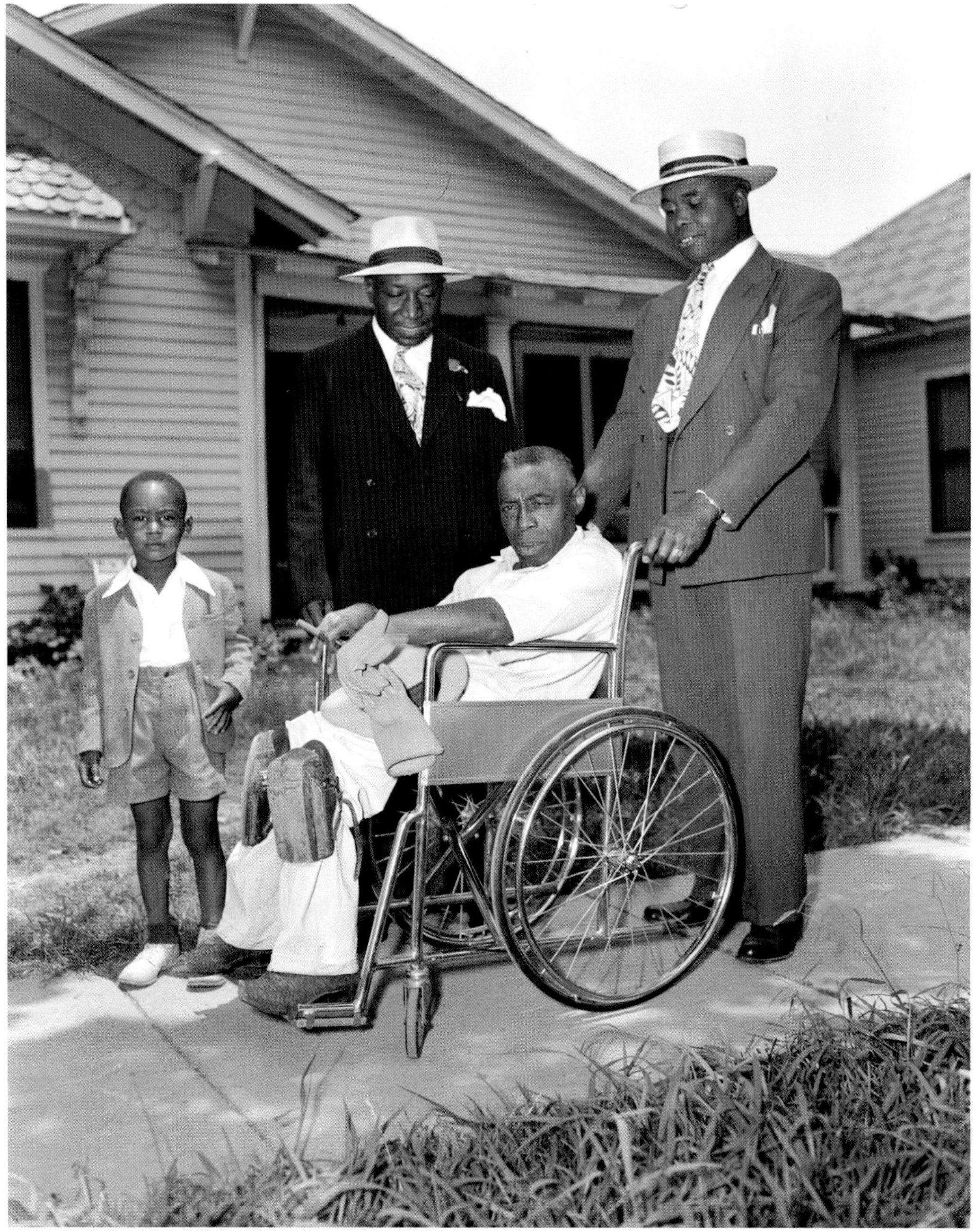

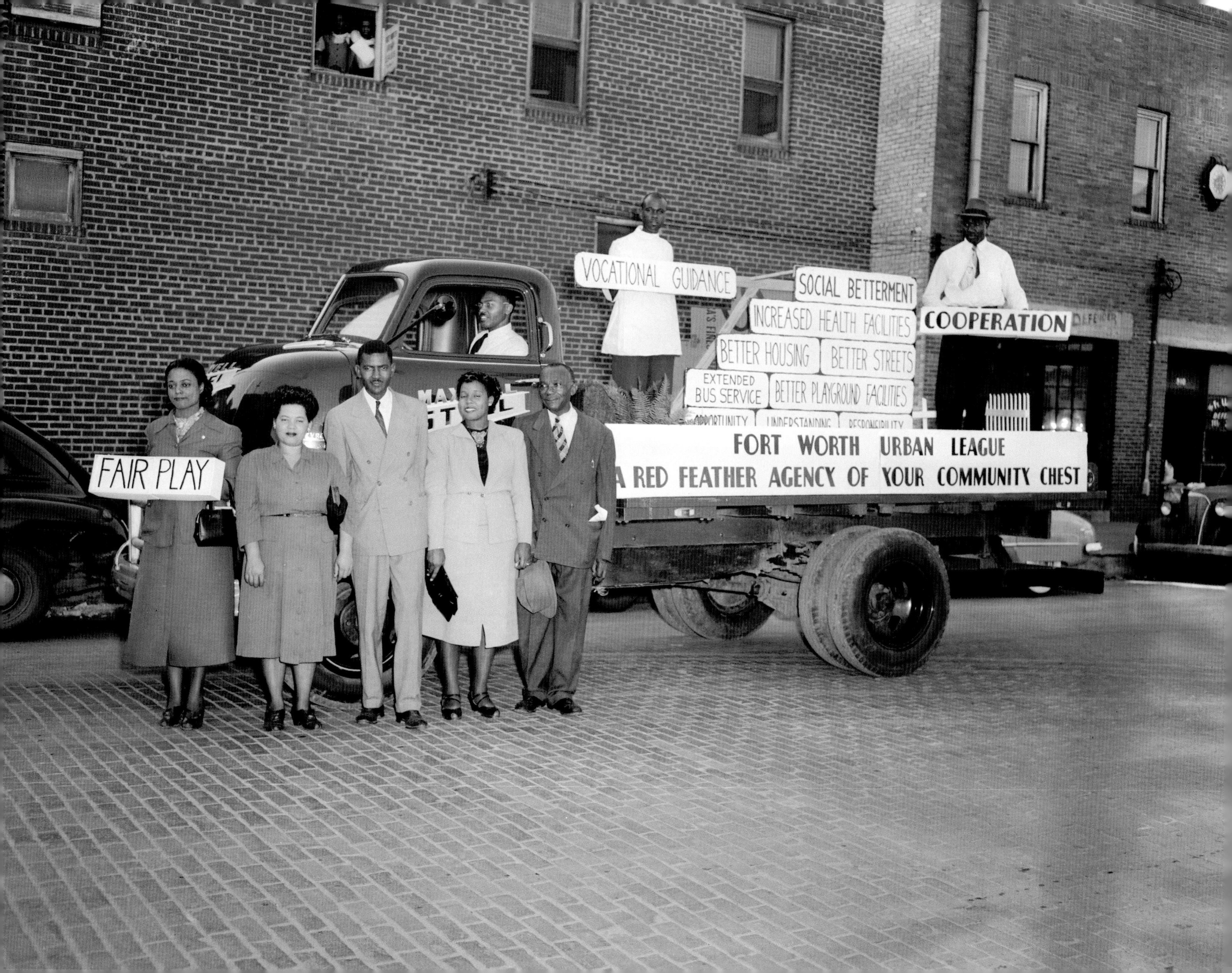
VOCATIONAL GUIDANCE
SOCIAL BETTERMENT
INCREASED HEALTH FACILITIES
BETTER HOUSING
BETTER STREETS
EXTENDED BUS SERVICE
BETTER PLAYGROUND FACILITIES
COOPERATION
FAIR PLAY
FORT WORTH URBAN LEAGUE
A RED FEATHER AGENCY OF YOUR COMMUNITY CHEST

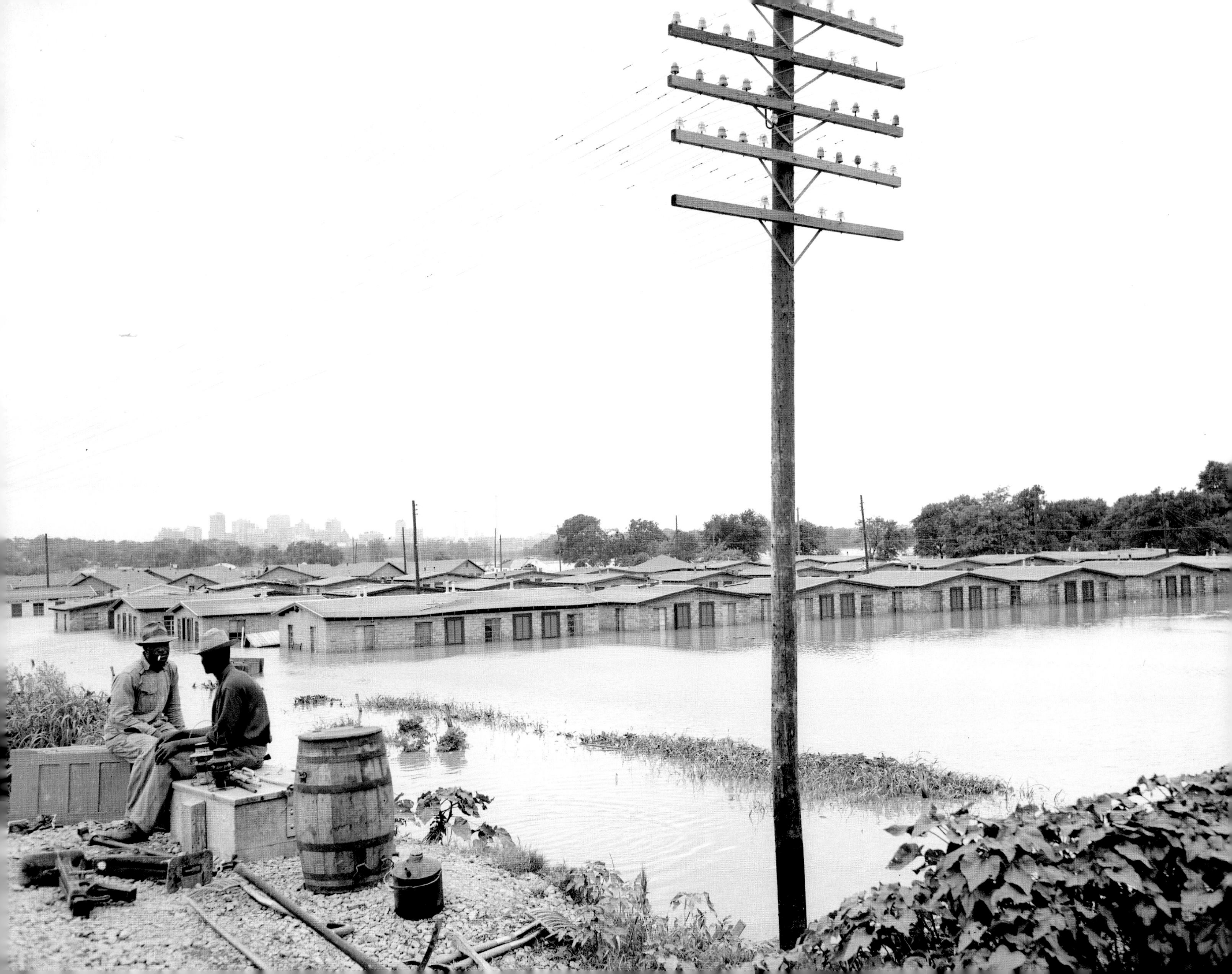

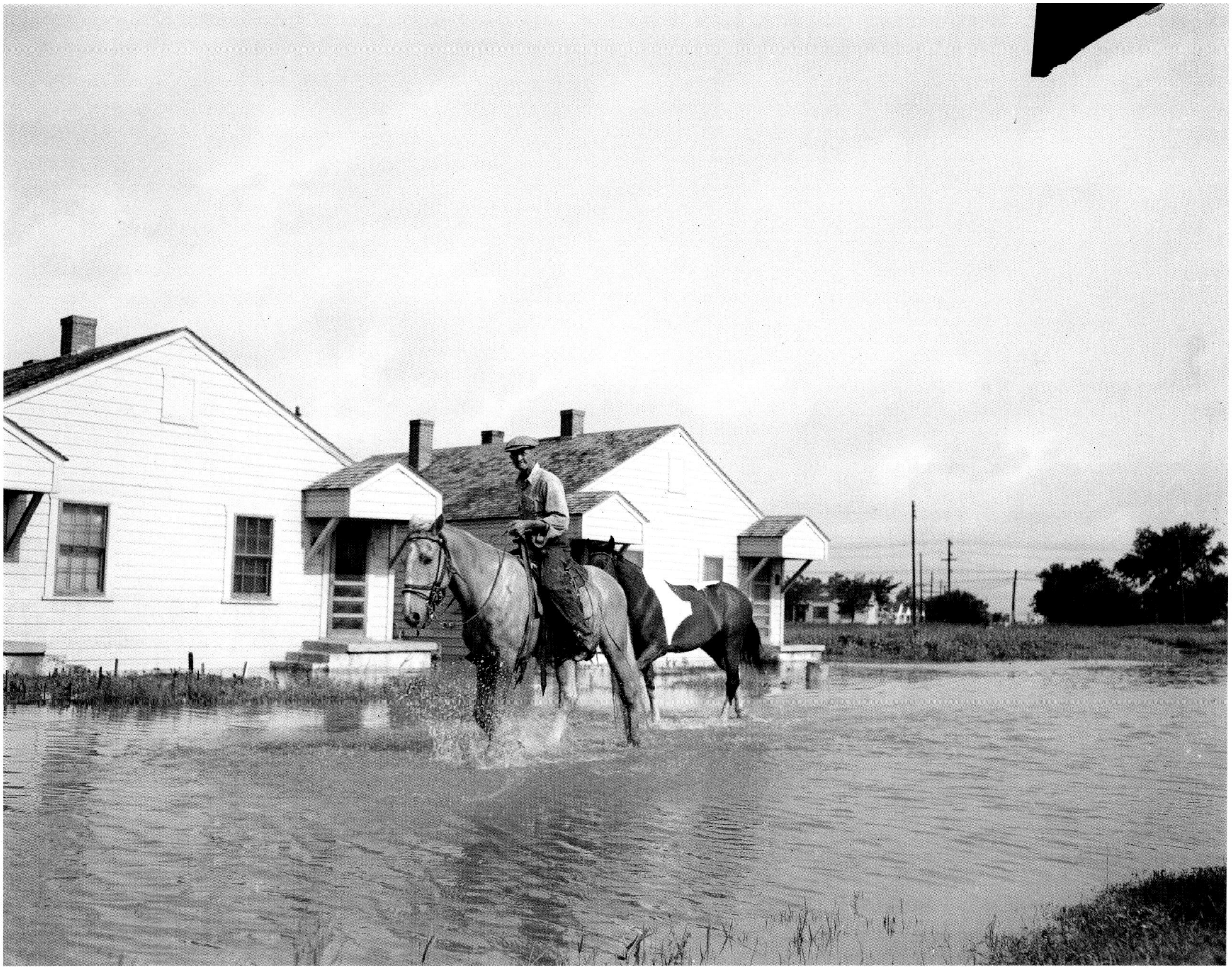

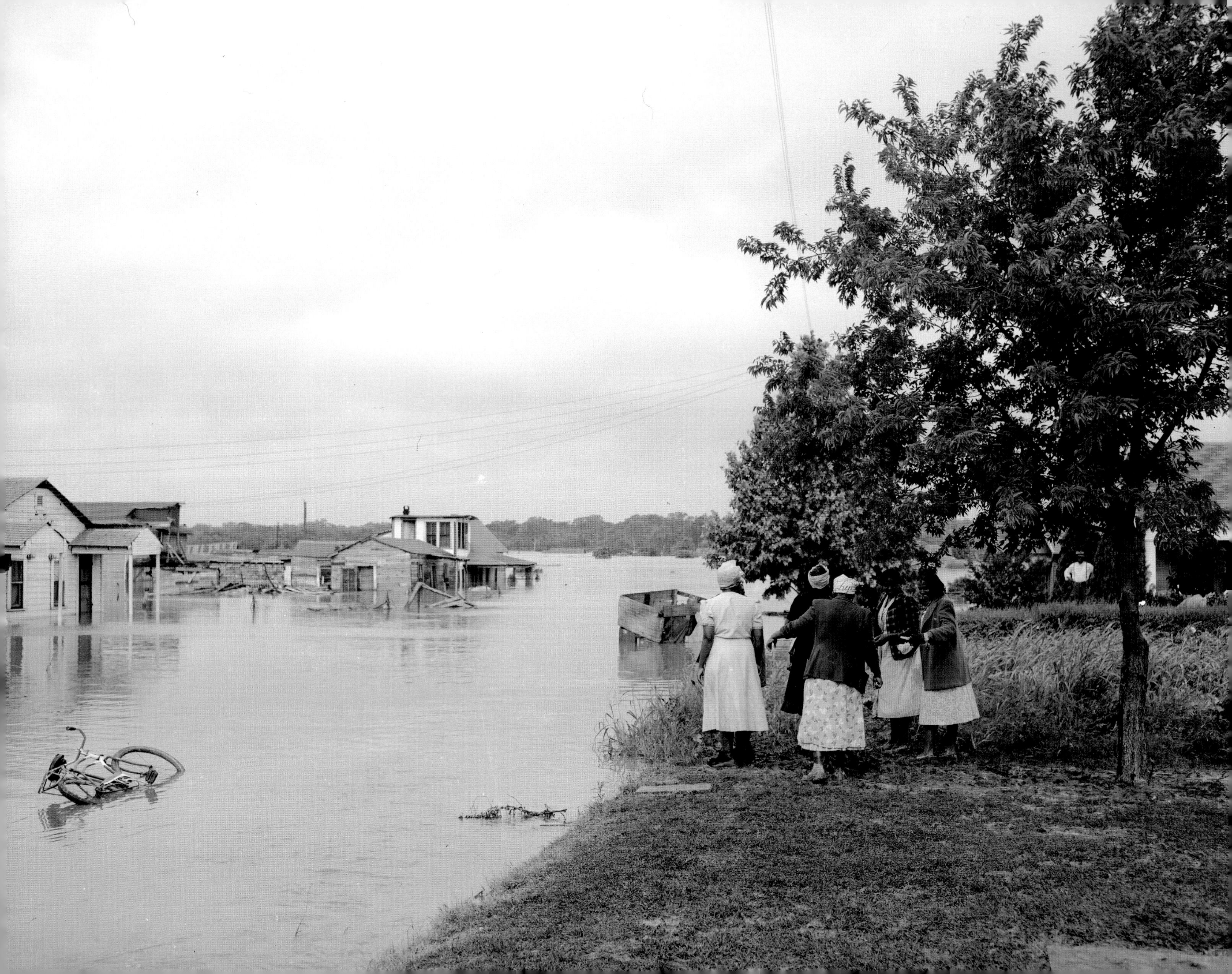

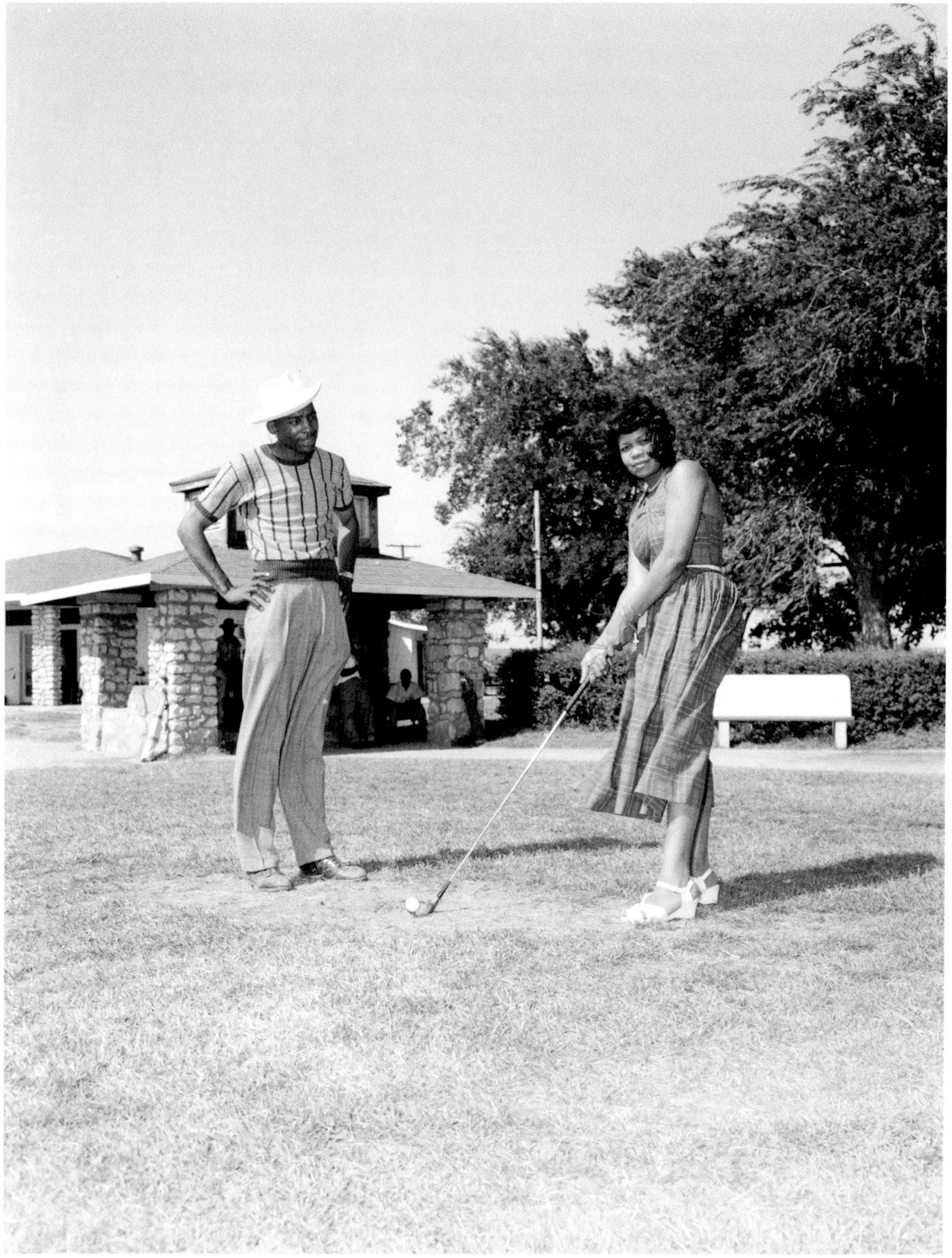

Far Left: Women standing on dry ground looking out over flooded street and homes in the Rock Island Bottom neighborhood, May 17, 1949.

Left: Golfers at Worth Hills Golf Course, June 19, 1951.

Right: Bathing beauty at the Rosedale Apartments.

Far Right: Children with hula hoops at the Fort Worth Recreation Center, November 16, 1958.

Next Page, Left: Boy Scouts, November 1964.

Next Page, Right: Boy Scouts, December 5, 1964.

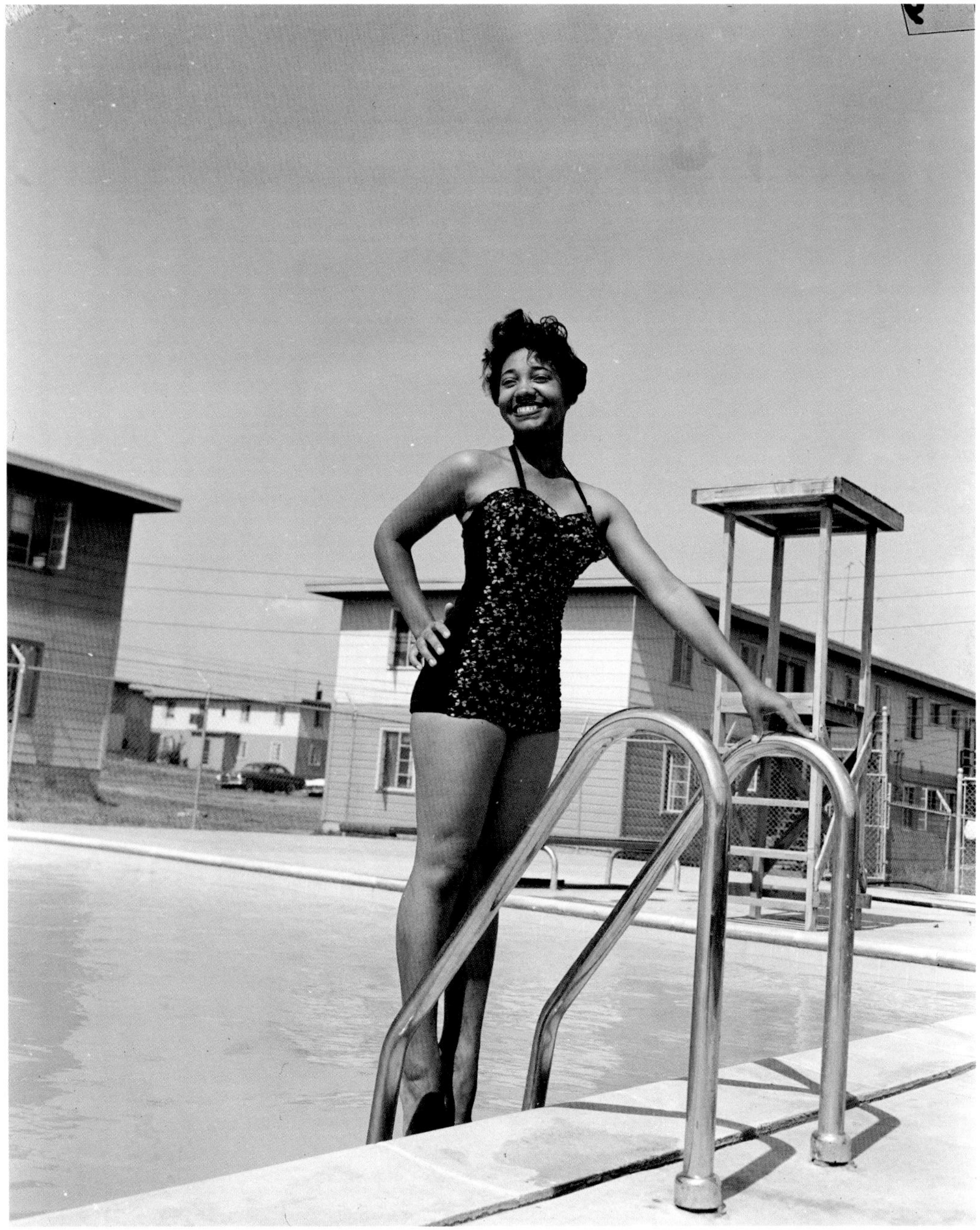

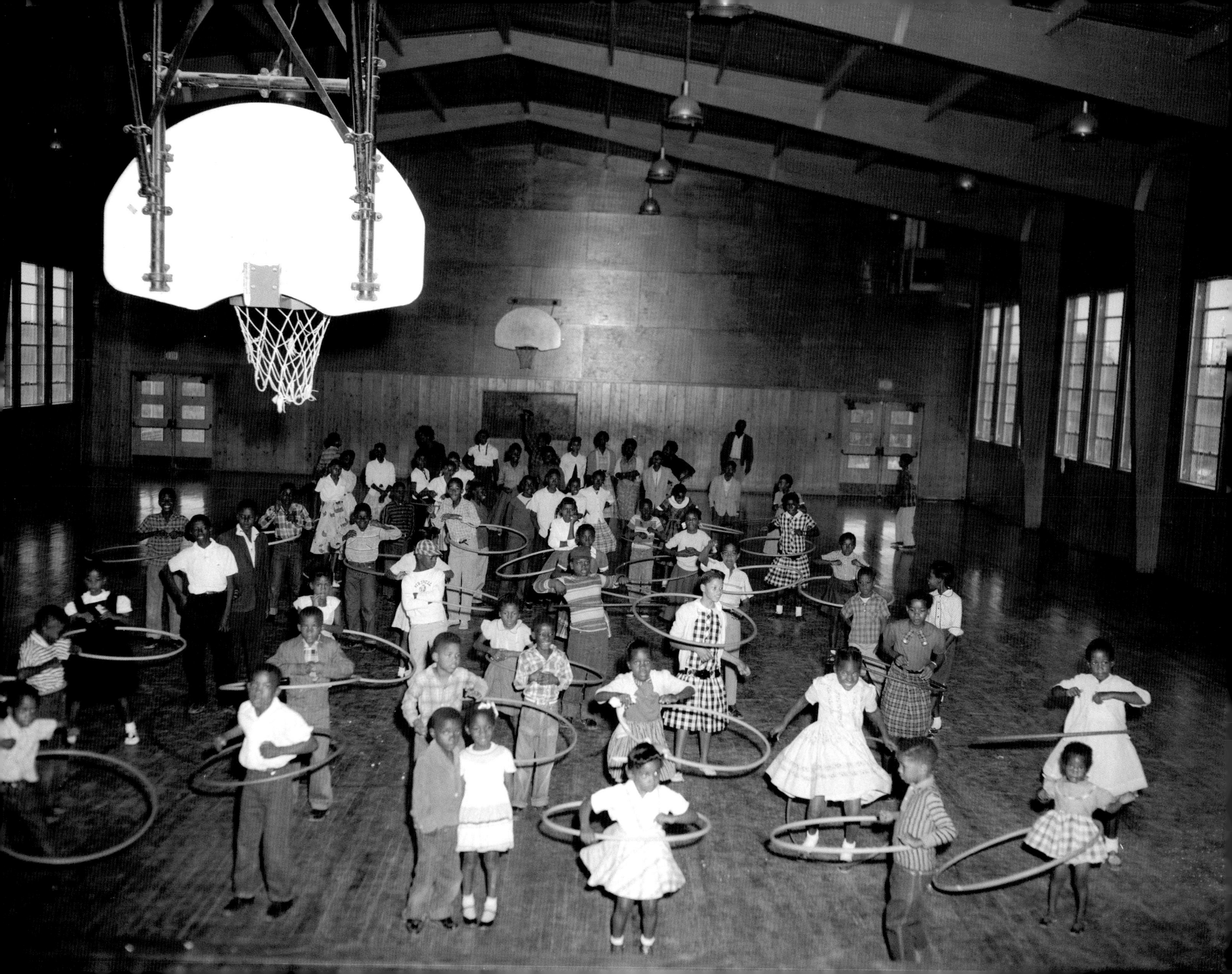

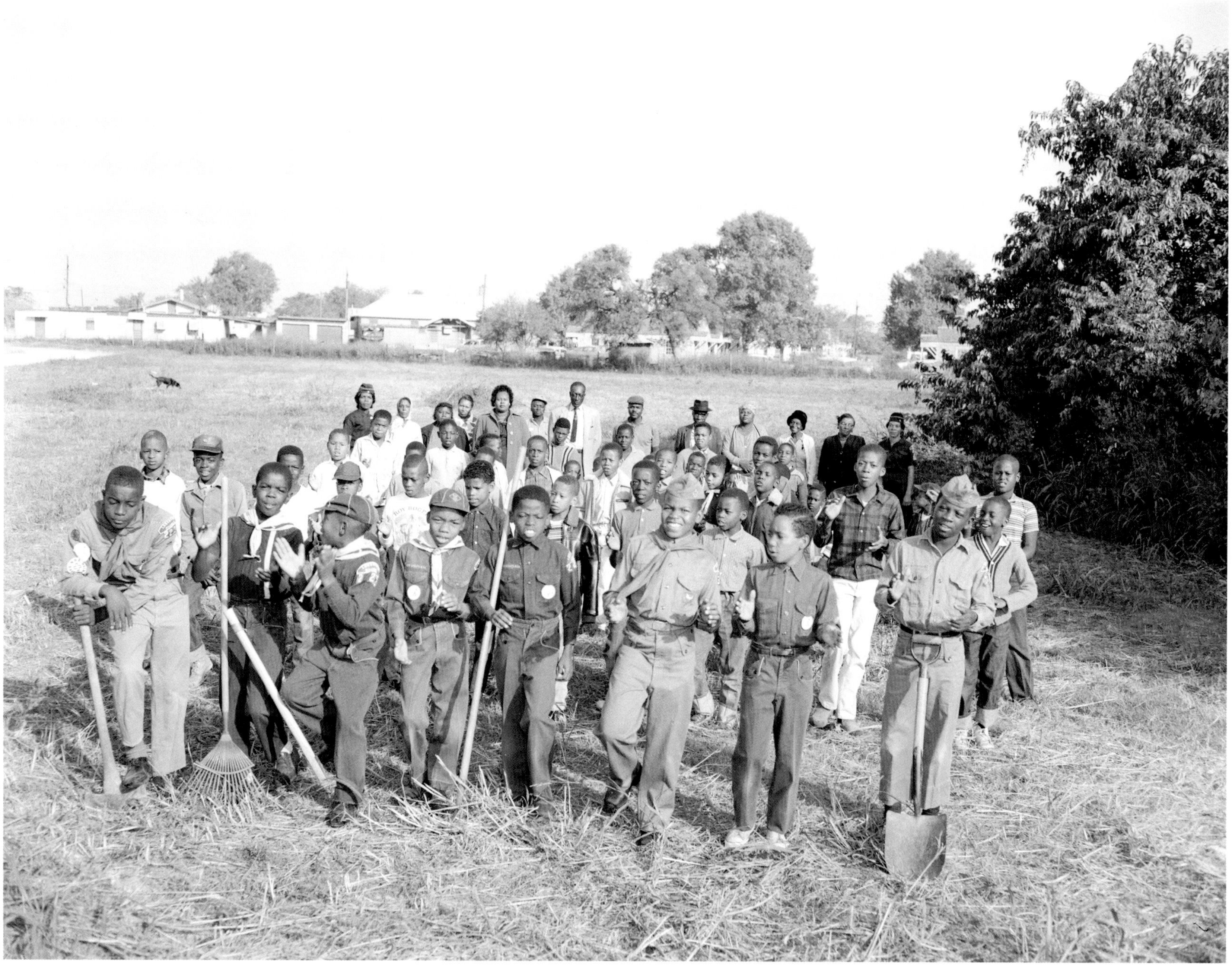

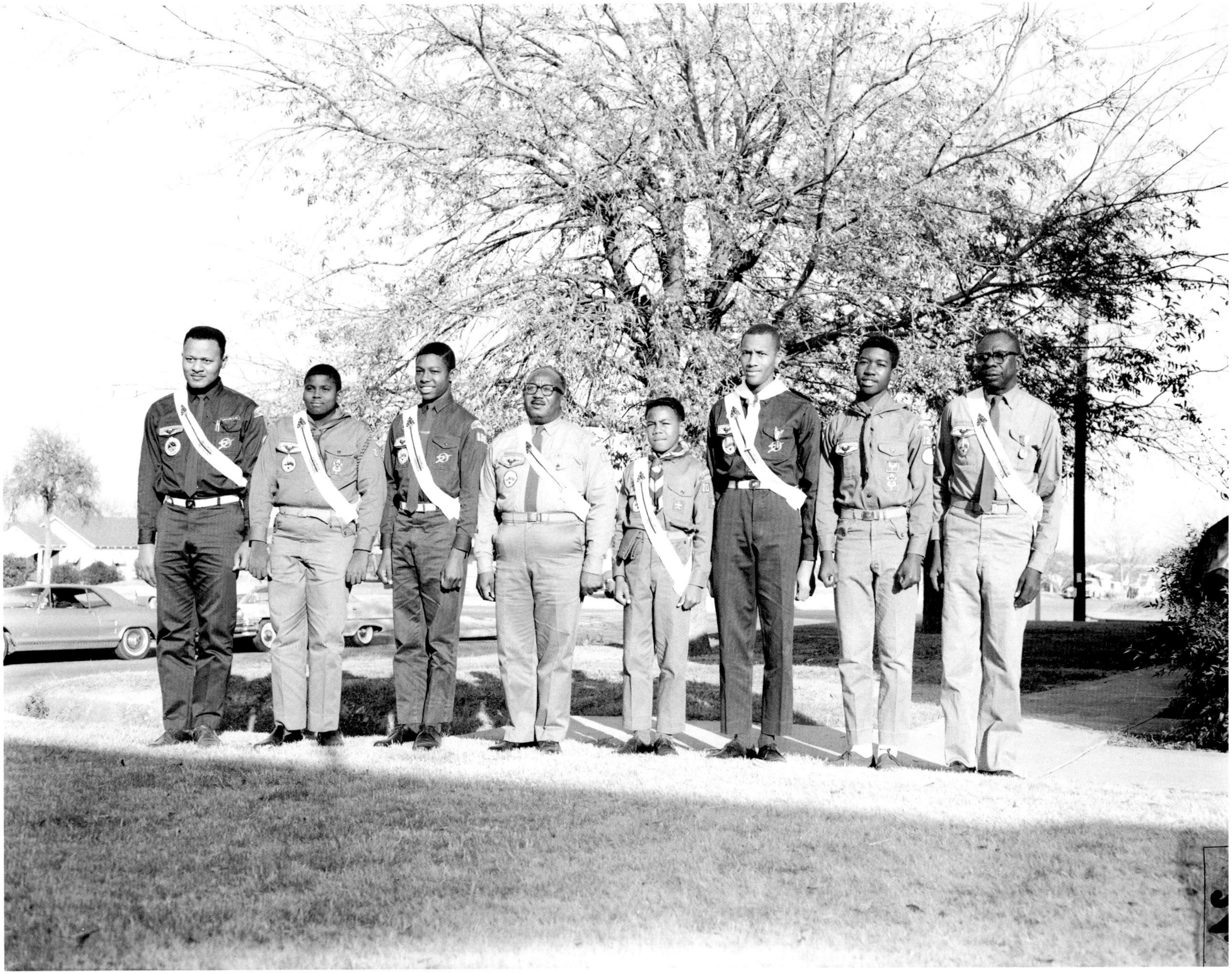

Right: Mrs. Opal Roland's children with Christmas tree at their home on Terrell Avenue, December 26, 1950.

Far Right: Mrs. Roland's children with bicycles and Christmas tree, 1954.

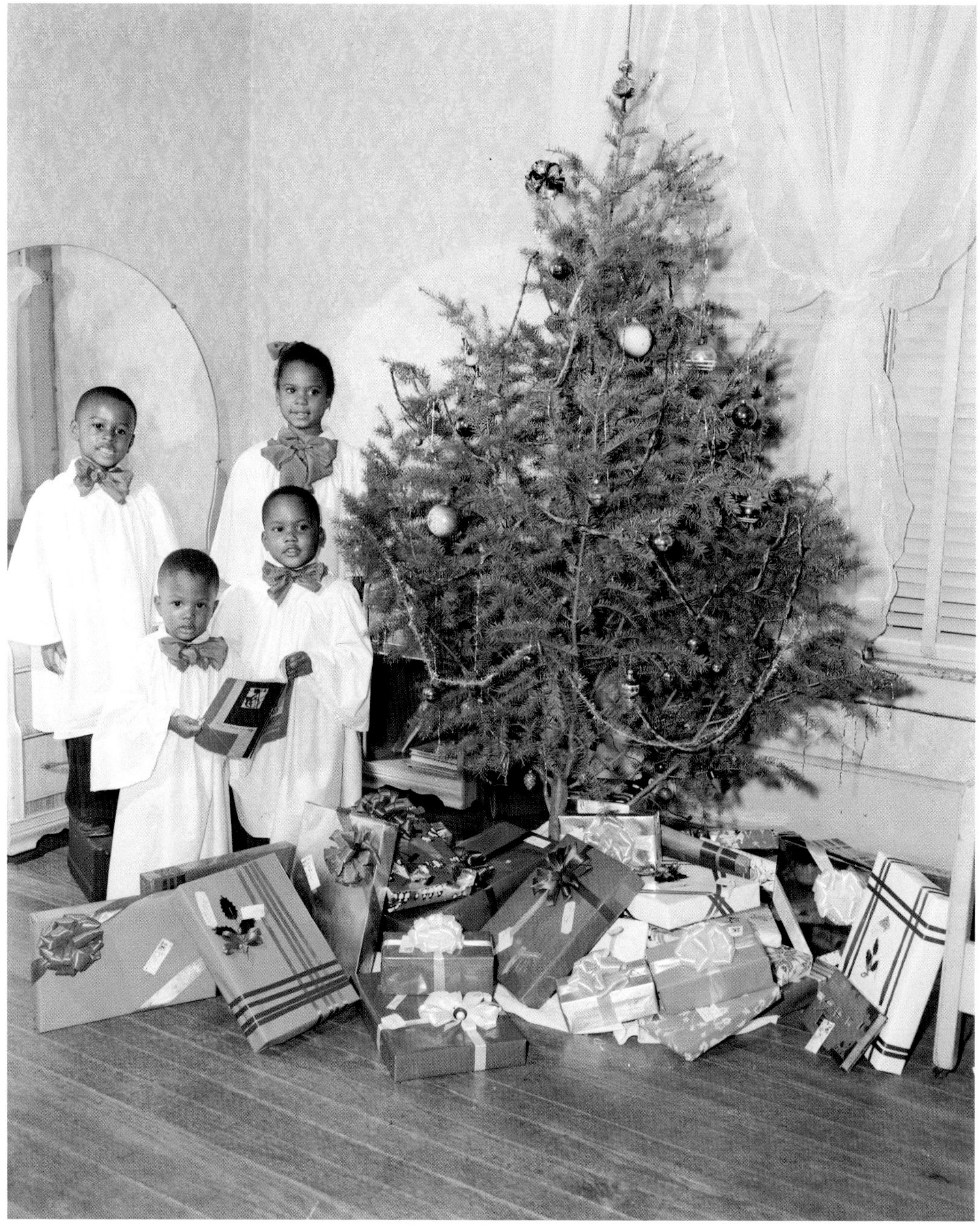

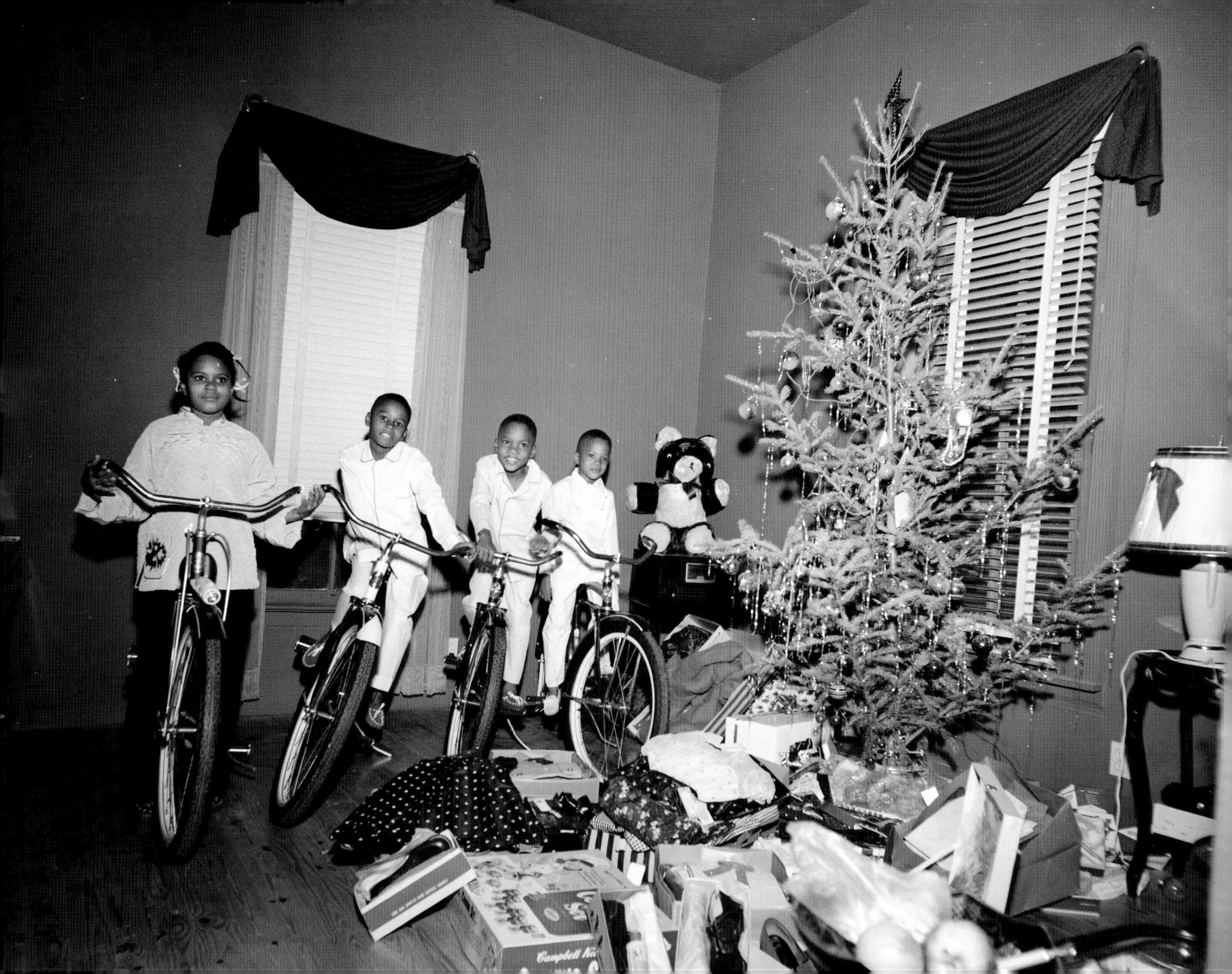
Campbell

Right: Studio portrait of a girl, for Christmas cards, December 8, 1949.

Far Right: Turner baby, March 1, 1949.

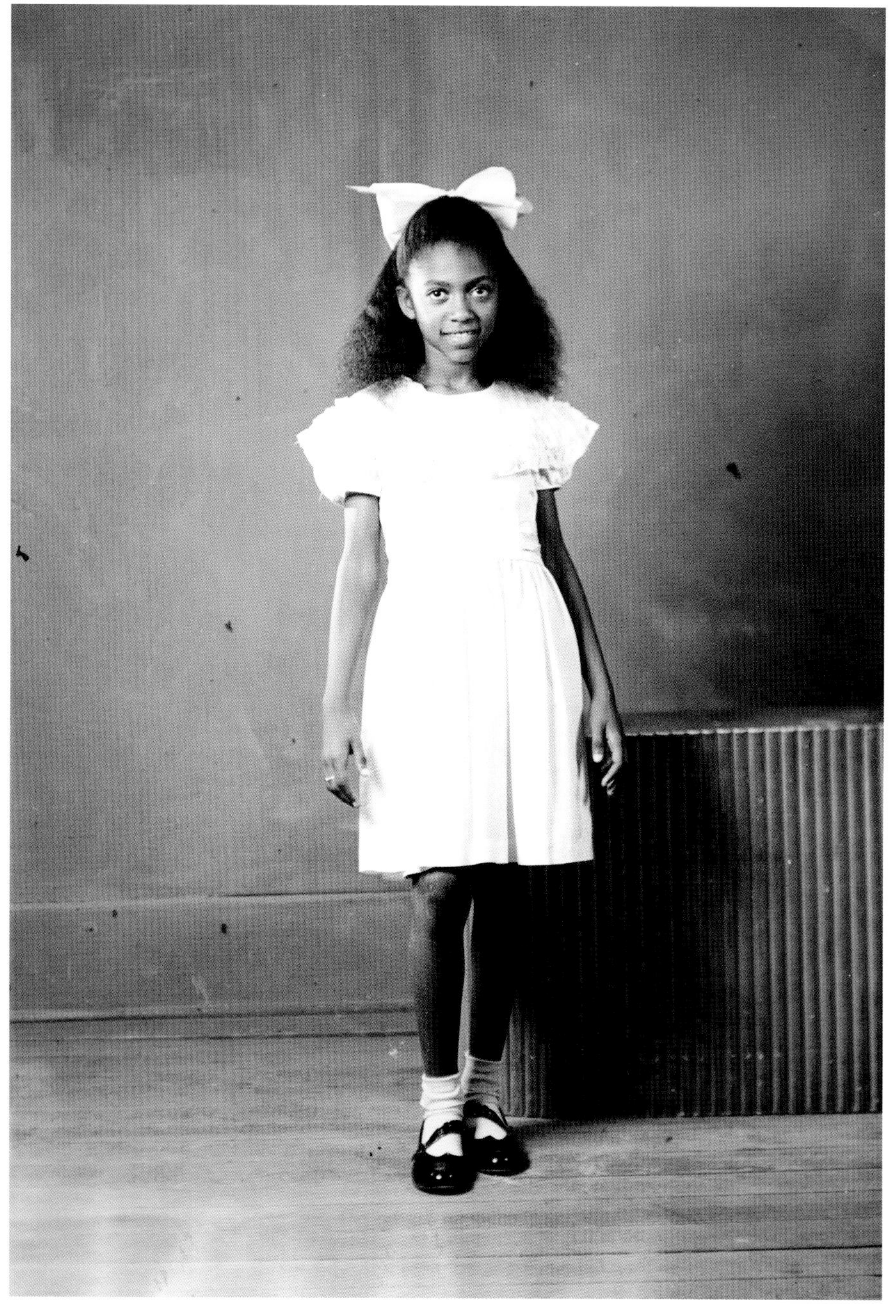

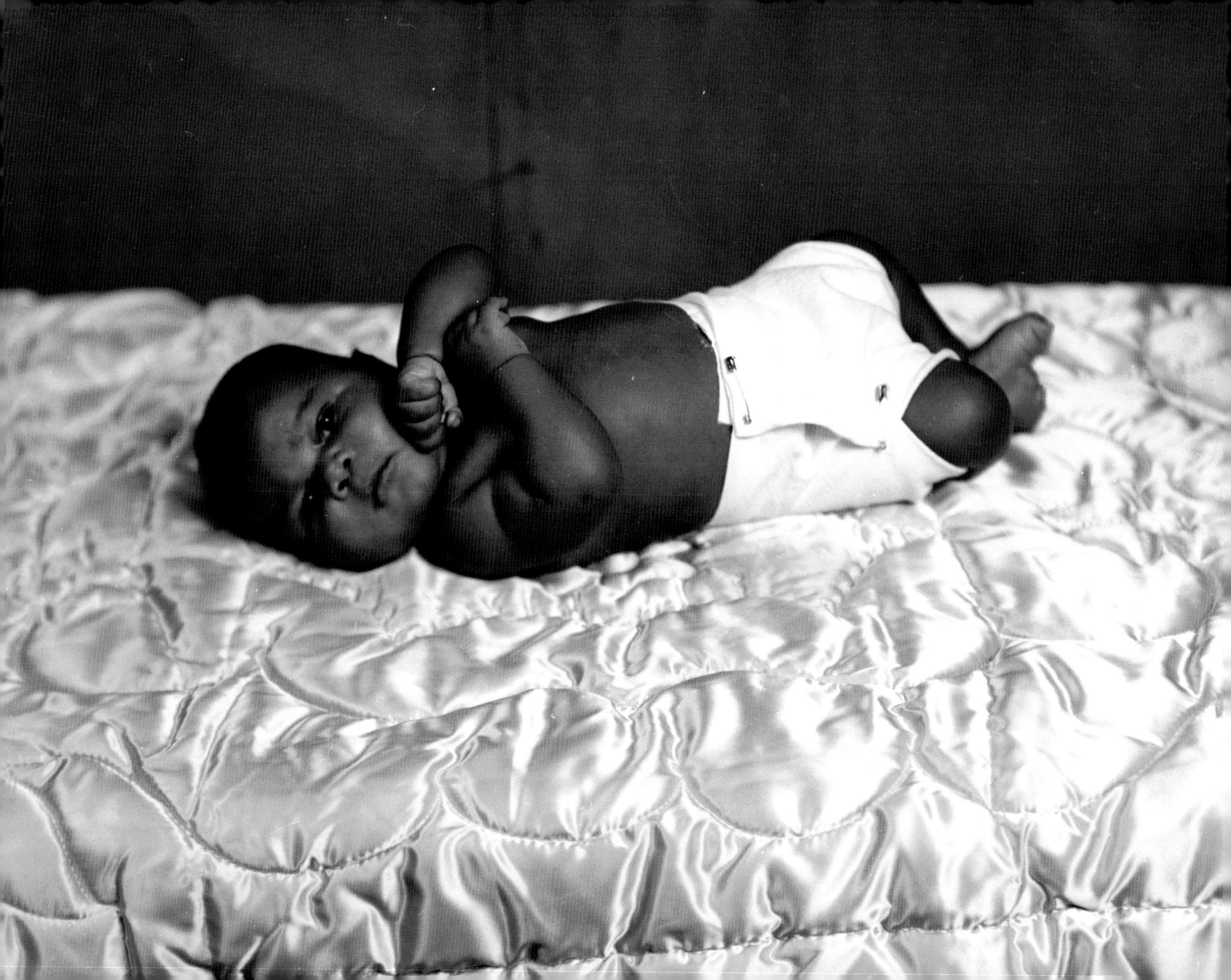

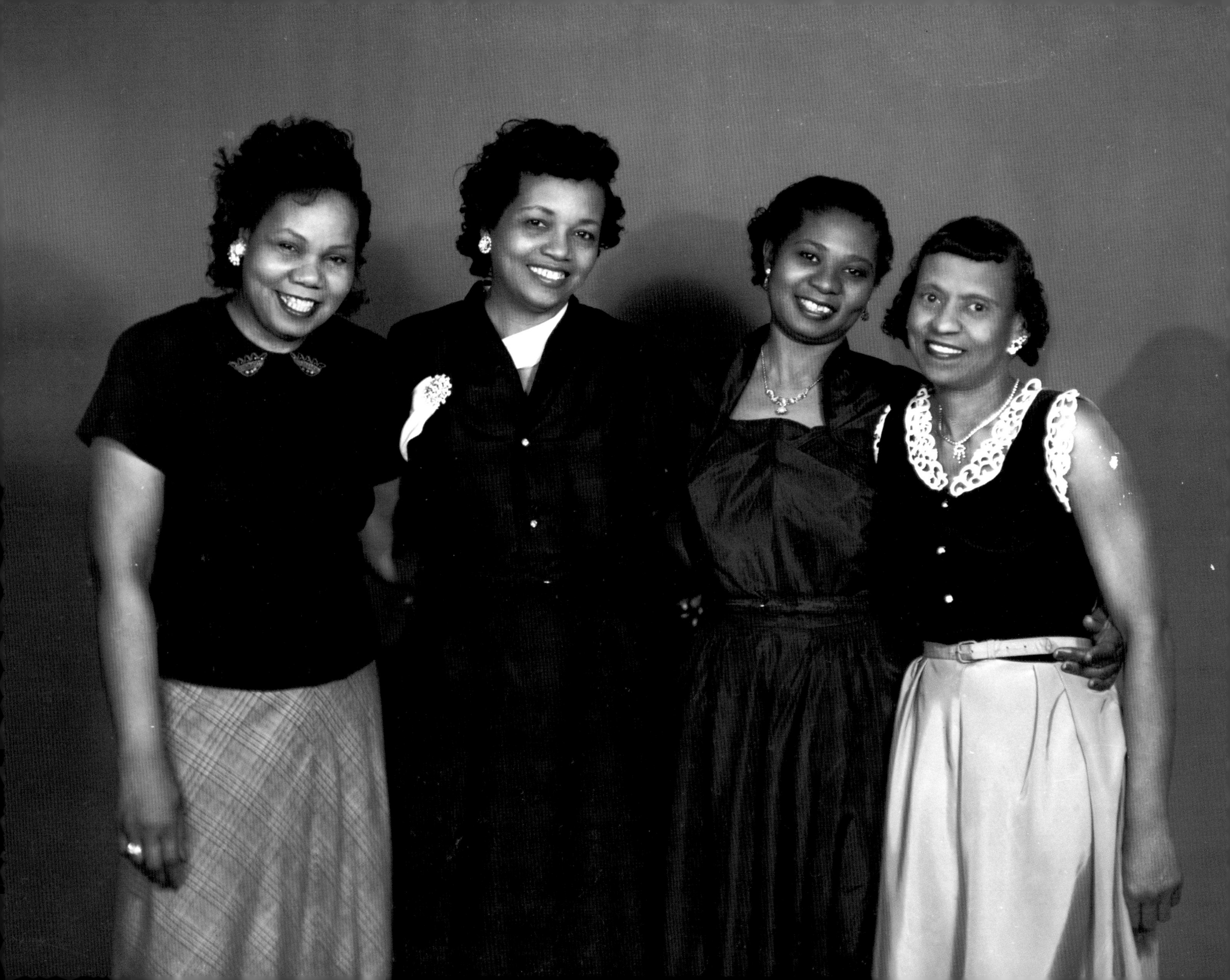

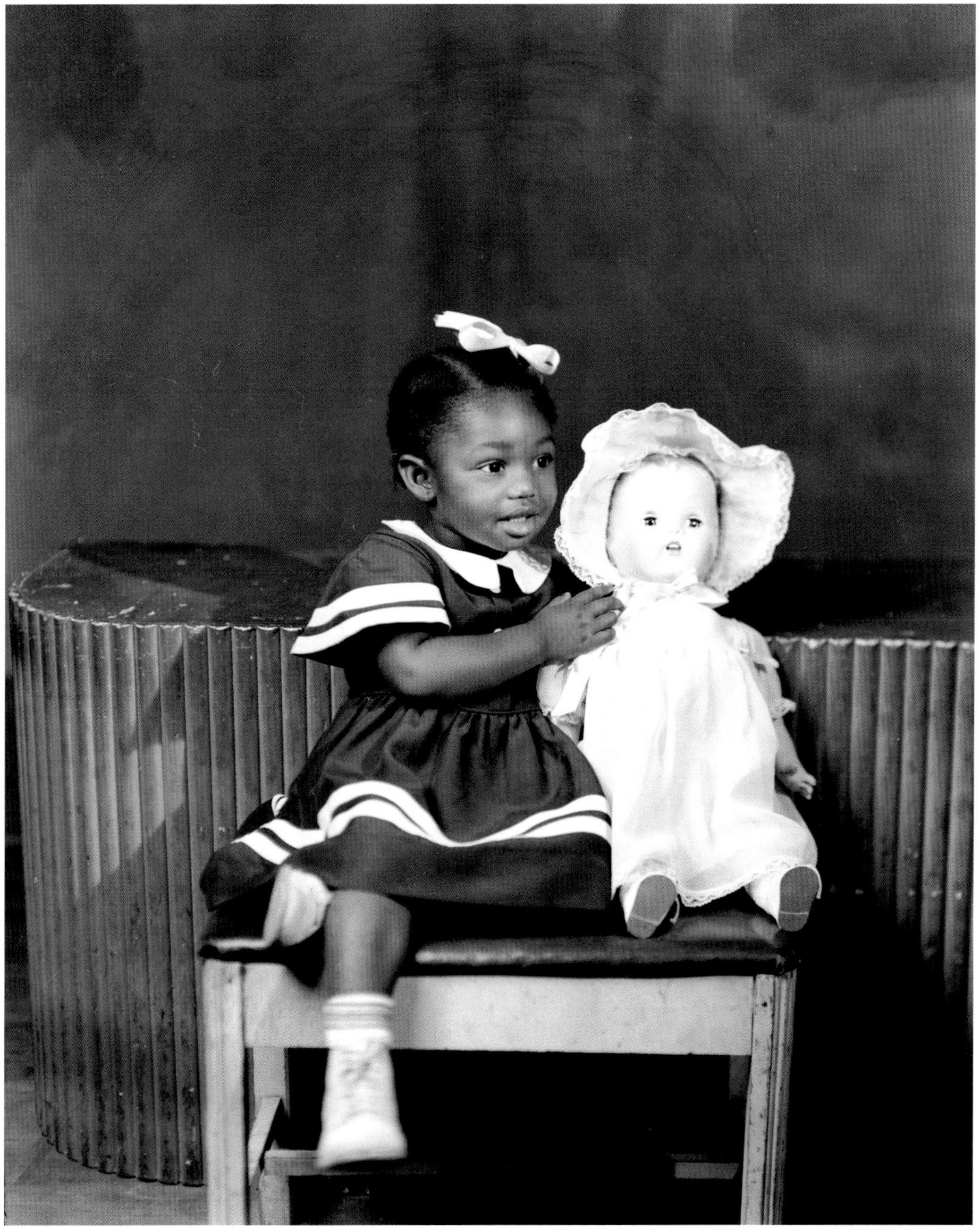

Far Left: Mrs. E. A. White and sisters, studio portrait.

Left: Girl and doll, December 31, 1949.

Right: Studio portrait of a girl, August 30, 1949.

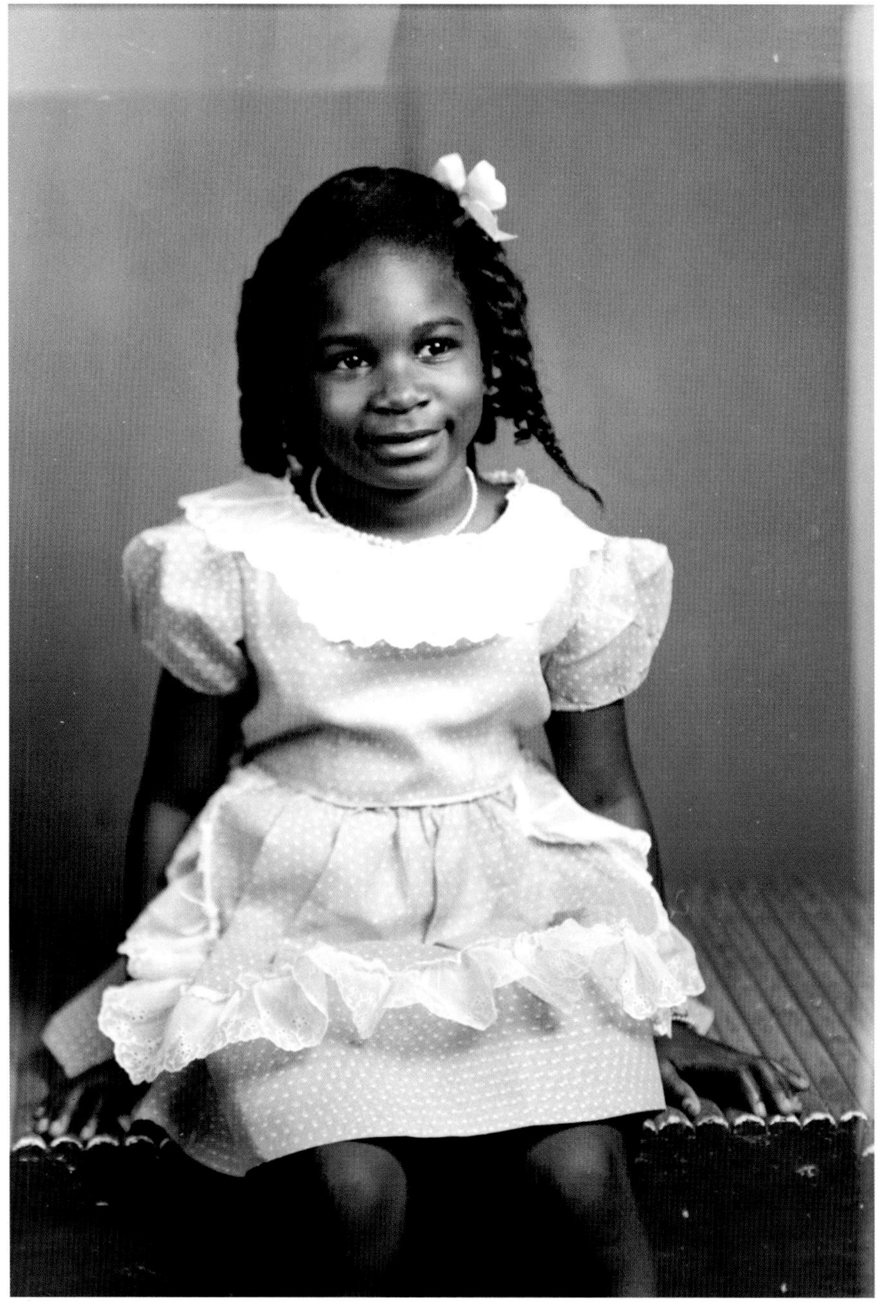

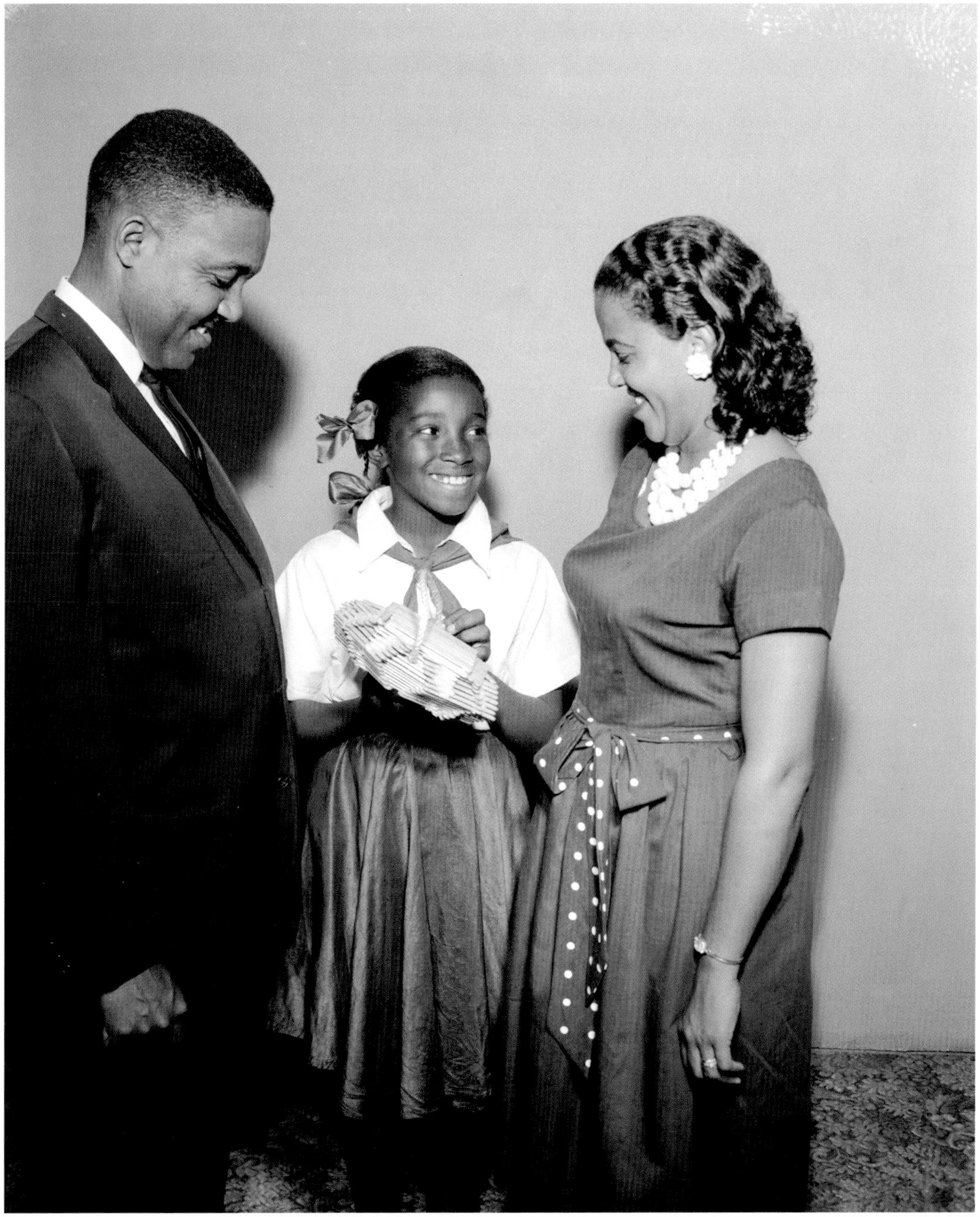

Left: Camp Fire Girl Cynthia Cook, a student at Riverside Elementary School, was the 1960 recipient of the Beta Mu Omega Campship for a deserving girl. She is pictured showing a bag made of slap sticks during her stay at Camp El Tesoro. With her are Rev. Albert E. Chew, longtime pastor of Shiloh Missionary Baptist Church, who was chairman of the Tejas Camp Committee of the United Way Agency, and Marguerite J. Johnson, a teacher at East Van Zandt Elementary School and Basileus-elect of Alpha Kappa Alpha Sorority at the time. Mrs. Johnson would go on to become principal of three other elementary schools in Fort Worth: Oaklawn, Maudrie M. Walton and Morningside. (1961)

Right: Dillie Mae Wilson, studio portrait, May 10, 1950.

Far Right: Mr. and Mrs. R. L. Wormley and family, December 21, 1954.

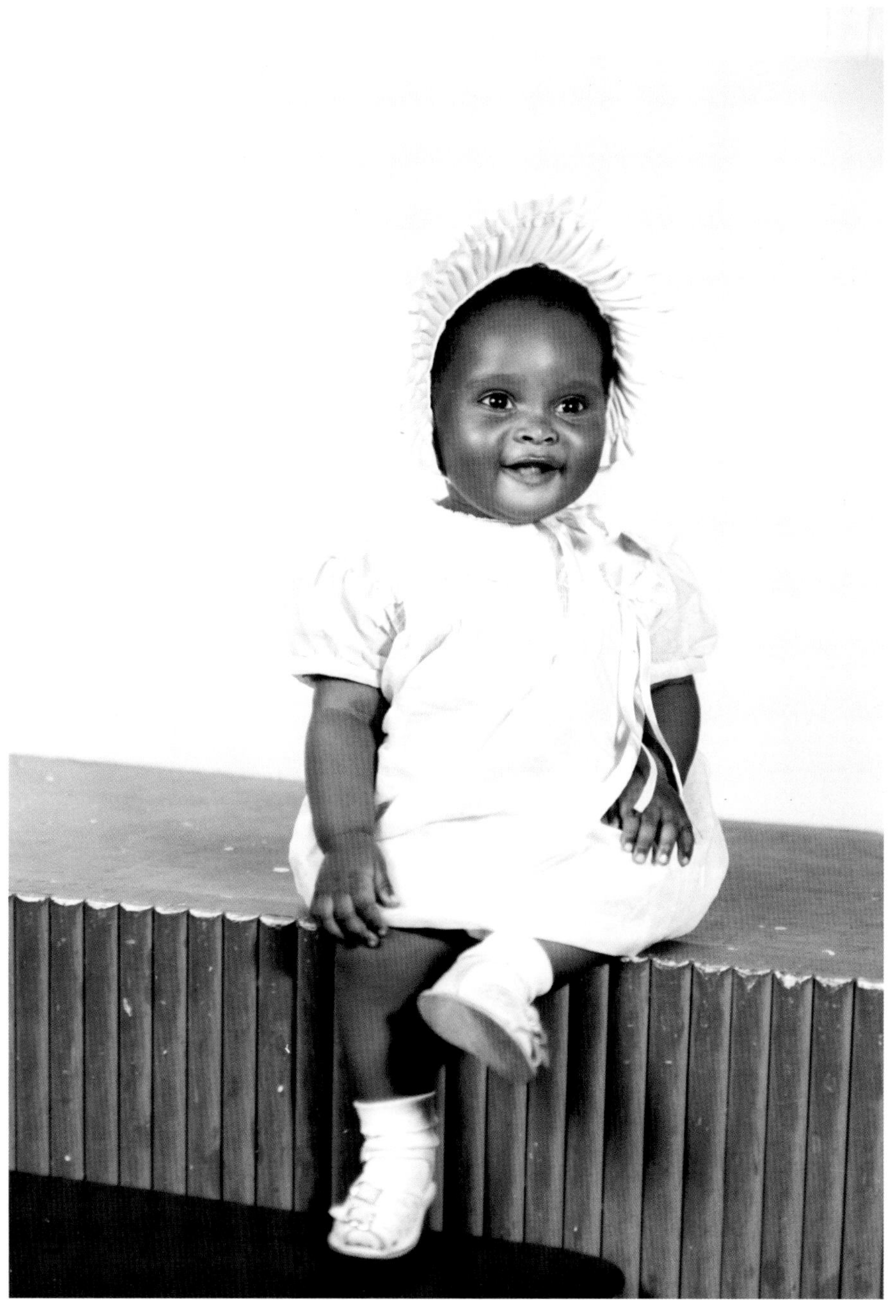

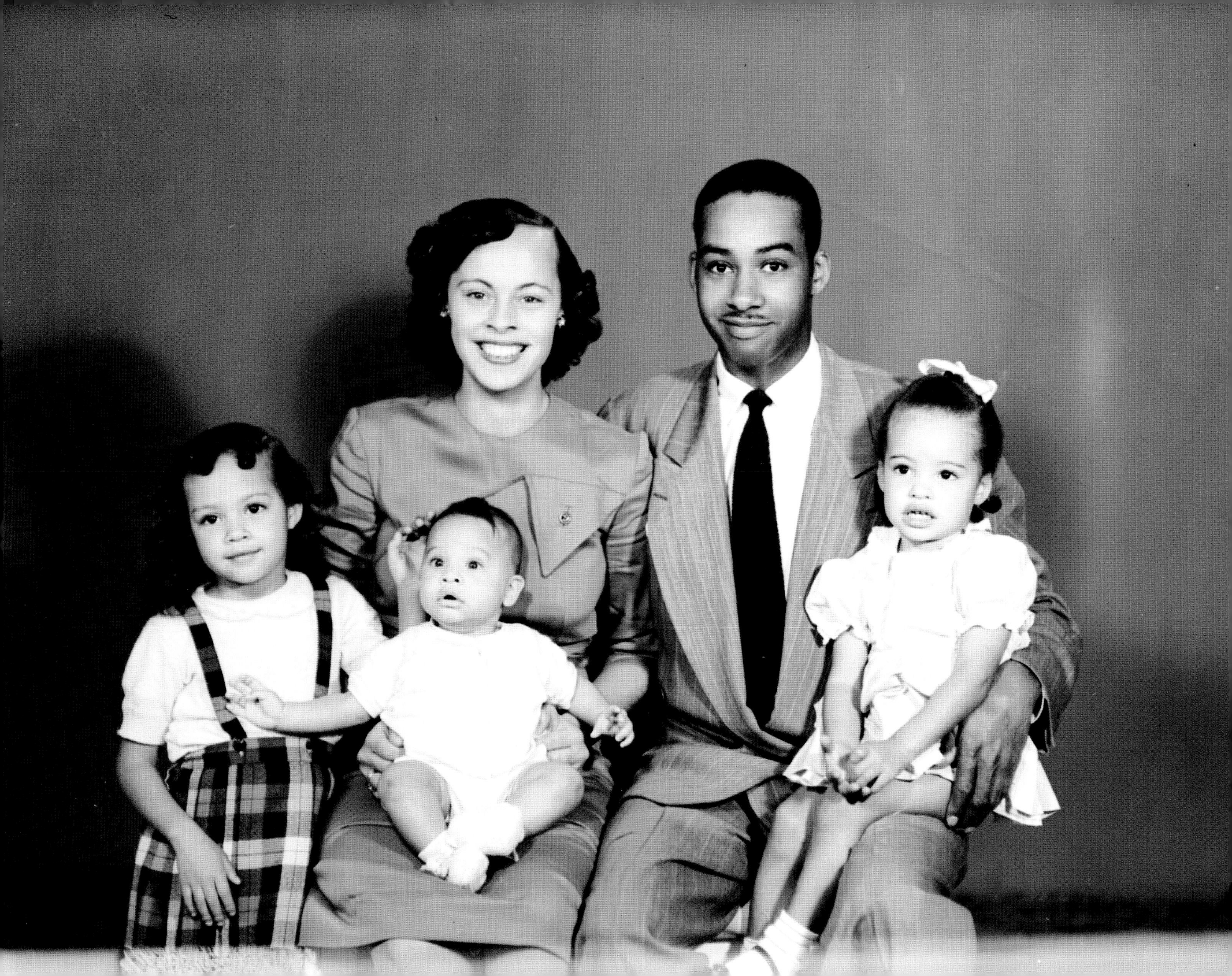

Right: Williams boy on tricycle, October 1949.

Far Right: R. L. Taylor's children, March 31, 1960.

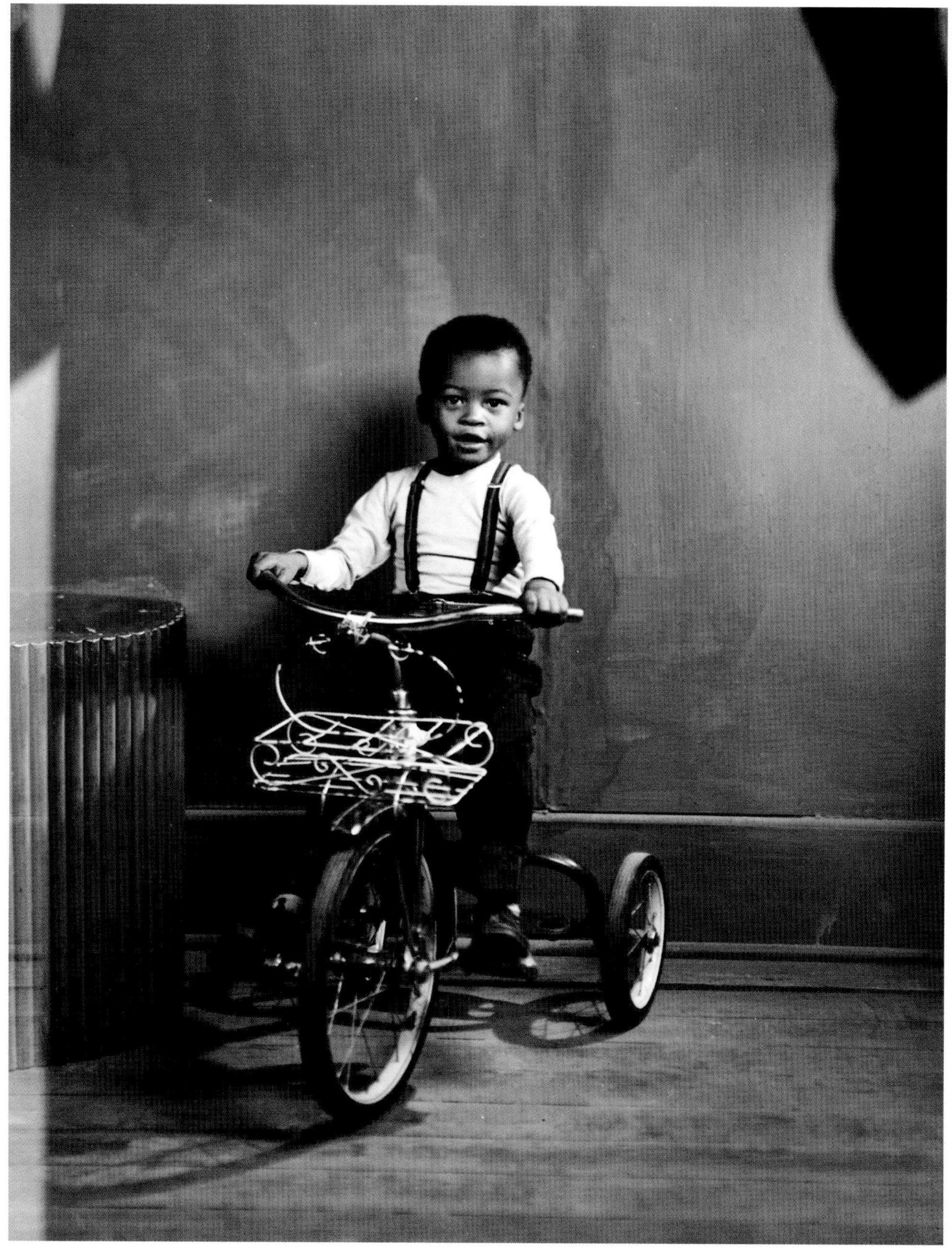

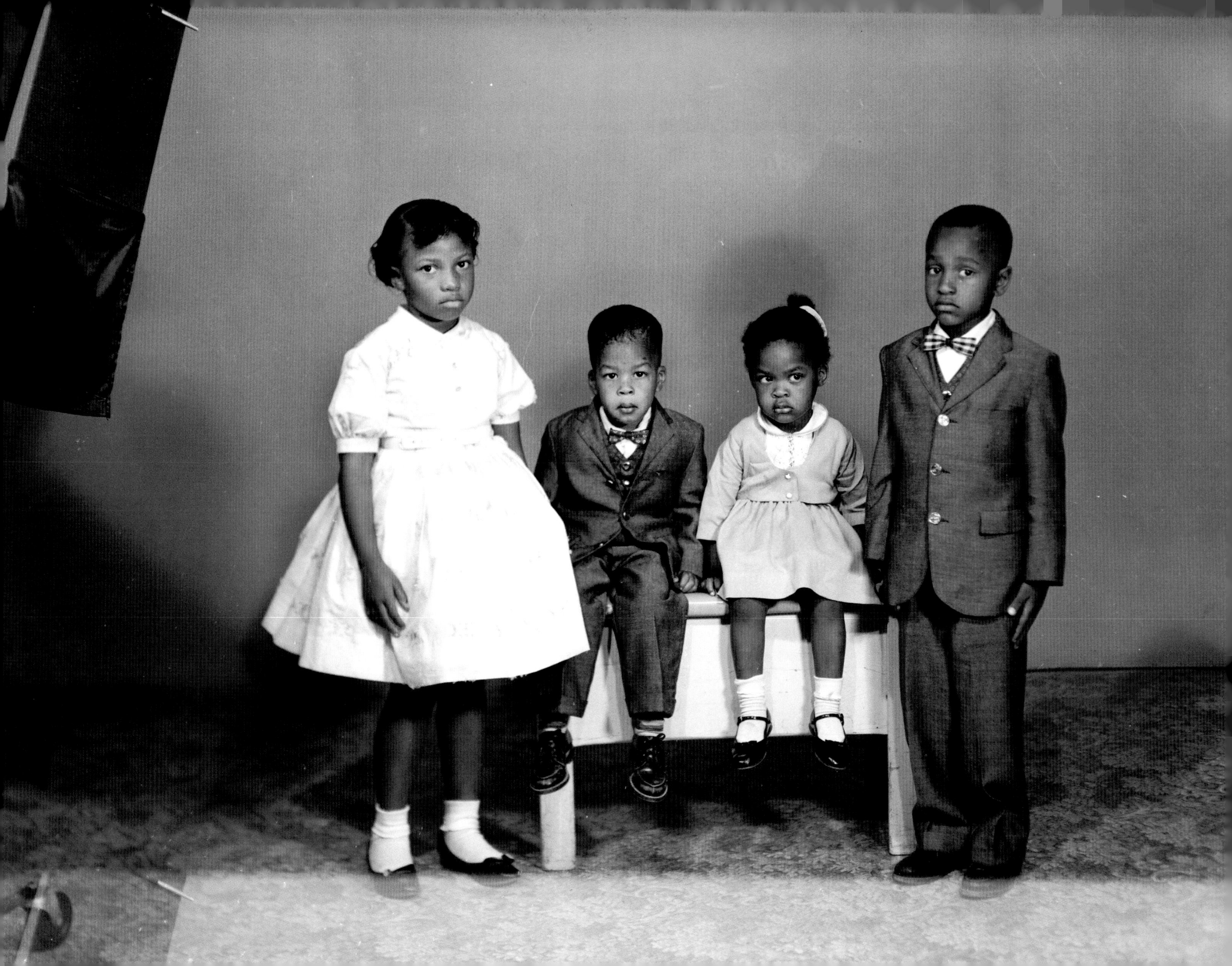

Right: Studio portrait of a couple, December 3, 1949.

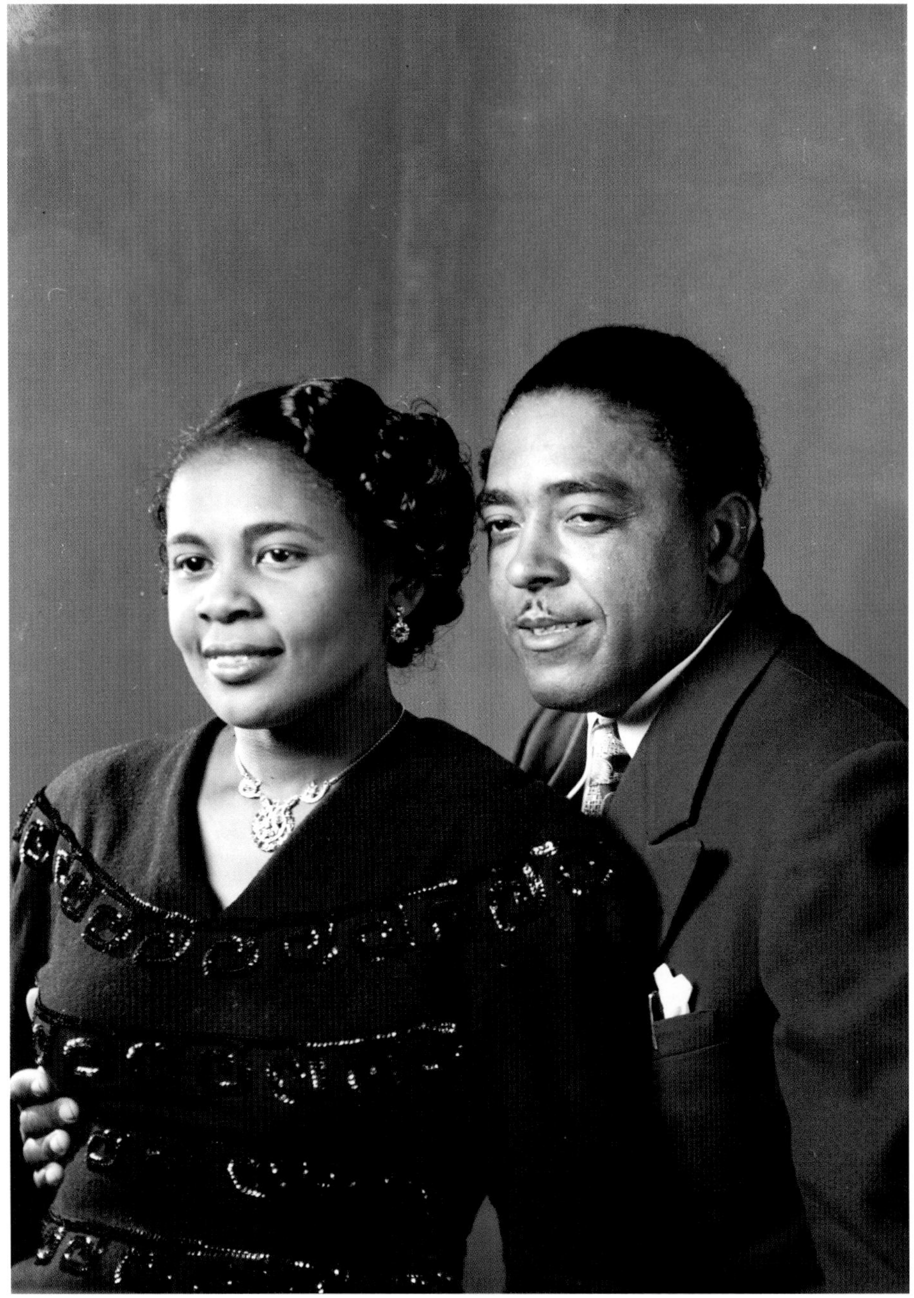

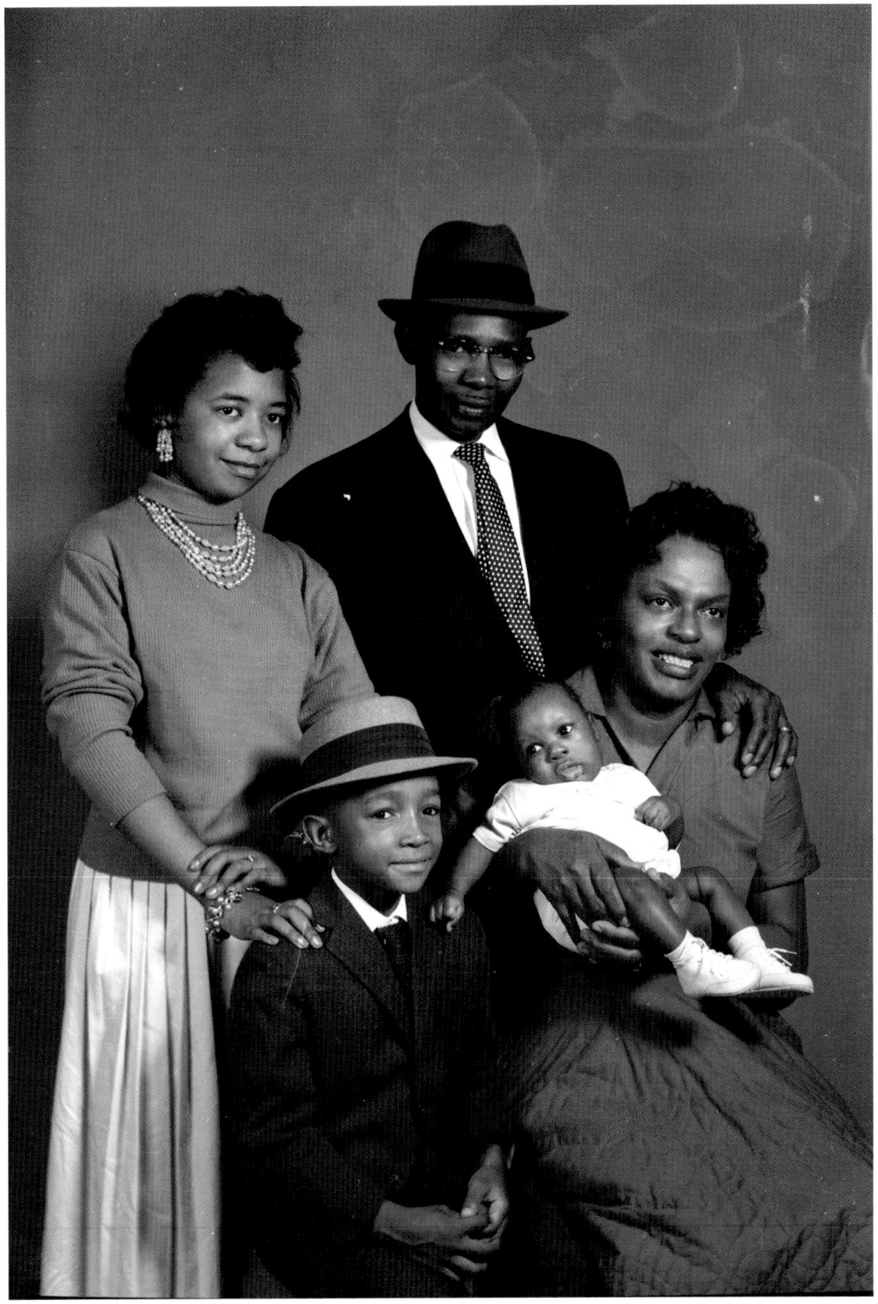

Left: Mr. and Mrs. Edwin Thomas and family, studio portrait, December 9, 1959.

Right: Birthday party, 1951.

Far Right: Birthday party, January 1953.

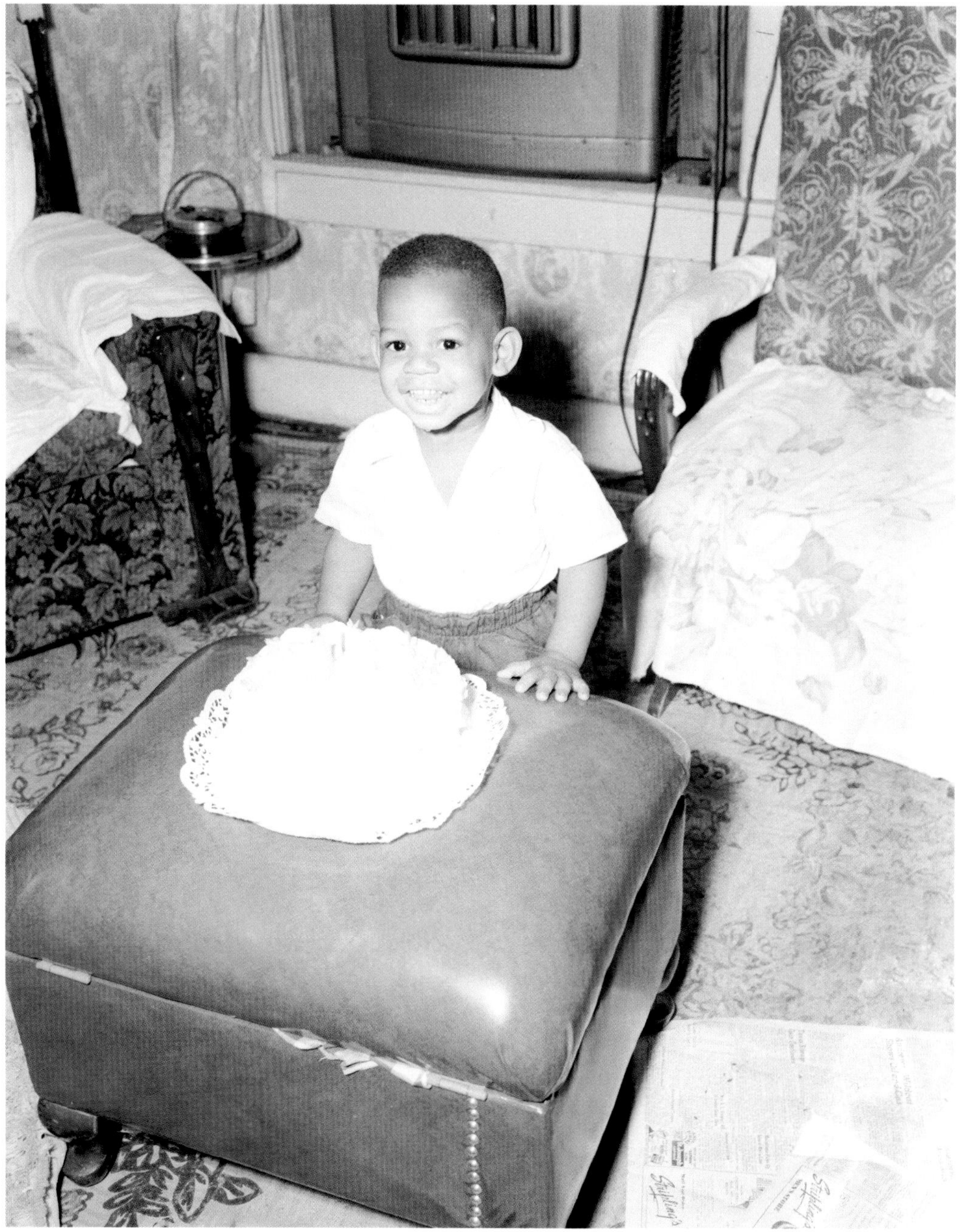

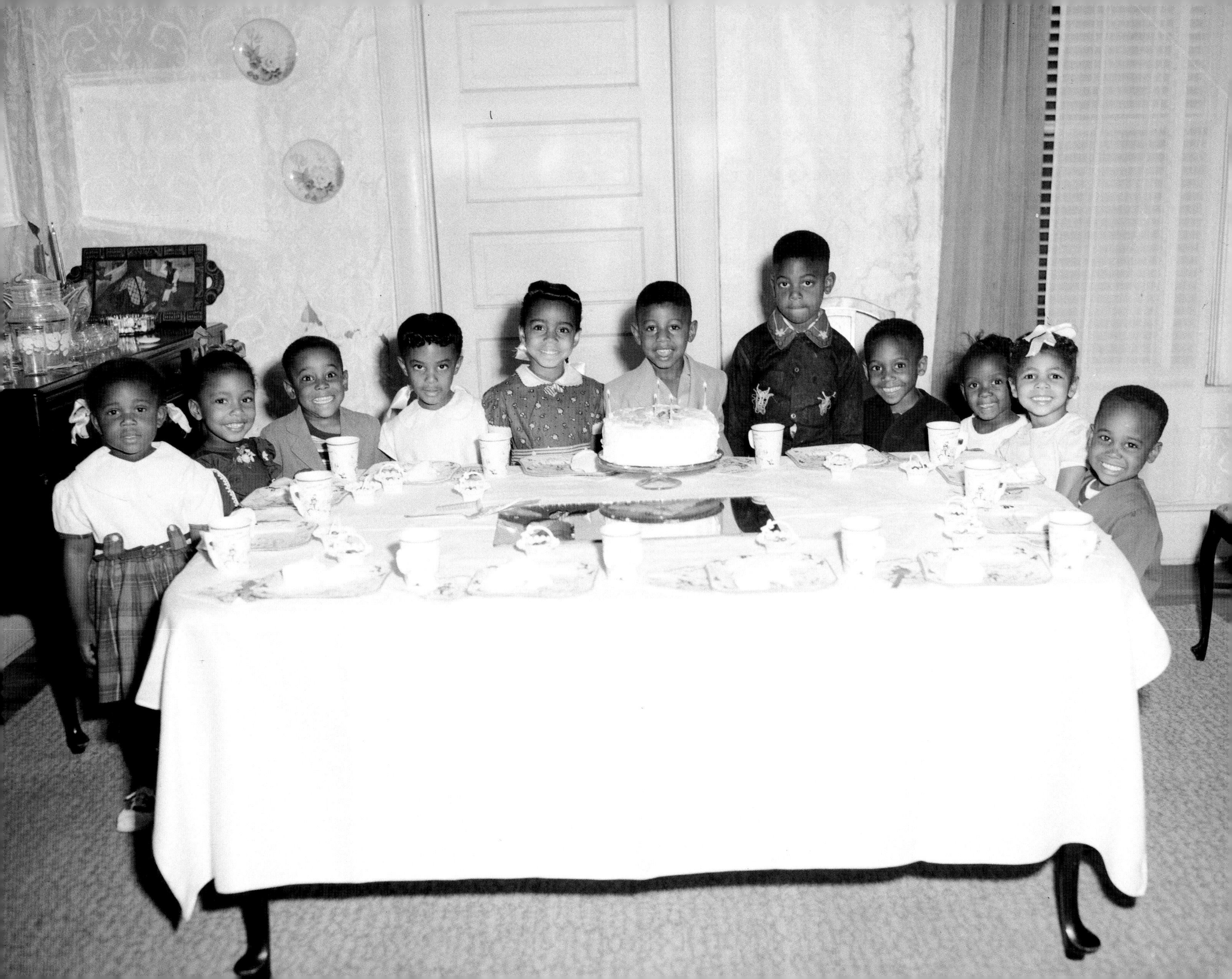

Right: Mrs. Edmonds' three children.

Far Right: Birthday party, perhaps for a child or grandchild of Thomas "Snooks" Russell, a Como civic leader, bail bondsman, and funeral director, 1956.

Next Page, Left: Playground in Central City, 1971.

Next Page, Right: Playground in Central City, 1971.

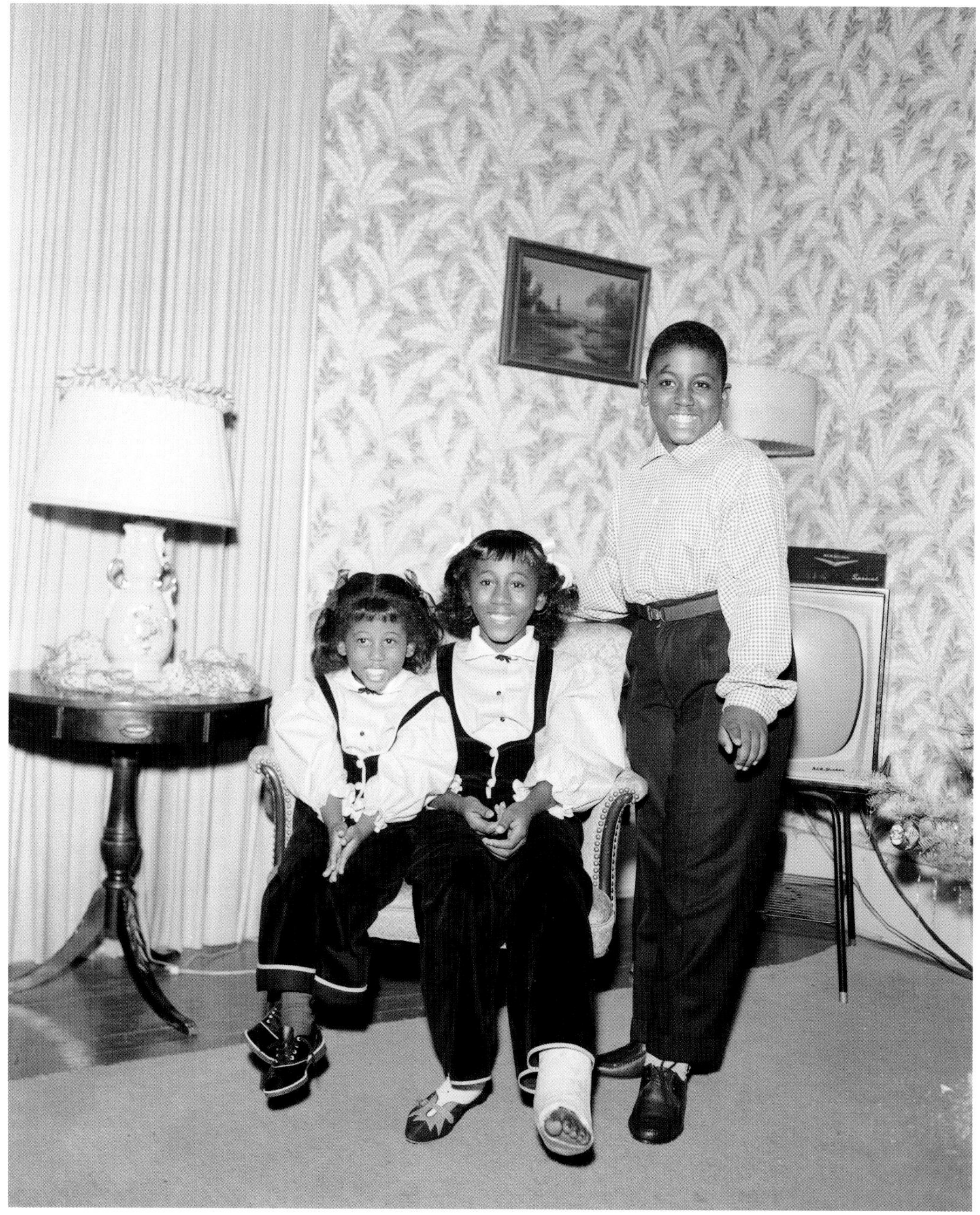

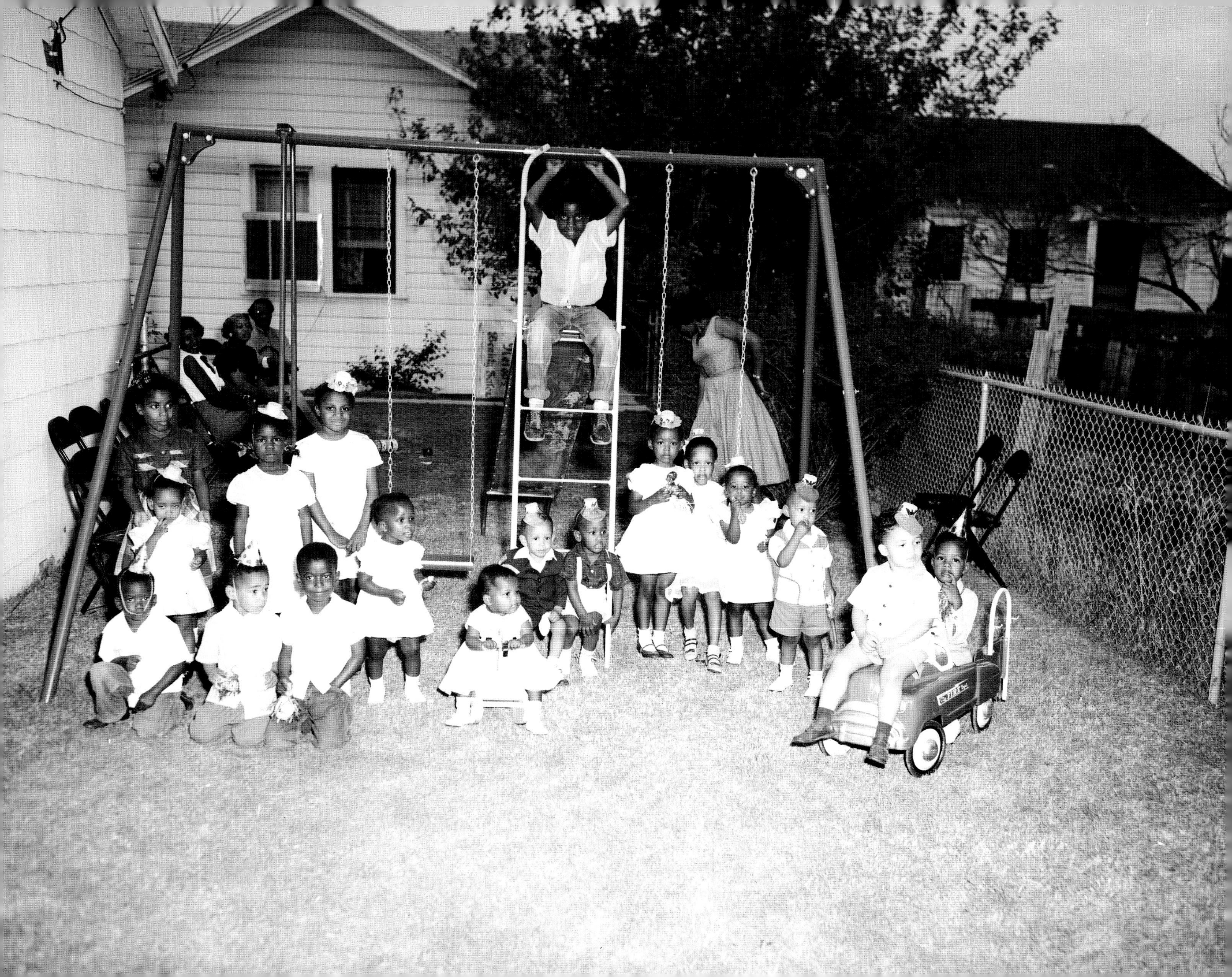

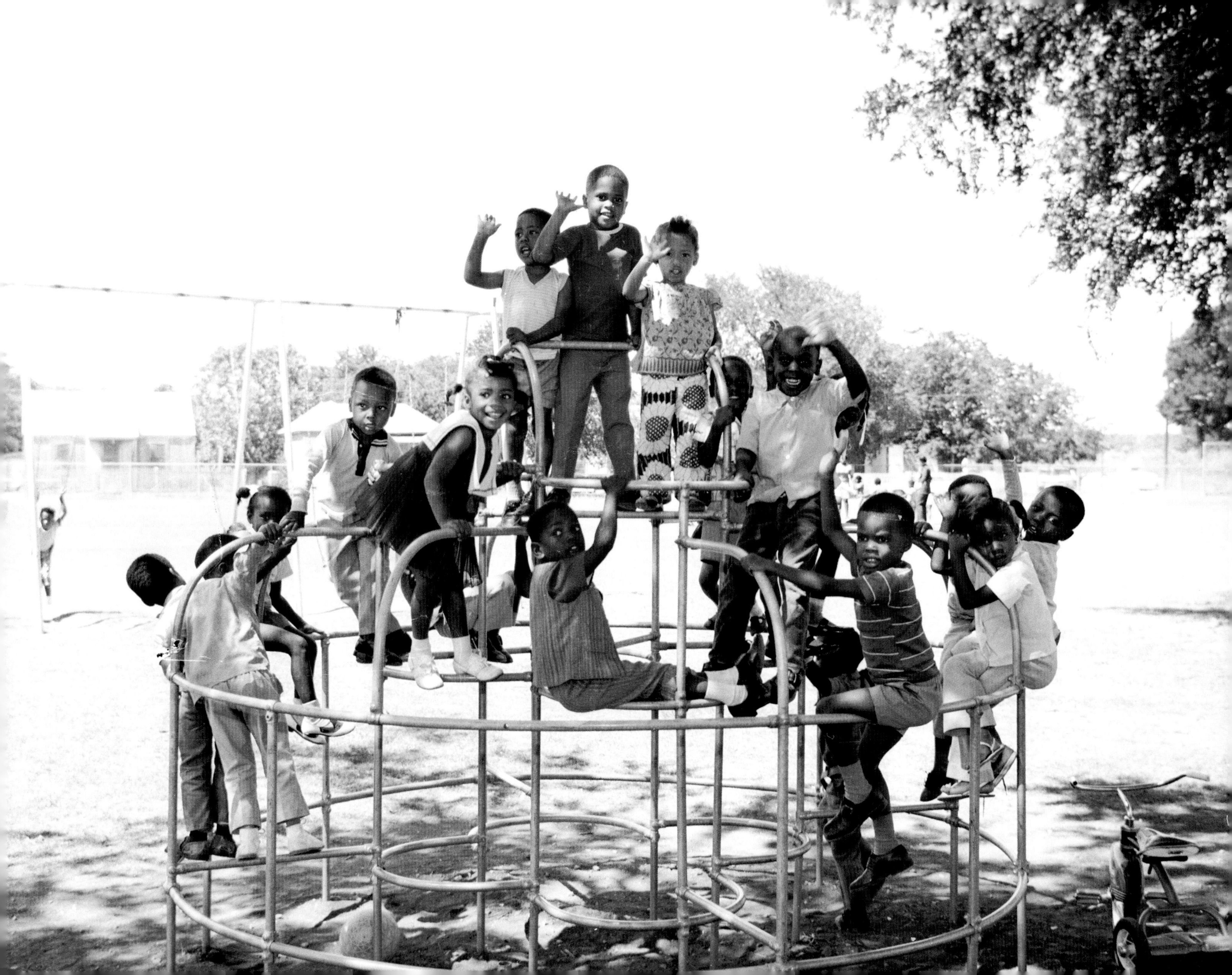

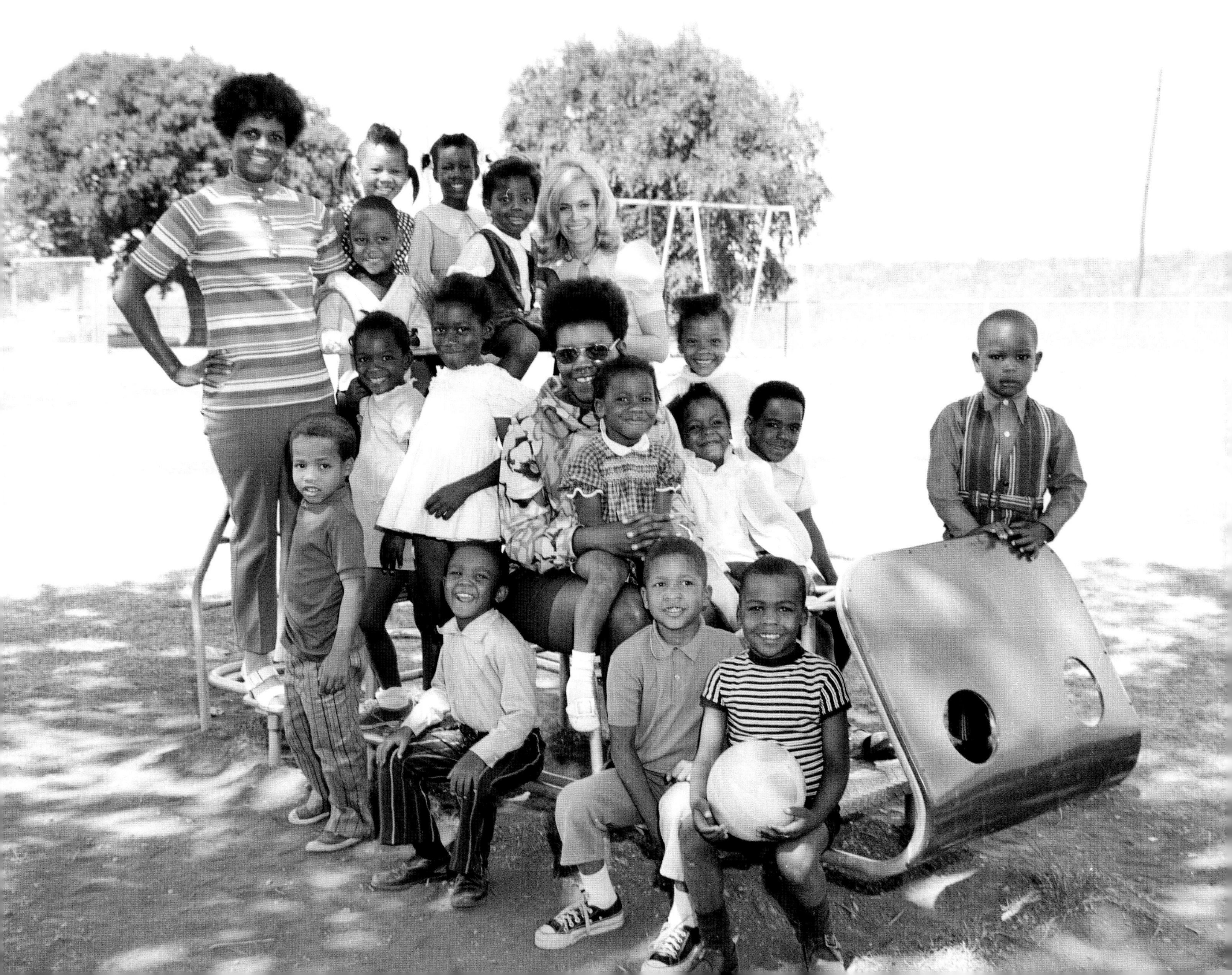

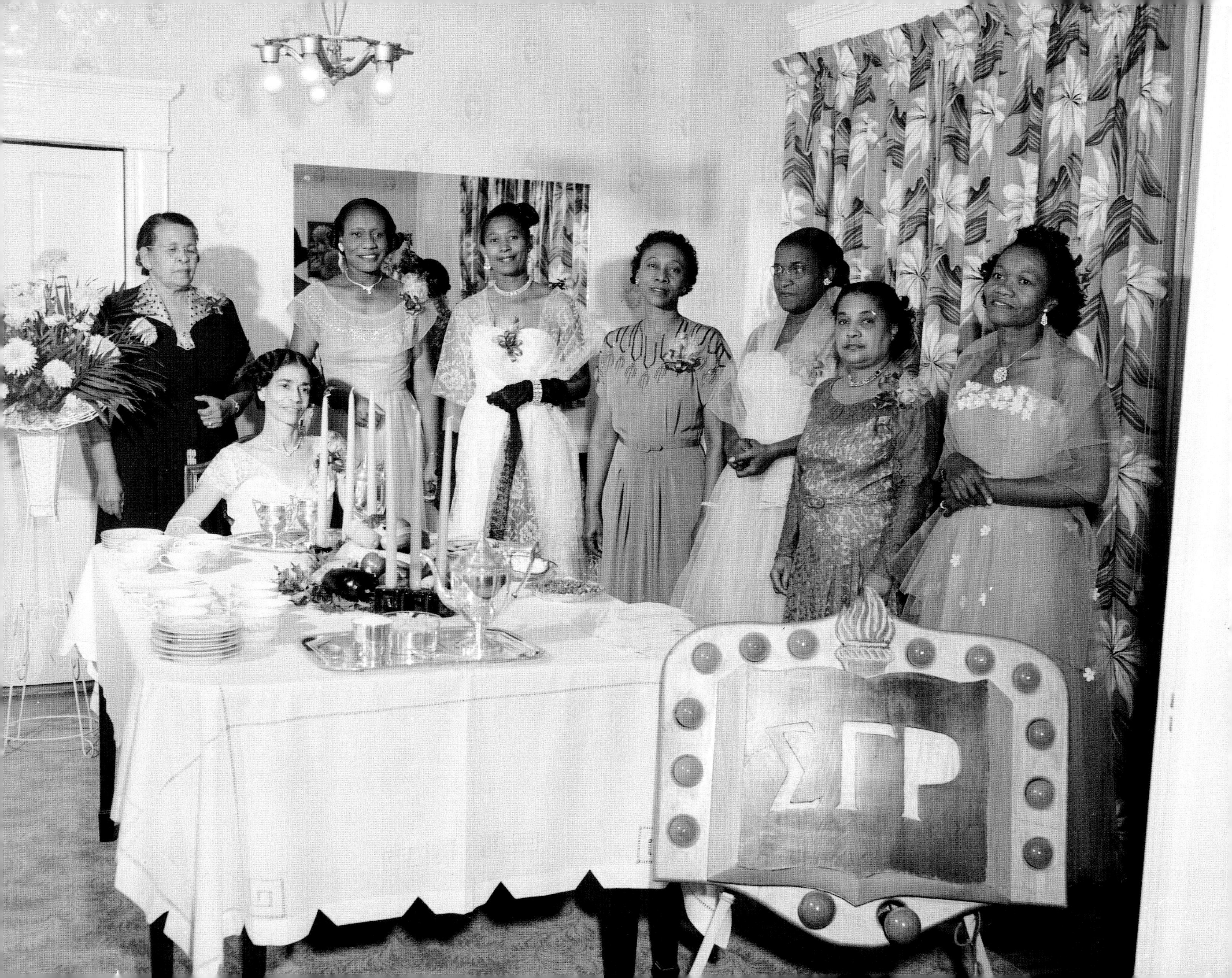
ΣΓΡ

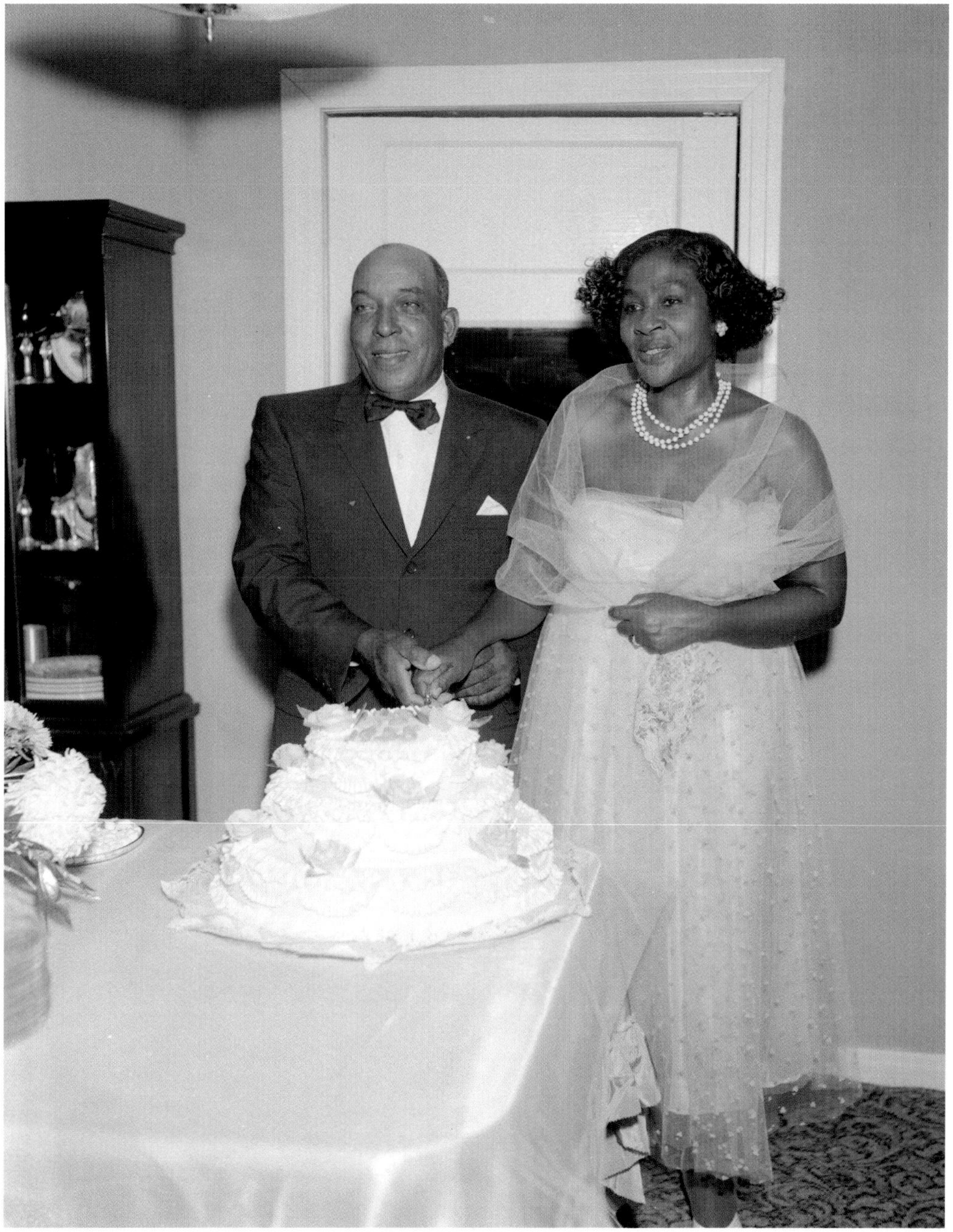

Far Left: Zeta Phi Beta Sorority Party. Most of the people pictured are educators, principals, and teachers. Seated is Mrs. Versia L. Williams who was principal of the "colored" Riverside Elementary School, which was later named for her. Standing at left is Mrs. Maude Logan, who also would have a school named for her.

Left: Twenty-fifth anniversary party, 1950s.

Right: Bride, studio portrait, 1980s.

Far Right: Eastern Stars honoring Mrs. Burnett (first name unknown) for forty-two years of service. Hortense Chapman is on left.

Next Page, Left: Four women at home on Wainwright Drive in the Stop Six neighborhood.

Next Page, Right: Funeral for Mrs. Maggie B. Cary, the "First Lady" of Rising Star Baptist Church where her husband, the Reverend Smith Cary (seated on front row left) was the pastor. Their son, Reby Cary (front row, center), would become the first black school board member in Fort Worth, the first black administrator at UT-Arlington and one of the first blacks elected to the state legislature from Tarrant County.

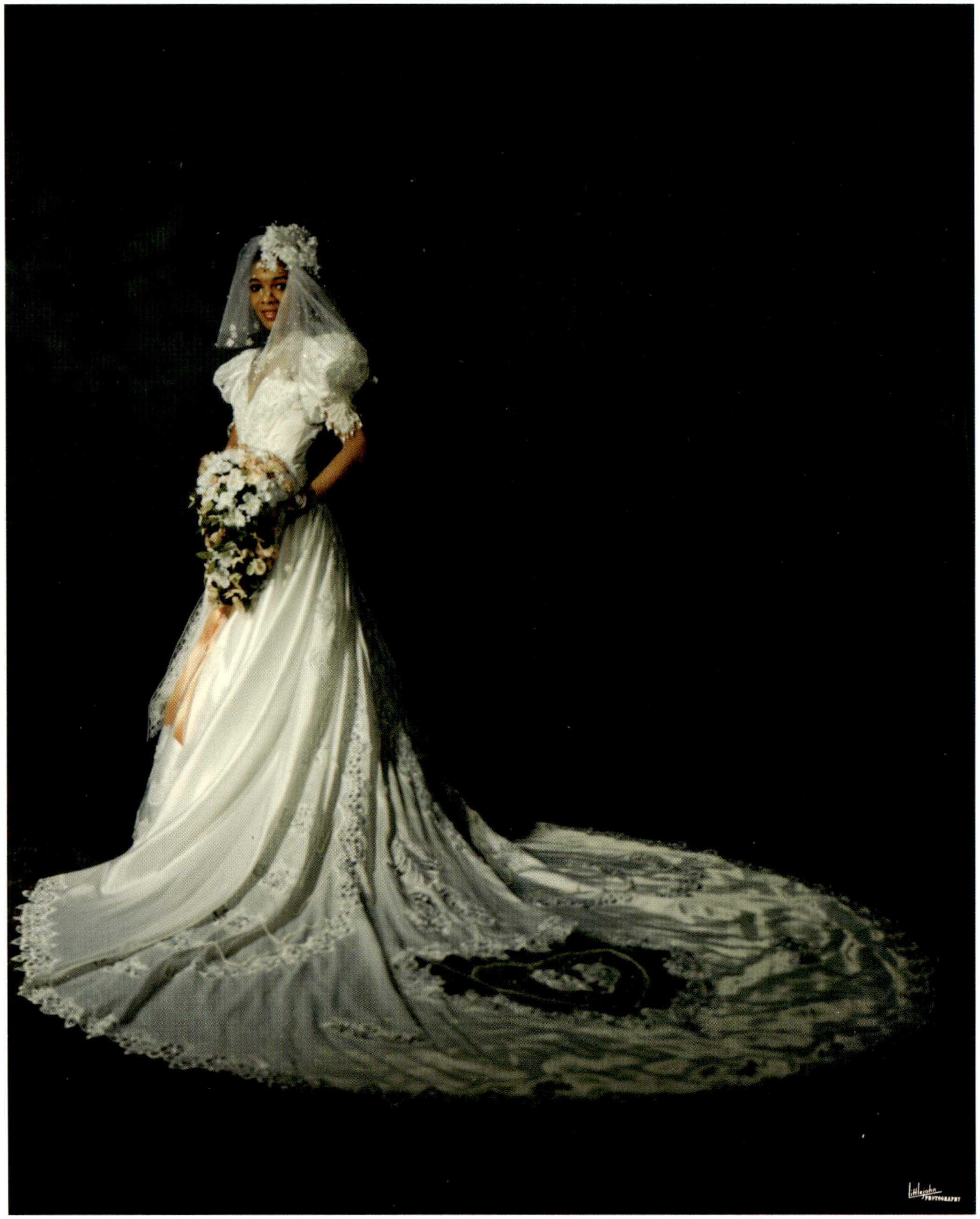

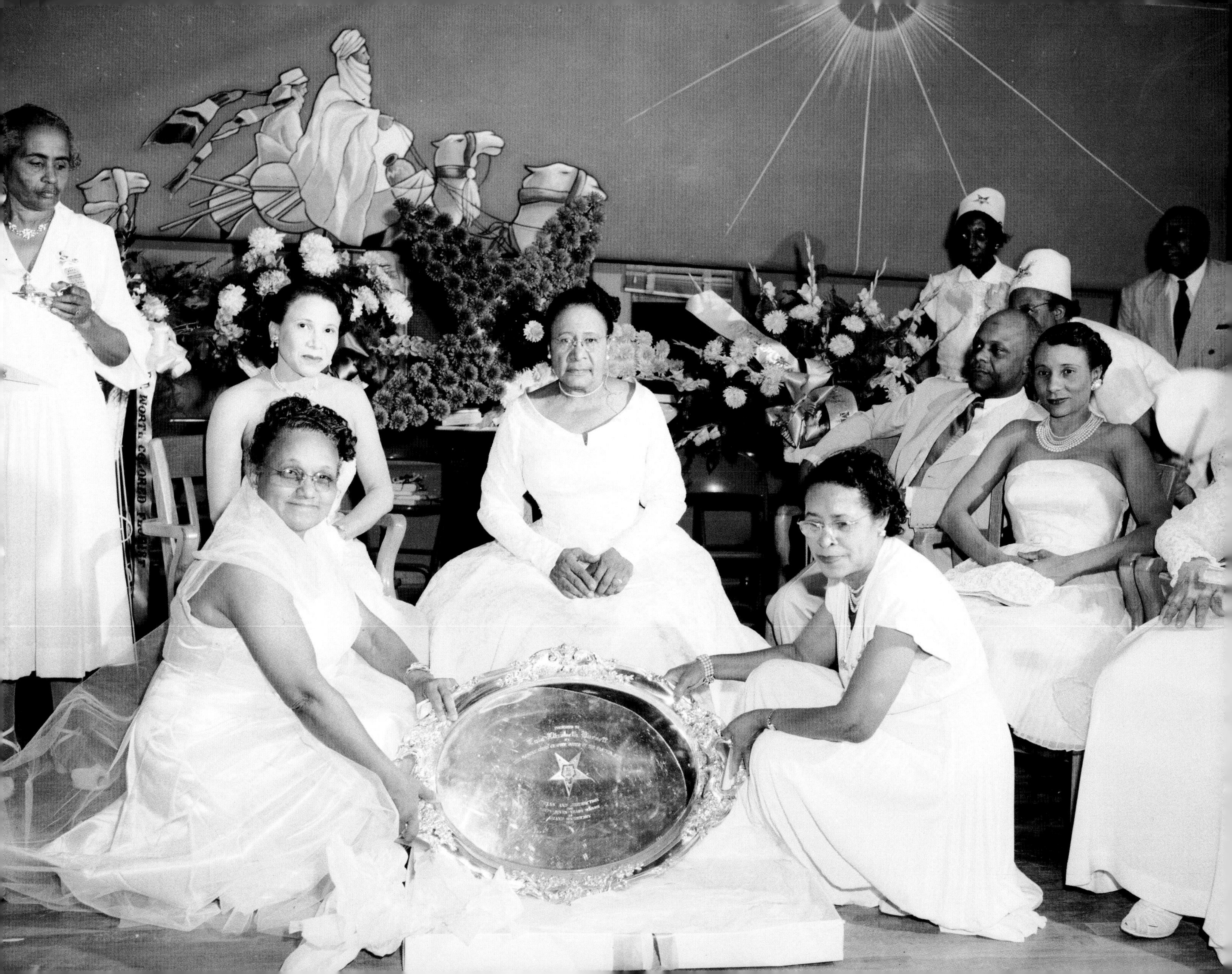

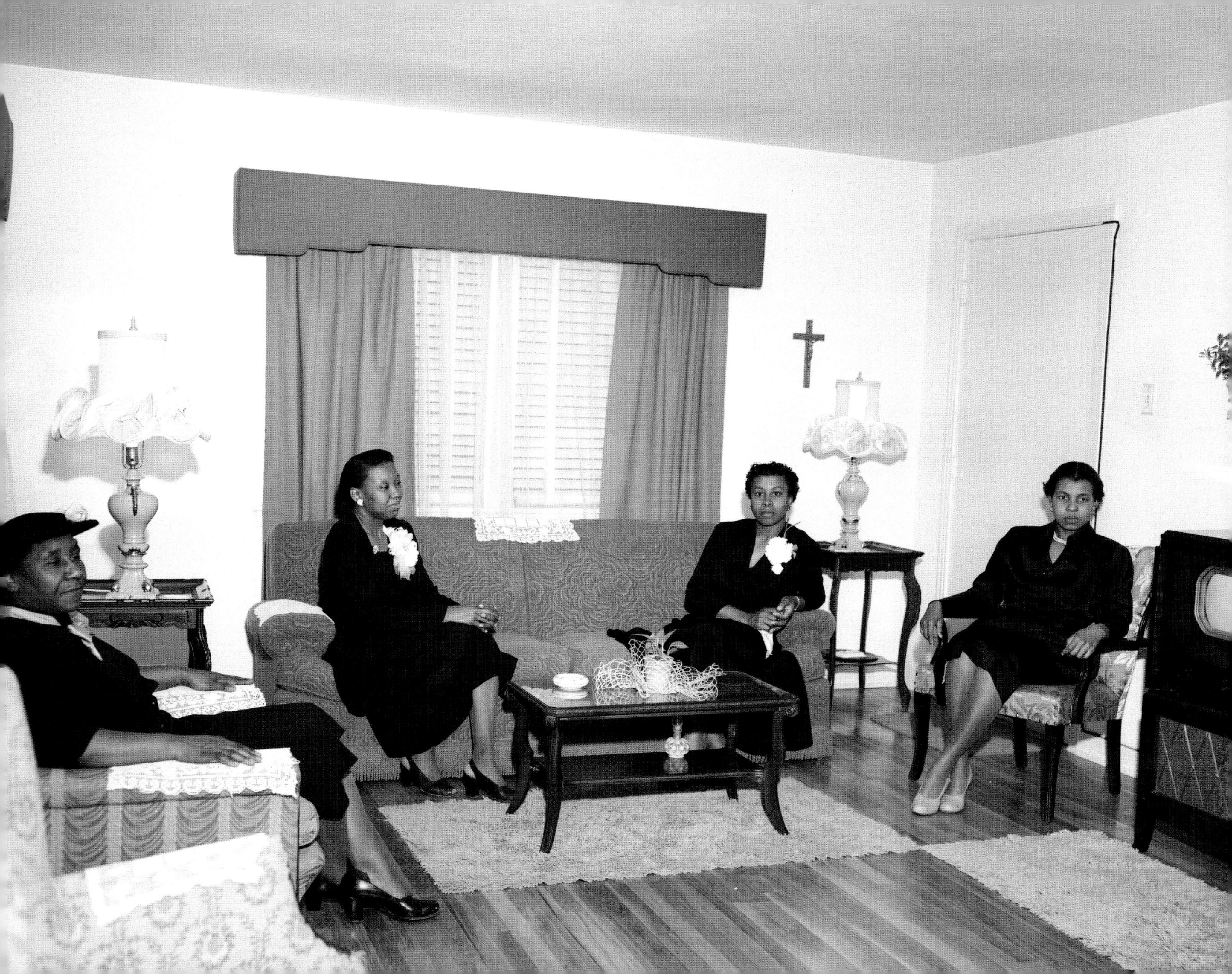

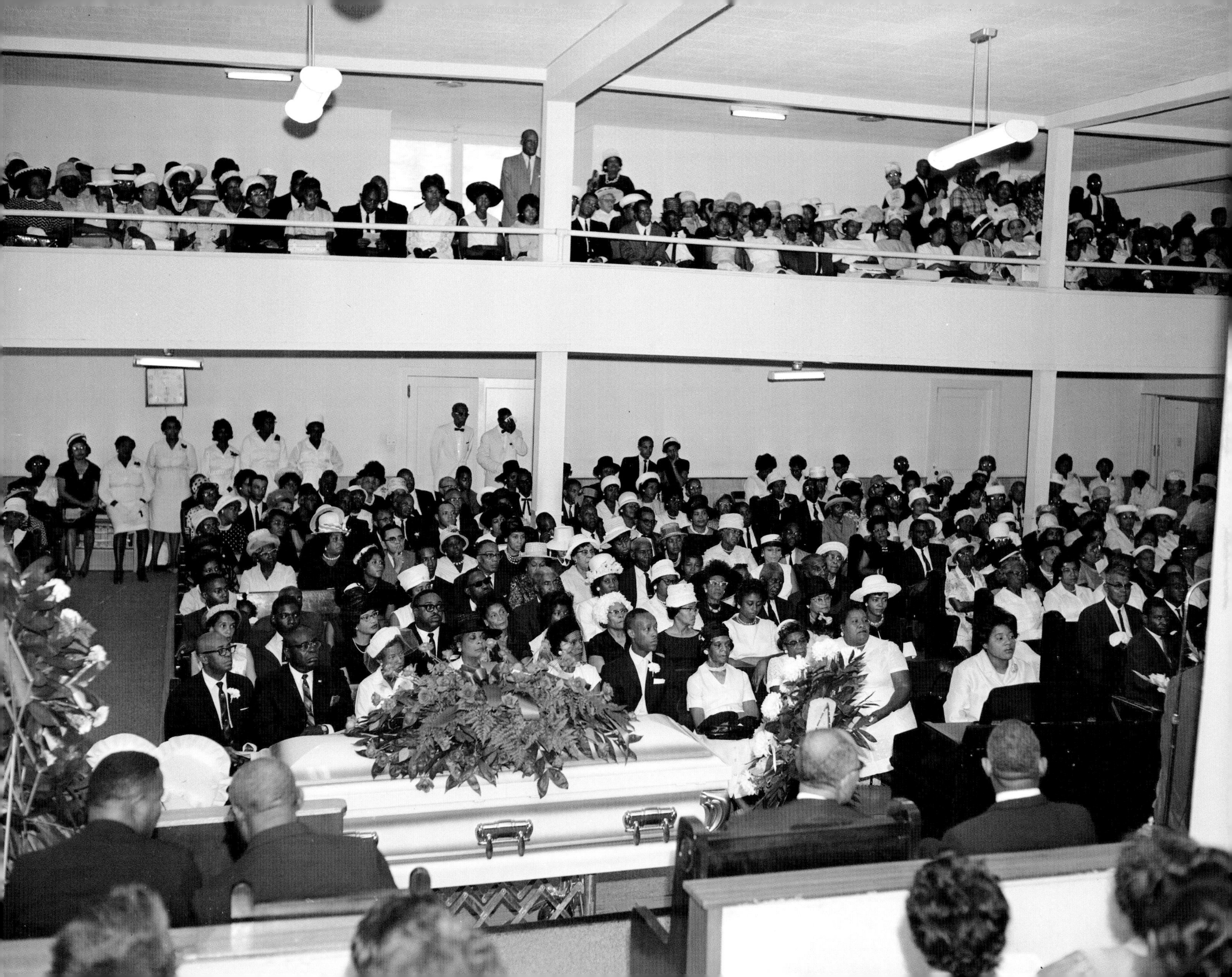

Right: Funeral of Dr. Riley Andrew Ransom, Jr., held Wednesday, June 6, 1963 at 2:00 p.m., Greater St. James Baptist Church. Dr. Ransom died June 1, 1963, at Parkland Hospital, Dallas, after a long illness.

Far Right: Mr. Pressley Jones lying in state at Baker Funeral Home's reposing room.

Next Page, Left: Funeral of Dr. Riley Andrew Ransom, Jr.

Next Page, Right: Viewing for Mr. Wheat's aunt, October 9, 1952. Baker Funeral Home Chapel.

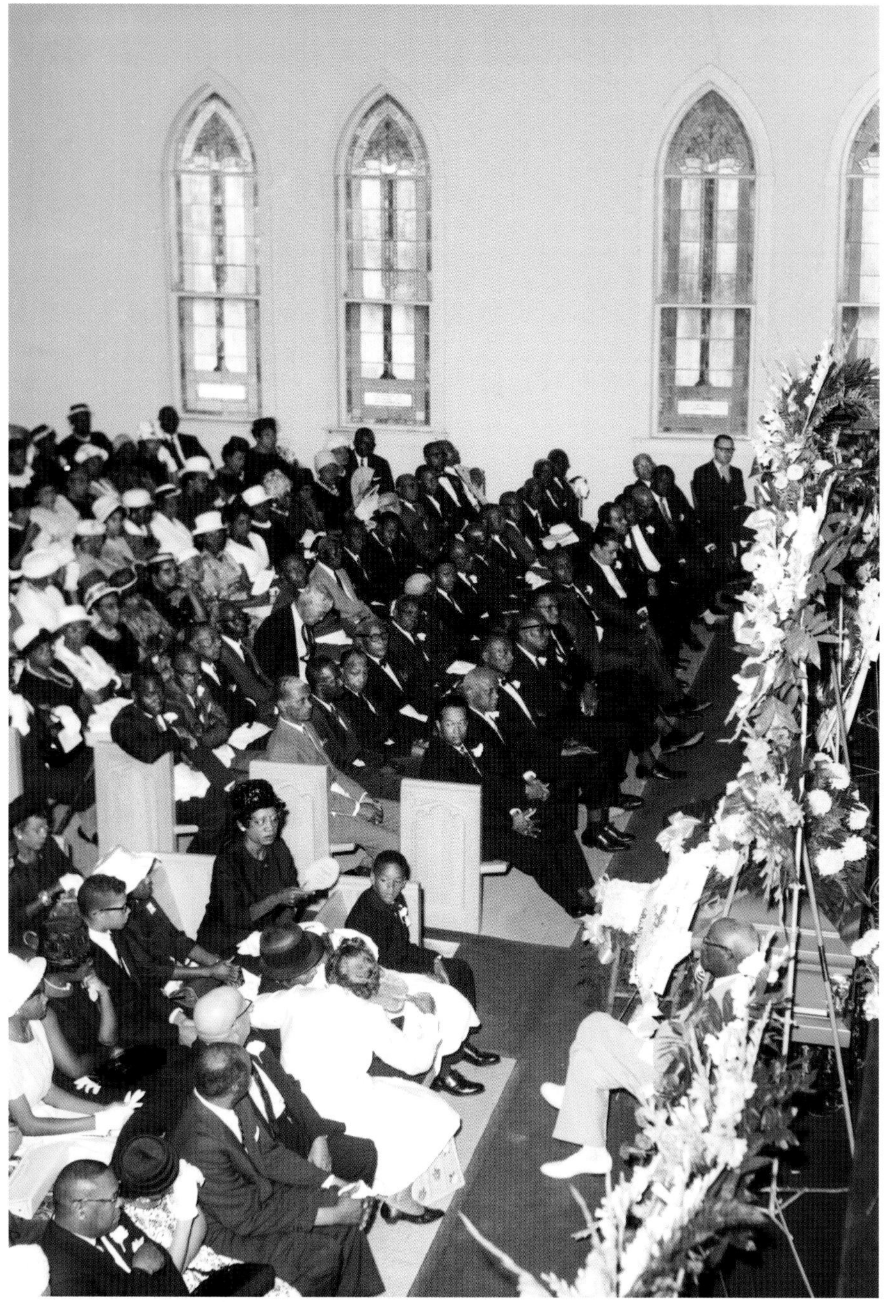

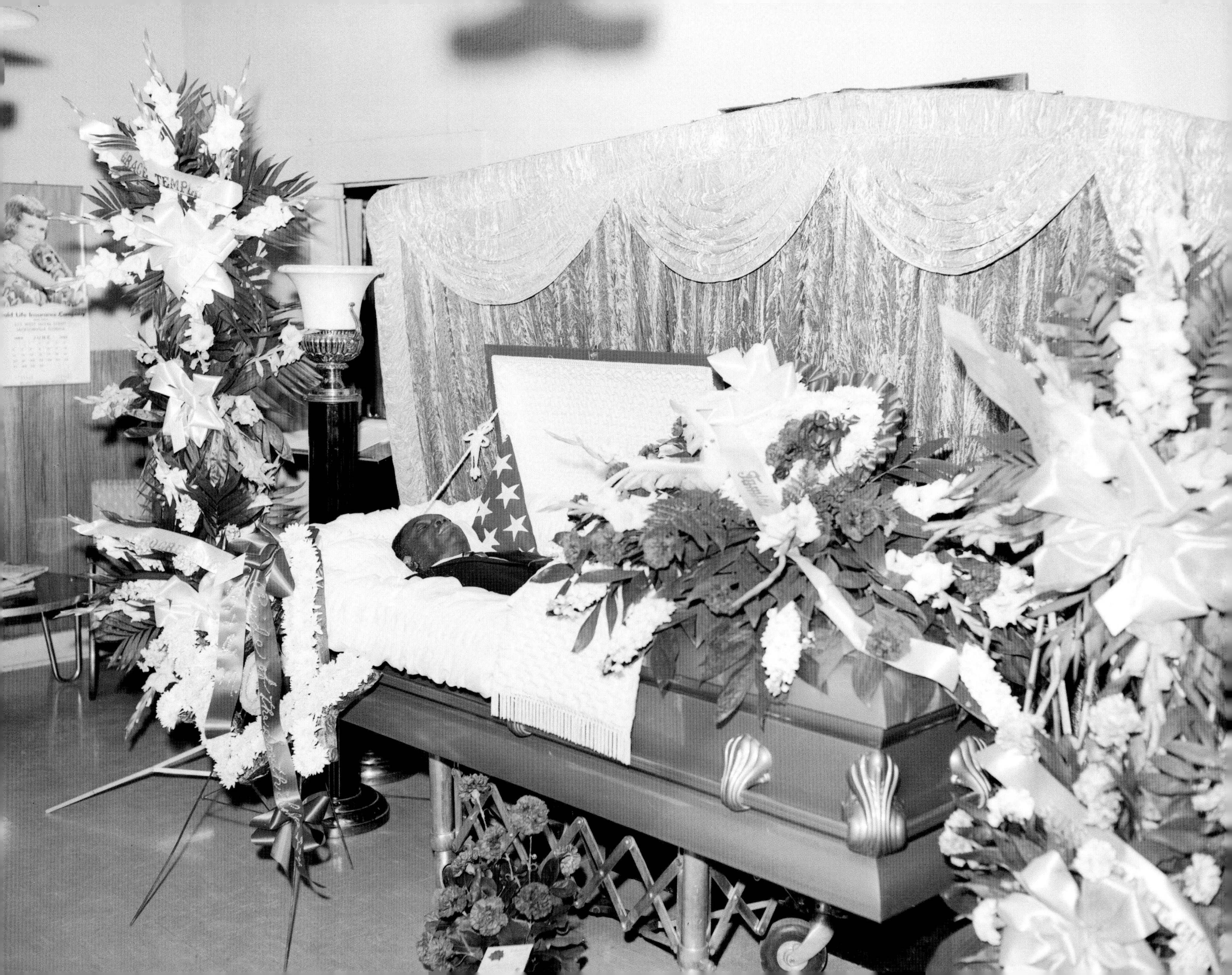
Family
JUNE

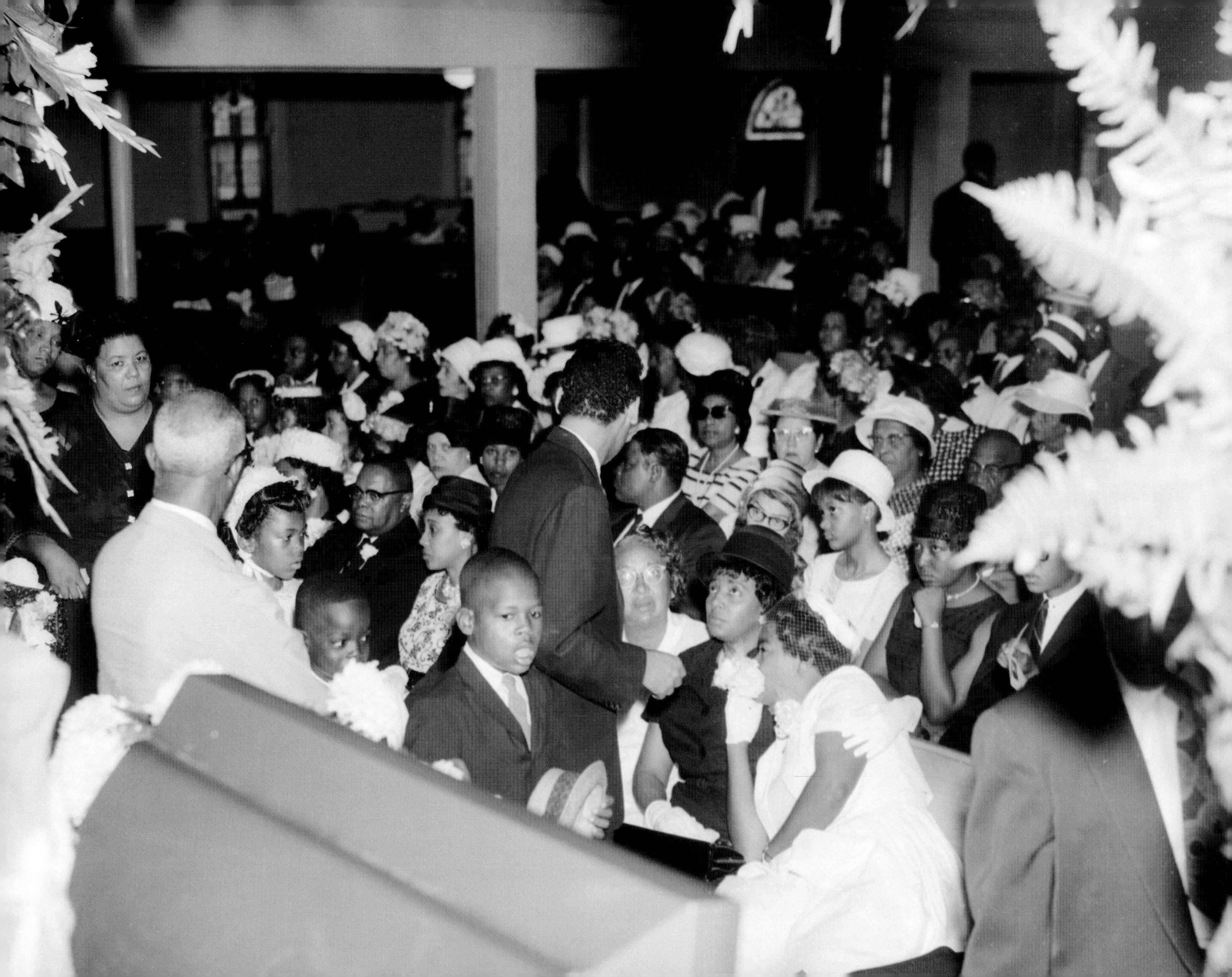

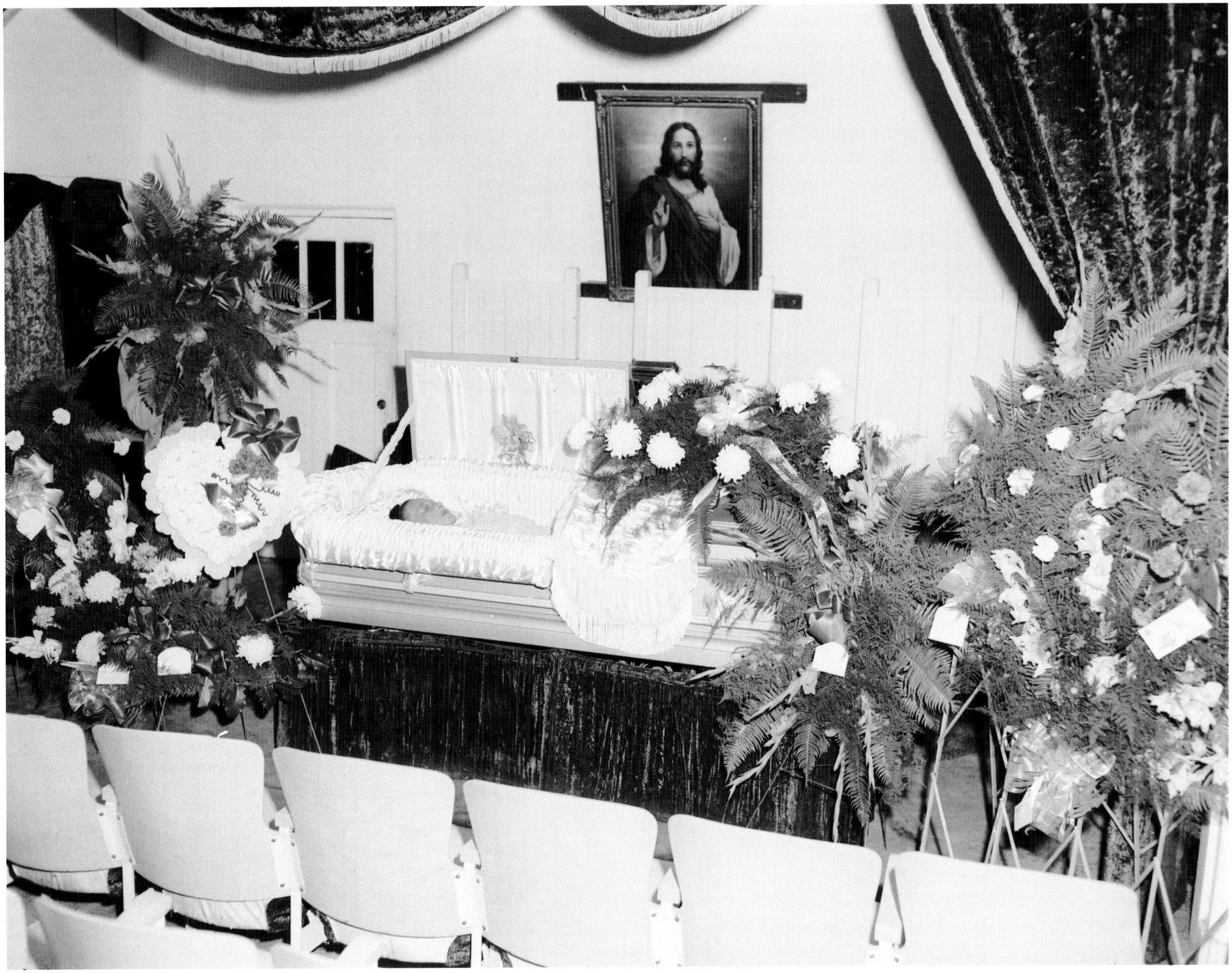

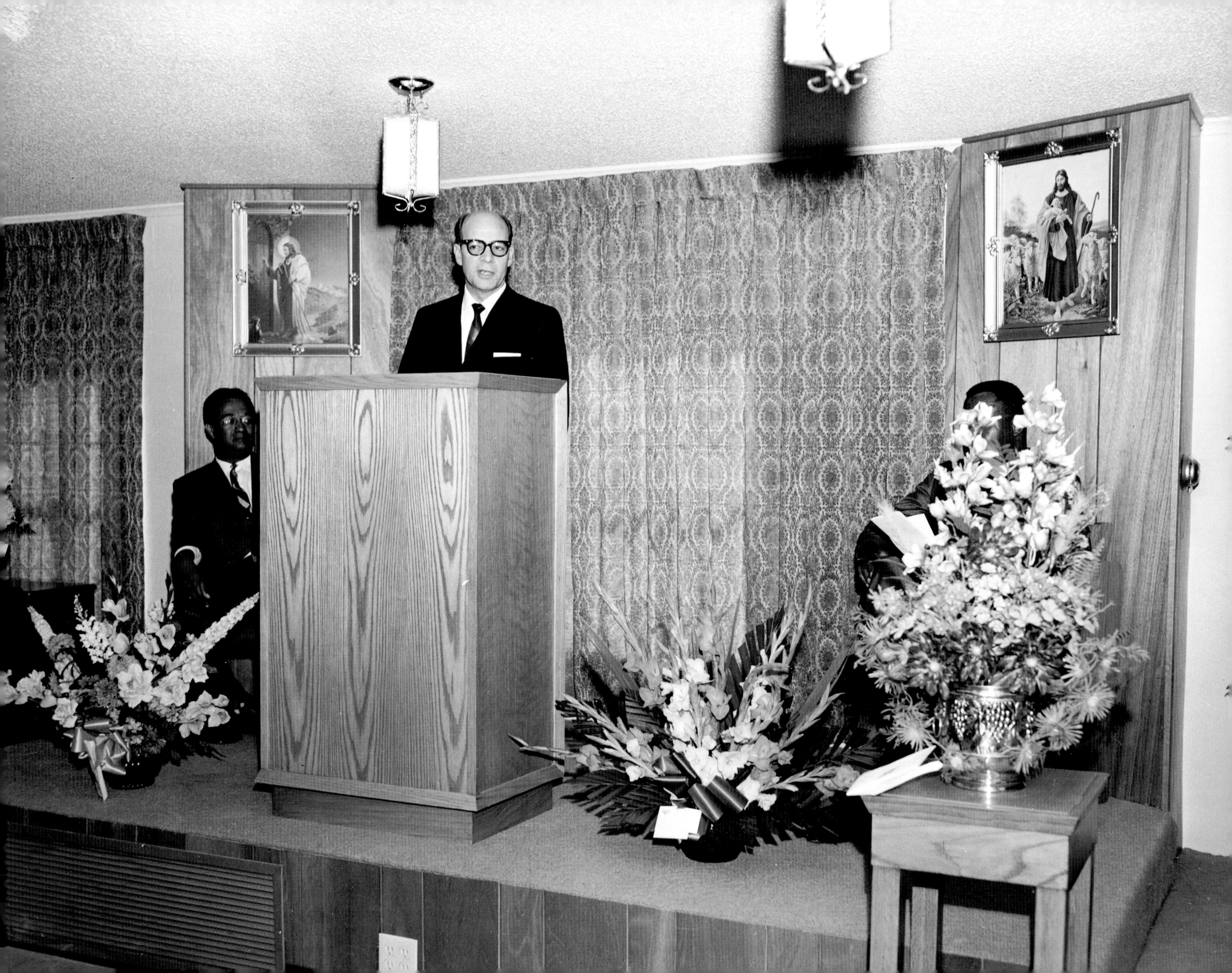

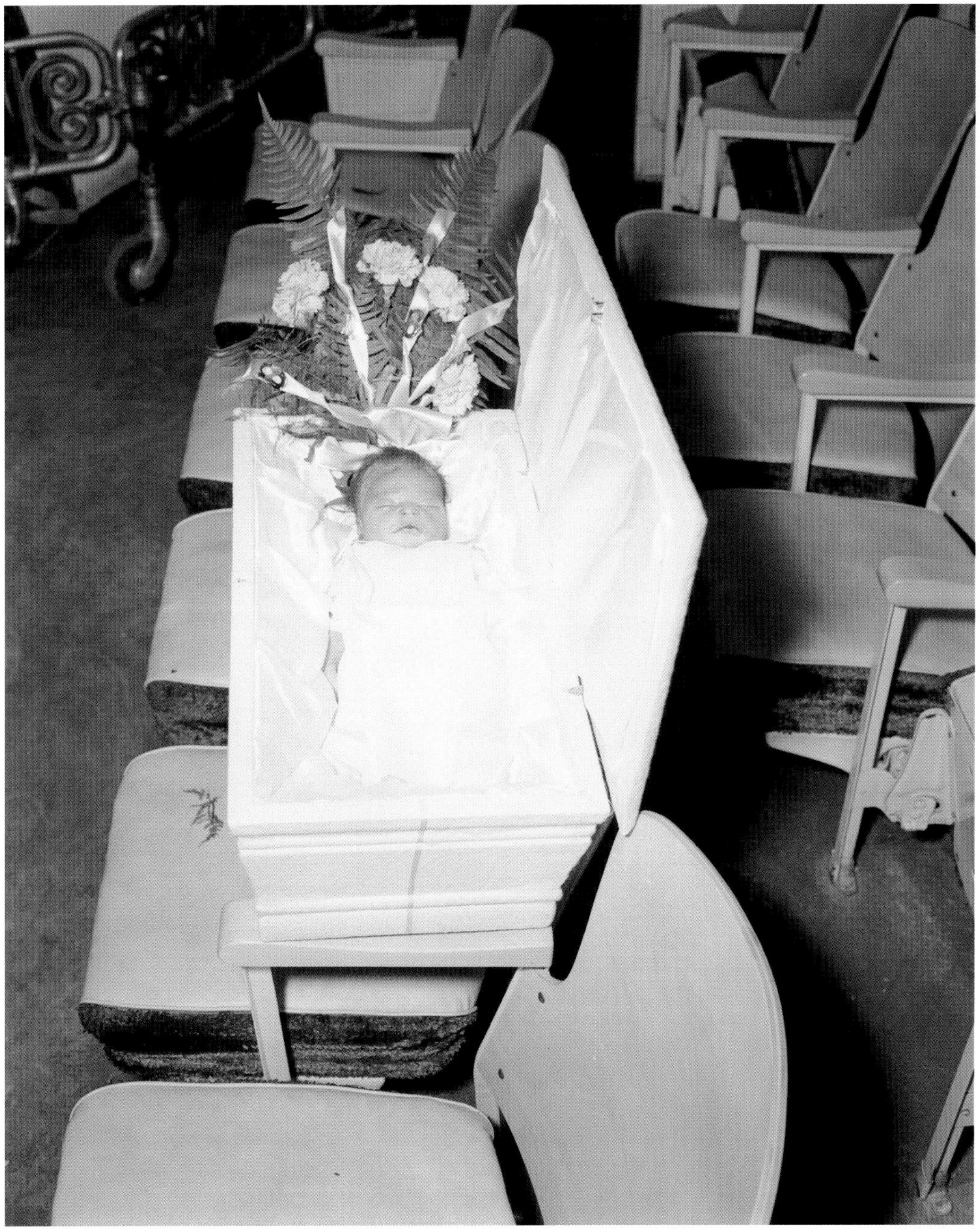

Far Left: Morris-Bates Funeral Home, July 4, 1965.

Left: Gray baby, Baker Funeral Home Chapel, March 1, 1951.

Next Page, Left: Funeral at Morris-Bates Funeral Home, July 4, 1965. Sitting on the front row are, second from left, Herbert V. Baker and third from left, James N. Baker, Sr., owners of Baker Funeral Home.

Next Page, Right: Lila Howard funeral, April 23, 1959.

Following Page, Left: Unidentified funeral scene, not dated.

Following Page, Right: Leroy Ford, an American Woodman, lies in state at Williams Funeral Home in Fort Worth.

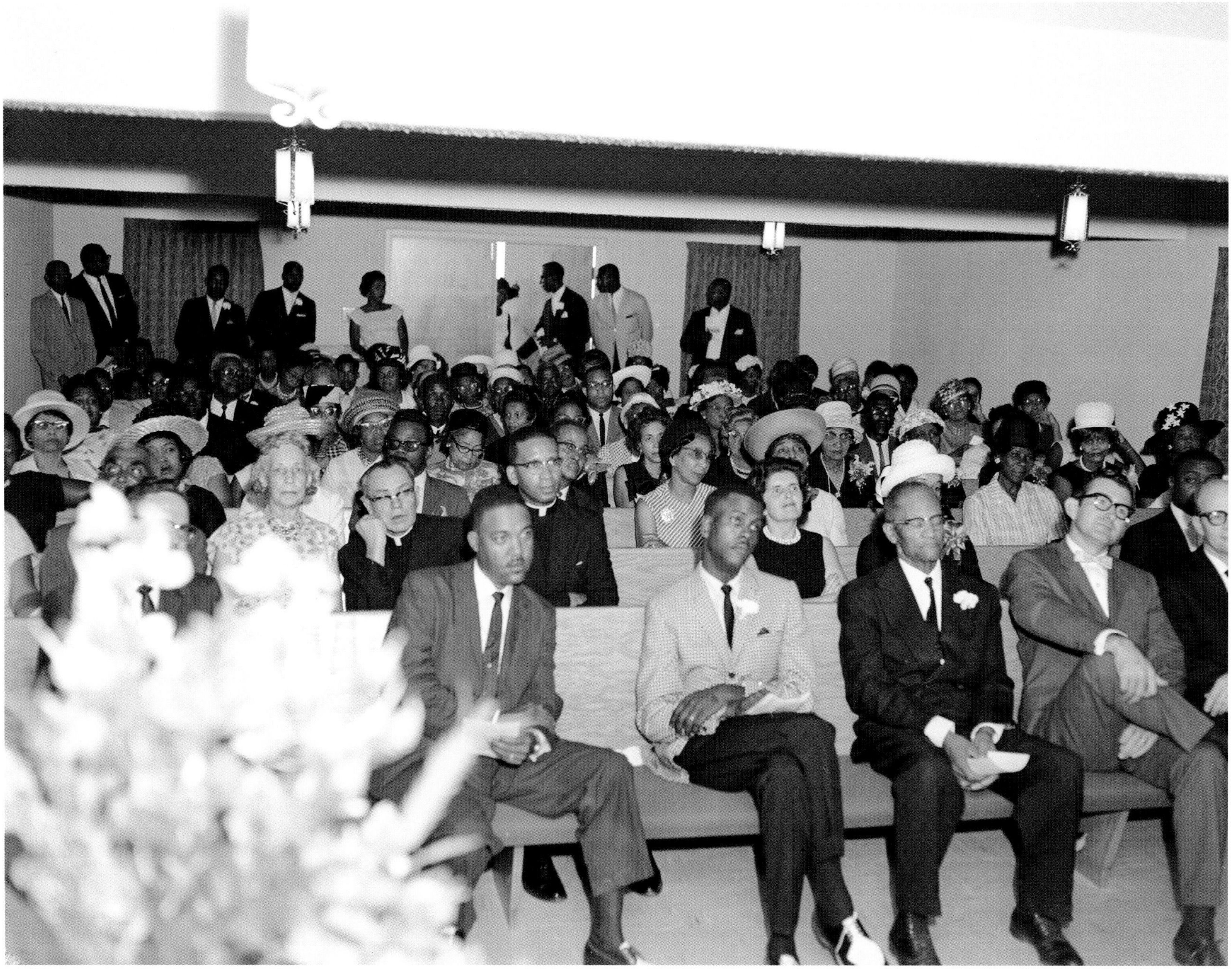

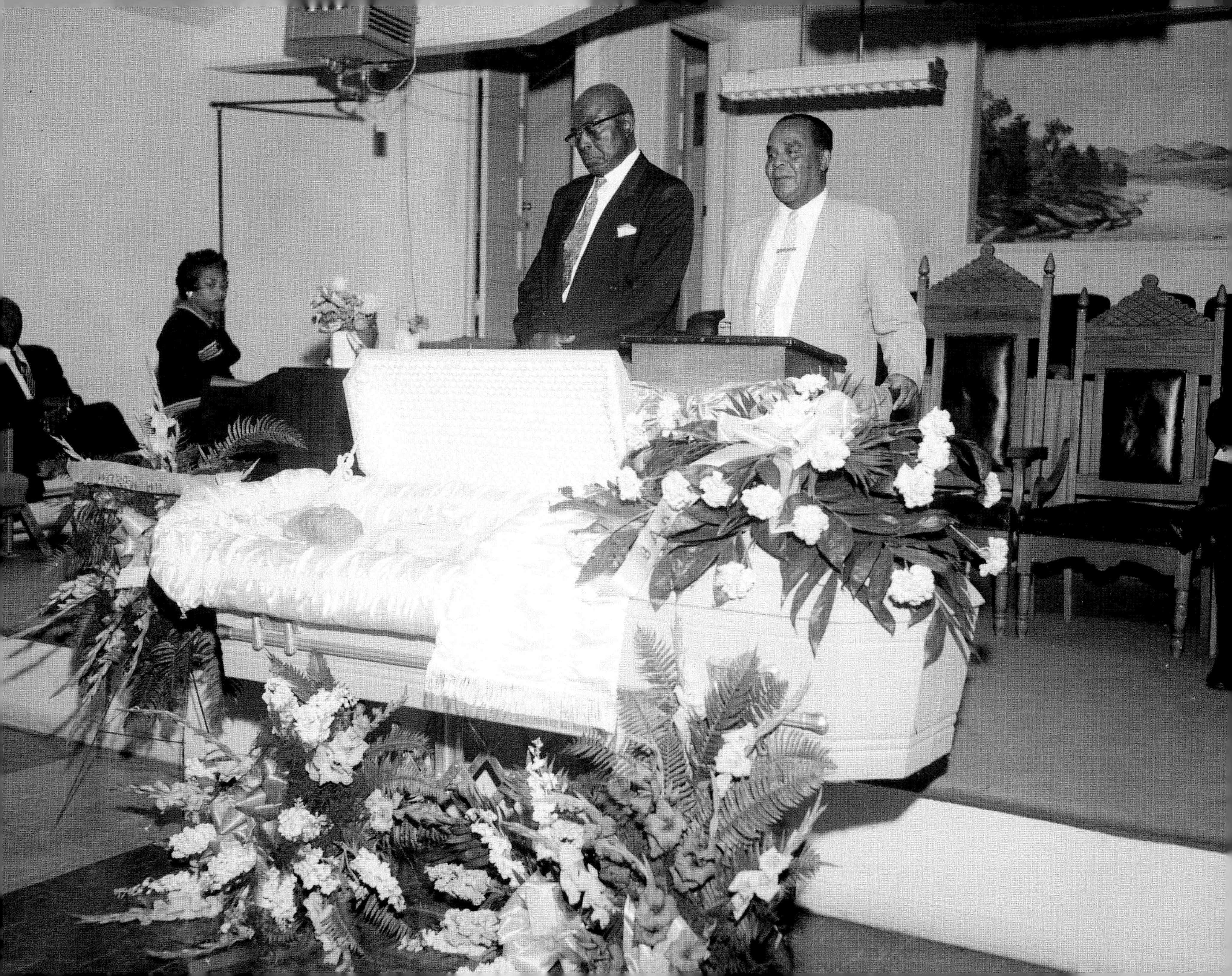

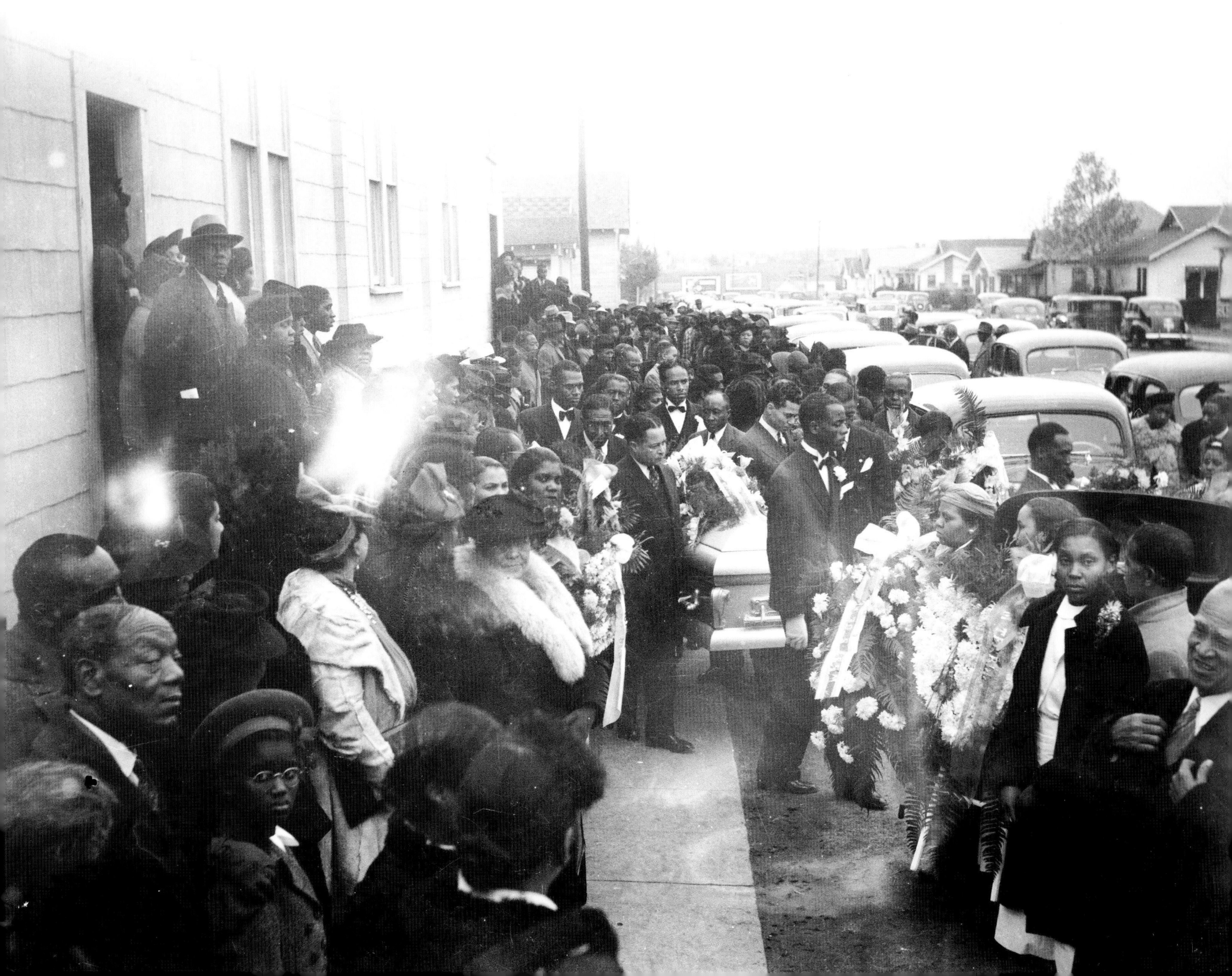

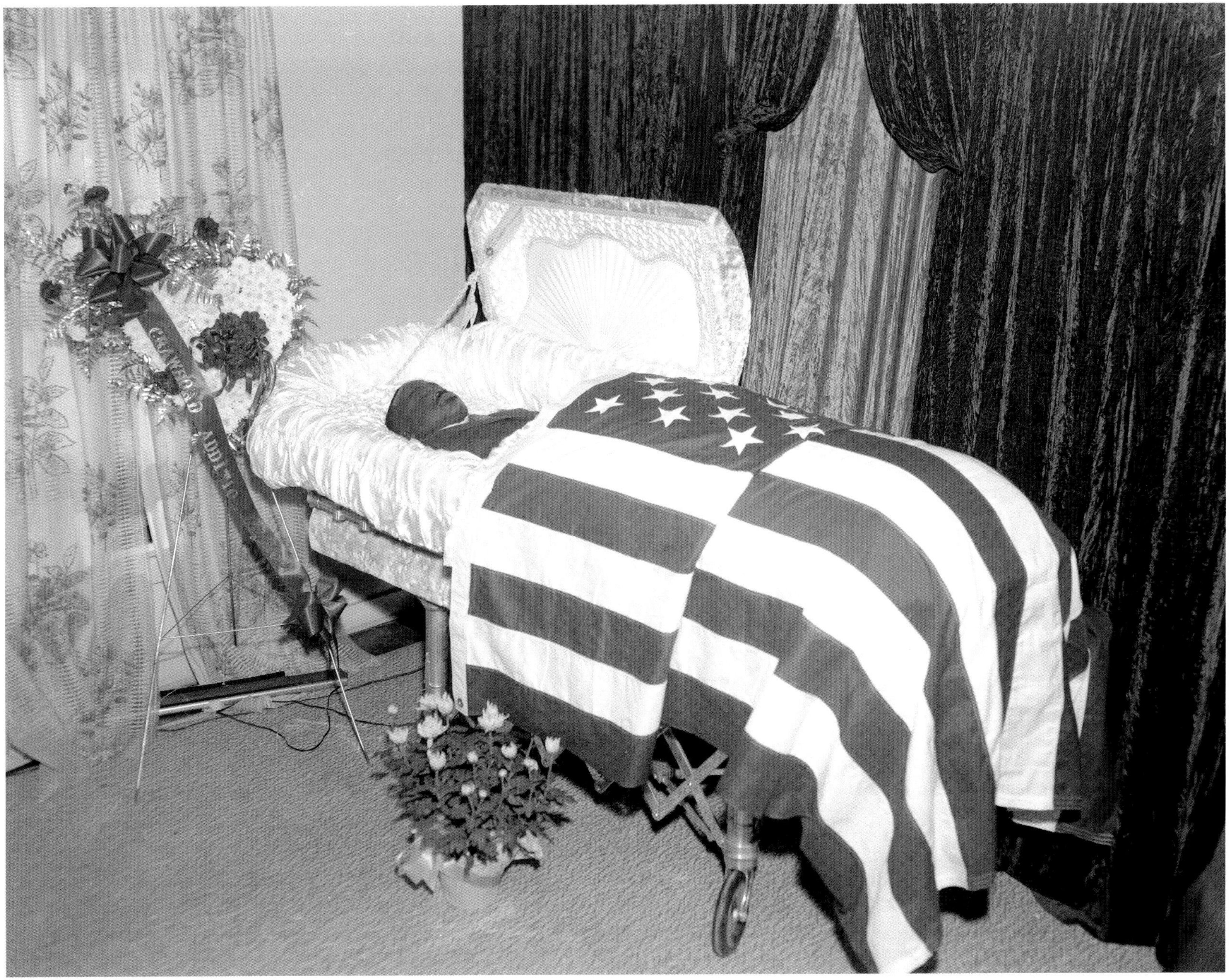

PART 4 CHURCHES

"One of my largest, biggest contracts was in 1941. A preacher came here. He was a very flamboyant preacher, St. James Church, and he wanted to get known to the public and everything. Called me; says 'Come over here, Littlejohn.' Said, 'I want you to be here at morning service, make some pictures for me—of me—at the church. But I want 150 pictures by three o'clock today. Five-by-sevens.' I delivered."

—Calvin Littlejohn

The church in the African American community was the one gathering place where black folk could not/would not be denied. It was a place where all, whether a member or not, felt comfortable because they felt welcomed.

Those sanctuaries scattered throughout black neighborhoods were not just places of worship, each was a refuge, a security zone, a solid rock in a land that sometimes seemed alien for a people who faced constant discrimination.

Beside the home, it was often the first place a child received any form of education, through Sunday schools, training unions, and vacation Bible schools. The church was the site of Saturday night suppers, dinners on the ground, and the natural setting for the feeding of the mind through intellectual discussion often led by prominent scholars.

It was the place people wanted to be married and, of course, even the unrepentant "sinner" expected to have his funeral in the church house.

The black preacher was a natural leader in the community, often being the counselor, the negotiator, and the official spokesperson and liaison to the white leadership.

From the late 1800s, black people in Fort Worth found ways to build magnificent edifices of worship that would become monuments not only to their God but to their own ingenuity, vision, and sacrifice.

They remained proud of those structures that commanded a certain reverence, requiring those who attended services to come attired in their very best. Some preachers had a saying, "If you can dress up for the devil on Saturday night, you can dress up for Jesus on Sunday morning."

For special occasions—building dedications, musicals, weddings and even funerals—the people often wanted a photographic record, and Calvin Littlejohn was there.

Right: Congregation entering Paradise Baptist Church on opening of new sanctuary.

Far Right: Ribbon-cutting ceremony, Paradise Baptist Church. The church's pastor, the Reverend J. F. Singleton, is the man at right.

Next Page, Left: Congregation gathering outside Paradise Baptist Church for the dedication.

Next Page, Right: C. B. Spence standing by car at Mt. Rose Baptist Church, August 16, 1944.

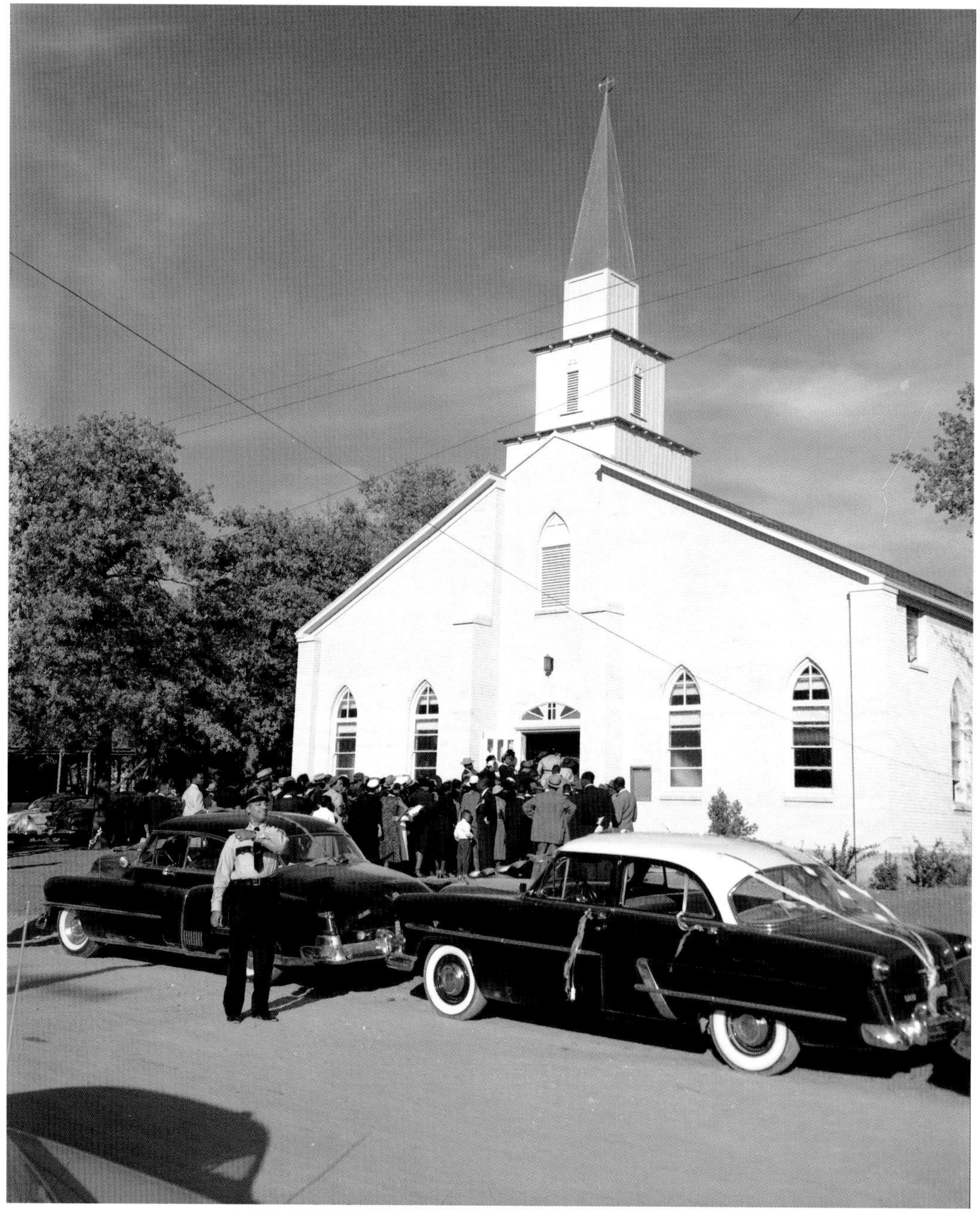

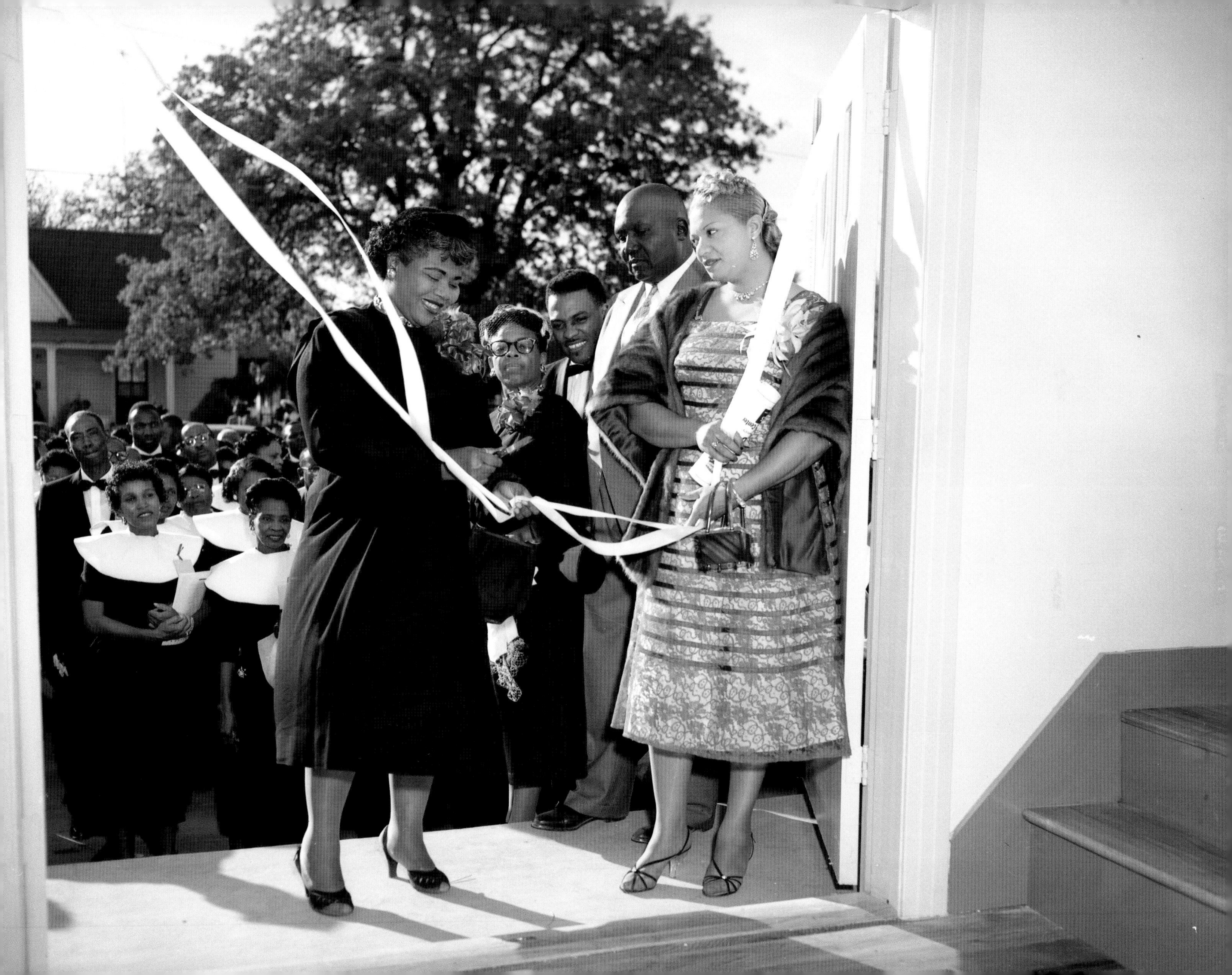

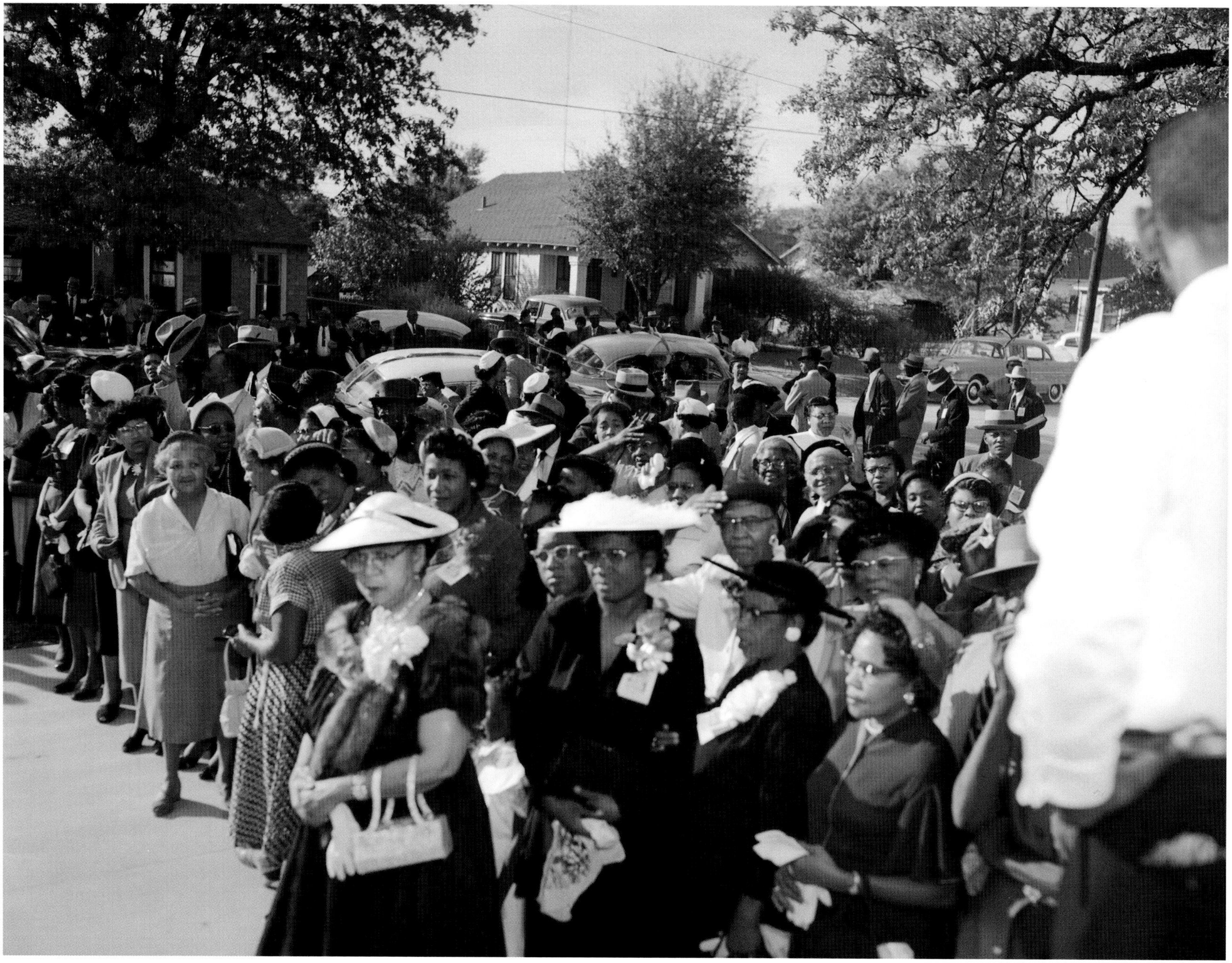

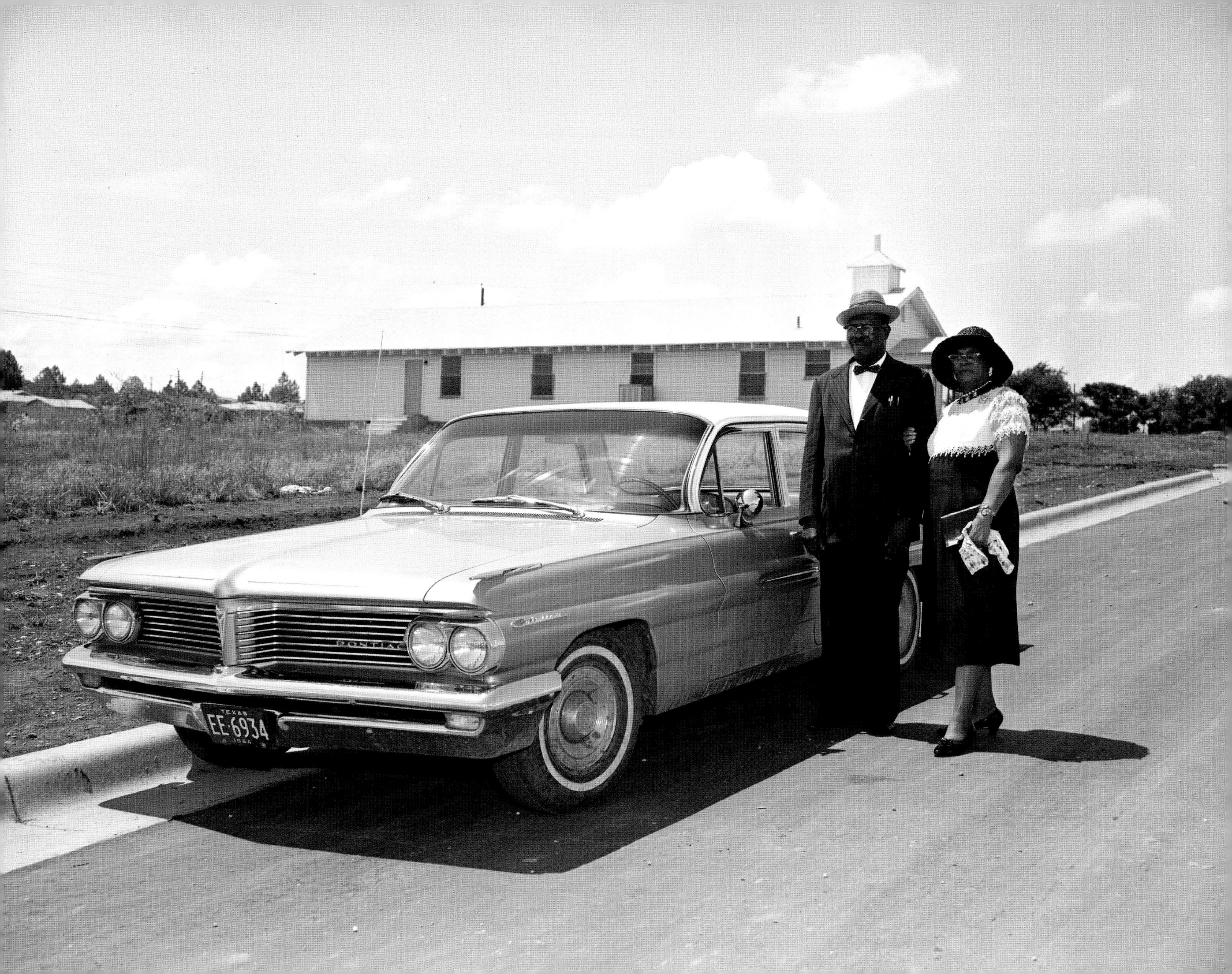
PONTIAC
TEXAS
EE-6934
1964

Right: Mt. Zion Baptist Church delegation to the National Baptist Convention, September 14, 1958.

Far Right: Procession for the opening of the eighteenth National Sunday School and Young People's Union Congress, Fort Worth, June 22, 1950.

Next Page, Left: St. Mark Missionary Baptist Church, located in the Stop Six neighborhood, 1952.

Next Page, Right: Opening of church convention, truck with a sign reading, "We thank God for our President, Bishop A. B. Williams, who has led us for 18 yrs," Fort Worth, June 22, 1950.

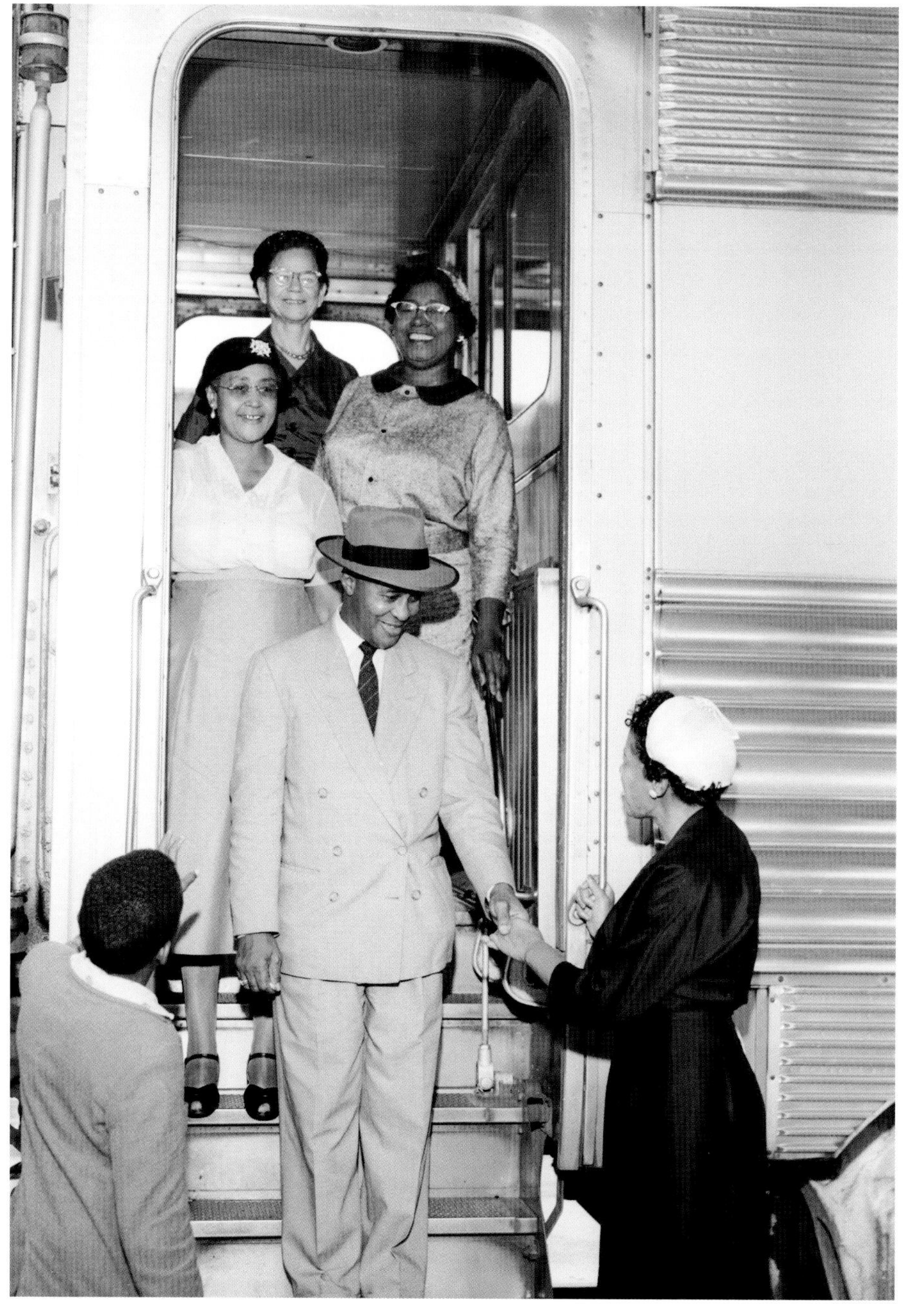

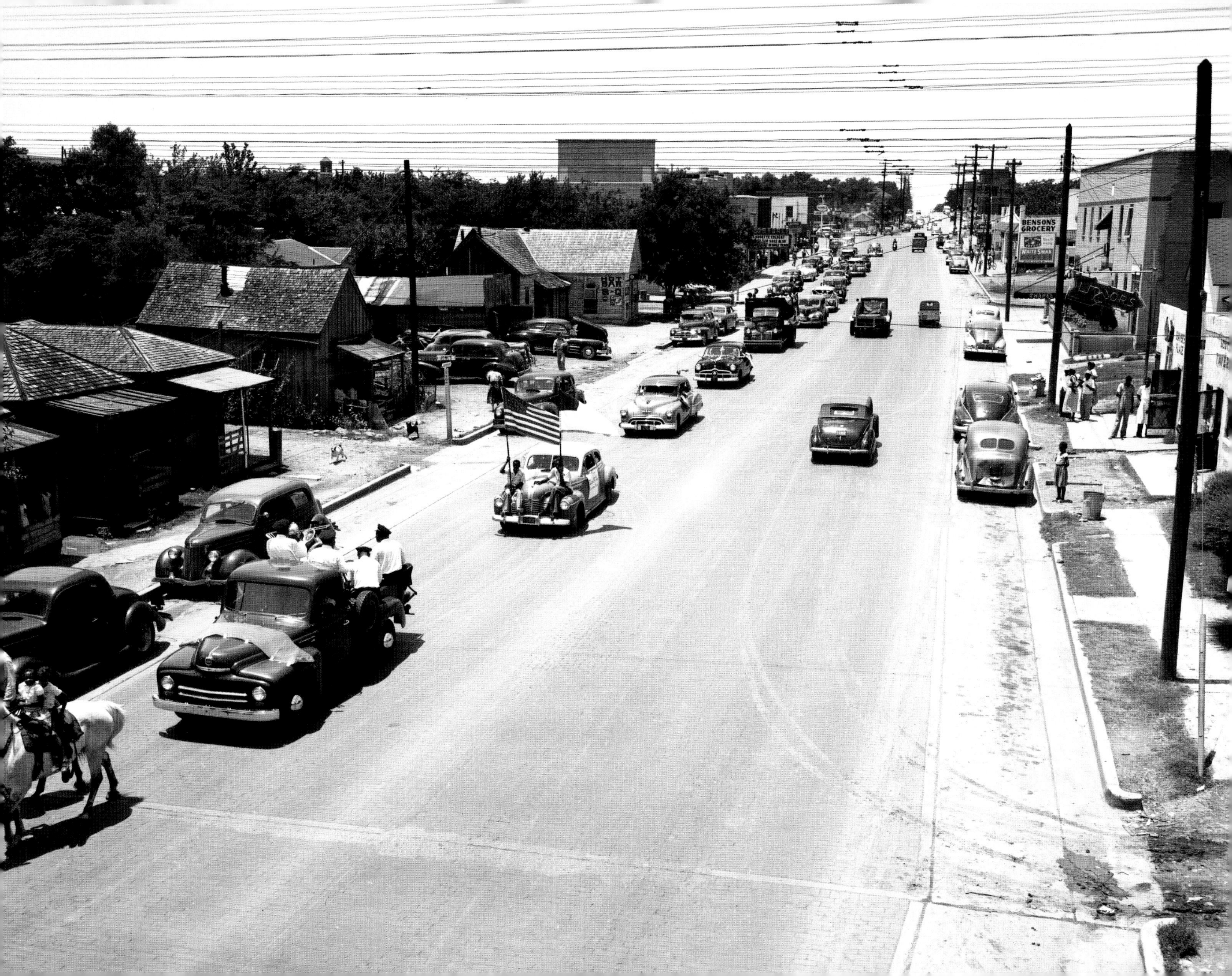
HOT
BAR
B-Q
BENSON'S
GROCERY
WHITE SWAN

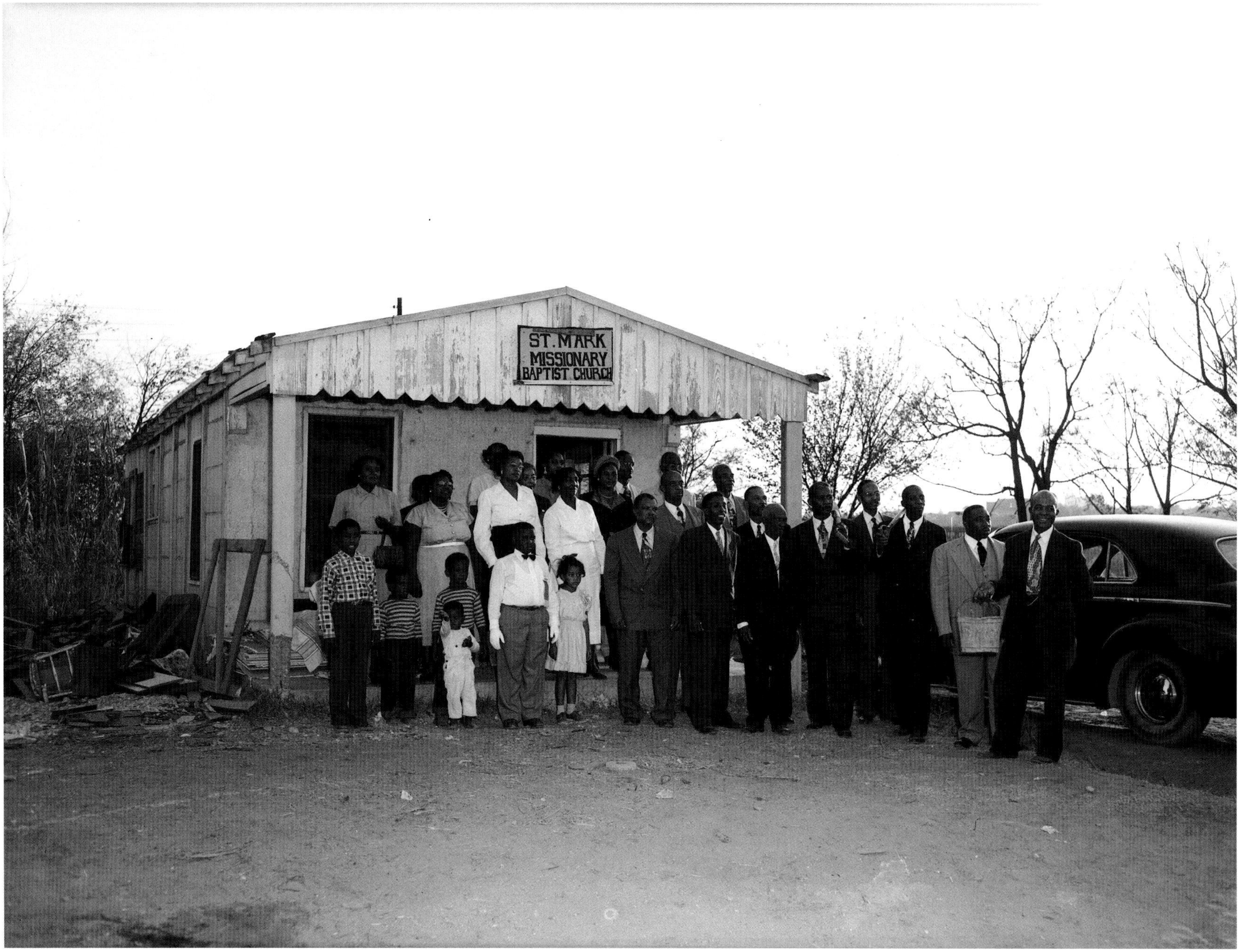
ST. MARK
MISSIONARY
BAPTIST CHURCH

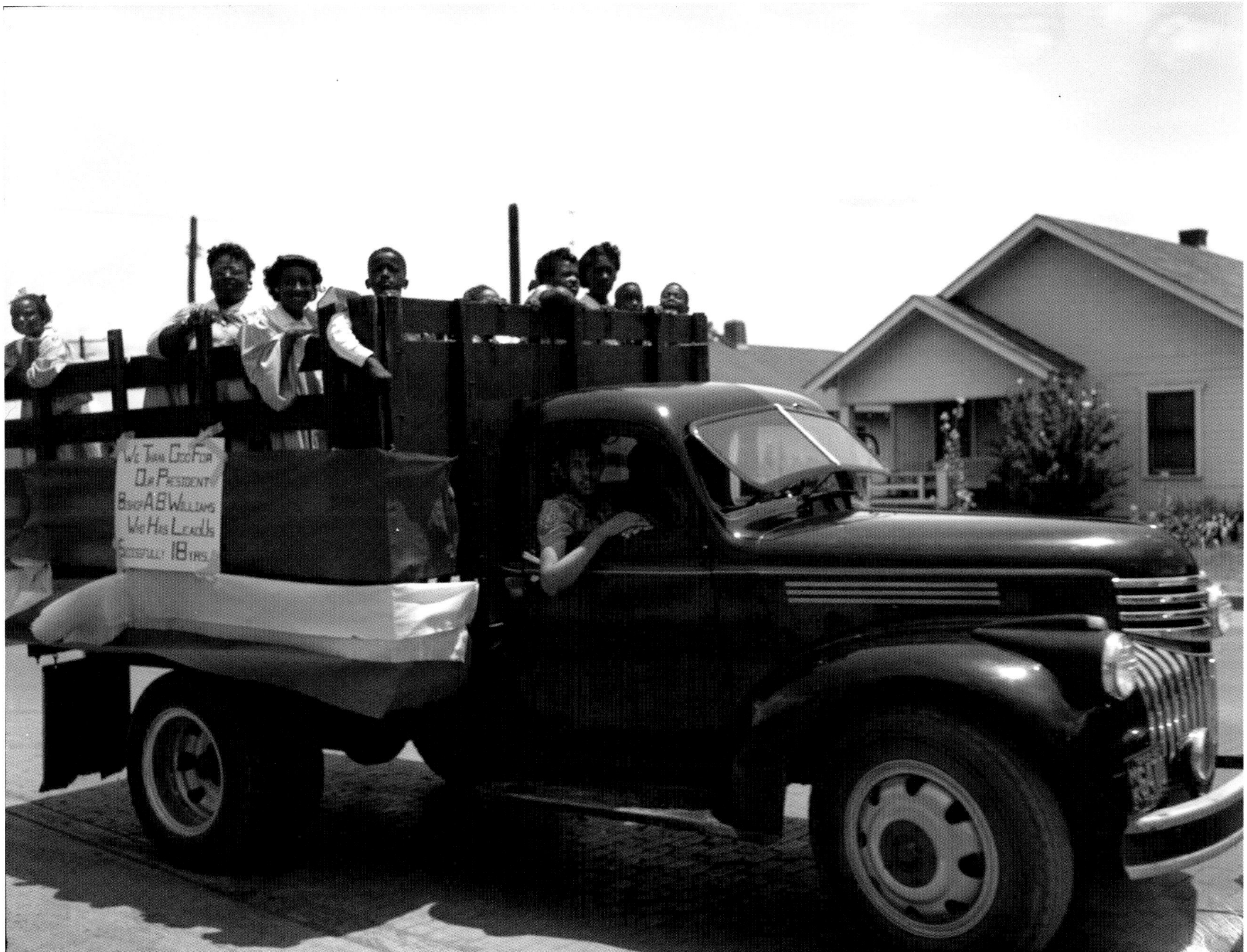
We Thank God For
Our President
Bishop A.B. Williams
Who Has Lead Us
18 yrs.

Right: Morning Chapel CME Church, Easter picture.

Far Right: Christmas tree and Santa Claus at church, 1952.

Next Page, Left: Congregation posing in front of the Immanuel Independent AME Church.

Next Page, Right: Christmas tree at church, 1952.

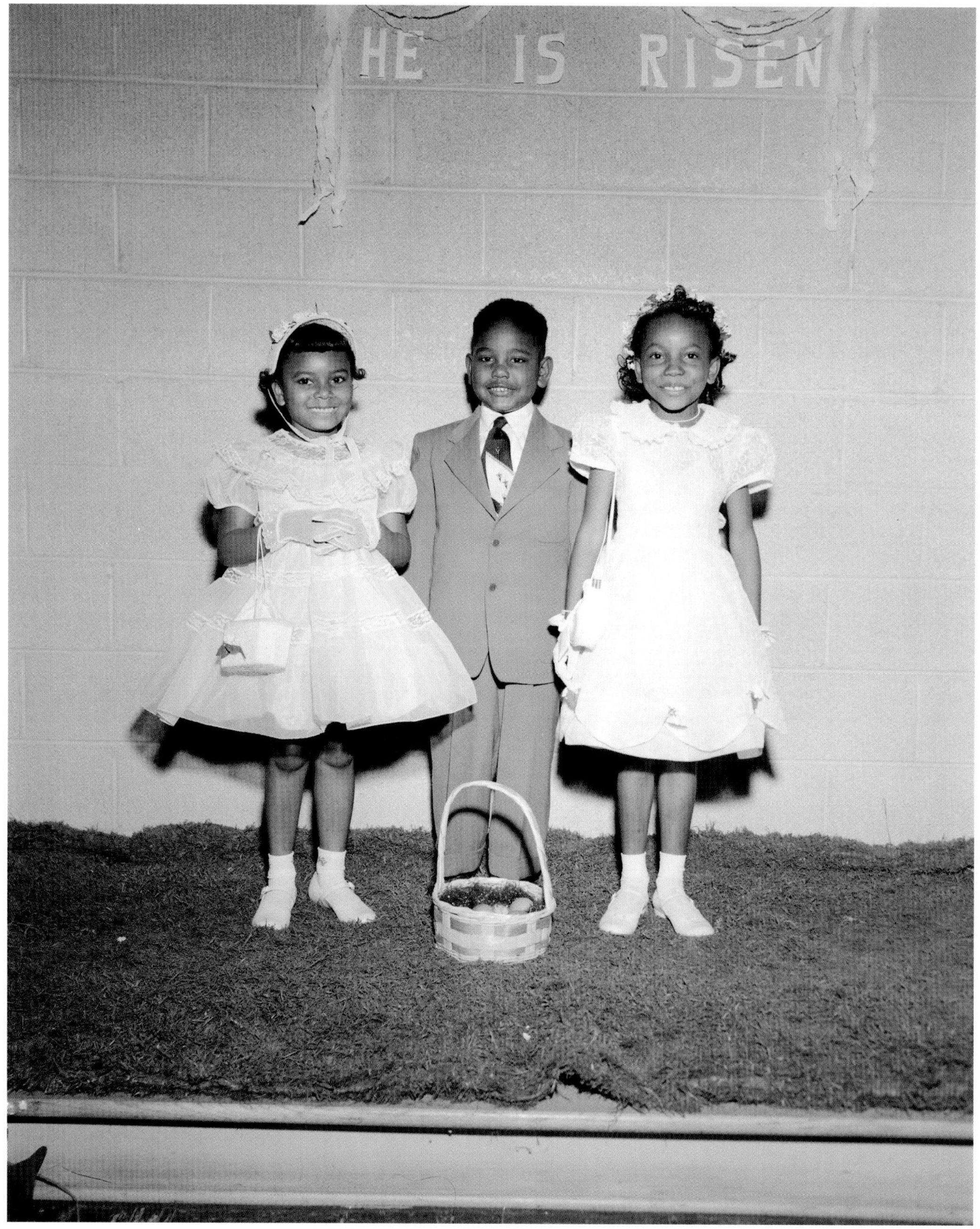

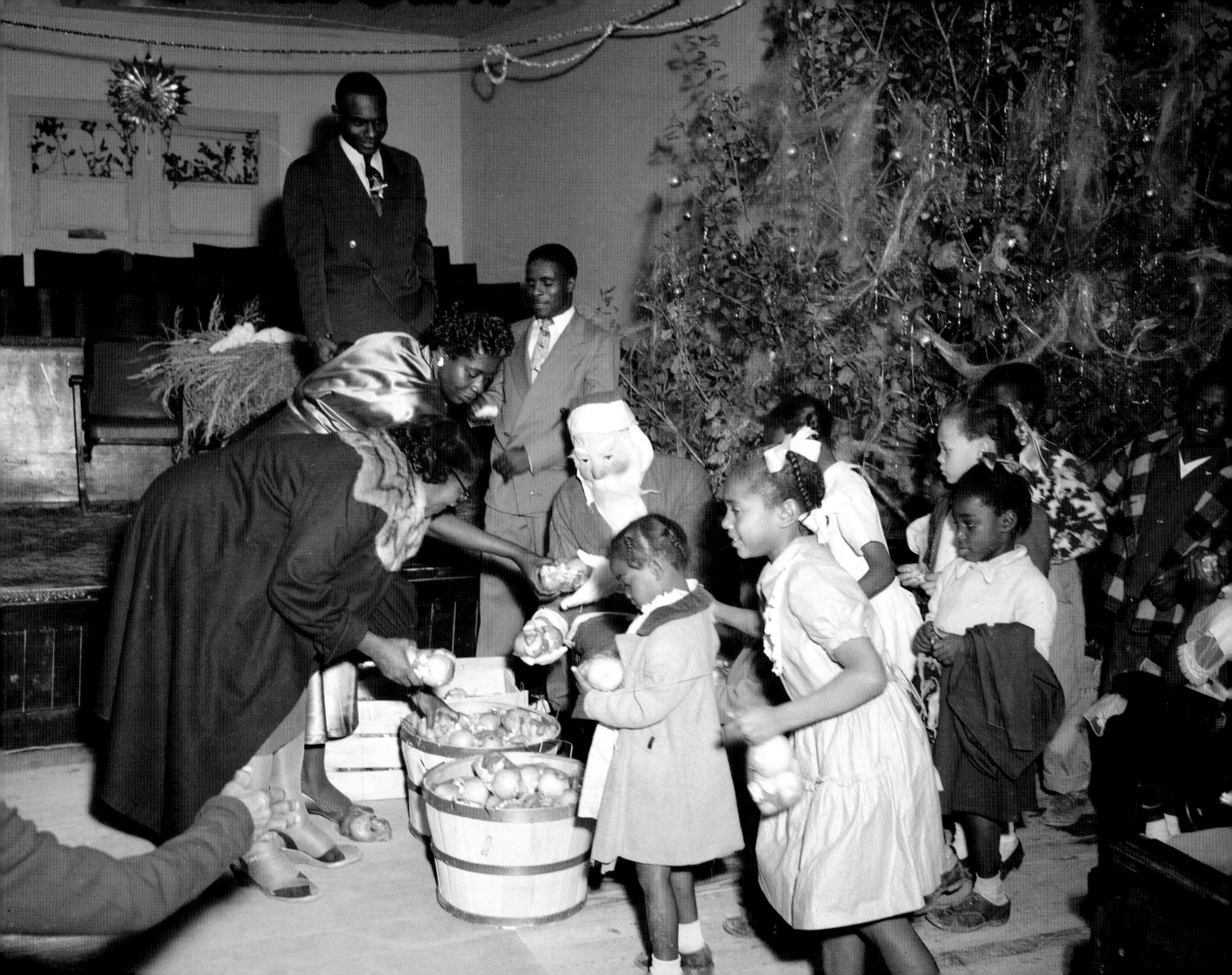

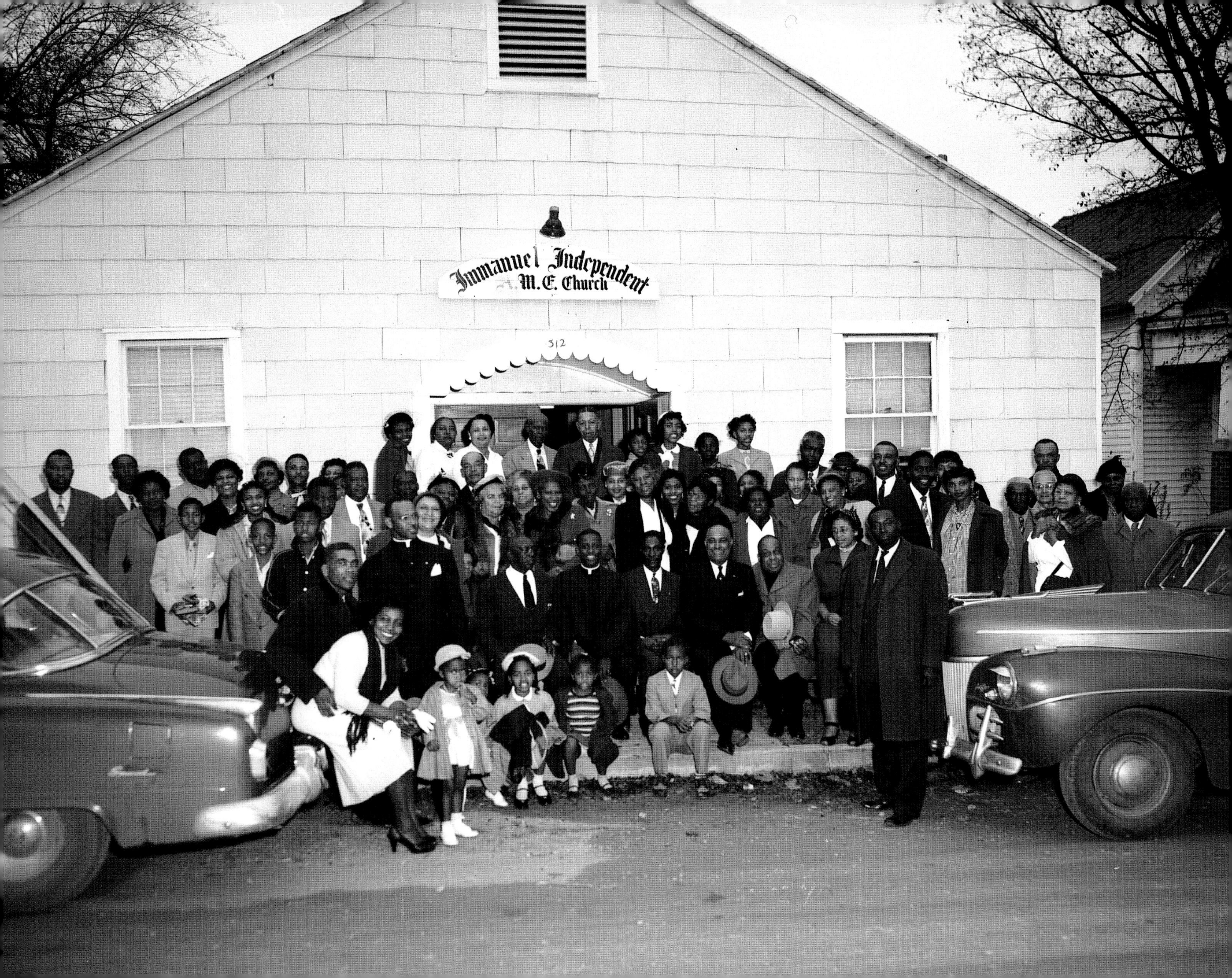
Immanuel Independent
A. M. E. Church
312

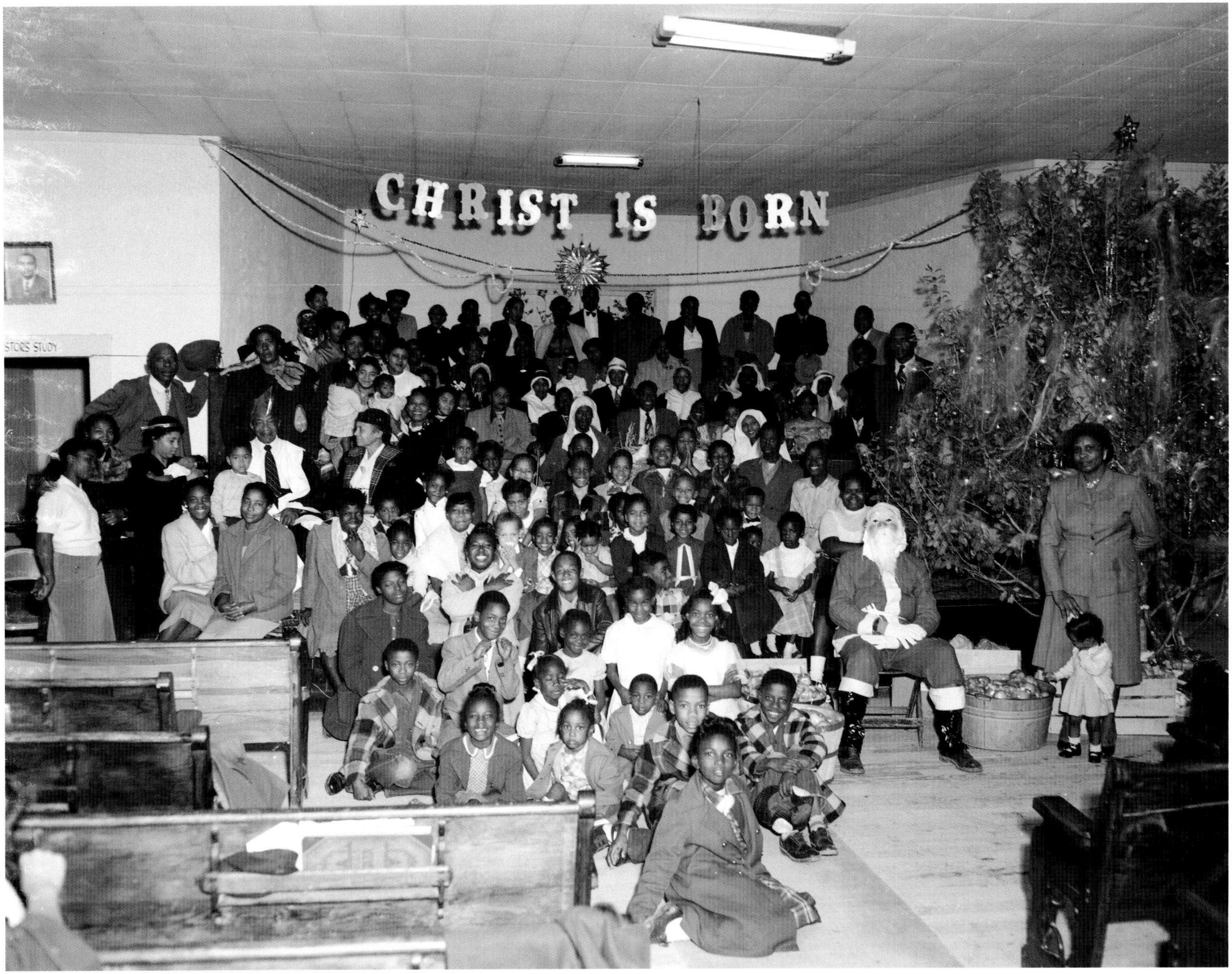
CHRIST IS BORN

Right: Mrs. Moch, Allen Chapel Church Queen, February 20, 1951.

Far Right: The Reverend H. R. Bradley, new pastor of Mount Pisgah Baptist Church, 1952.

Next Page, Left: Morningside Methodist Church, cornerstone laying, February 16, 1964.

Next Page, Right: In the center of this photo of the cornerstone laying for Morningside Methodist Church is Rev. Marshall Hodge, the church's first minister, who later became a leading civil rights advocate in Dallas. At right is Dr. Marion "Jack" Brooks, a leading Fort Worth physician and civil rights leader who was a founding member of the church.

Following Page, Left: Annie Street Christian Church, children and caretakers in the nursery, 1952. Annie Street Christian later became Community Christian Church, which is now located at the corner of Riverside and Vickery.

Following Page, Right: Children napping in the nursery at Annie Street Christian Church, 1952.

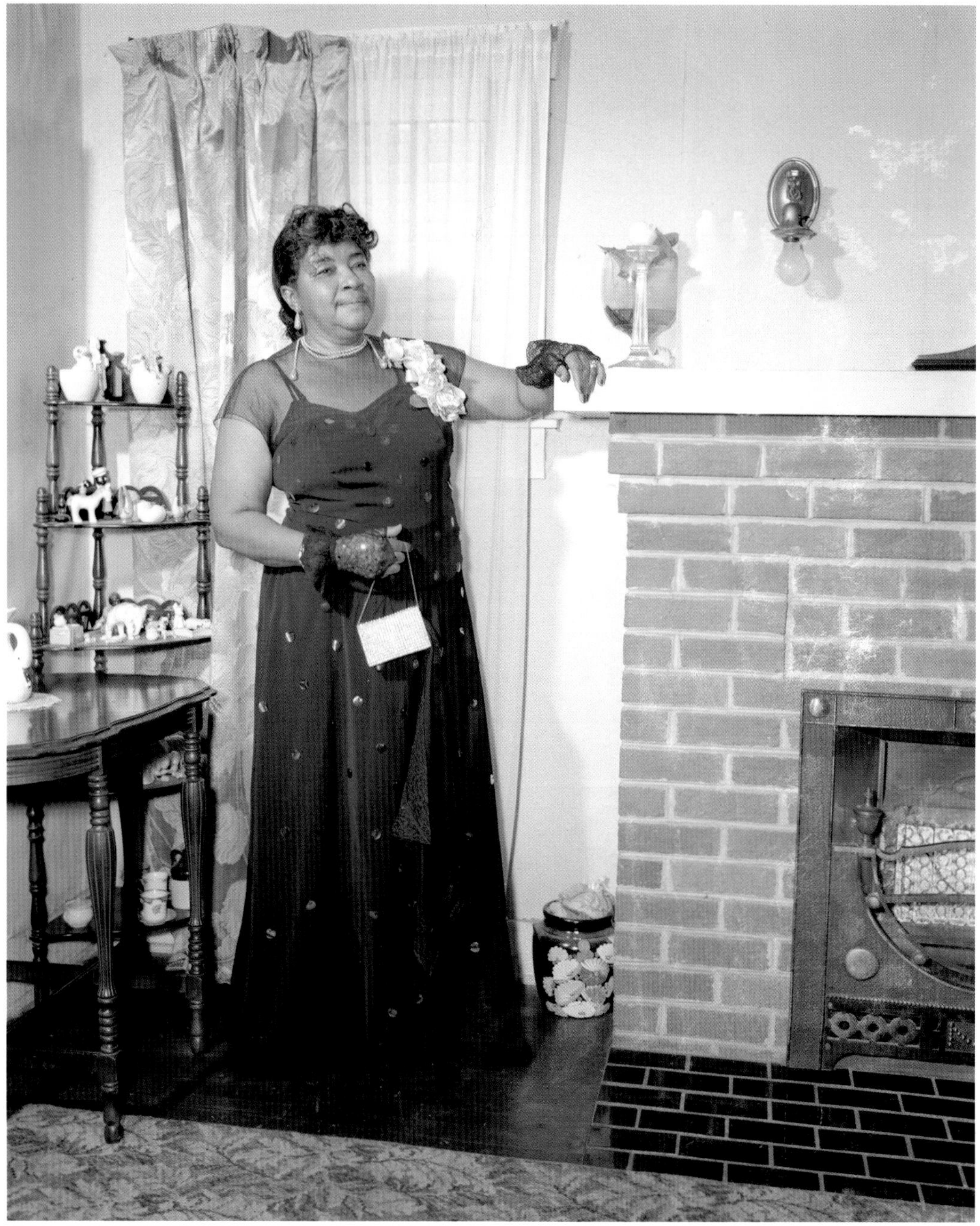

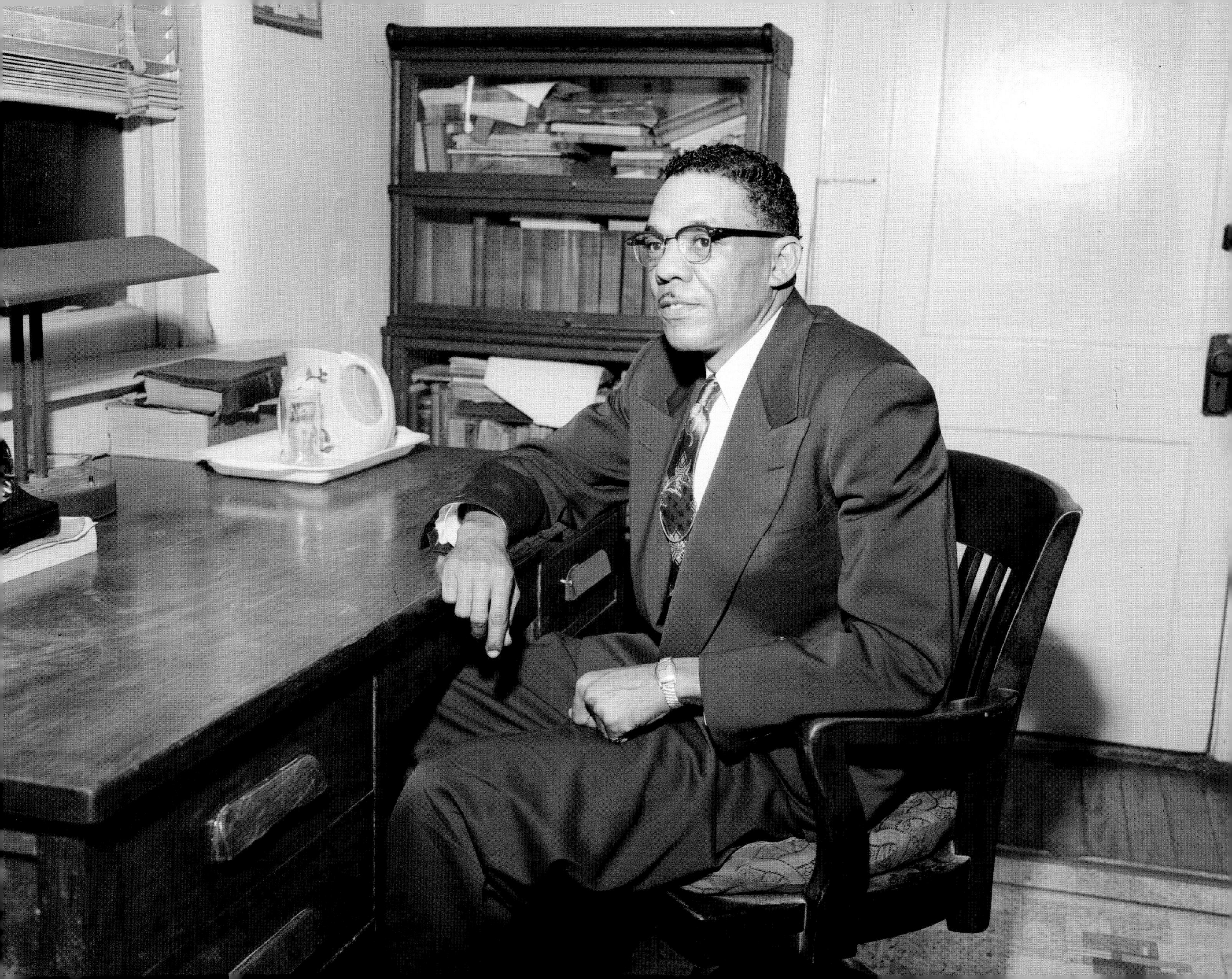

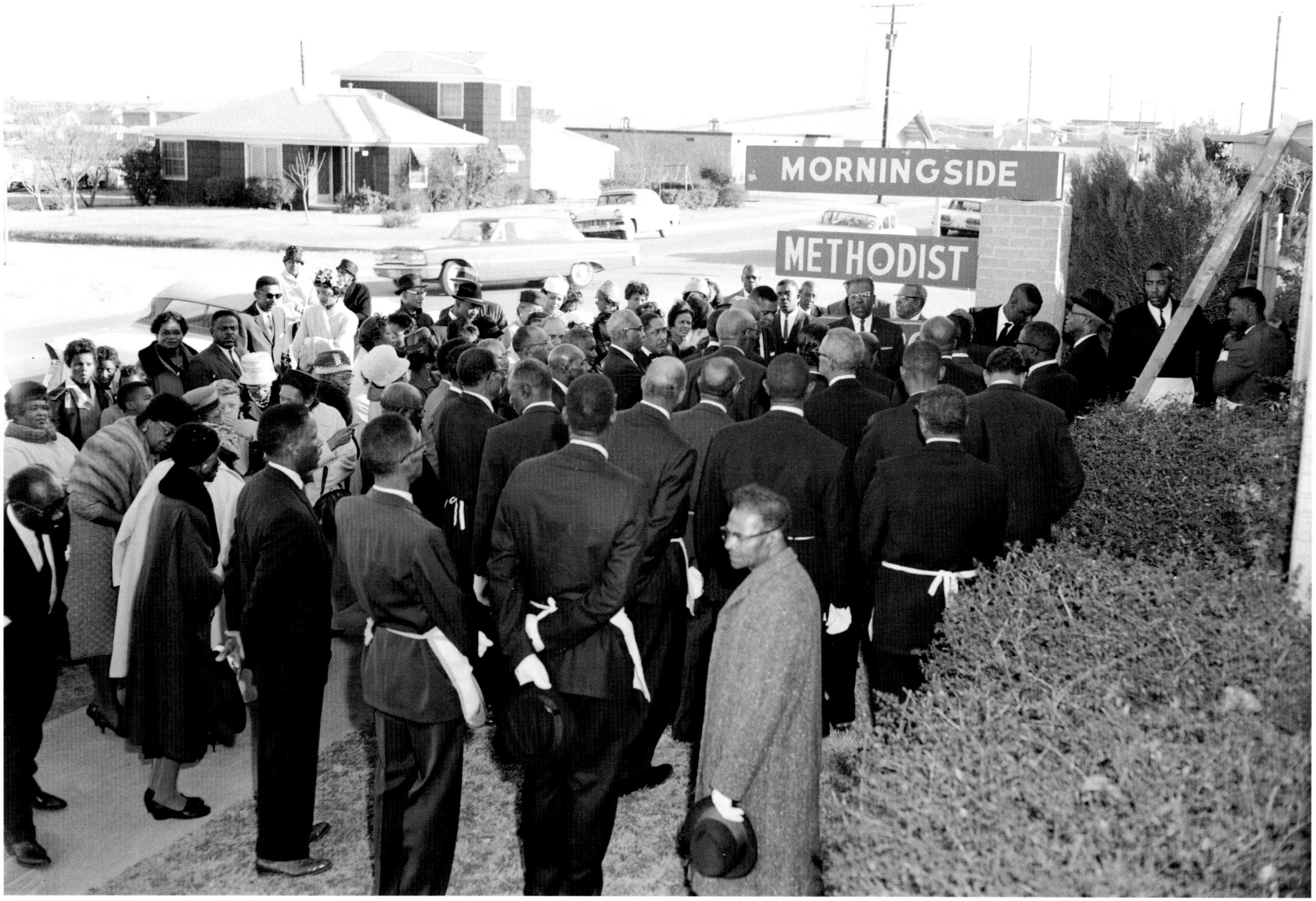
MORNINGSIDE
METHODIST

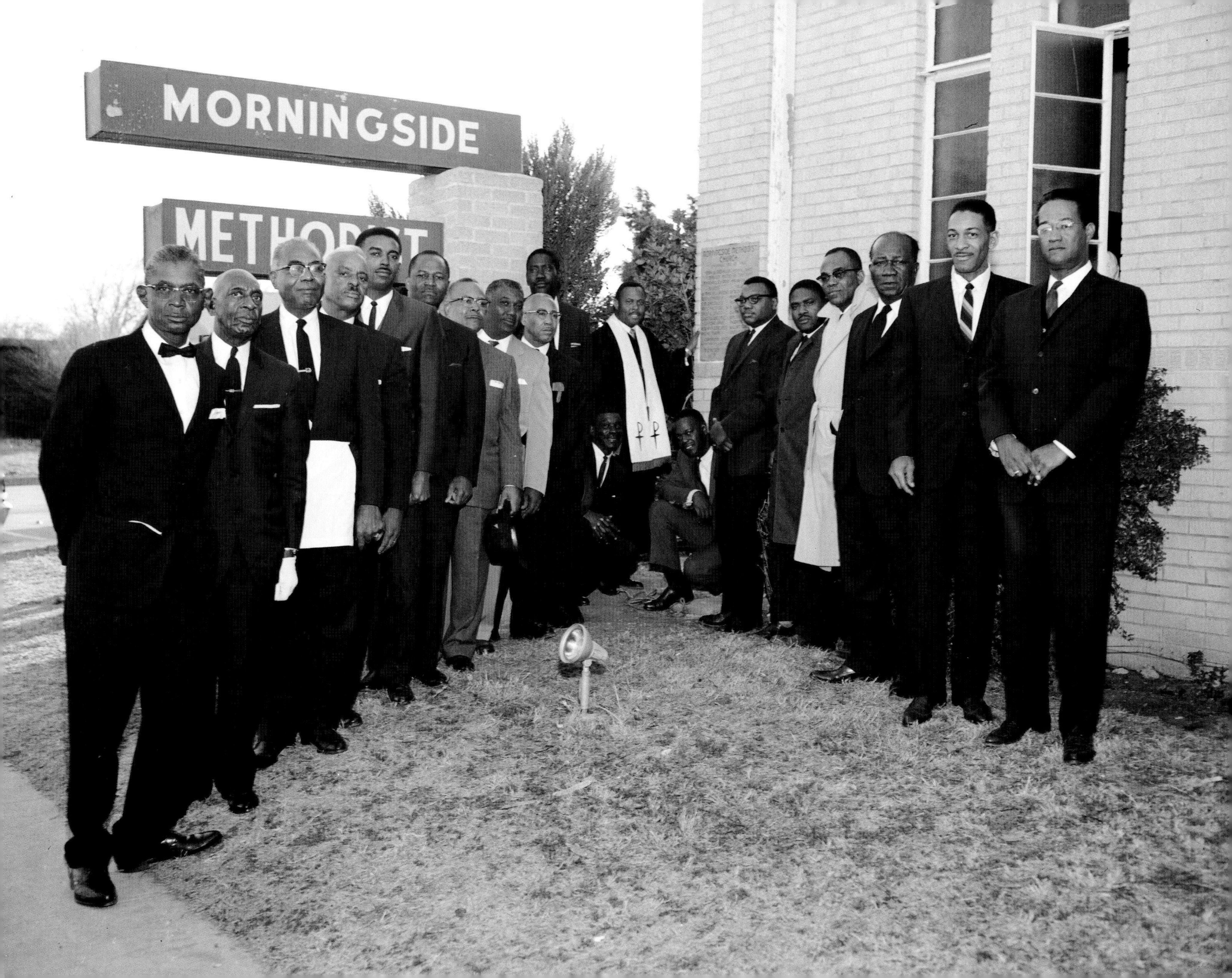
MORNINGSIDE
METHODIST

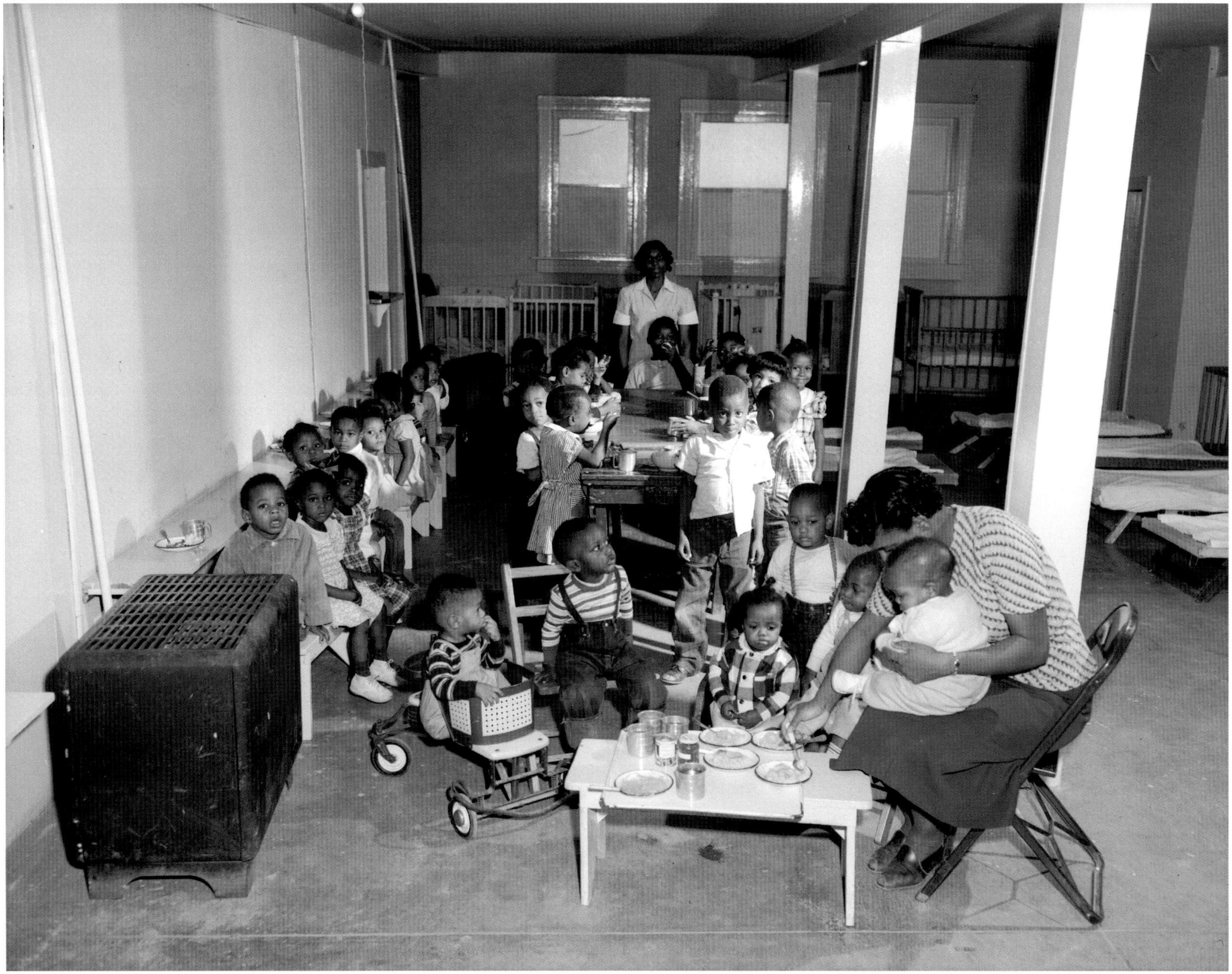

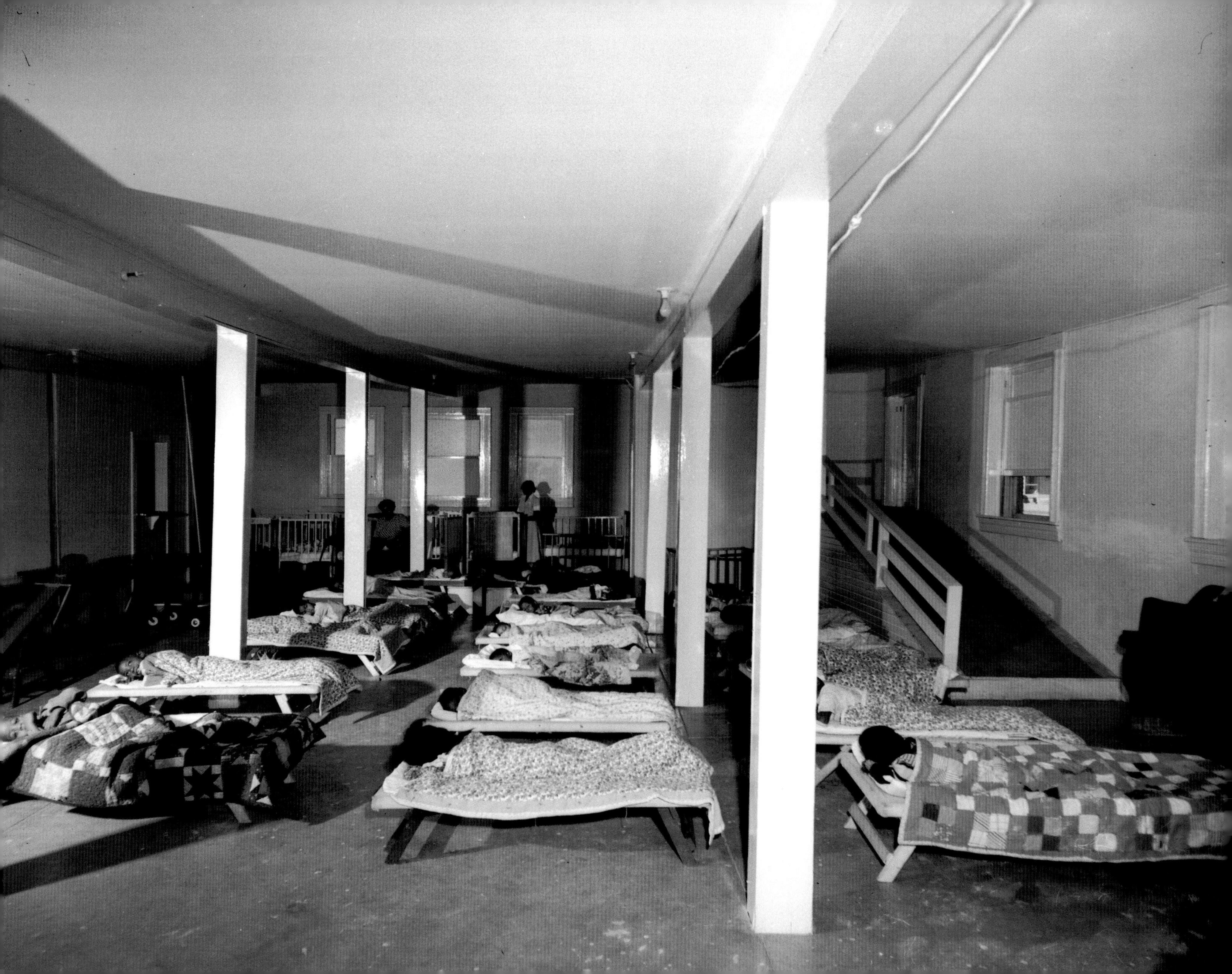

Right: Morningside Methodist Church, sign, March 1964.

Far Right: The Ferguson Bible Class. Mrs. Ferguson is seated on the right.

Next Page, Left: Mount Pisgah Baptist Church Building, September 1969.

Next Page, Right: Mount Pisgah Baptist Church Sunday School, August 6, 1948.

Following Page, Left: Ayers Church, 1964.

Following Page, Right: New edifice, St. Andrew's United Methodist Church, 1951.

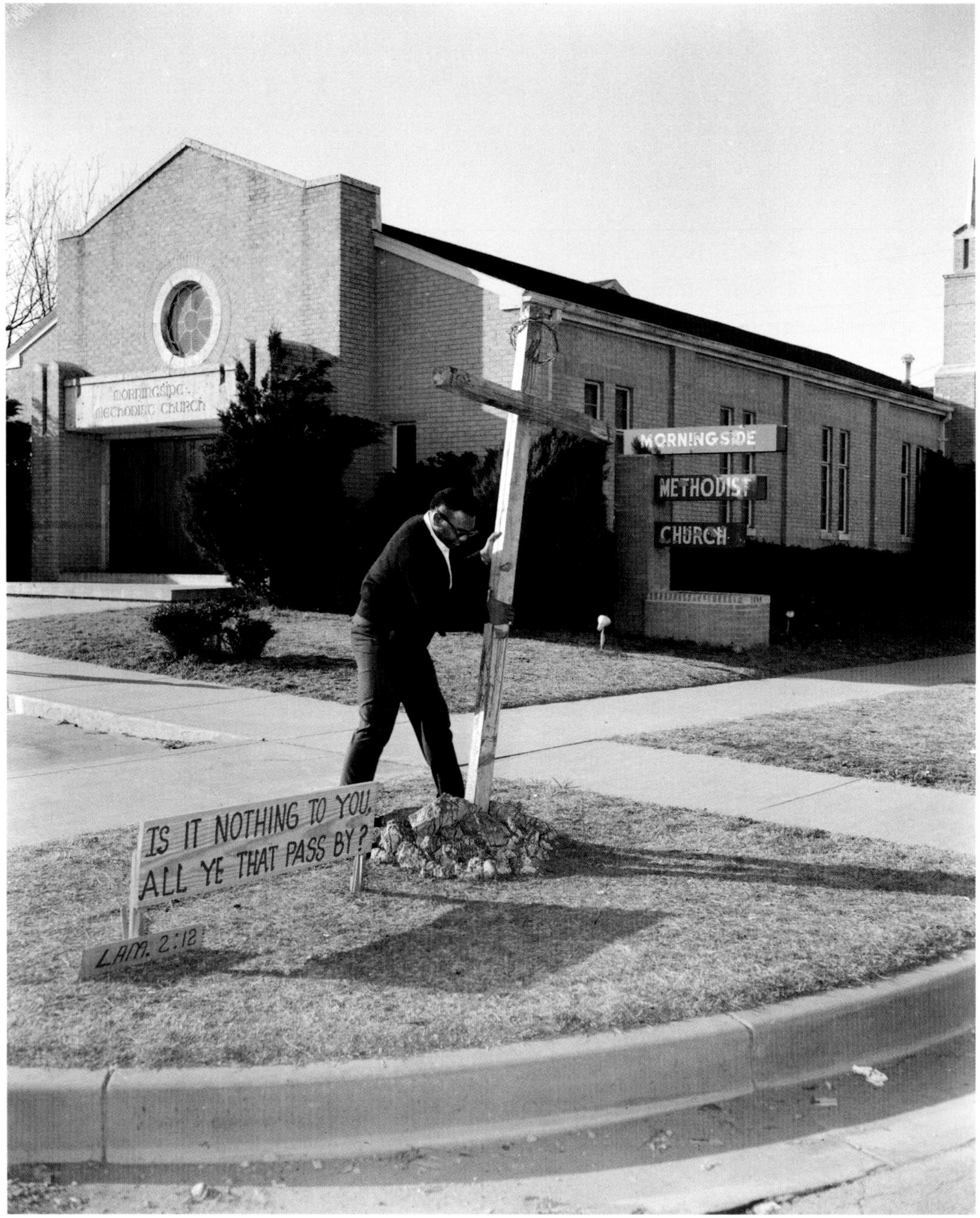

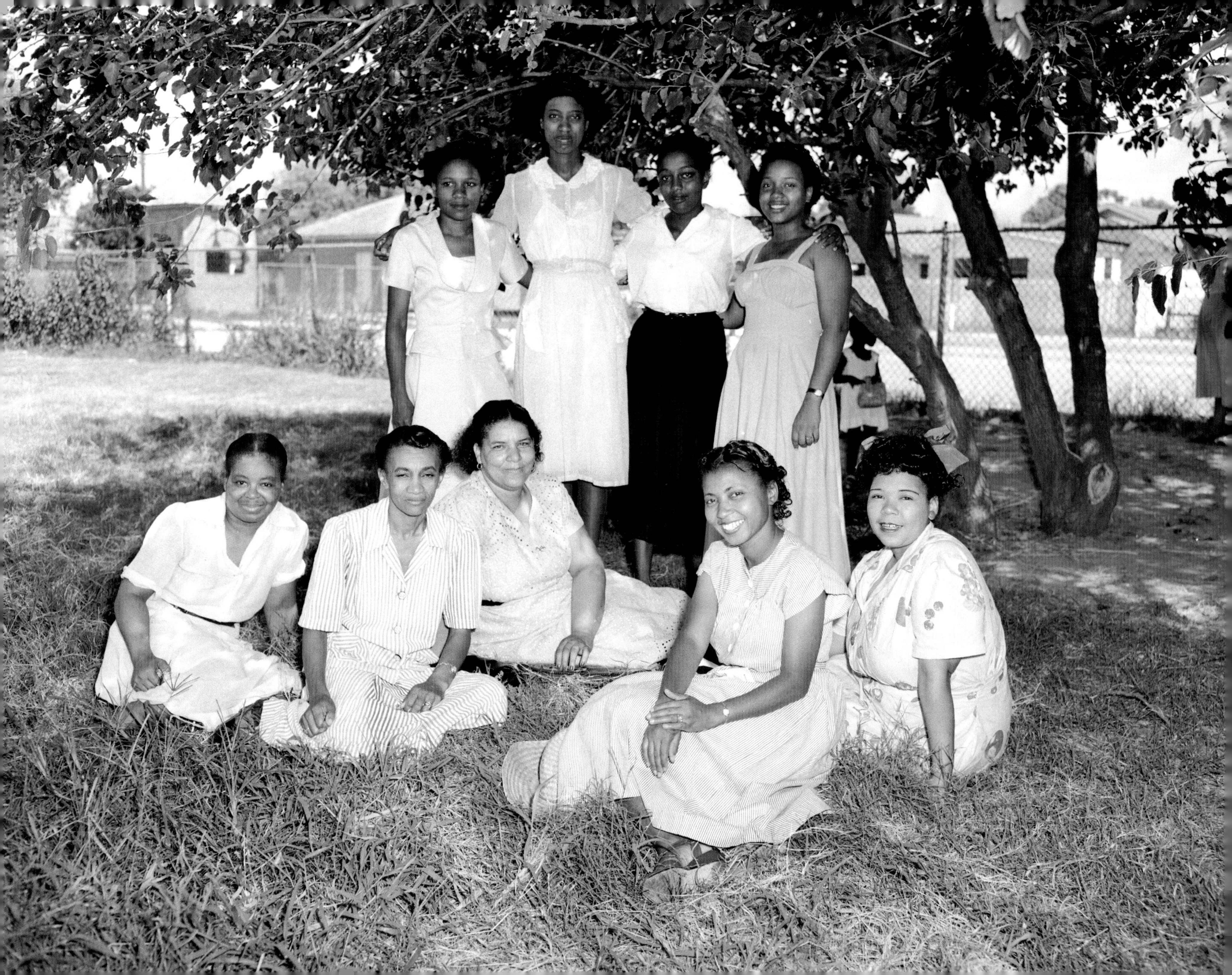

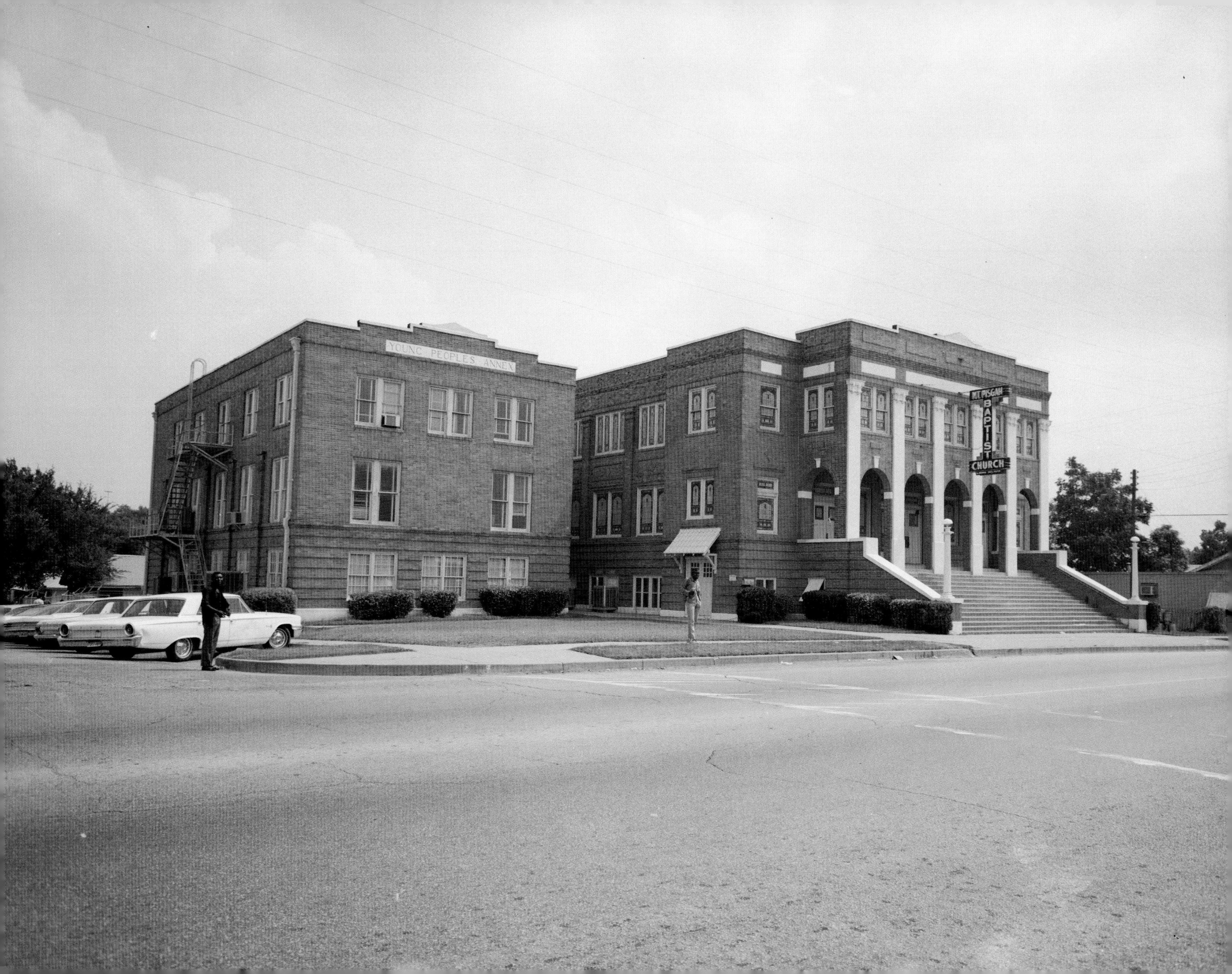
YOUNG PEOPLES ANNEX
MT. PISGAH
BAPTIST
CHURCH

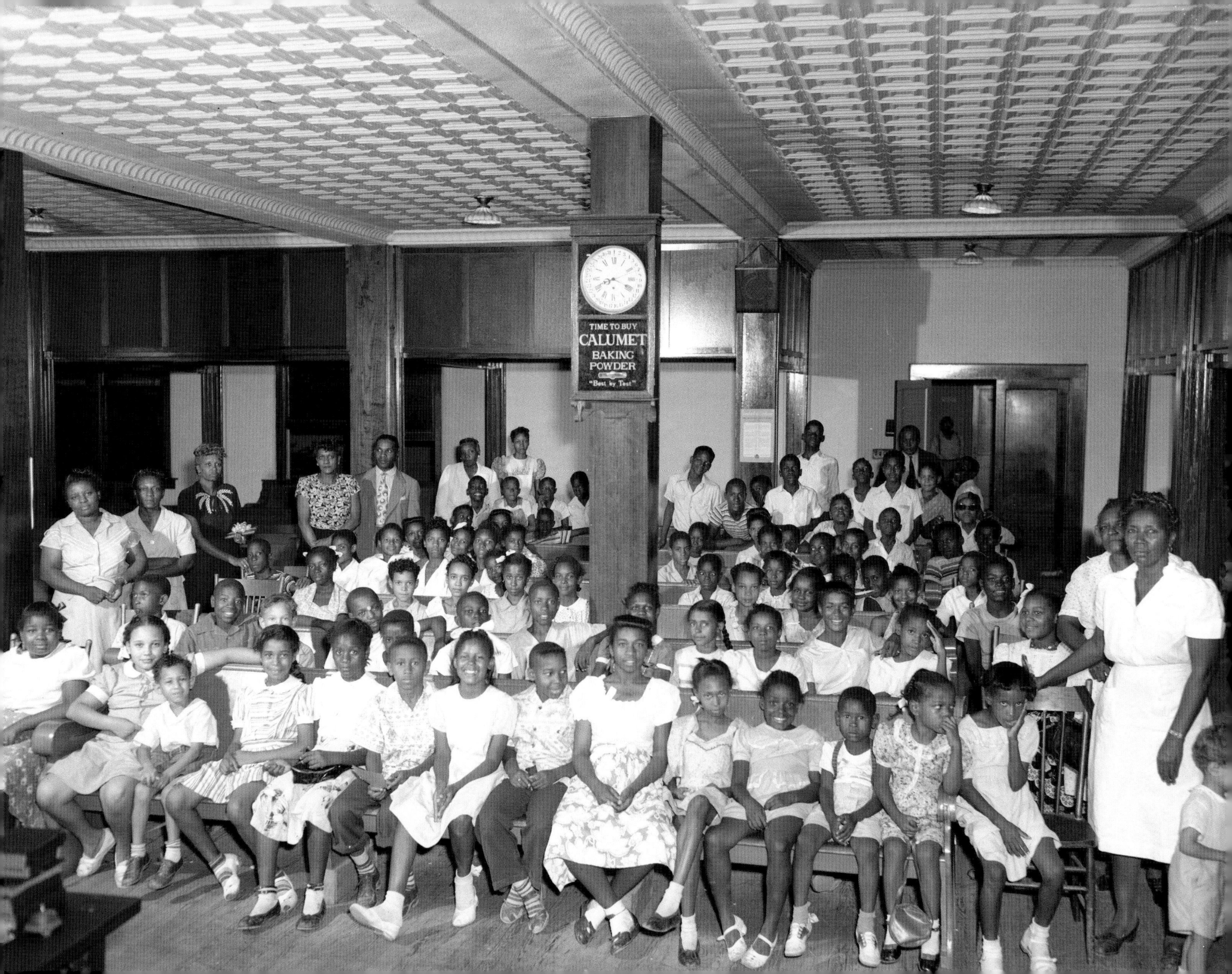
TIME TO BUY
CALUMET
BAKING
POWDER
"Best by Test"

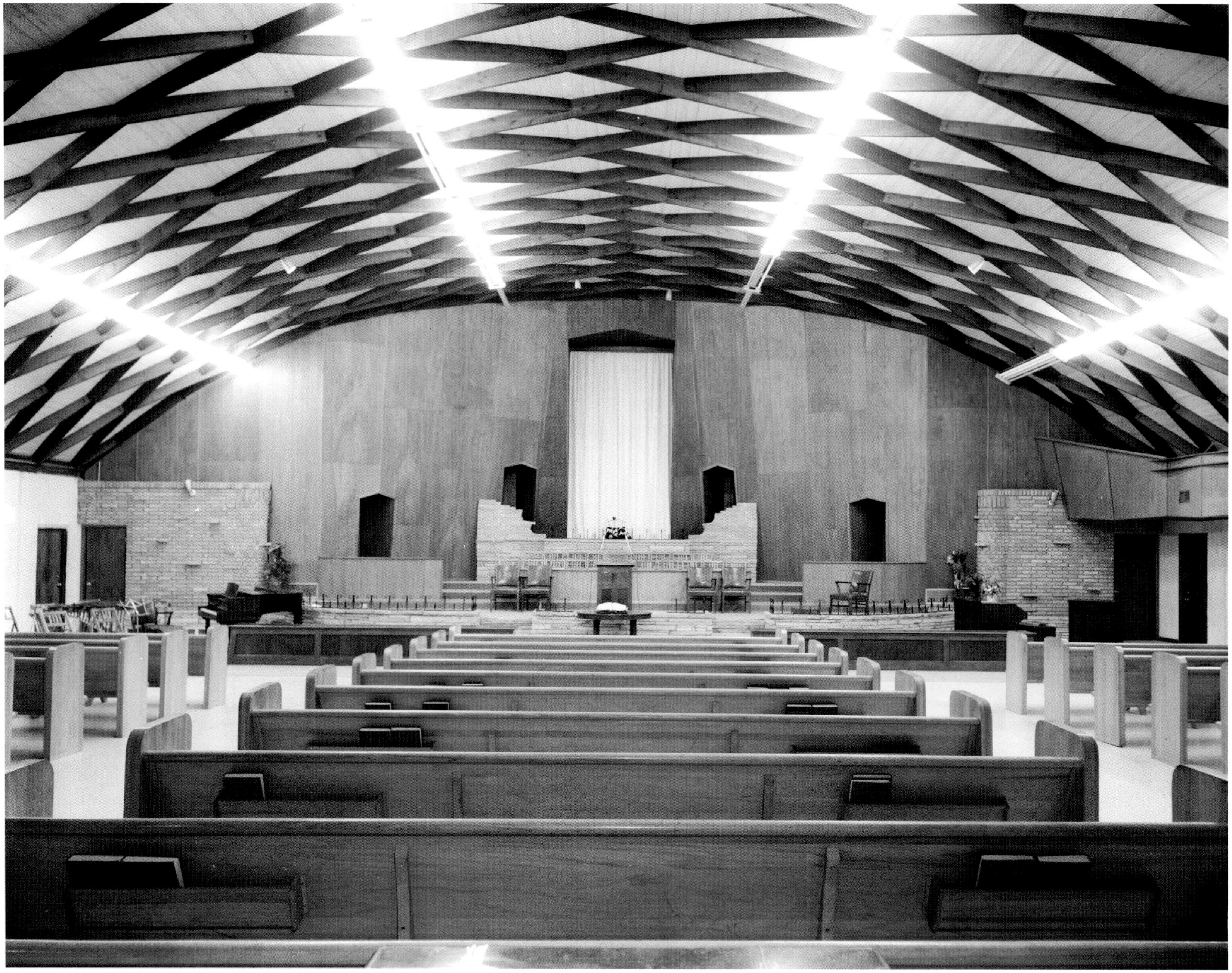

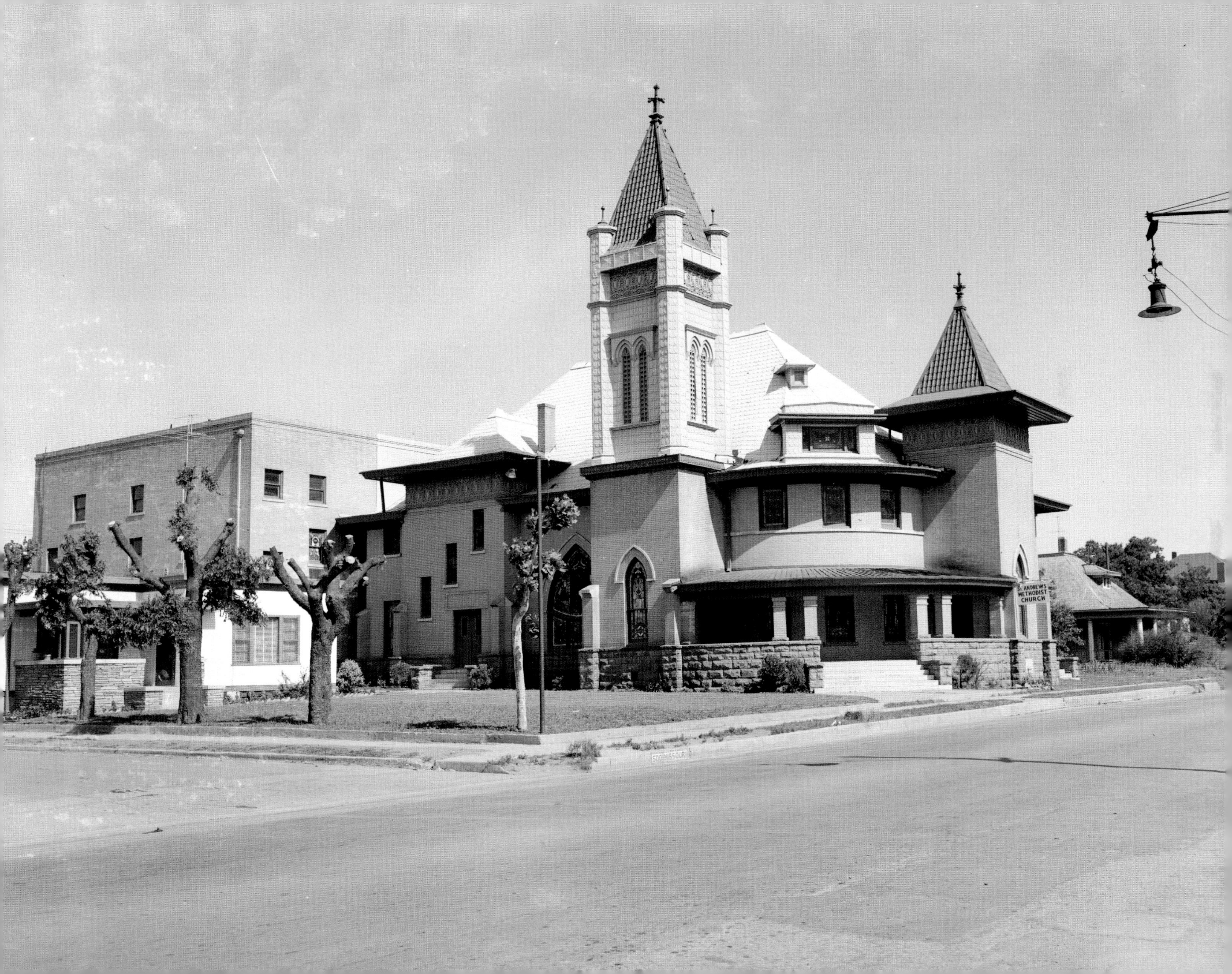
St. ANDREWS
METHODIST
CHURCH

Right: Mt. Zion Baptist Church delegation to National Baptist Convention, September 14, 1958.

Far Right: Baker Chapel AME choir, March 1953.

Next Page, Left: Hillary Thomas, church wedding, August 11, 1964.

Next Page, Right: Hillary Thomas, church wedding, bouquet toss, August 11, 1964.

Following Page, Left: Allen Chapel AME baptism, 1969.

Following Page, Right: Immanuel Independent AME Church, Rev. Brown and men in church service.

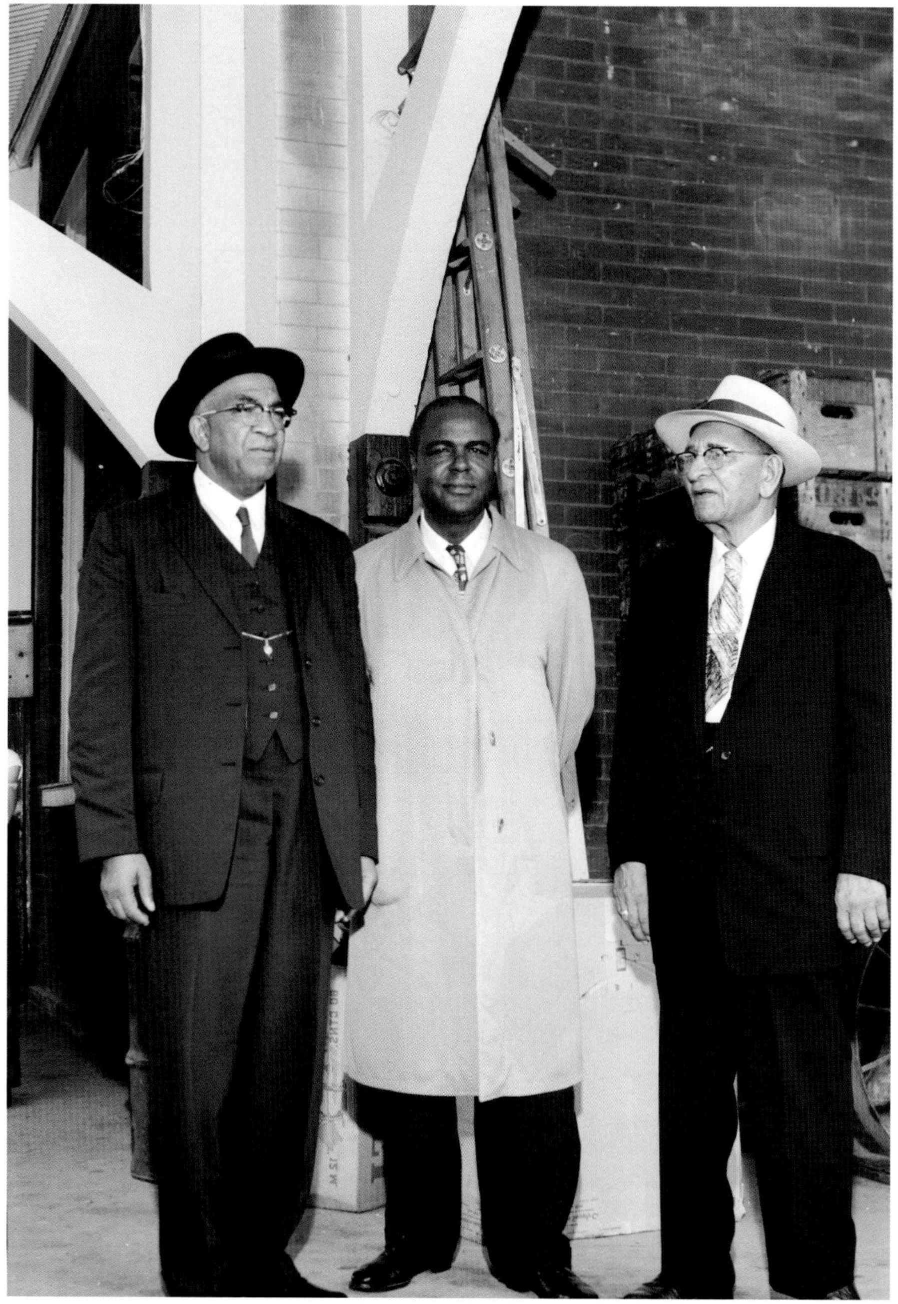

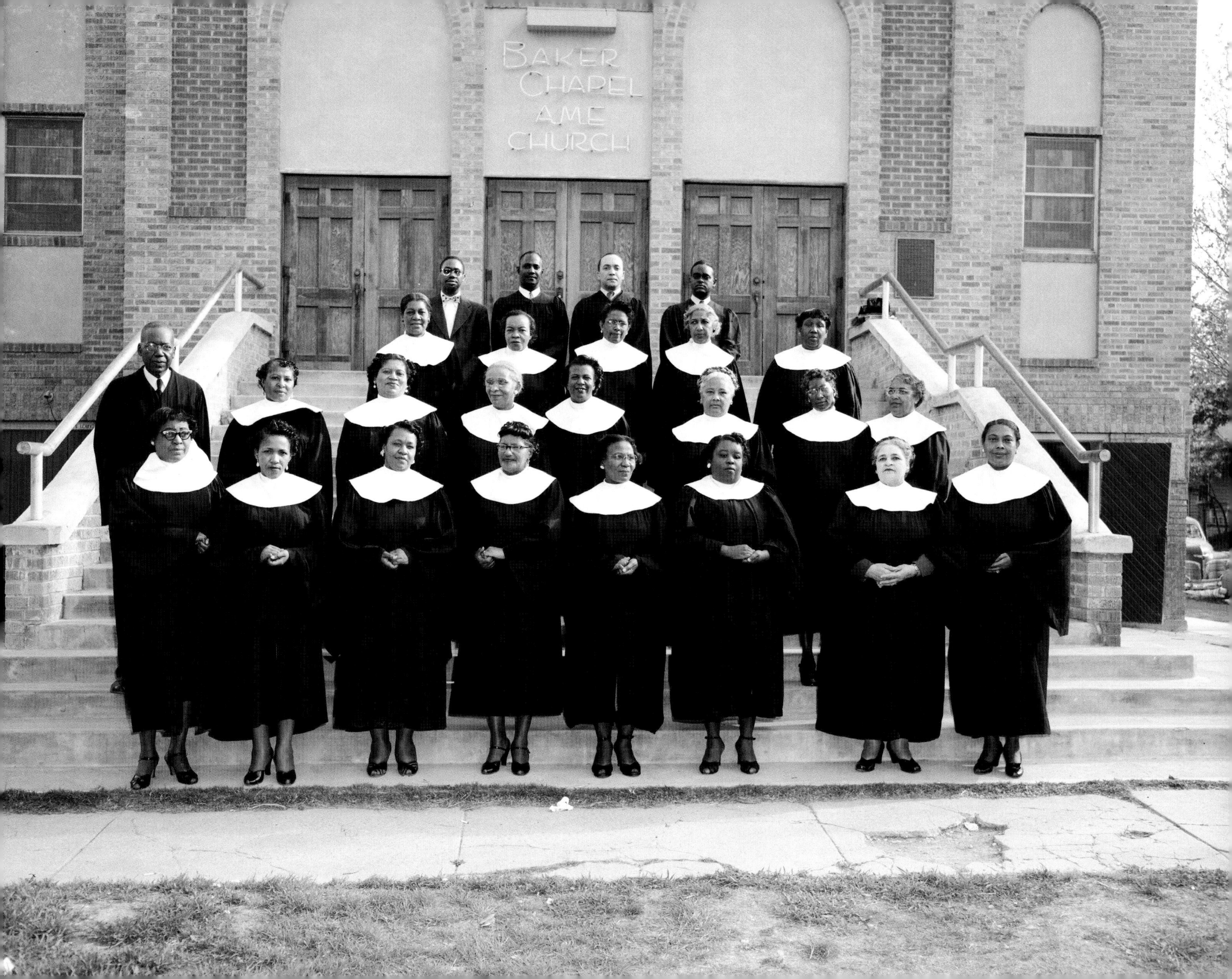
BAKER
CHAPEL
A.M.E
CHURCH

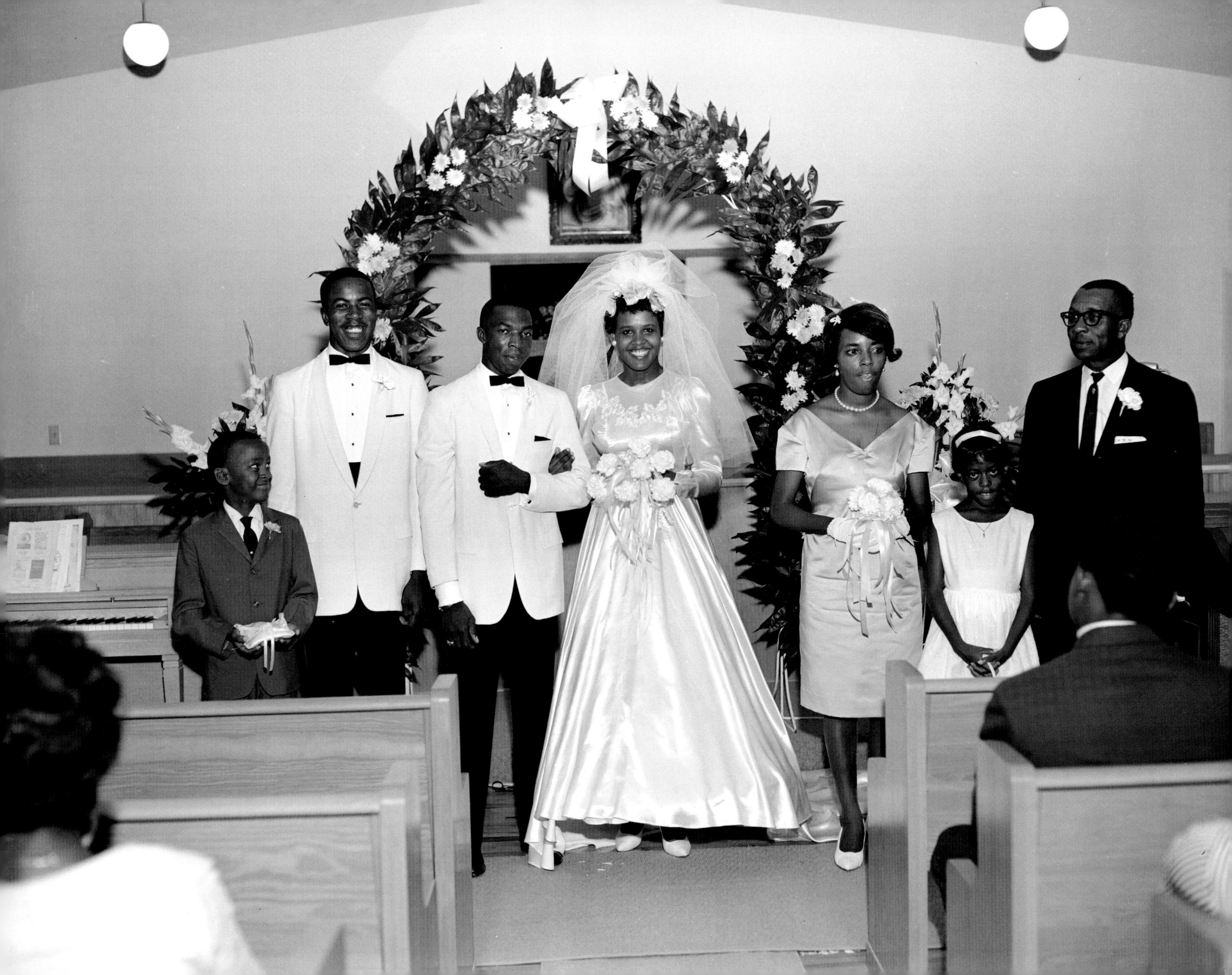

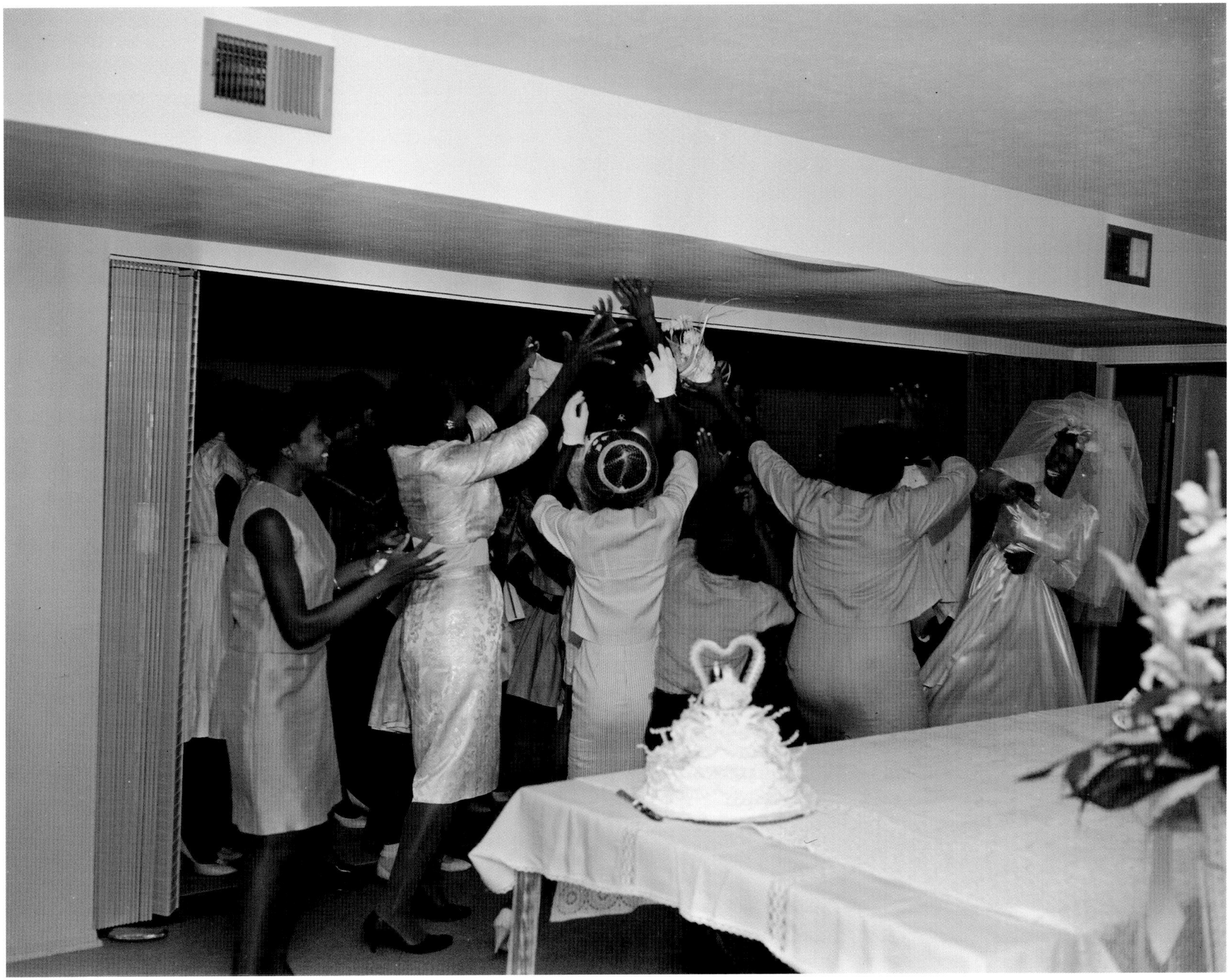

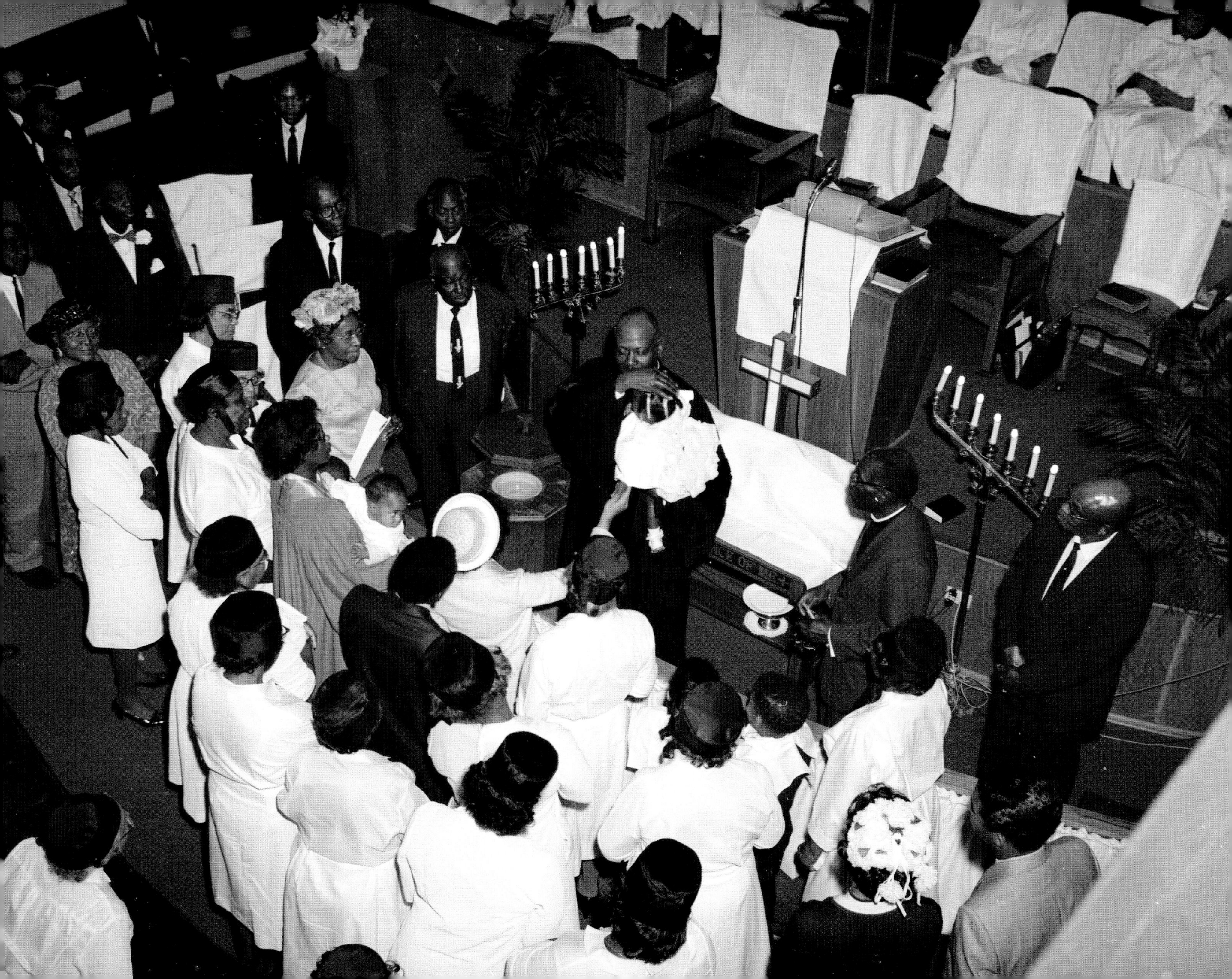

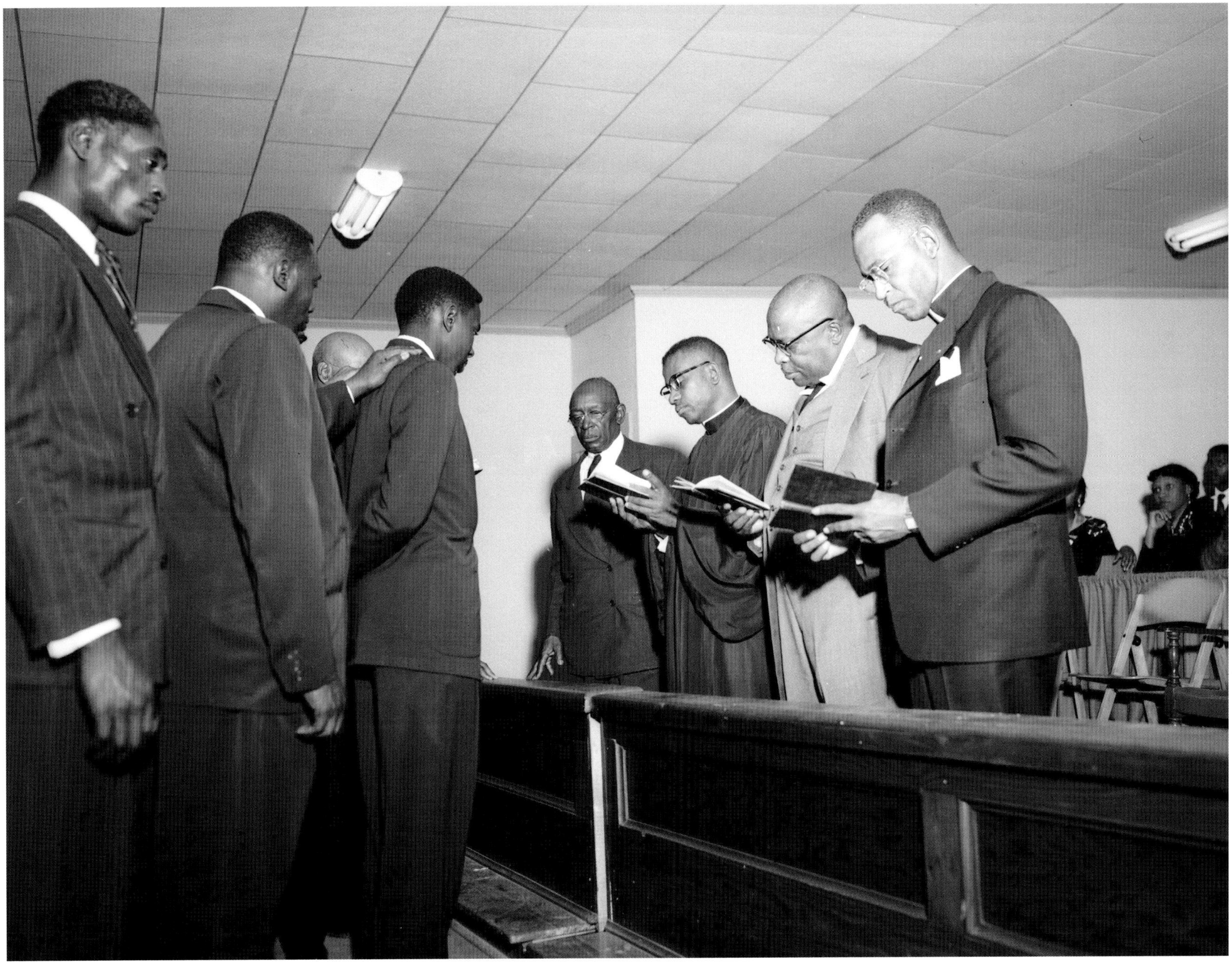

PART 5 SPORTS & ENTERTAINMENT

"I did a little bit for the Star-Telegram. *But they had a thing that, at that time, they weren't publishing very many black people's pictures. Consequently, it wasn't in demand. And you might be interested to know that when the big bands would come here—Duke Ellington, Cab Calloway... and all those guys—I covered 'em for the local papers. But, when they played for white audiences... [the newspapers] wouldn't print it. They had artists to conceptualize it."*

—Calvin Littlejohn

With Fort Worth being one of the largest cities in Texas and having a large African American population, black entertainers were often booked in the city. In those days, they would play Dallas one night and Fort Worth the next, or vice versa.

The city's active club scene and its reputation for having produced some of the greatest jazz musicians in the country (Ornette Coleman, Dewey Redman and "King" Curtis Ousley, to name three), made Fort Worth a natural stop for jazz, blues, and pop artists touring the country. After musicians finished their booked performances, they would often find their way to the local clubs for jam sessions long into the night and hang out with the locals.

Fort Worth also had a long minor league baseball history and, while there were no major league teams in town, black and white citizens were avid fans of teams in other cities. Blacks tended to be fans of the Brooklyn (later Los Angeles) Dodgers, primarily because the team was the first to integrate when it signed Jackie Robinson in 1947. The Fort Worth Cats was a Dodger farm team where the great Maury Wills was assigned in the 1950s.

At both entertainment and sporting events, if blacks were allowed to attend with whites, they had to sit in special segregated sections. And, like in church, when they attended such occasions, they were well dressed for them.

Some of the country's most renowned performers in music and sports found themselves on the other side of Calvin Littlejohn's lens when they visited Cowtown.

Right: Ruth Brown singing with band at Masonic Mosque, Fort Worth, November 14, 1959.

Far Right: Charles Brown playing with band at Masonic Mosque, Fort Worth, November 14, 1956.

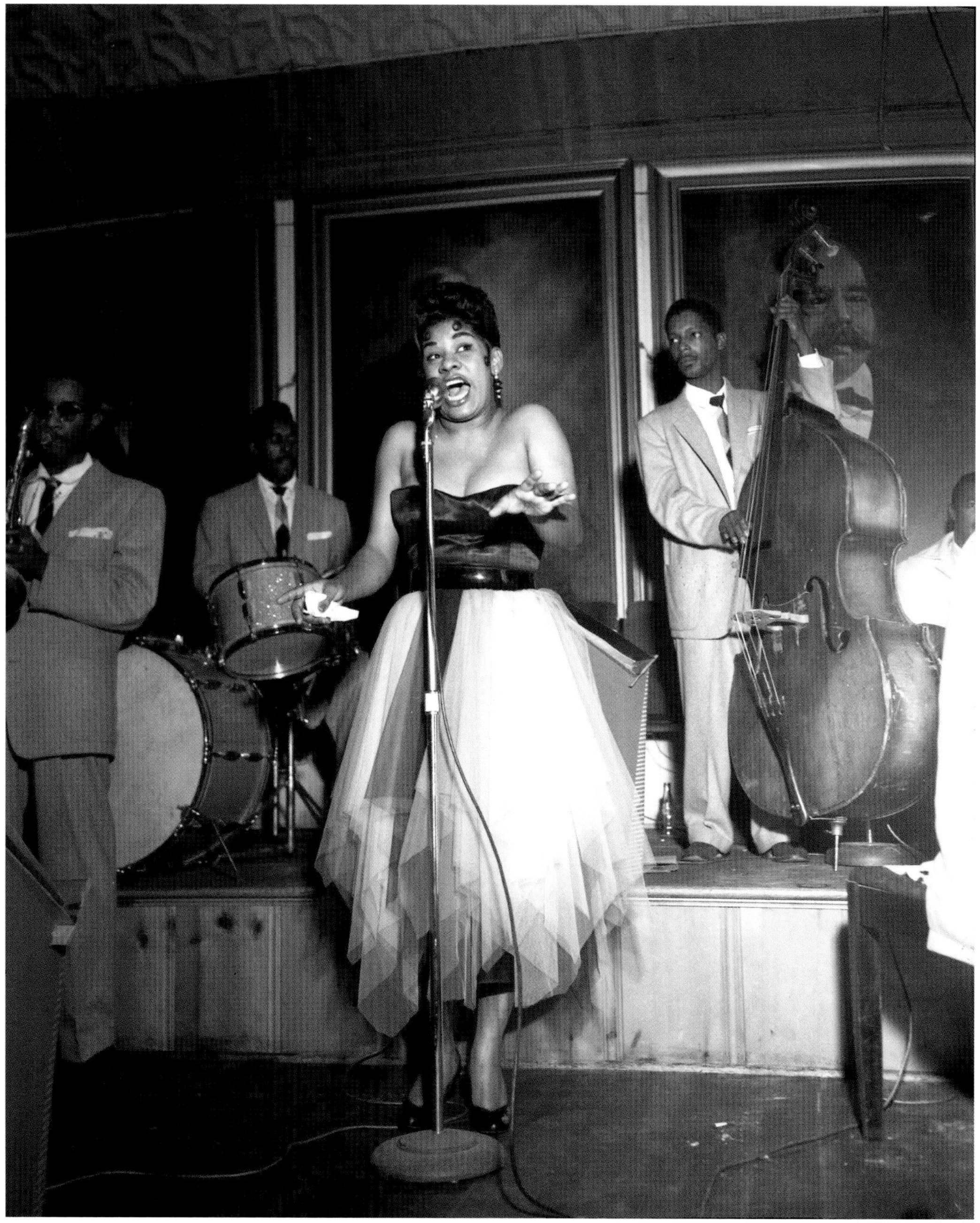

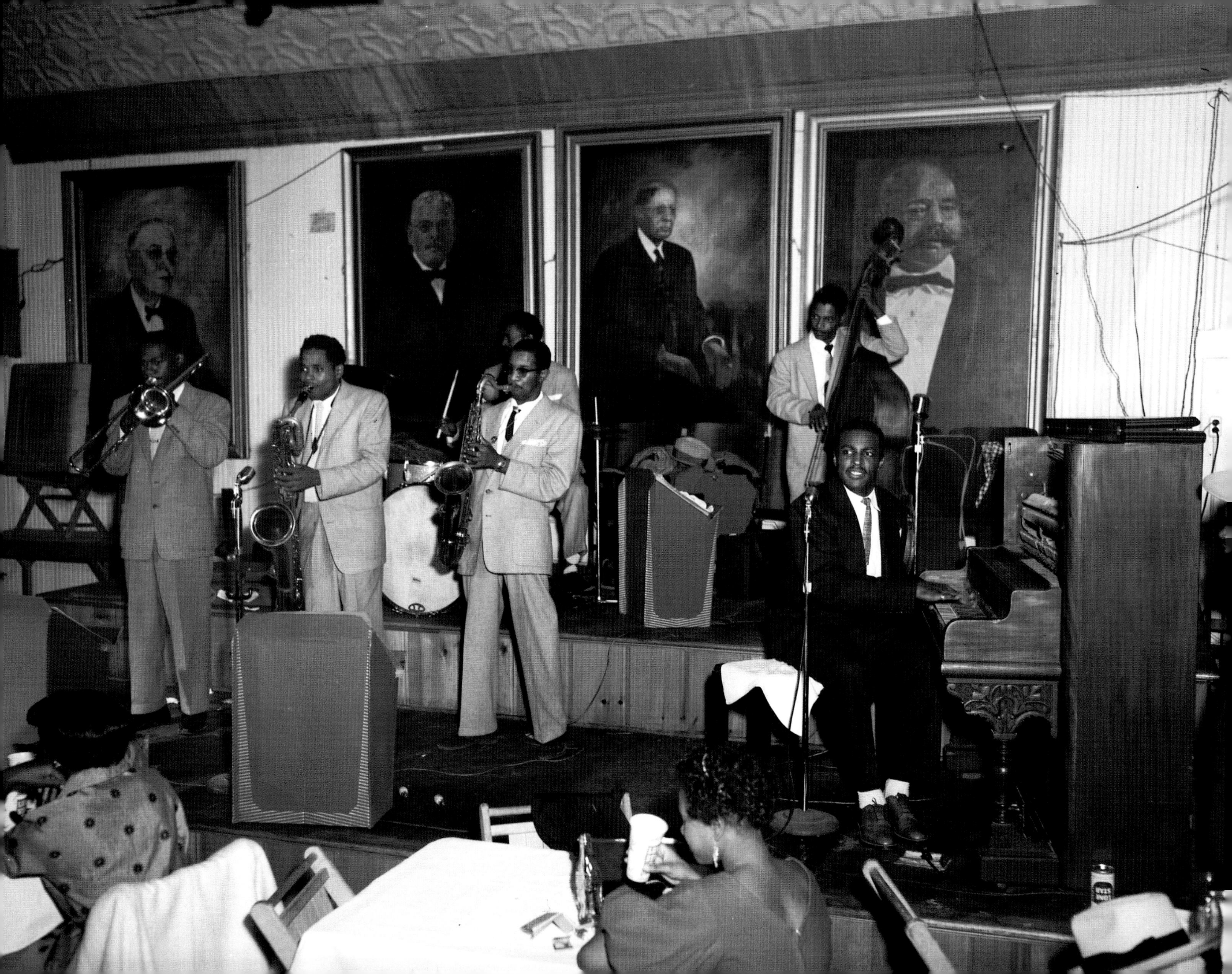

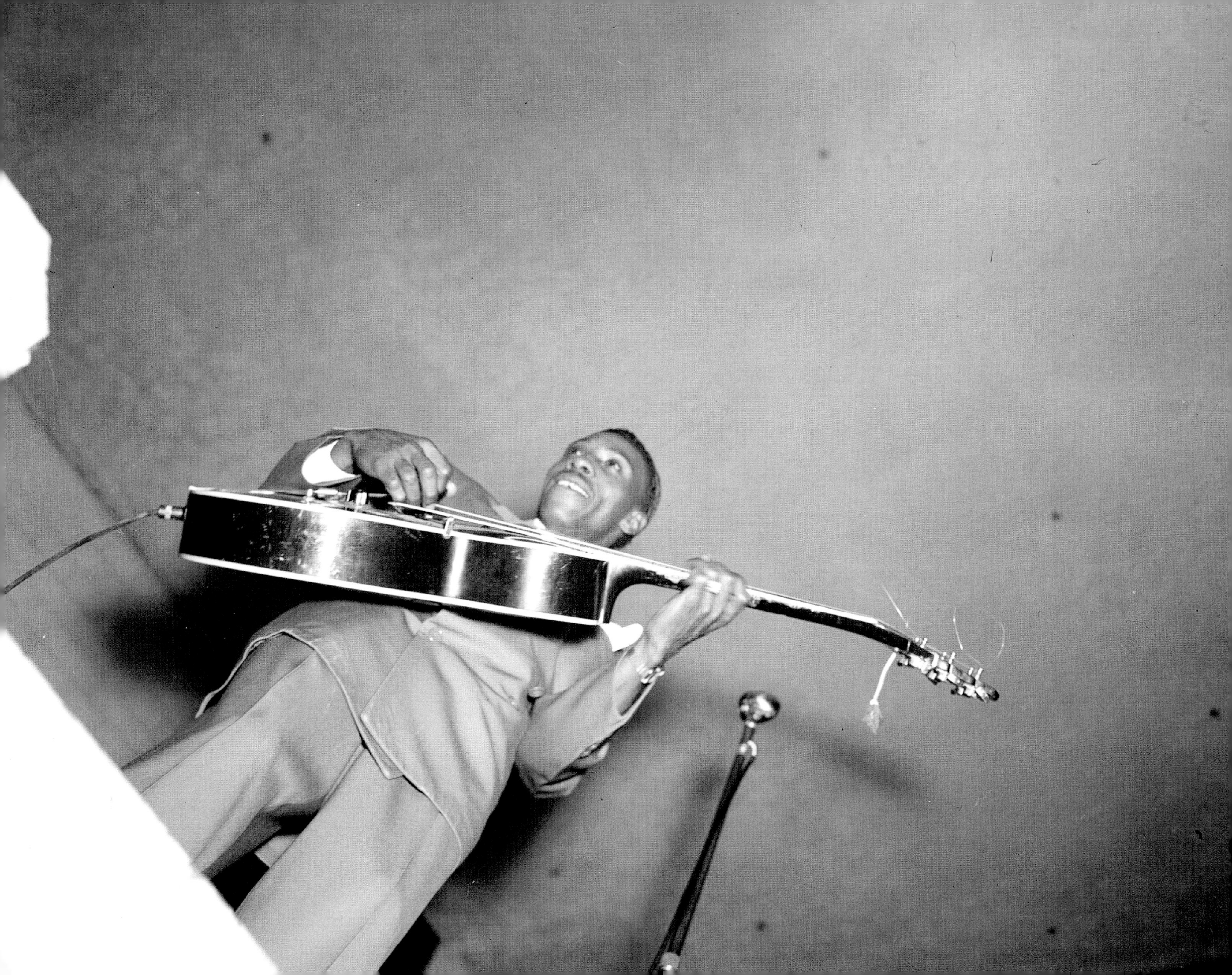

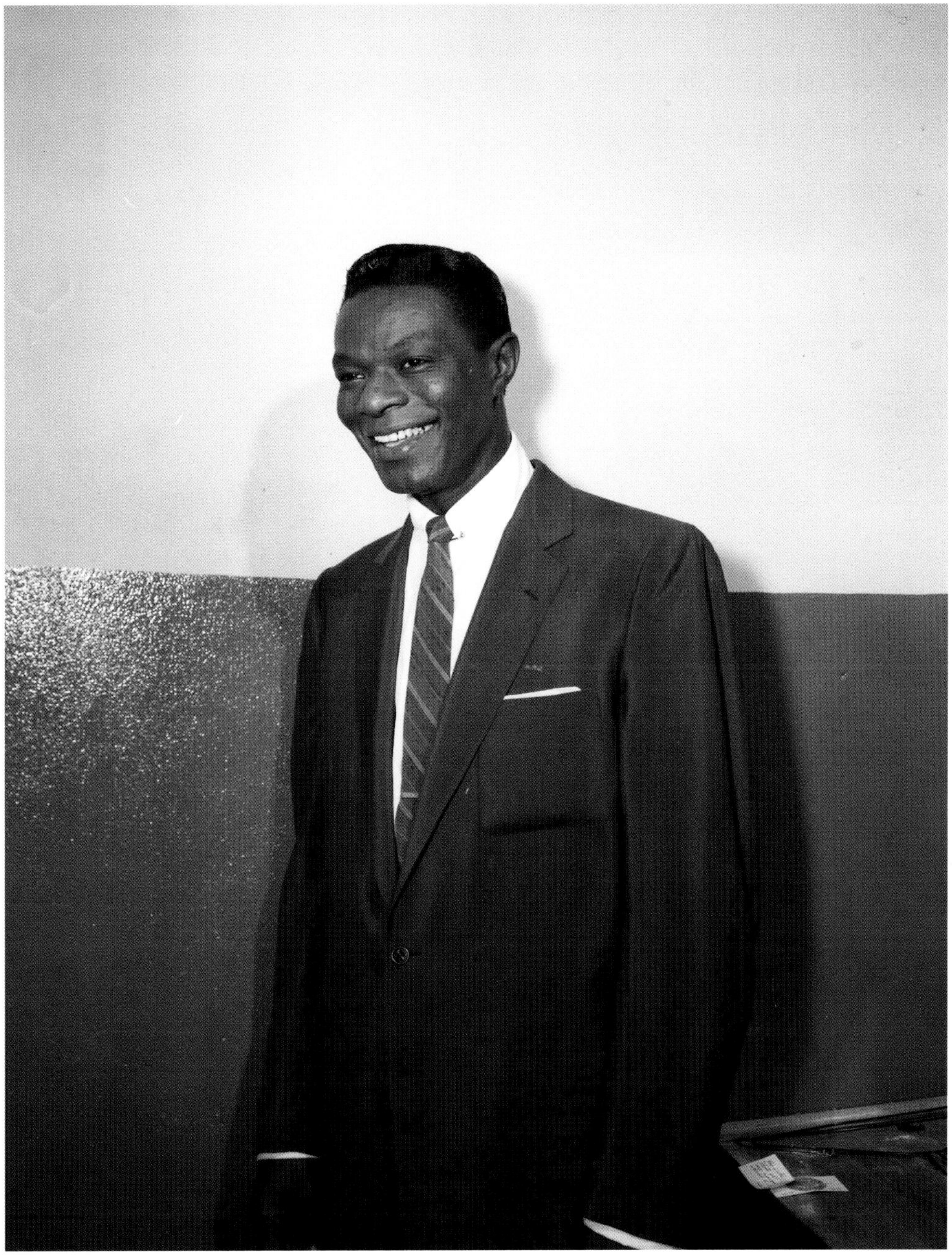

Far Left: T. Bone Walker playing the guitar onstage, 1946.

Left: Nat "King" Cole in Fort Worth, 1950s.

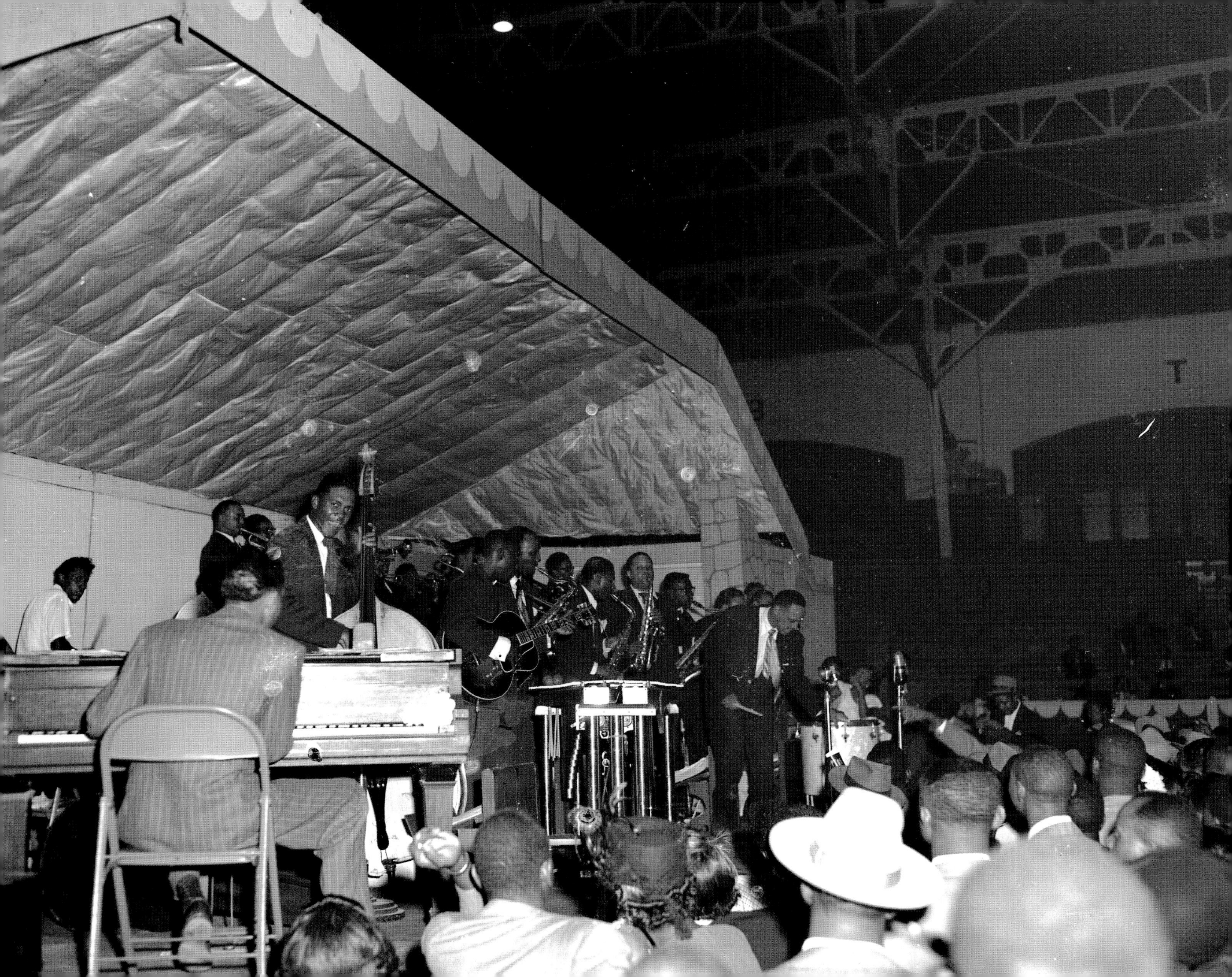

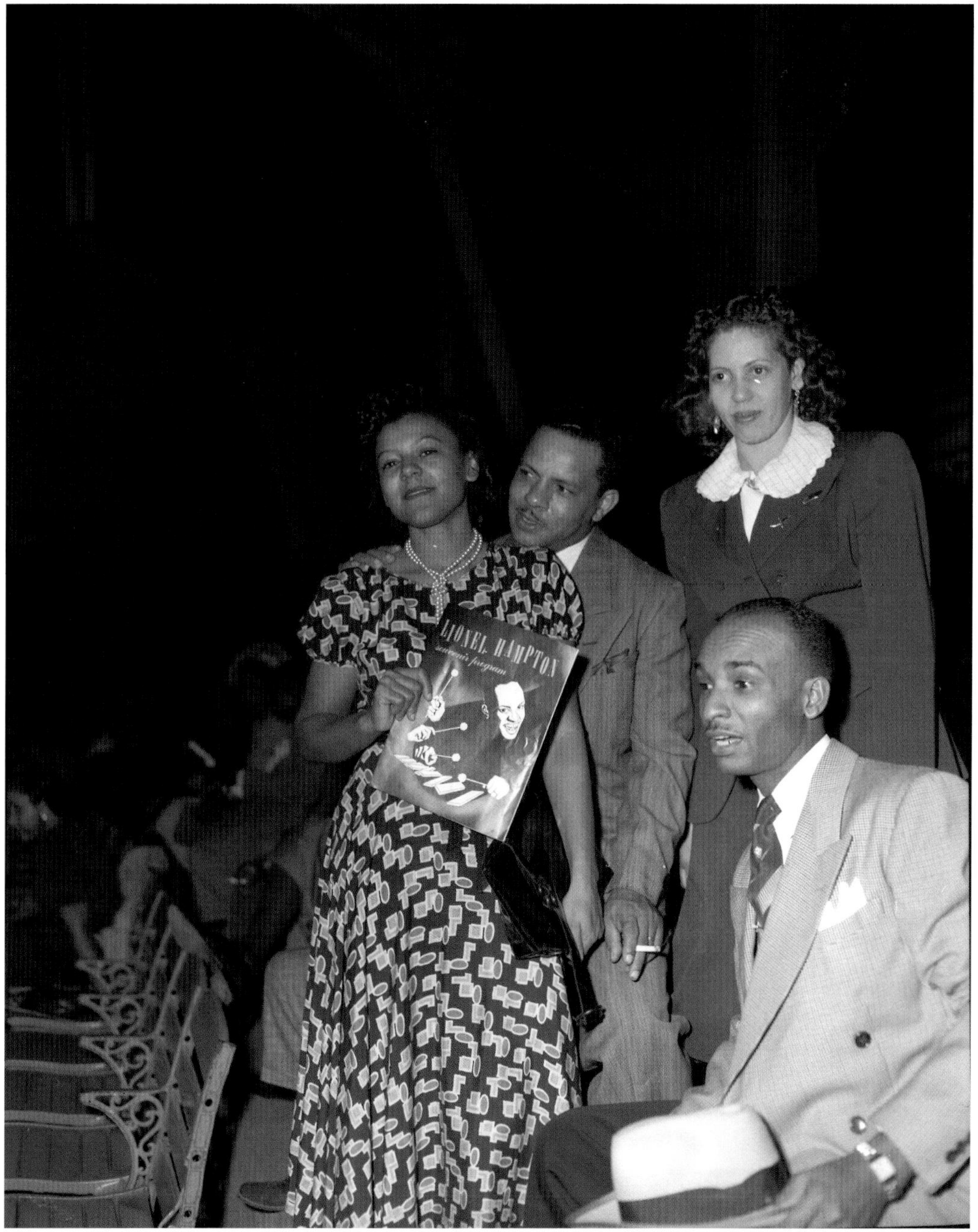

Far Left: Lionel Hampton performance at the North Side Coliseum (now the Cowtown Coliseum), October 12, 1948.

Left: Part of the audience at the Lionel Hampton performance, October 12, 1948.

Right: Oscar Peterson Trio in Fort Worth, 1950s.

Far Right: Ella Fitzgerald singing with band onstage at the Philharmonic Club, Dallas, 1955.

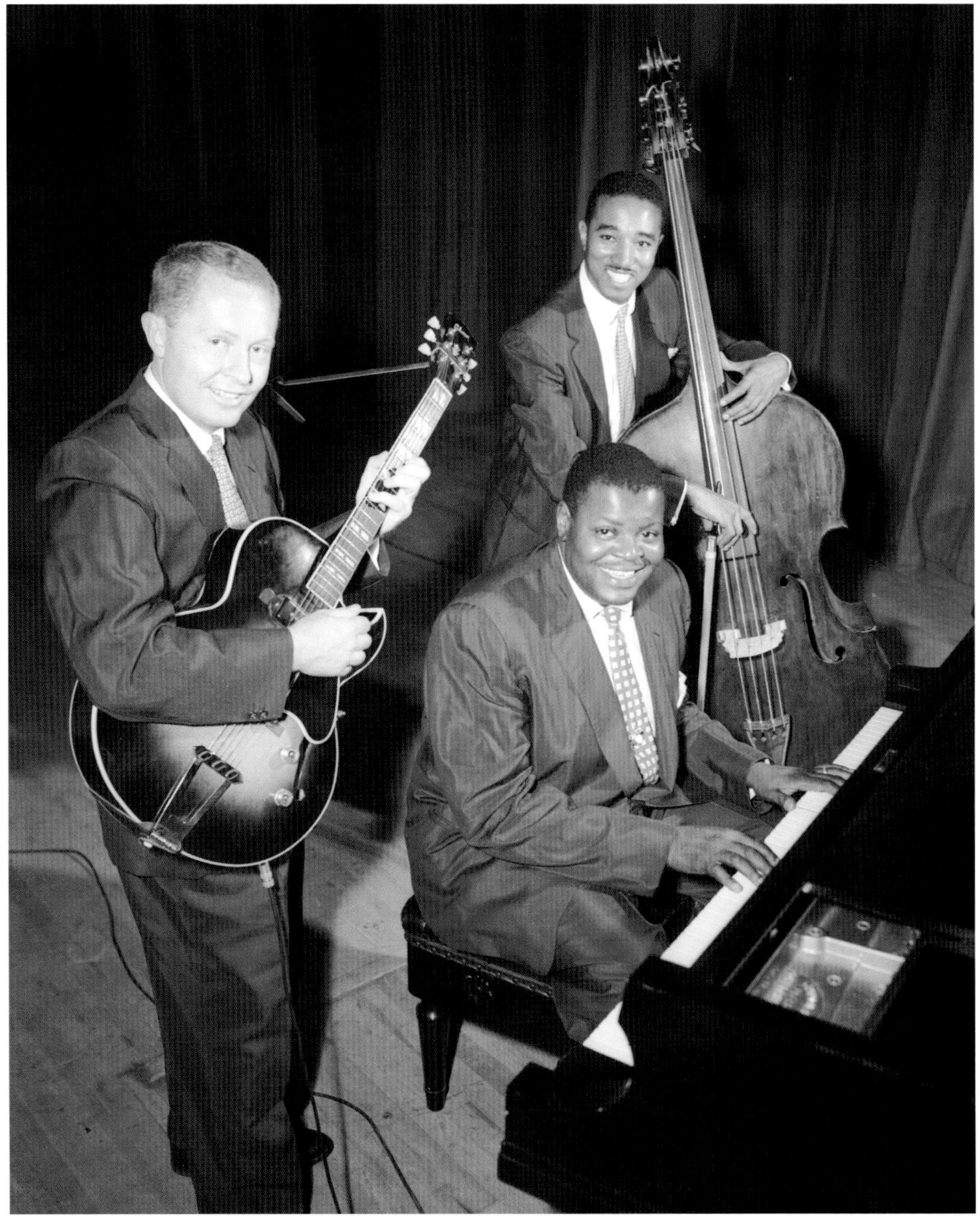

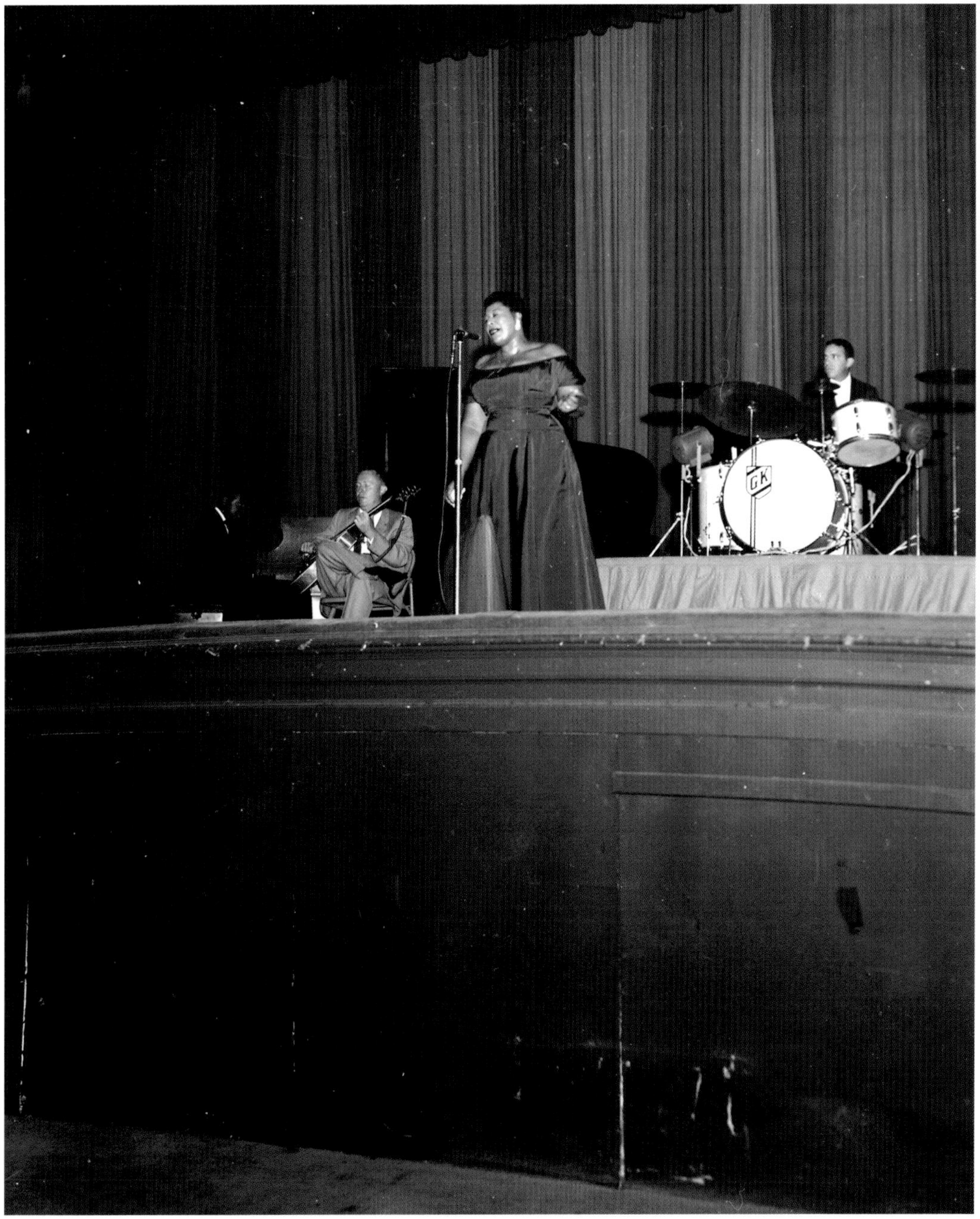

Next Page, Left: Overflow crowd seated on the edge of the baseball field for the exhibition game of Jackie Robinson and the Brooklyn Dodgers, November 11, 1949.

Next Page, Right: The photo, with woman holding up baseball, is great unto itself. But the man in the foreground is one of Fort Worth's most famous ministers, Brother Kirby Holmes.

Following Page, Left: Jackie Robinson speaking into a microphone at LaGrave Field for an exhibition game, November 11, 1949. With him are, from left: Raymond L. "Pie" Melton, co-founder of The Fort Worth Mind, *and James Clemons, well-known promoter and radio deejay.*

Following Page, Right: Boxer Joe Louis, left, Fort Worth, March 18, 1950.

Following Page, Left: Mrs. Lucille Smith serving lunch to boxer Joe Louis, March 18, 1950. Seated at the table with Louis is H. L. King, principal of I. M. Terrell High School. R. L. "Pie" Melton, co-founder of The Fort Worth Mind, *takes notes in the background.*

Following Page, Right: Joe Louis knocking down an opponent at a boxing exhibition, Fort Worth, March 18, 1950.

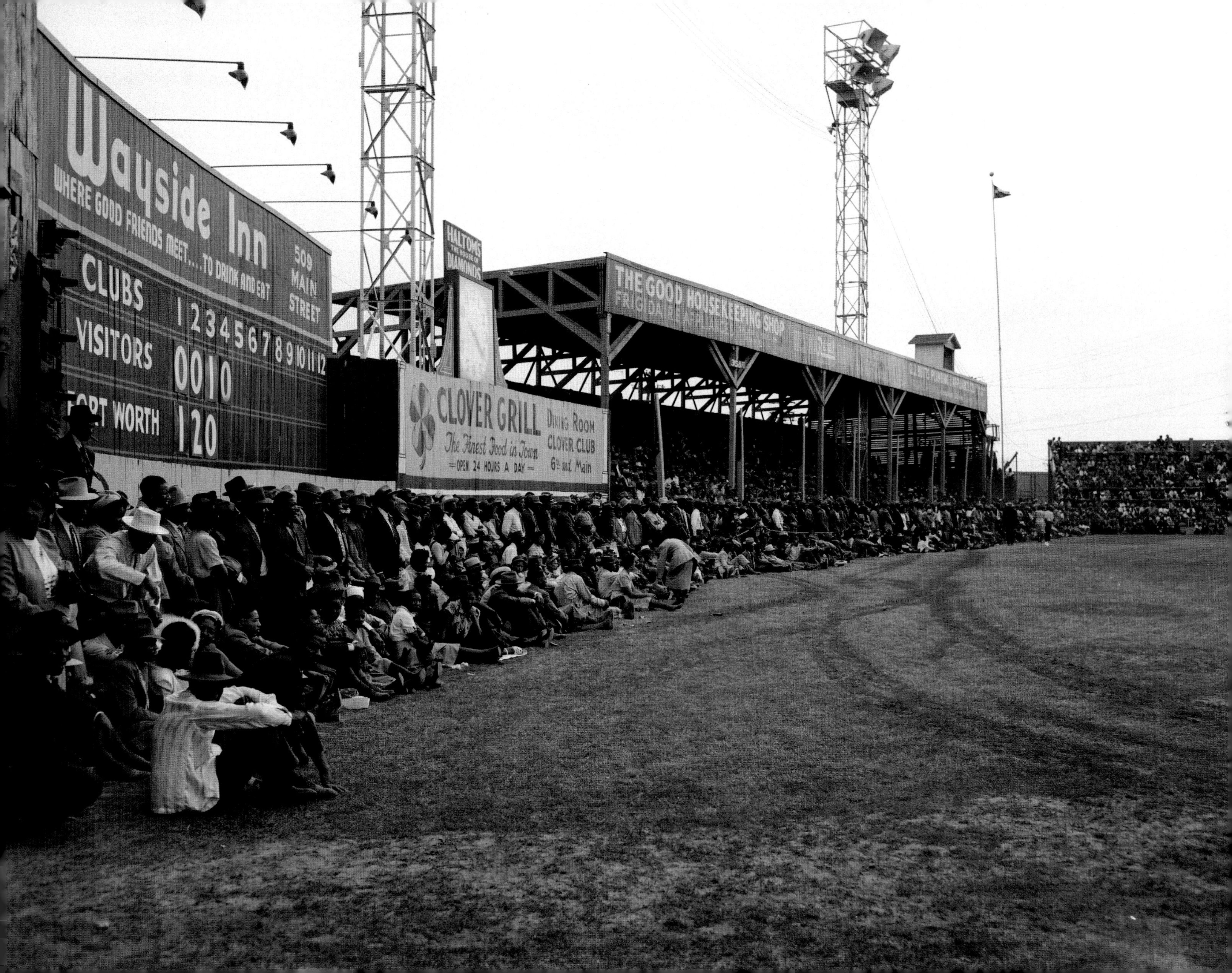
Wayside Inn
WHERE GOOD FRIENDS MEET.....TO DRINK AND EAT
509 MAIN STREET
CLUBS
1 2 3 4 5 6 7 8 9 10 11 12
VISITORS
0 0 1 0
ORT WORTH
1 2 0
HALTOMS
THE HOUSE OF DIAMONDS
CLOVER GRILL
The Finest Food in Town
OPEN 24 HOURS A DAY
DINING ROOM
CLOVER CLUB
6th and Main
THE GOOD HOUSEKEEPING SHOP

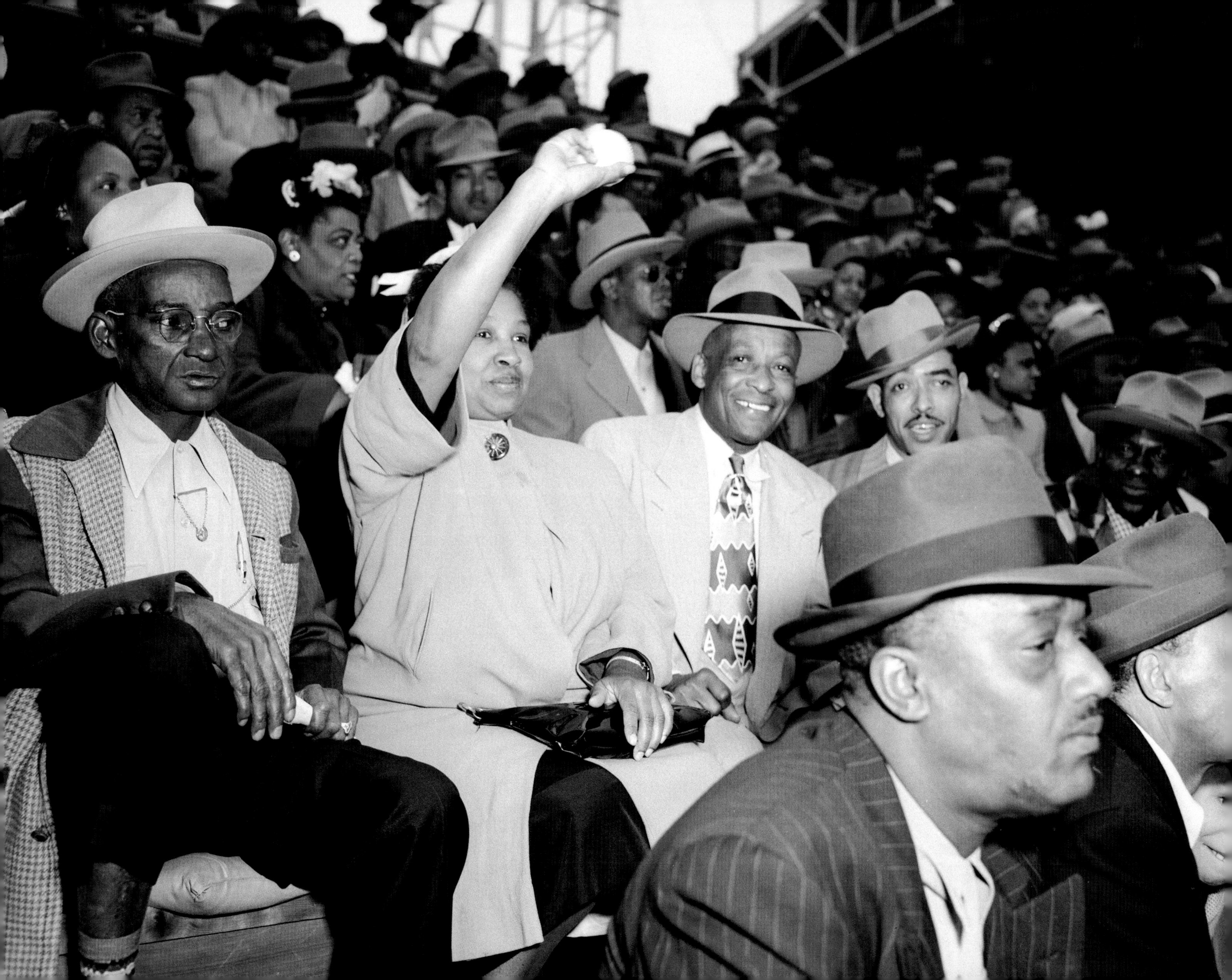

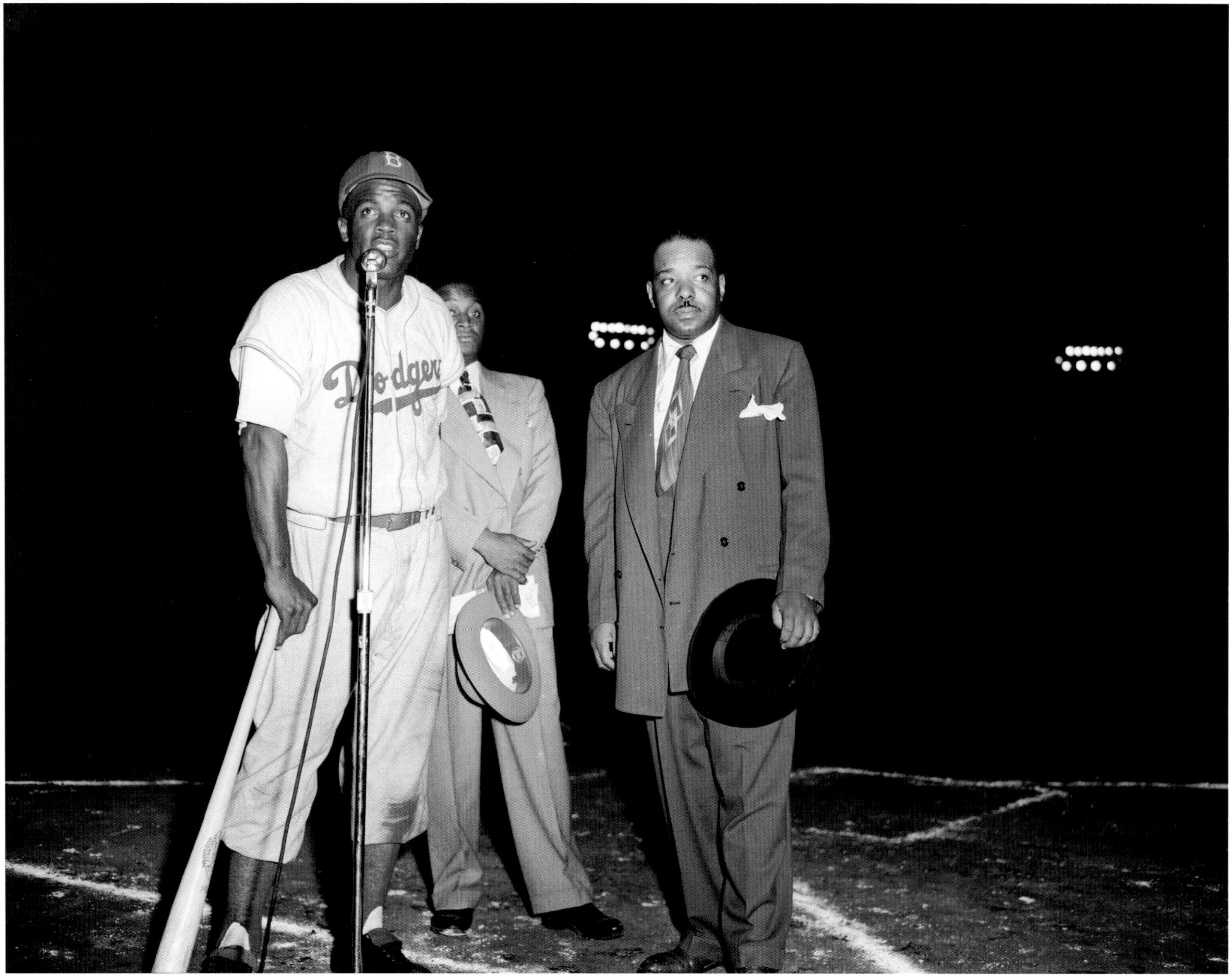
Dodgers

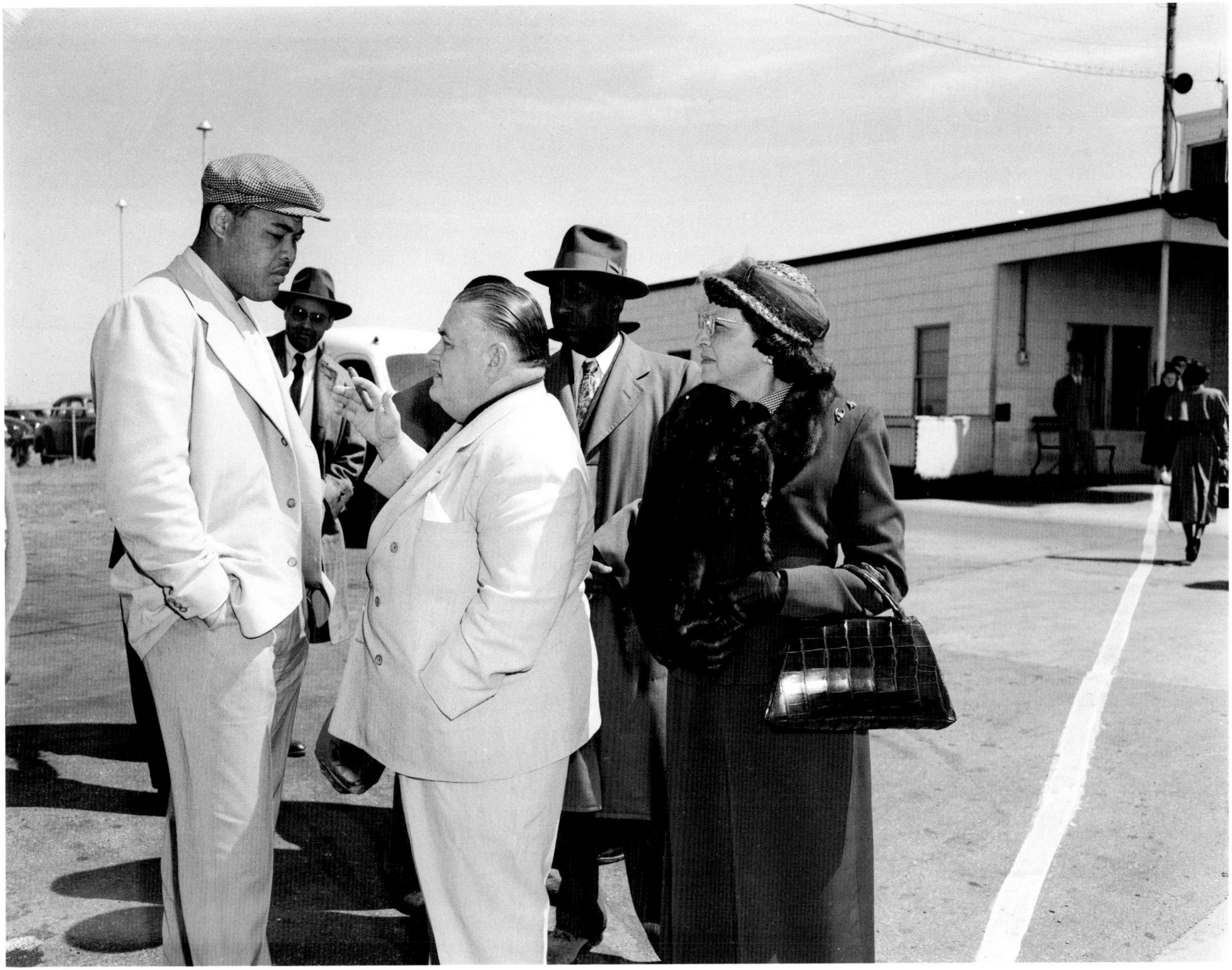

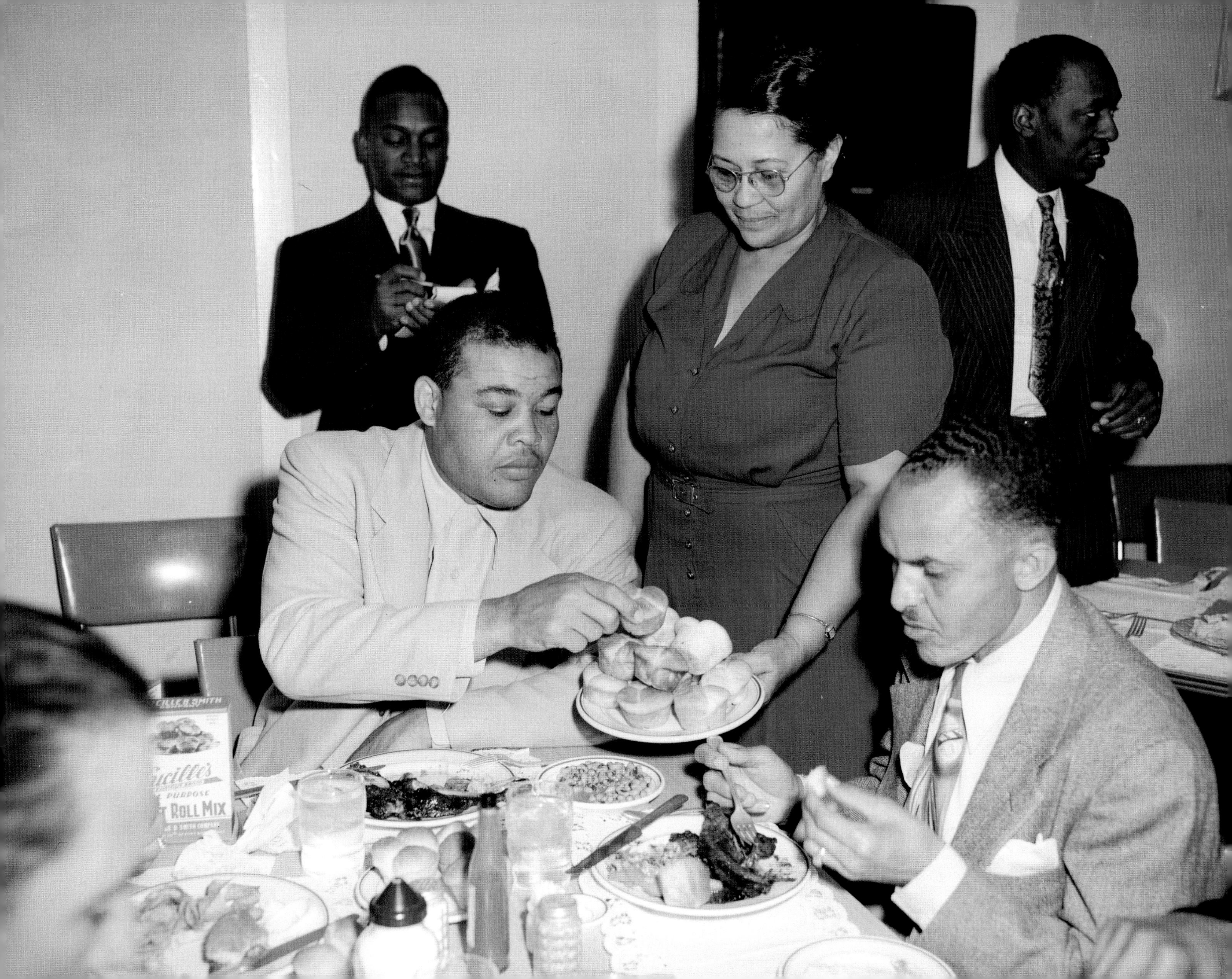
PURPOSE
ROLL MIX

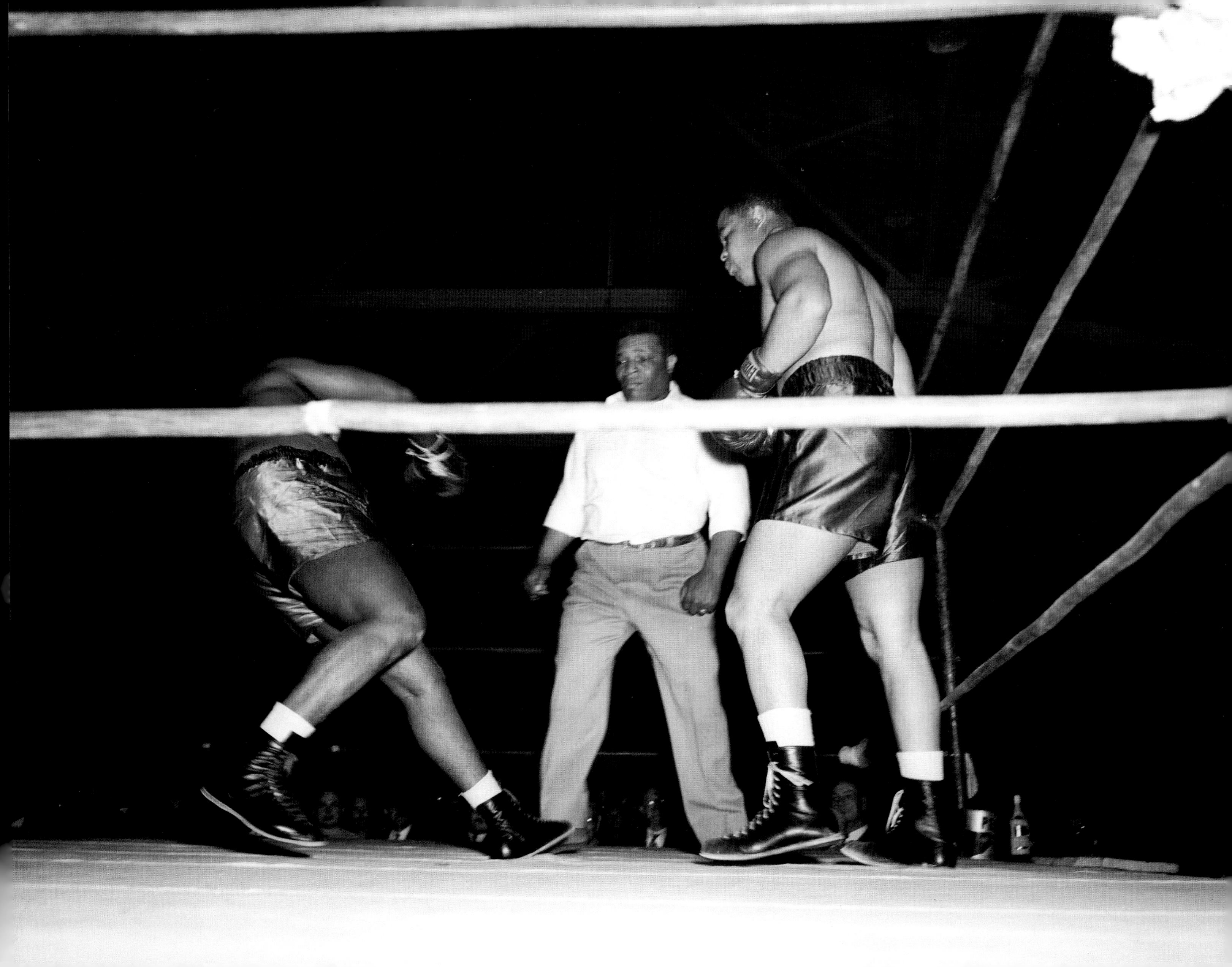

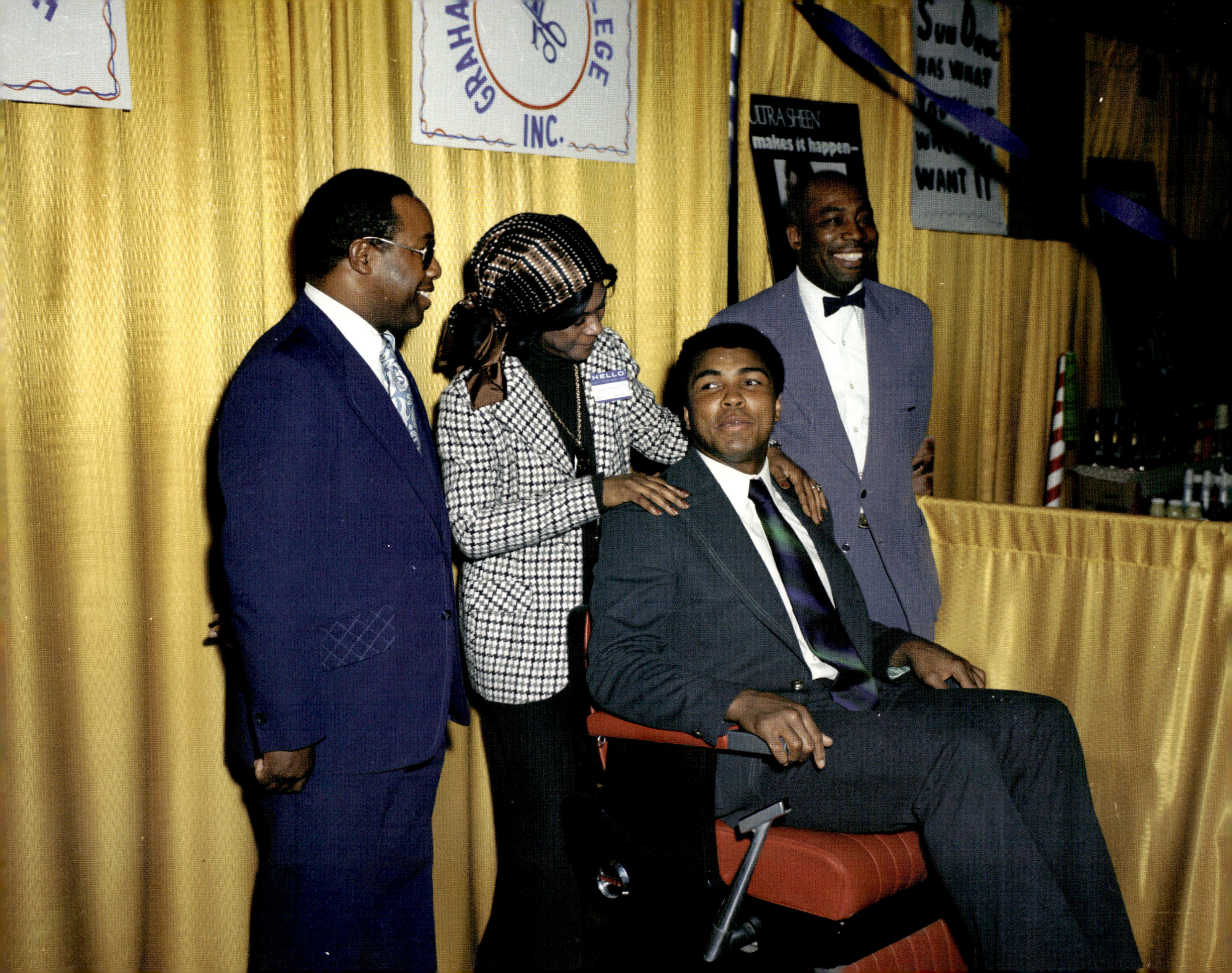
GRAHA
LEGE
INC.
ULTRA SHEEN
makes it happen—
HAS WHAT
WANT IT
HELLO

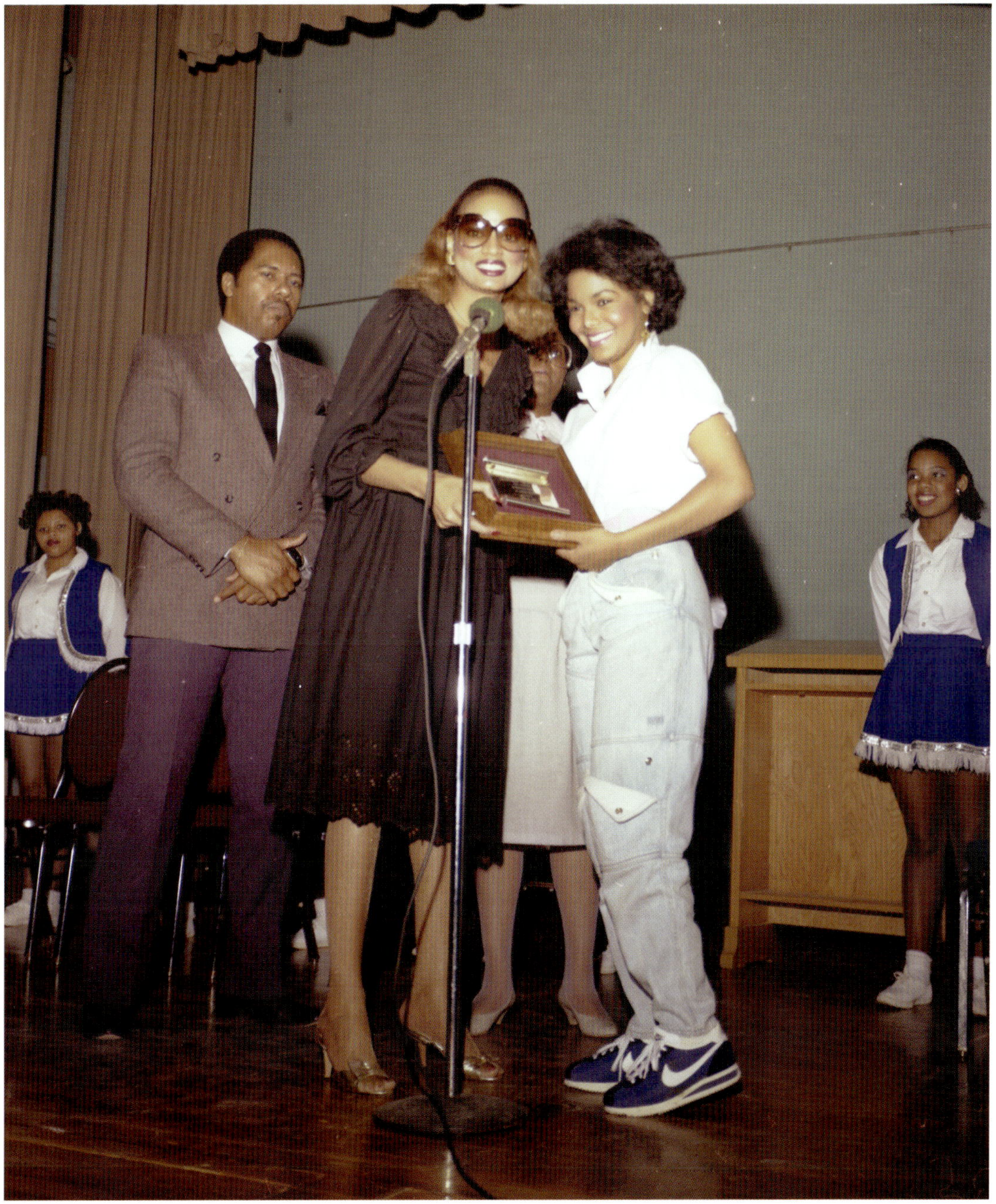

Far Left: Muhammad Ali at Dallas Black Business Expo, 1975.

Left: Singer Janet Jackson receiving an award from teacher Lavern Rowe-Williams at Dunbar High School during an album promotional tour sponsored by KKDA-FM radio, 1983.

PART 6 WORLD LEADERS

"Margaret Truman...This is MacArthur there...right after he was fired, you know...Thurgood Marshall...when he was here for the NAACP...Adam Clayton Powell here..."

—*Calvin Littlejohn*
(While thumbing through a photo album of his work)

Because Texas long had political influence in Washington, DC, and because many wealthy Fort Worth residents were large financial contributors to some of the most influential state and national elected officials, well-known politicians usually included Fort Worth on their itineraries. The city also was a major railhead, with several passenger trains a day stopping at the T&P Terminal or Santa Fe Station, and that made it a convenient destination for those presidential candidates and war heroes who wanted to make whistle-stop appearances.

Nationally known black figures often came at the invitation of the local NAACP chapter, a national church convention, or a civic group wanting to expose the local community to some of the "Negro" leaders who were trying to change the status quo.

Authentic American heroes, black and white, were sometimes welcomed with parades, and there was always an audience eager to hear words from some famous individual they had only read about in the newspapers, heard on the radio, or seen in newsreels in between movies at segregated theaters.

Calvin Littlejohn was there for the arrival of presidents, generals, ambassadors and, in 1959, for the city's only visit by the country's most famous and revered civil rights leader, Dr. Martin Luther King, Jr.

He was also there when Air Force One touched down at Carswell Air Force Base one Thursday night in November 1963, bringing a young first-term president who would spend his last night, deliver his last speech, and perhaps hear his last prayer in Fort Worth before leaving for a very short flight to Dallas the next morning.

Few of those leaders who had their photos snapped by Littlejohn ever knew his name, for he was always more concerned about getting the picture than being introduced to national celebrities.

Right: President Harry S. Truman, Lyndon B. Johnson, Tom Clark, and Beauford Jester at a Truman campaign appearance, Fort Worth, September 27, 1948.

Far Right: Crowd gathered at the T&P Station for a speech by President Truman, Fort Worth, September 27, 1948.

Next Page, Left: Paul Robeson giving a speech at a Progressive Party rally for Henry A. Wallace's presidential campaign, Dallas, August 10, 1948.

Next Page, Right: Rally for the Henry A. Wallace Progressive Party campaign, Fort Worth, October 29, 1948.

Following Page, Left: General Douglas MacArthur and family riding in a downtown Fort Worth parade, June 16, 1951.

Following Page, Right: Senator Adlai Stevenson shaking hands with Sam Rayburn while campaigning with Lyndon Johnson in Fort Worth, October 1952.

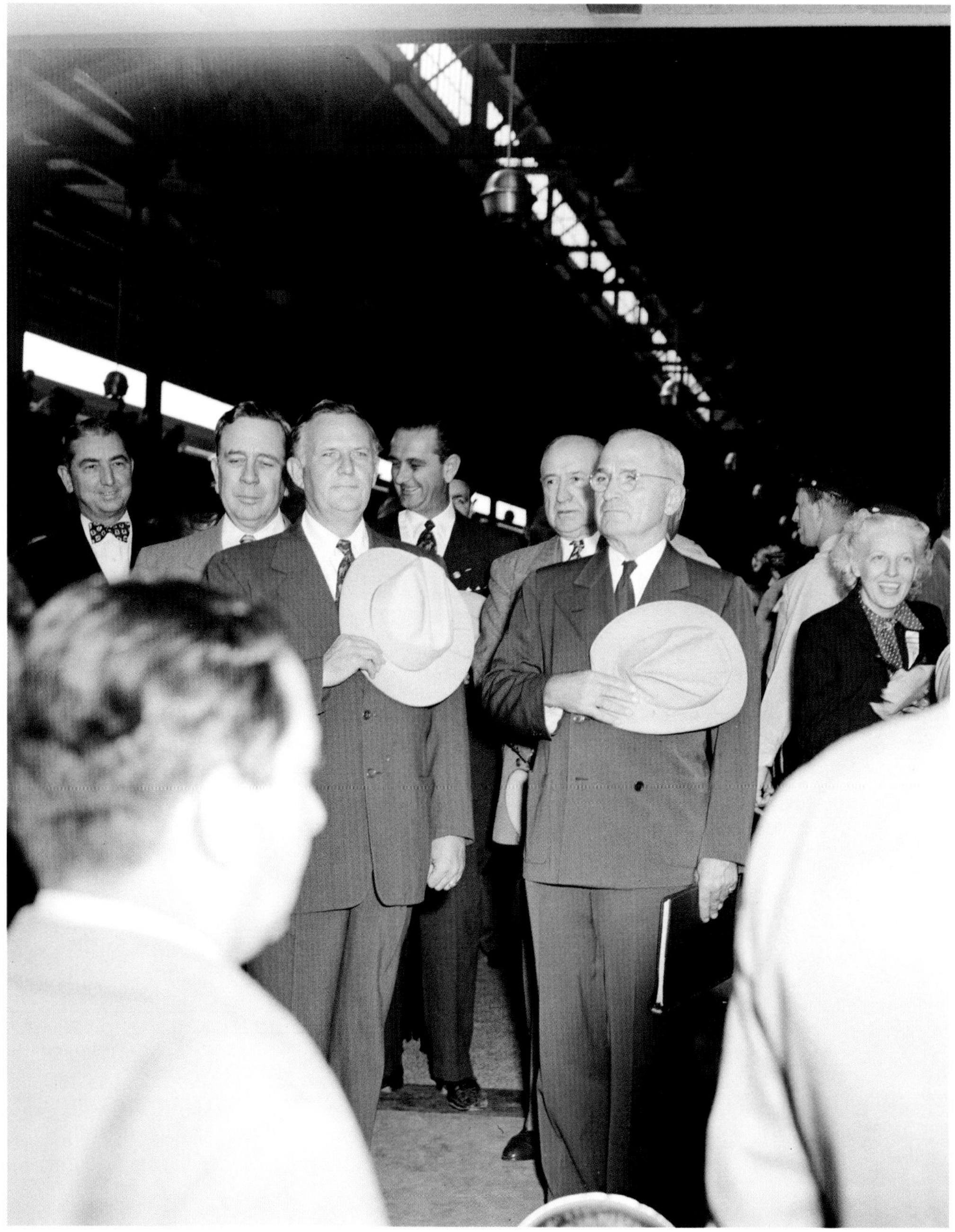

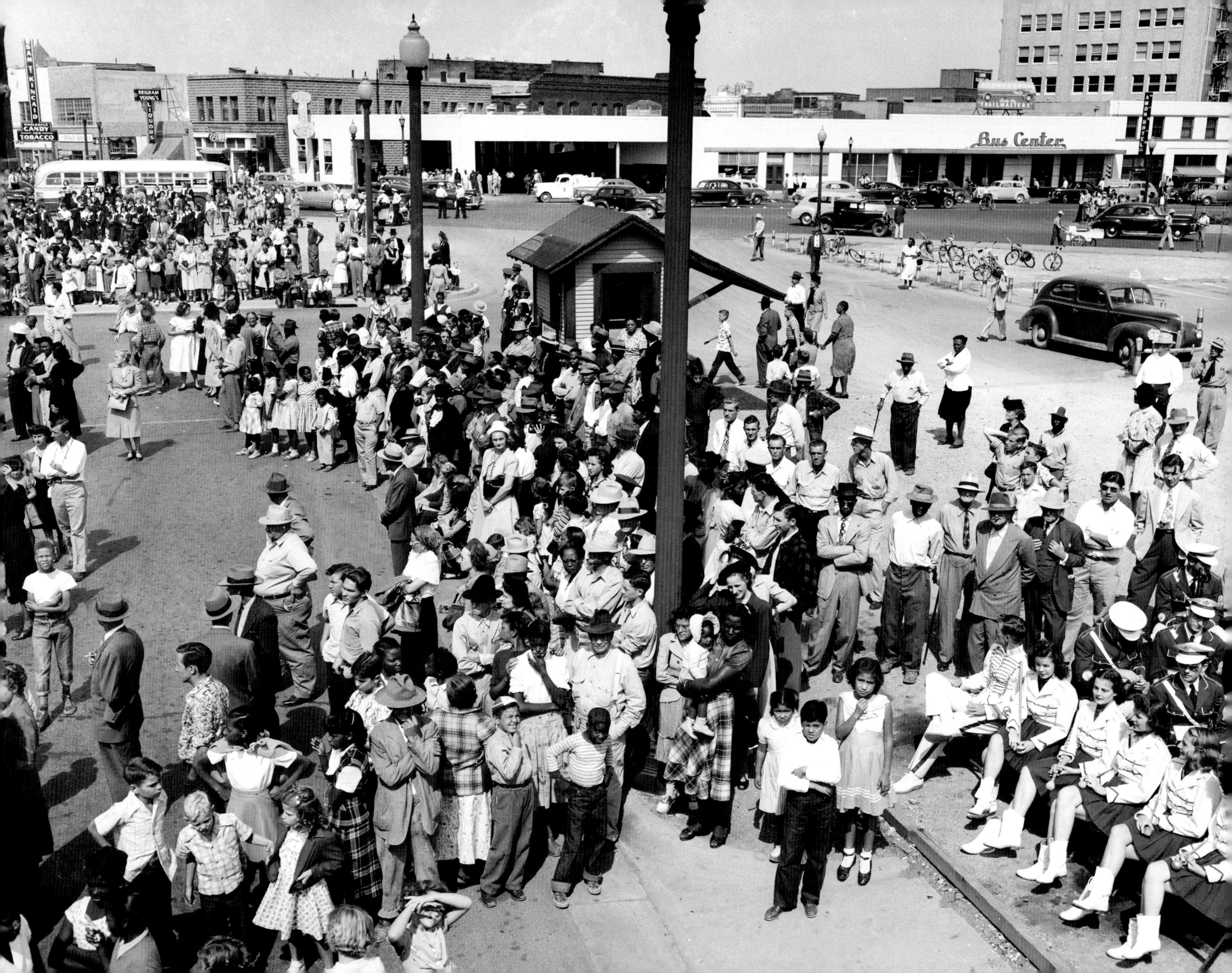
SAM T. KINCAID
WHOLESALE
CANDY
AND
TOBACCO
BRIGHAM YOUNG'S
LIQUORS
TRAILMASTERS
Bus Center

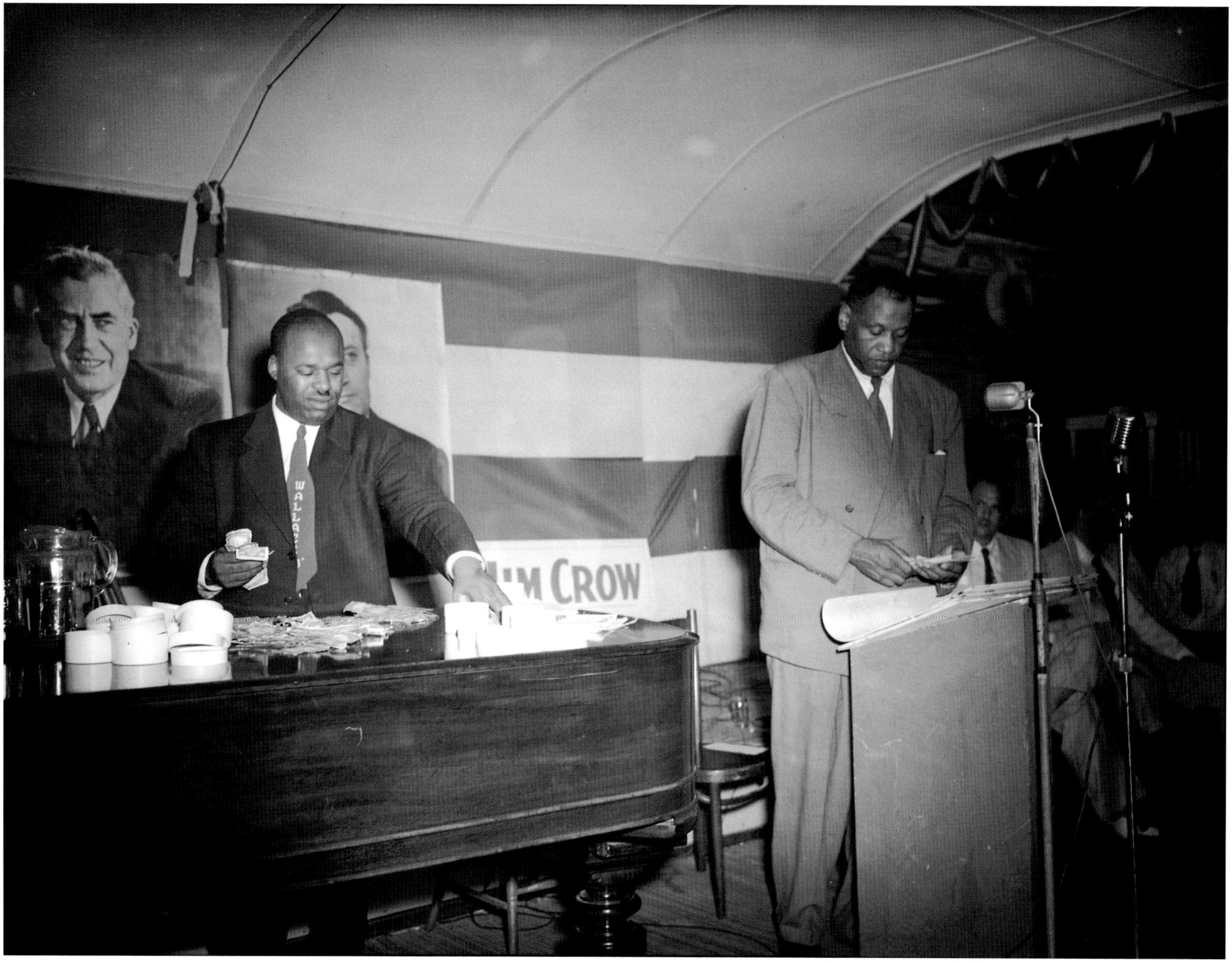
CROW

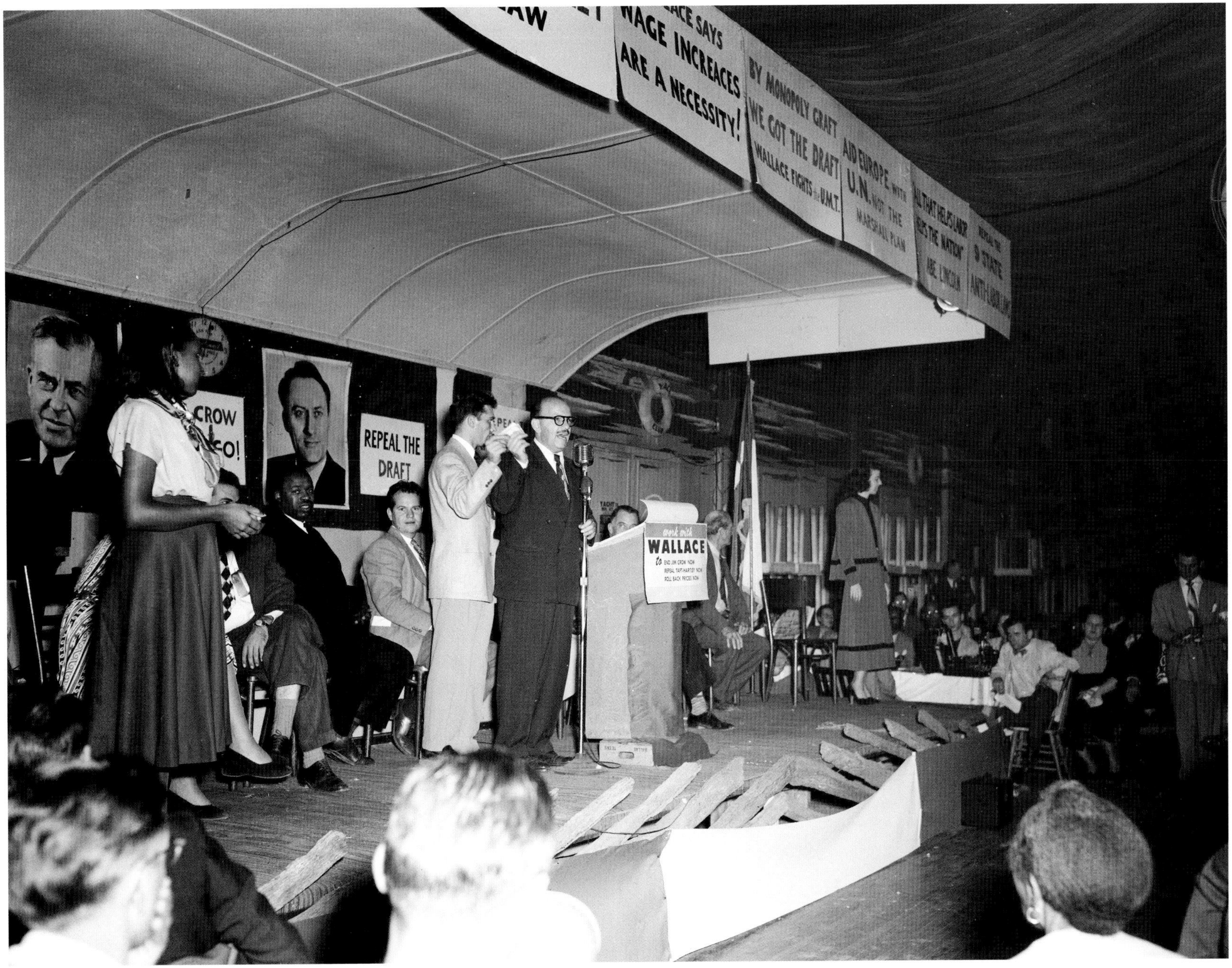
WAGE INCREACES
ARE A NECESSITY!
BY MONOPOLY GRAFT
WE GOT THE DRAFT
AID EUROPE WITH
U.N. NOT THE
MARSHALL PLAN
REPEAL THE
DRAFT
WALLACE

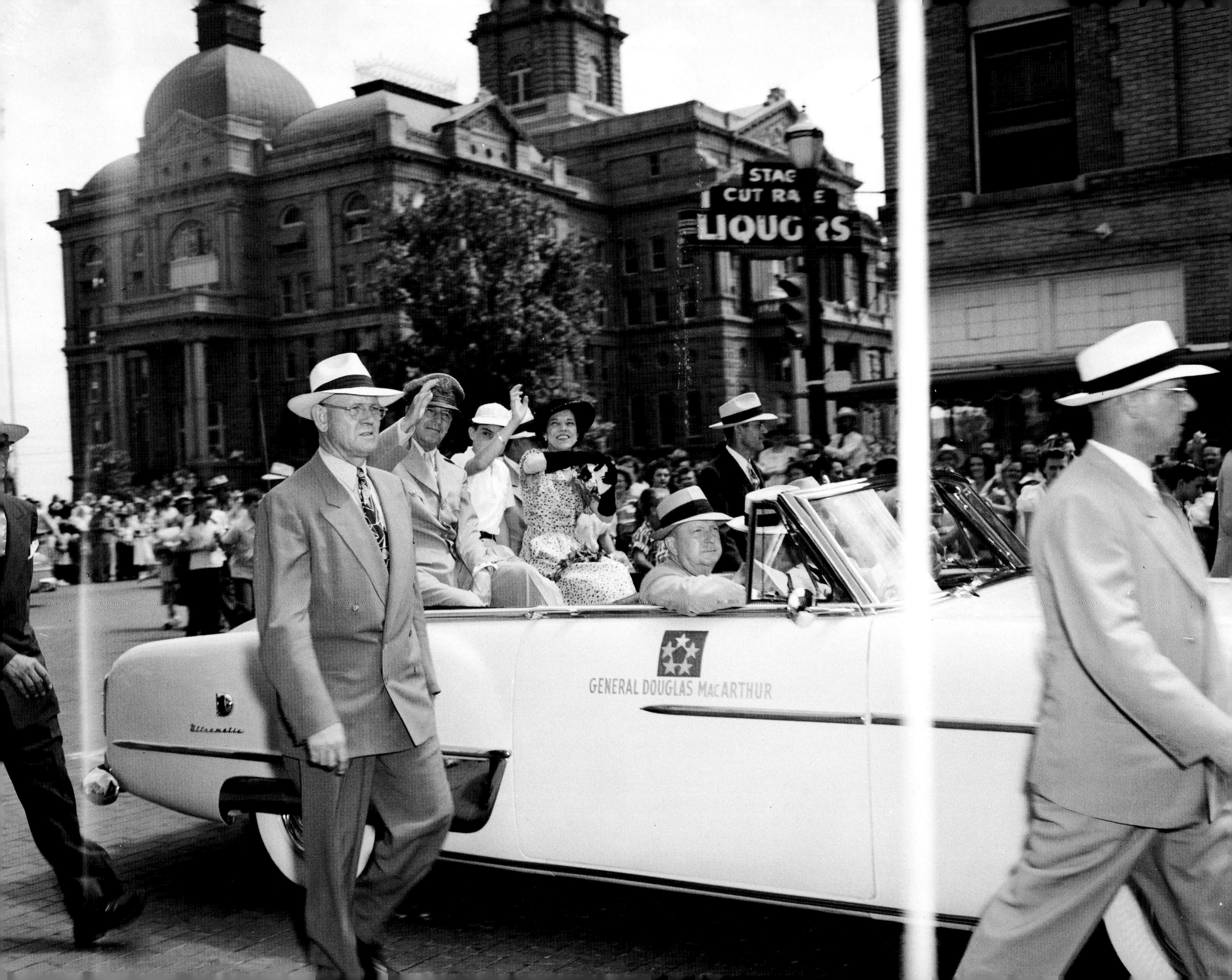
STAG
CUT RATE
LIQUORS
GENERAL DOUGLAS MacARTHUR
Ultramatic

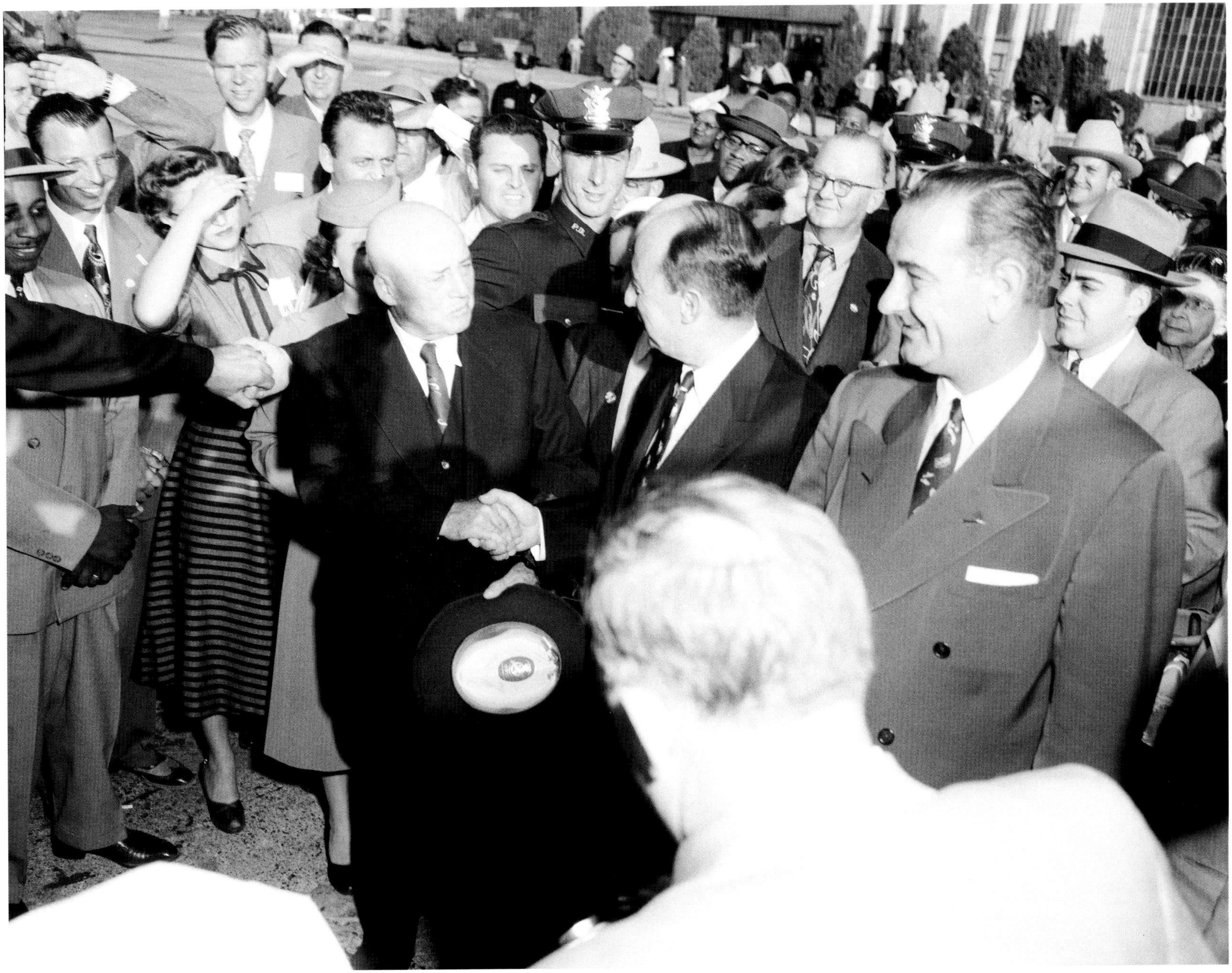

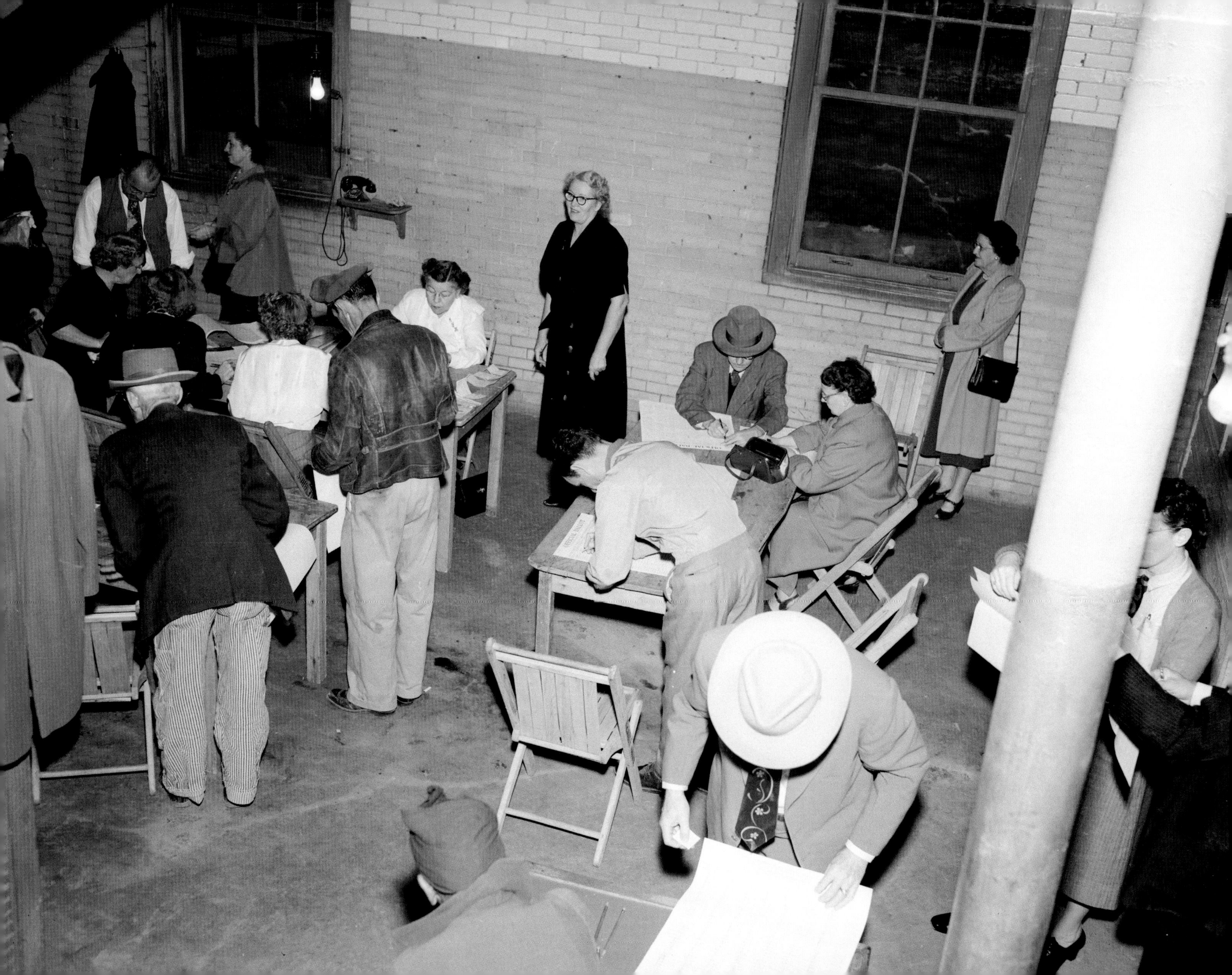

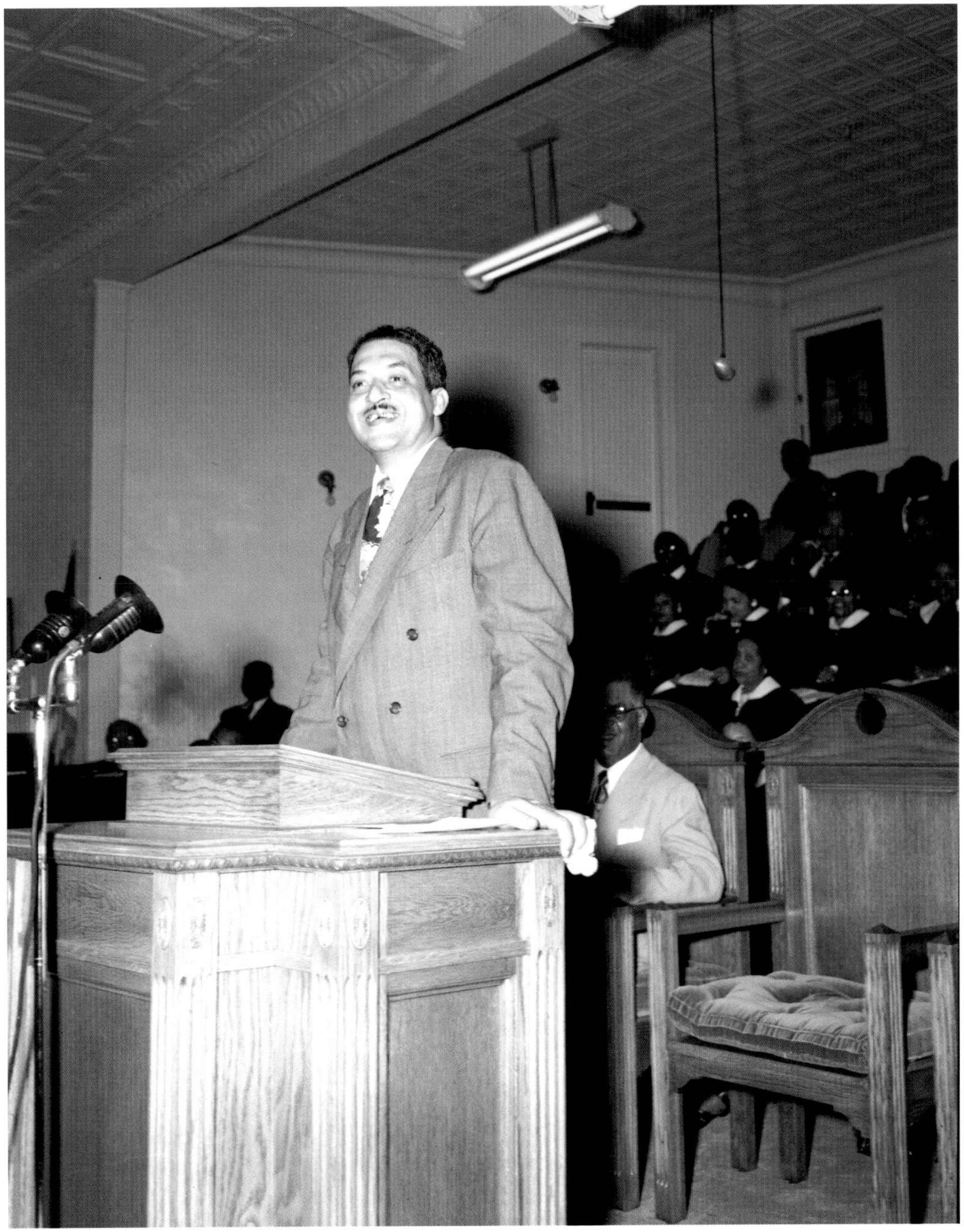

Far Left: Voters and election workers at a voting precinct in Fort Worth, 1952.

Left: Thurgood Marshall giving a speech at the 1954 NAACP convention, Dallas, July 1954.

Right: *U. N. Ambassador Ralph Bunche speaking at the NAACP convention, Dallas, July 1954.*

Far Right: Ralph Bunche being interviewed at Love Field, Dallas, July 1954. With him are, from left: Dr. R. A. Ransom, C. W. Flint Jr., and Ollis Malloy.

Next Page, Left: Dr. Martin Luther King greeting a woman at the Majestic Theater in downtown Fort Worth. The woman next to Dr. King is Mrs. Vada Felder, who had invited him to the city.

Next Page, Right: With Dr. King at Love Field are, from left: Brother Kirby Holmes, Mrs. Vada Felder, singer Francine Reese Morrison, two unidentified people, Fannie Mae Williams, and Reverend Calvin Browning.

Following Page, Left: Dr. King visiting Dr. Aurelia Harris' home in Fort Worth, with gospel artist Francine Morrison seated on Dr. King's left. At left is R. L. "Pie" Melton of The Fort Worth Mind. *Dr. Harris is the second woman from right, seated on the edge of sofa, and the Reverend Ahnin H. Forbes on right, October 22, 1959.*

Following Page, Right: President John F. Kennedy and First Lady Jacqueline Kennedy departing Air Force One upon arrival at Carswell Air Force Base, Fort Worth, November 21, 1963.

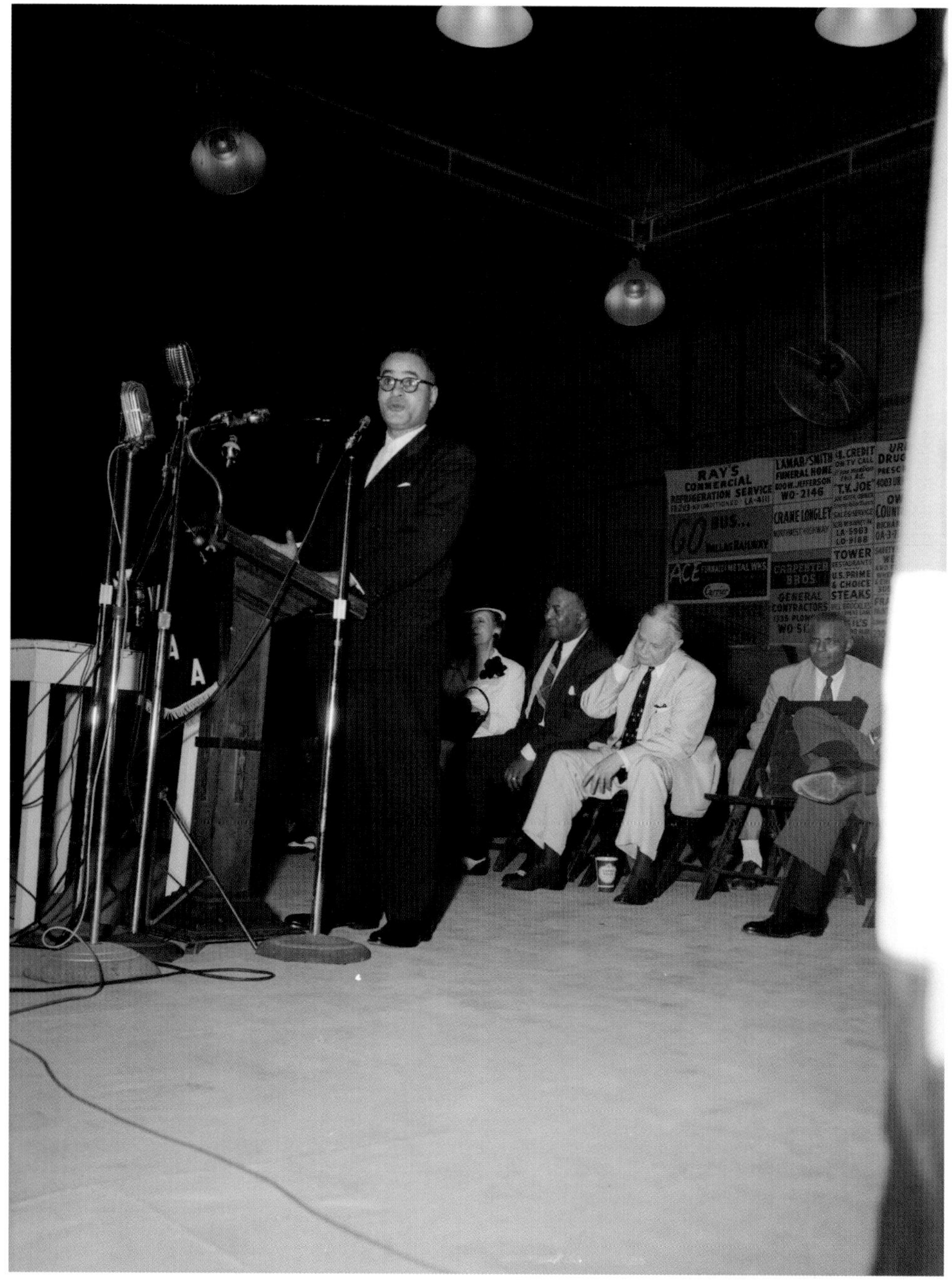

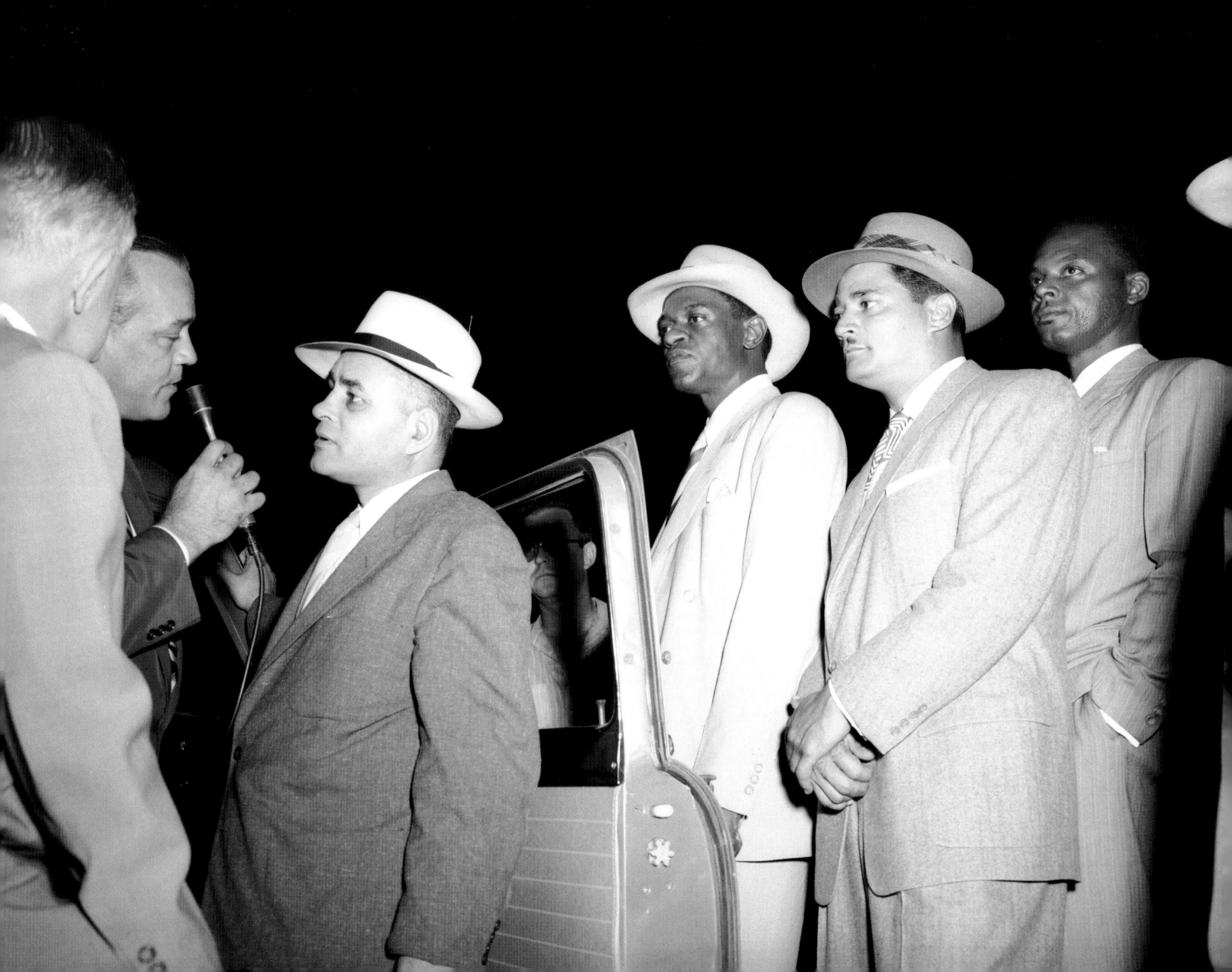

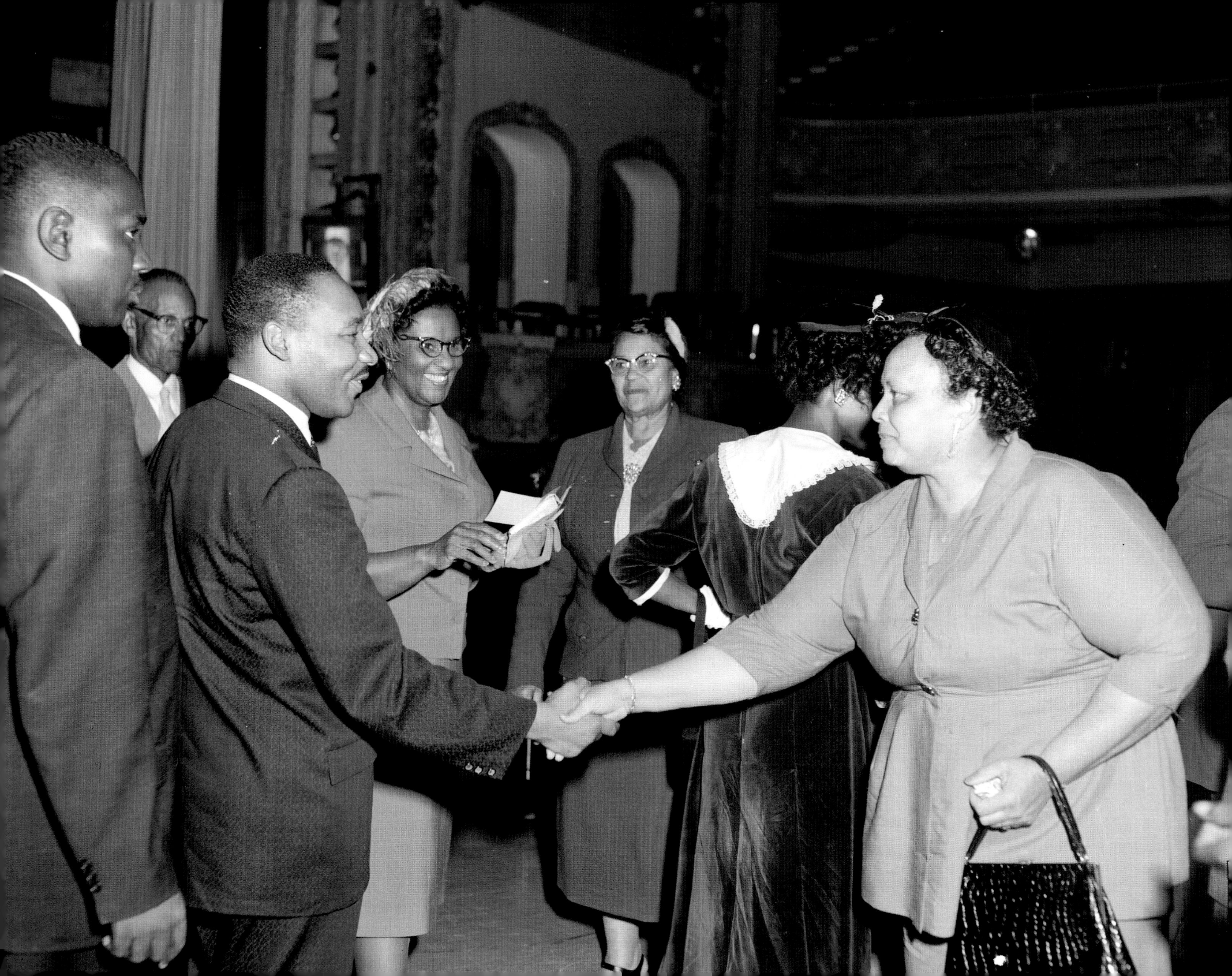

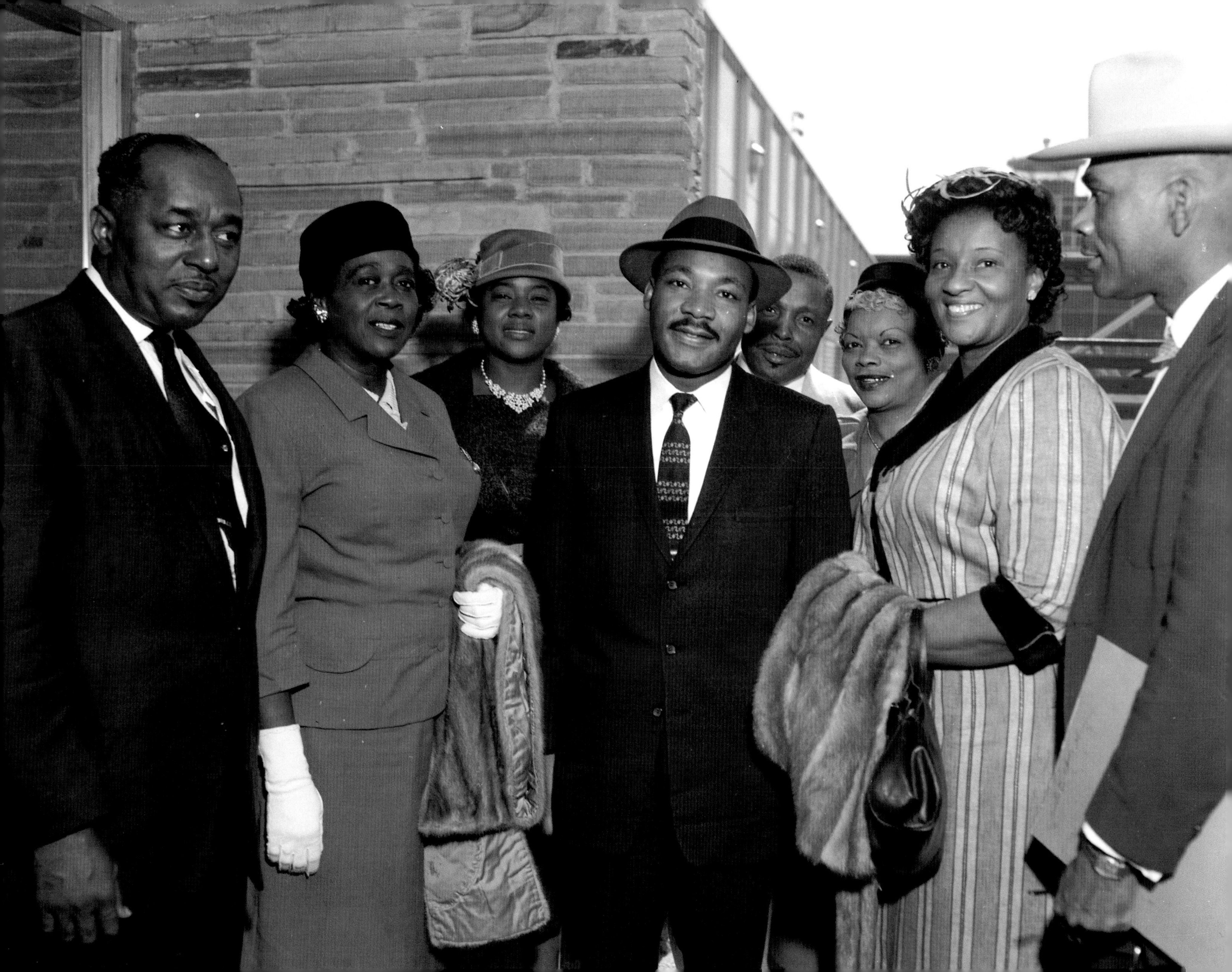

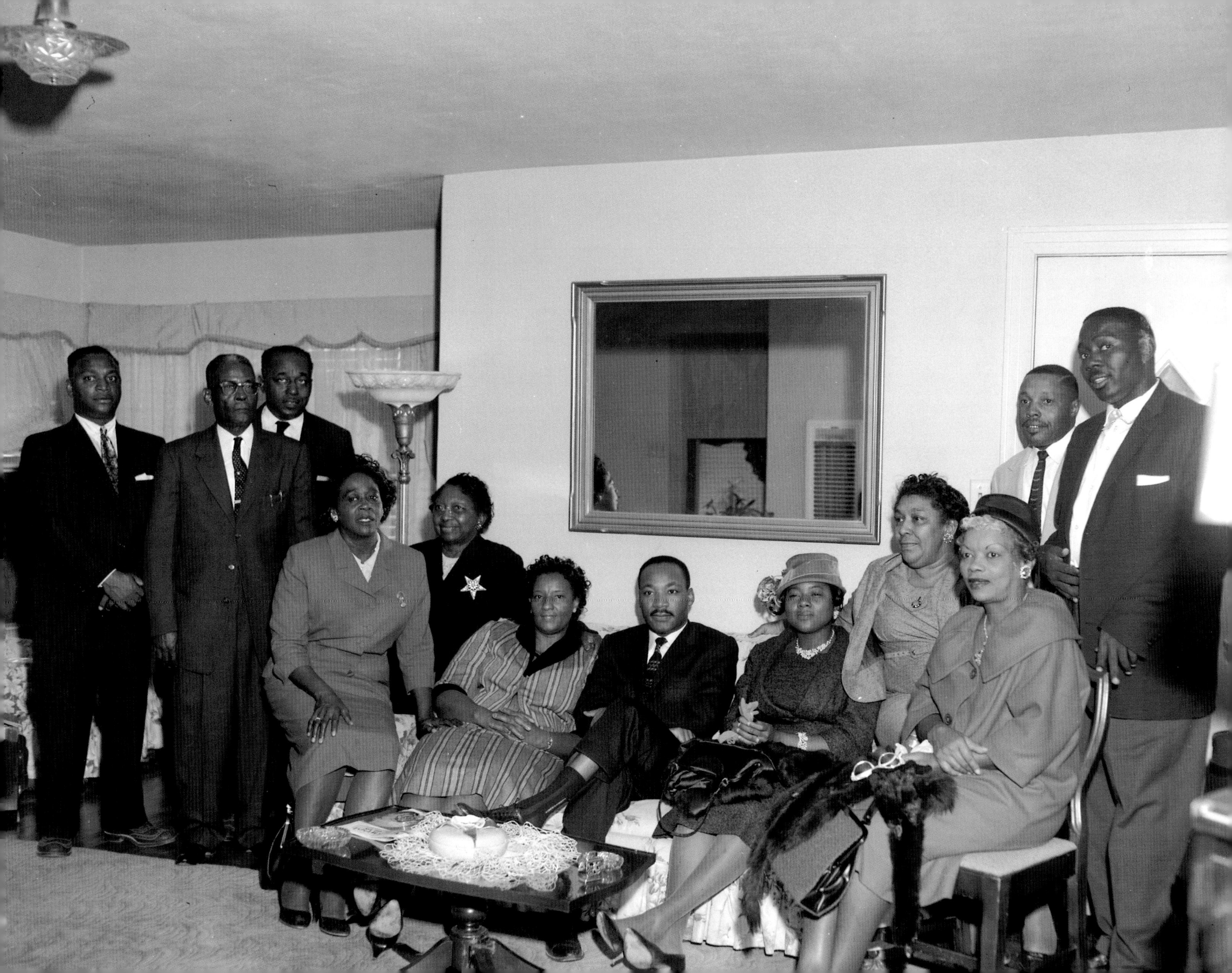

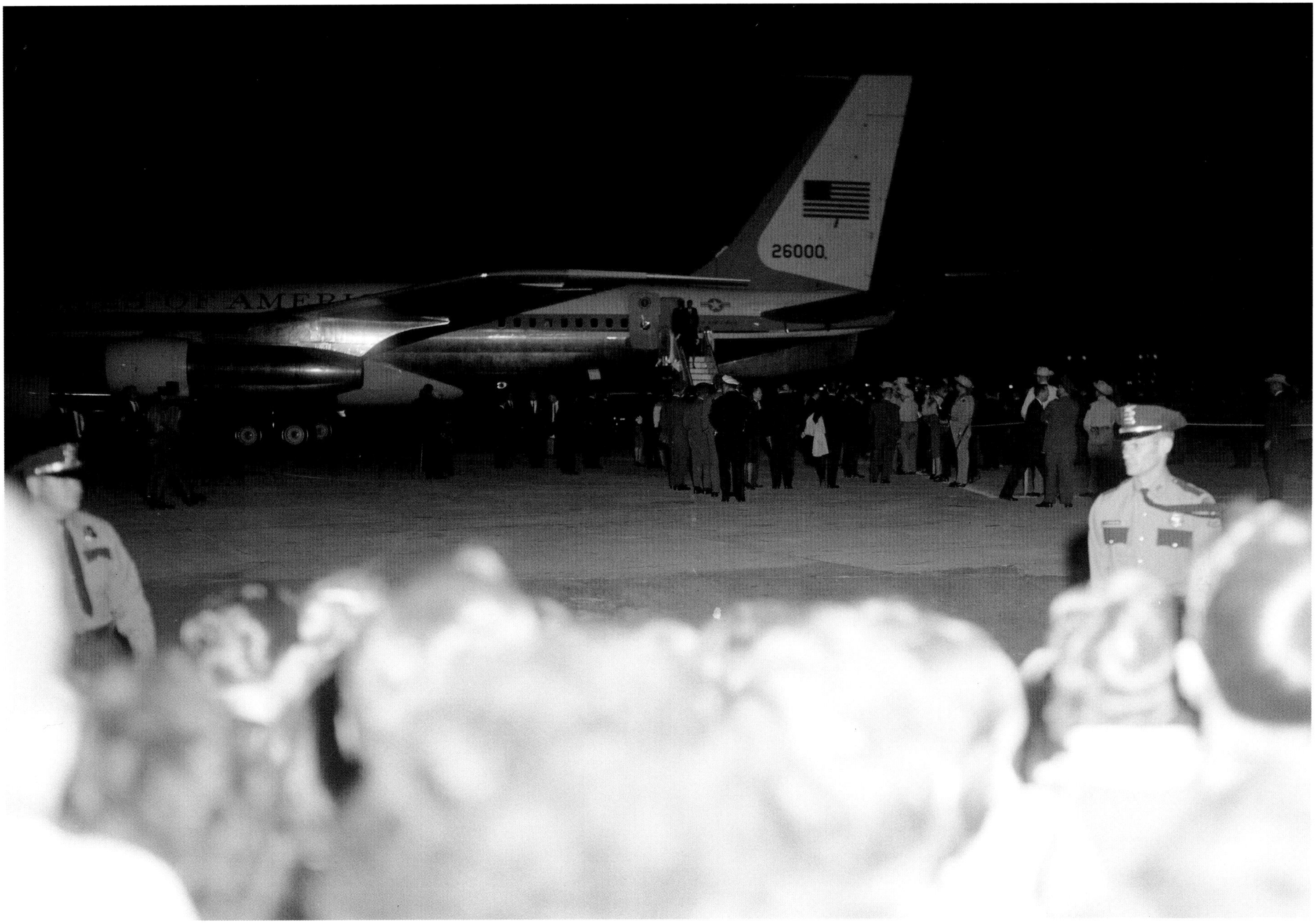
26000

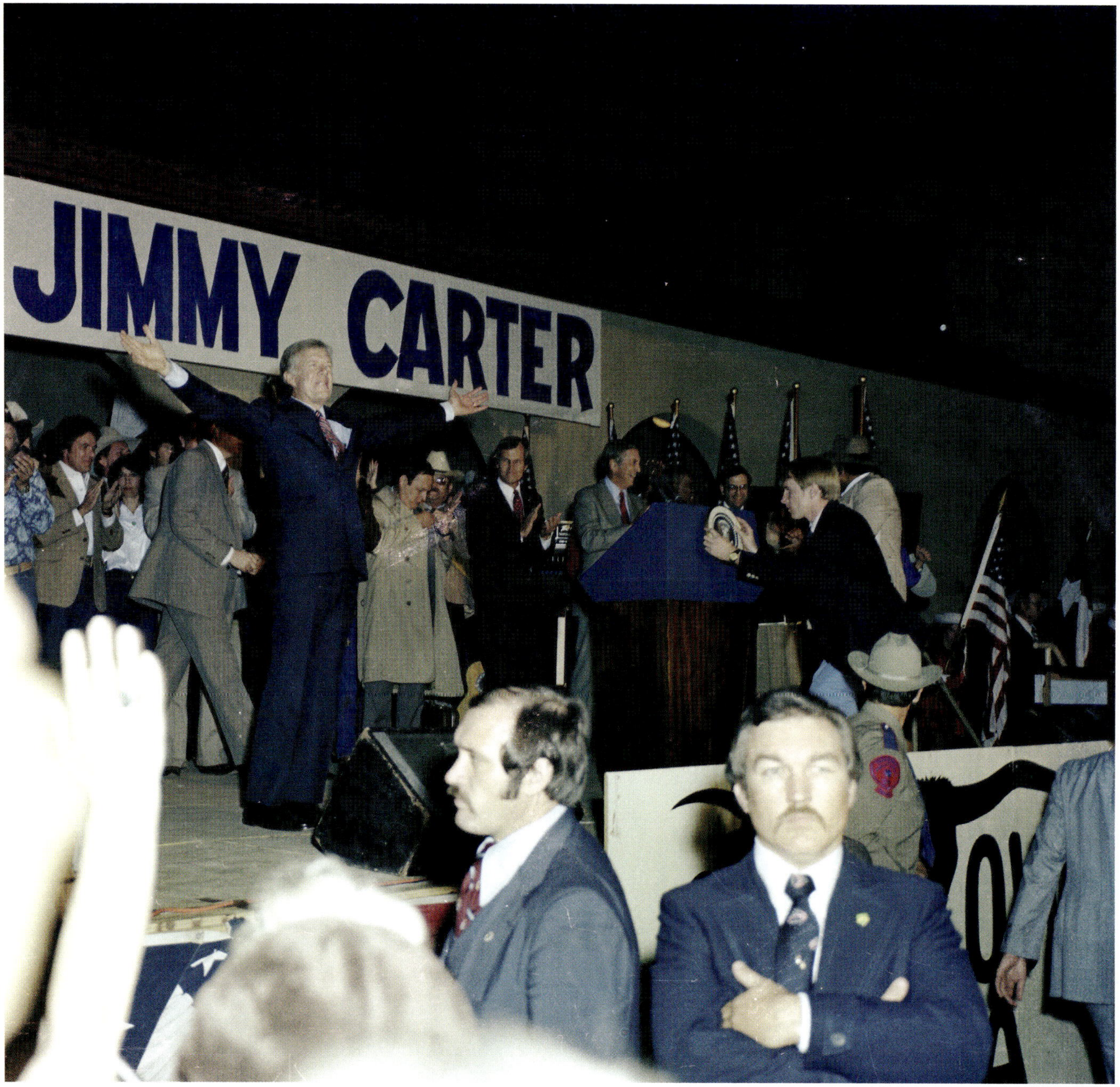
JIMMY CARTER

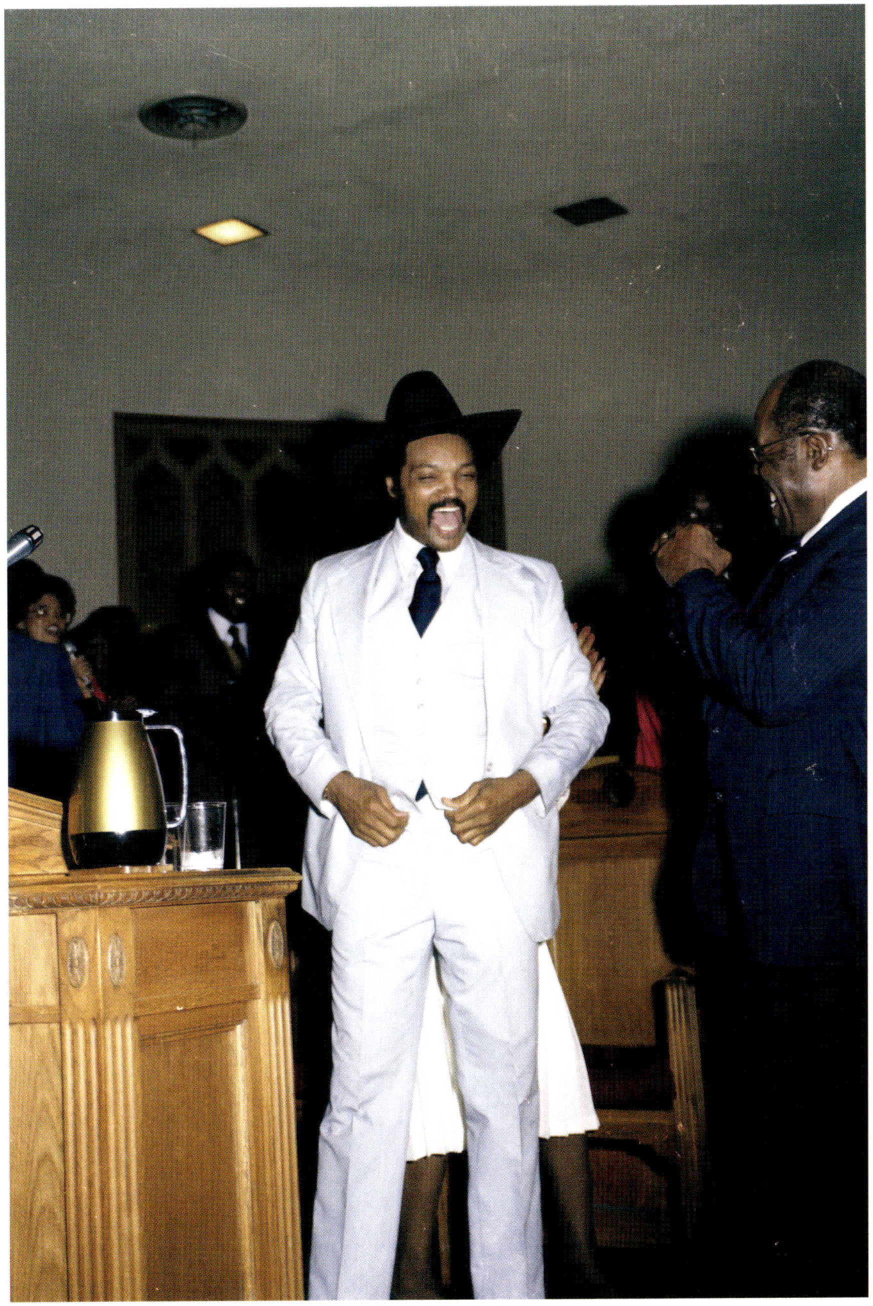

Far Left: President Jimmy Carter at campaign rally at Fort Worth Stockyards, 1980.

Left: The Reverend Jesse Jackson, 1980.

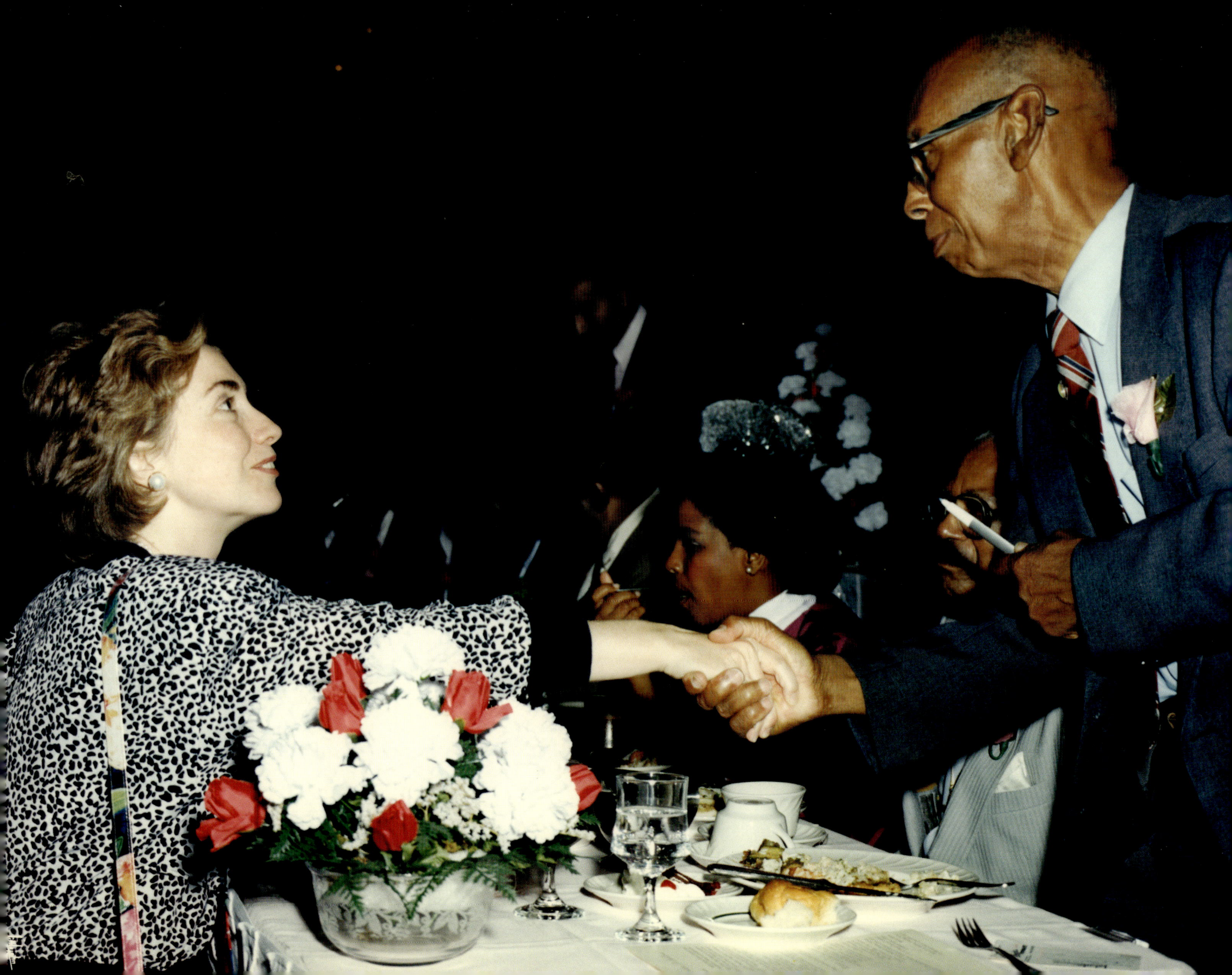

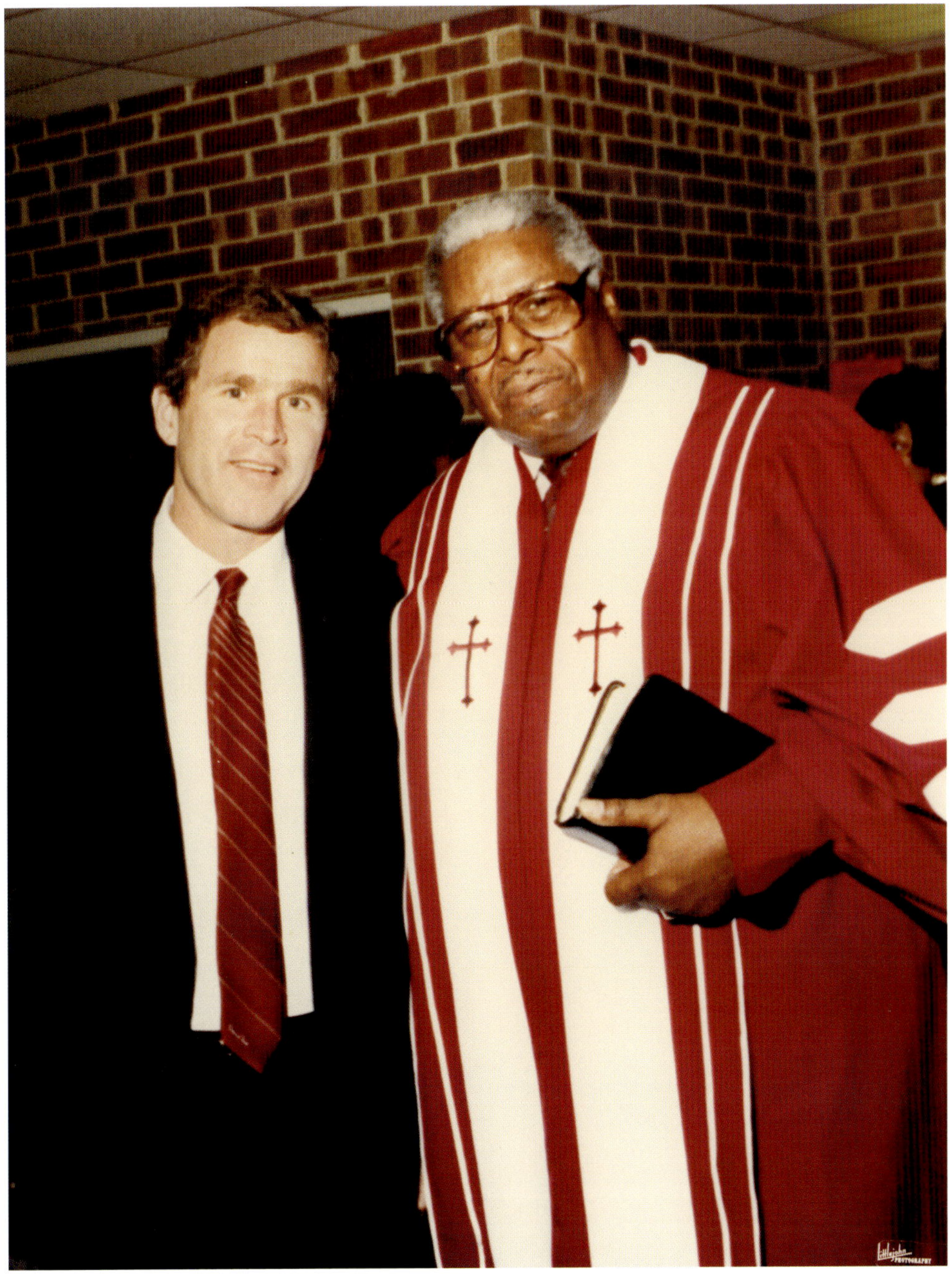

Far Left: Hillary Clinton, c. 1986.

Left: George W. Bush at Mt. Olive Baptist Church in Arlington, with the church's pastor, Reverend N. L. Robinson, 1991.

LIST OF IMAGES

All images are from the Calvin Littlejohn Photographic Archive at the Dolph Briscoe Center for American History, The University of Texas at Austin. *(The number is the Center's electronic file name.)*

Hardee Funeral Home, August 20, 1950. e_cl_0321.

Page 46 Jazz saxophonist Illinois Jacquet (left) at the Flint Hotel, with C. W. Flint, Jr. e_cl_0024.

Page 47 A soldier's funeral at Baker Funeral Home, April 6, 1949. e_cl_0267.

Page 48 Rodger Payne, pharmacist, at work at Payne's Drug Store, c. 1949. e_cl_0149.

Page 49 Ethel Ransom Memorial Hospital, c. 1940. e_cl_0160.

Page 50 Mrs. Lucille Smith demonstrating Lucille's Hot Roll Mix, Dallas grocery store, March 18, 1950. e_cl_0155.

Page 51 U. S. Smith's Famous Bar-B-Q building and parking lot, located on the city's North Side. e_cl_0157.

Page 52 Customers in the main lobby of Fraternal Bank and Trust, 1950. e_cl_0135.

Page 53 Two women seated in the school room of Dickerson's Beauty School, located on Rosedale Street and Illinois Avenue. e_cl_0137.

Page 54 Fashion Dress Shop—Mrs. Bertha Mitchell, proprietor, is on the right. March 9, 1951. e_cl_0201.

Page 55 A "George Washington Tea" at Dickerson's Beauty School. e_cl_0199.

Page 56 Dickerson's Beauty School, February 22, 1949. e_cl_0200.

Page 57 Barbershop owner Homer Williams at work, 1951. e_cl_0161.

Page 58 Mrs. Robinson's grandson, studio portrait, December 10, 1950. e_cl_0060.

Page 59 Pee Wee's Shoe Shop on Terrell Avenue, December 29, 1959. e_cl_0152.

Page 60 Milbane Grocery on New York Avenue, 1954. e_cl_0147.

Page 61 Fresh Air Taxi Stand on Magnolia Avenue. e_cl_0141.

Page 62 Mr. U. S. Smith, studio portrait in chef's uniform, March 23, 1949. e_cl_0100.

Page 63 Bill "Gooseneck" McDonald, founder and president of Fraternal Bank and Trust, seated at the desk in his office, 1950. e_cl_0101.

Page 64 Brothers Oscar Cooper, Jr., (left) and Lonnell Cooper (center) with friend Hugh Talton at the main bar of the Jim Hotel in downtown Fort Worth, 1947. Lonnell Cooper became one of the first black police officers hired by the city of Fort Worth in the 1950s. The hotel was owned by brothers Oscar Cooper, Sr., and Levi Cooper. e_cl_0143.

Page 65 Flint Hotel, 1400 Jones Street, 1949. e_cl_0139.

Page 66 The soda fountain counter at Dr. Ransom's Drug Store. The man in the photo is Dr. R. A. Ransom, Sr. The woman on his right is his wife Davila. e_cl_0154.

Page 67 Dr Pepper commercial, May 1980. e_cl_0286.

Page 68 High Hat Beauty Salon demonstration, October 18, 1965. e_cl_0296.

Page 69 Children at Randel Howard's Laundromat, 1989. e_cl_0291.

Page 72 Herman Milton, studio portrait, December 22, 1948. e_cl_0057.

Page 73 Mechanics, c. 1941. e_cl_0334.

Page 74 Mr. Paris Holmes, car wreck, January 10, 1956. e_cl_0266.

Page 75 The first black graduates of Fort Worth's Police School, January 1951. From left: Charles Wright, Jack Gray, Benny Griffin, and Travis Bell. e_cl_0268.

Page 76 Fort Worth Urban League's Red Feather Parade, October 15, 1949. e_cl_0210.

Page 77 Soldier, studio portrait, September 3, 1948. e_cl_0058.

Page 78 Masons' Party—Harold Baker (of Baker Funeral Home family) is at left; Lonnie "Fat" Dixon is center, December 4, 1948. e_cl_0236.

Page 79 Black Masons in Fort Worth prepare to distribute boxes at Christmas time, 1965. e_cl_0277.

Page 80 Homer Williams, a barber, is the man in the wheelchair. He is pictured in other photos. e_cl_0303.

Page 81 The Fort Worth Urban League's Red Feather Parade, October 15, 1949. In the center is C. R. "Coot" Wise, one of the owners of *The Fort Worth Mind*, a black weekly newspaper. e_cl_0209.

Page 82 Two men sitting on dry land near flooded street and houses in the Rock Island Bottom neighborhood Fort Worth, May 17, 1949. e_cl_0168.

Page 83 Man with two horses riding through a flooded street in front of homes in the Rock Island Bottom neighborhood, Fort Worth, May 17, 1949. e_cl_0165.

Page 84 Women standing on dry ground looking out over flooded street and homes in the Rock Island Bottom neighborhood, May 17, 1949. e_cl_0166.

Page 85 Golfers at Worth Hills Golf Course, June 19, 1951. e_cl_0213.

Page 86 Bathing beauty at the Rosedale Apartments. e_cl_0243.

Page 87 Children with hula hoops at the Fort Worth Recreation Center, November 16, 1958. e_cl_0244.

Page 88 Boy Scouts, November 1964. e_cl_0275.

Page 89 Boy Scouts, December 5, 1964. e_cl_0276.

Page 90 Mrs. Opal Roland's children with Christmas tree at their home on Terrell Avenue, December 26, 1950. e_cl_0304.

Page 91 Mrs. Roland's children with bicycles and Christmas tree, 1954. e_cl_0246

Page 92 Studio portrait of a girl, for Christmas cards, December 8, 1949. e_cl_0309.

Page 93 Turner baby, March 1, 1949. e_cl_0253.

Page 94 Mrs. E. A. White and sisters, studio portrait. e_cl_0255.

Page 95 Girl and doll, December 31, 1949. e_cl_0305.

Page 96 Studio portrait of a girl, August 30, 1949. e_cl_0258.

Page 97 Rev. Albert E. Chew, Cynthia Cook, Marguerite J. Johnson, May 27, 1961. e_cl_0273.

Page 98 Dillie Mae Wilson, studio portrait, May 10, 1950. e_cl_0299.

Page 99 Mr. and Mrs. R. L. Wormley and family, December 21, 1954. e_cl_0252.

Page 100 Williams boy on tricycle, October 1949. e_cl_0251.

Page 101 R. L. Taylor's children, March 31, 1960. e_cl_0249

Page 102 Studio portrait of a couple, December 3, 1949. e_cl_0063.

Page 103 Mr. and Mrs. Edwin Thomas and family, studio portrait, December 9, 1959. e_cl_0067.

Page 104 Birthday party, 1951. e_cl_0237.

Page 105 Birthday party, January 1953. e_cl_0263.

Page 106 Mrs. Edmonds' three children. e_cl_0240.

Page 107 Birthday party, perhaps for a child or grandchild of Thomas "Snooks" Russell, a Como civic leader, bail bondsman, and funeral director, 1956. e_cl_0262.

Page 108 Playground in Central City, 1971. e_cl_0294.

Page 109 Playground in Central City, 1971. e_cl_0295.

Page 110 Zeta Phi Beta Sorority Party. Most of the people pictured are educators, principals, and teachers. Seated is Mrs. Versia L. Williams who was principal of the "colored" Riverside Elementary School, which was later named for her. Standing at left is Mrs. Maude Logan, who also would have a school named for her. e_cl_0235.

Page 111 Twenty-fifth-anniversary party, 1950s. e_cl_0272.

Page 112 Bride, studio portrait, 1980s. e_cl_0287

Page 113 Eastern Stars honoring Mrs. Burnett (first name unknown) for forty-two years of service. Hortense Chapman is on left. e_cl_0234.

Page 114 Four women at home on Wainwright Drive in the Stop Six neighborhood. e_cl_0265.

Page 115 Funeral for Mrs. Maggie B. Cary, the "First Lady" of Rising Star Baptist Church where her husband, the Reverend Smith Cary (seated on front row left) was the pastor. Their son, Reby Cary, would become the first black school board member in Fort Worth, the first black administrator at UT-Arlington and one of the first blacks elected to the state legislature from Tarrant County. e_cl_0184.

Page 116 Funeral of Dr. Riley Andrew Ransom, Jr., held Wednesday, June 6, 1963, at 2:00 p.m., Greater St. James Baptist Church. Dr. Ransom died June 1, 1963, at Parkland Hospital, Dallas, after a long illness. e_cl_0330.

Page 117 Mr. Pressley Jones lying in state at Baker Funeral Home's reposing room. e_cl_0338.

Page 118 Funeral of Dr. Riley Andrew Ransom, Jr. e_cl_0331.

Page 119 Viewing for Mr. Wheat's aunt, October 9, 1952. Baker Funeral Home Chapel. e_cl_0341.

Page 120 Morris-Bates Funeral Home, July 4, 1965. e_cl_0349.

Page 121 Gray baby, Baker Funeral Home Chapel, March 1, 1951. e_cl_0344.

Page 122 Funeral at Morris-Bates Funeral Home, July 4, 1965. Sitting on the front row are, second from left, Herbert V. Baker and third from left, James N. Baker, Sr., owners of Baker Funeral Home. e_cl_0350.

Page 123 Lila Howard funeral, April 23, 1959. e_cl_0345.

Page 124 Unidentified funeral scene, not dated. e_cl_0332.

Page 125 Leroy Ford, an American Woodman, lies in state at Williams Funeral Home in Fort Worth. e_cl_0329.

Page 128 Congregation entering Paradise Baptist Church on opening of new sanctuary. e_cl_0052.

Page 129 Ribbon-cutting ceremony, Paradise Baptist Church. The church's pastor, the Reverend J. F. Singleton, is the man at right. e_cl_0054.

Page 130 Congregation gathering outside Paradise Baptist Church for the dedication. e_cl_0053.

Page 131 C. B. Spence standing by car at Mt. Rose Baptist Church, August 16, 1944. e_cl_0188.

Page 132 Mt. Zion Baptist Church delegation to the National Baptist Convention, September 14, 1958. e_cl_0324.

Page 133 Procession for the opening of the eighteenth National Sunday School and Young People's Union Congress, Fort Worth, June 22, 1950. e_cl_0031.

Page 134 St. Mark Missionary Baptist Church, located in the Stop Six neighborhood, 1952. e_cl_0047.

Page 135 Opening of church convention, truck with a sign reading, "We thank God for our President, Bishop A. B. Williams, who has led us for 18 yrs," Fort Worth, June 22, 1950. e_cl_0033.

Page 136 Morning Chapel CME Church, Easter picture. e_cl_0207.

Page 137 Christmas tree and Santa Claus at church, 1952. e_cl_0196.

Page 138 Congregation posing in front of the Immanuel Independent AME Church. e_cl_0038.

Page 139 Christmas tree at church, 1952. e_cl_0195.

Page 140 Mrs. Moch, Allen Chapel Church Queen, February 20, 1951. e_cl_0204.

Page 141 The Reverend H. R. Bradley, new pastor of Mount Pisgah Baptist Church, 1952. e_cl_0315.

Page 142 Morningside Methodist Church, cornerstone laying, February 16, 1964. e_cl_0280.

Page 143 In the center of this photo of the cornerstone laying for Morningside Methodist Church is Rev. Marshall Hodge, the church's first minister, who later became a leading civil rights advocate in Dallas. At right is Dr. Marion "Jack" Brooks, a leading Fort Worth physician and civil rights leader who was a founding member of the church. e_cl_0281.

Page 144 Annie Street Christian Church, children and caretakers in the nursery, 1952. Annie Street Christian later became Community Christian Church, which is now located at the corner of Riverside and Vickery. e_cl_0048.

Page 145 Children napping in the nursery at Annie Street Christian Church, 1952. e_cl_0049.

Page 146 Morningside Methodist Church, sign, March 1964. e_cl_0282.

Page 147 The Ferguson Bible Class. Mrs. Ferguson is seated on the right. e_cl_0206.

Page 148 Mount Pisgah Baptist Church Building, September 1969. e_cl_0319.

Page 149 Mount Pisgah Baptist Church Sunday School, August 6, 1948. e_cl_0318.

Page 150 Ayers Church, 1964. e_cl_0190.

Page 151 New edifice, St. Andrew's United Methodist Church, 1951.e_cl_0205.

Page 152 Mt. Zion Baptist Church delegation to National Baptist Convention, September 14, 1958. e_cl_0325.

Page 153 Baker Chapel AME choir, March 1953. e_cl_0203.

Page 154 Hillary Thomas, church wedding, August 11, 1964. e_cl_0278.

Page 155 Hillary Thomas, church wedding, bouquet toss, August 11, 1964. e_cl_0279.

Page 156 Allen Chapel AME baptism, 1969. e_cl_0290.

Page 157 Immanuel Independent AME Church, Rev. Brown and men in church service. e_cl_0039.

Page 160 Ruth Brown singing with band at Masonic Mosque, Fort Worth, November 14, 1959. e_cl_0016.

Page 161 Charles Brown playing with band at Masonic Mosque, Fort Worth, November 14, 1956. e_cl_0017.

Page 162 T. Bone Walker playing the guitar onstage, 1946. e_cl_0172.

Page 163 Nat "King" Cole in Fort Worth, 1950s. e_cl_0019.

Page 164 Lionel Hampton performance at the North Side Coliseum (now the Cowtown Coliseum), October 12, 1948. e_cl_0022.

Page 165 Part of the audience at the Lionel Hampton performance, October 12, 1948. e_cl_0023.

Page 166 Oscar Peterson Trio in Fort Worth, 1950s. e_cl_0025.

Page 167 Ella Fitzgerald singing with band onstage at the Philharmonic Club, Dallas, 1955. e_cl_0020

Page 168 Overflow crowd seated on the edge of the baseball field for the exhibition game of Jackie Robinson and the Brooklyn Dodgers, November 11, 1949. e_cl_0127.

Page 169 The photo, with woman holding up baseball, is great unto itself. But the man in the foreground is one of Fort Worth's most famous ministers, Brother Kirby Holmes. e_cl_0128.

Page 170 Jackie Robinson speaking into a microphone at LaGrave Field for an exhibition game, November 11, 1949.With him are, from left: Raymond L. "Pie" Melton, co-founder of The Fort Worth Mind, and James Clemons, well-known promoter and radio deejay. e_cl_0123.

Page 171 Boxer Joe Louis, left, Fort Worth, March 18, 1950. e_cl_0114.

Page 172 Mrs. Lucille Smith serving lunch to boxer Joe Louis, March 18, 1950. Seated at the table with Louis is H. L. King, principal of I. M. Terrell High School. R. L. "Pie" Melton, co-founder of The Fort Worth Mind, takes notes in the background. e_cl_0115.

Page 173 Joe Louis knocking down an opponent at a boxing exhibition, Fort Worth, March 18, 1950. e_cl_0118.

Page 174 Muhammad Ali at Dallas Black Business Expo, 1975. e_cl_0098

Page 175 Singer Janet Jackson receiving an award from teacher Lavern Rowe-Williams at Dunbar High School during an album promotional tour sponsored by KKDA-FM radio, 1983. e_cl_0027.

Page 178 President Harry S. Truman, Lyndon B. Johnson, Tom Clark, and Beauford Jester at a Truman campaign appearance, Fort Worth, September 27, 1948. e_cl_0098.

Page 179 Crowd gathered at the T&P Station for a speech by President Truman, Fort Worth, September 27, 1948. e_cl_0109.

Page 180 Paul Robeson giving a speech at a Progressive Party rally for Henry A. Wallace's presidential campaign, Dallas, August 10, 1948. e_cl_0006.

Page 181 Rally for the Henry A. Wallace Progressive Party campaign, Fort Worth, October 29, 1948. e_cl_0113

Page 182 General Douglas MacArthur and family riding in a downtown Fort Worth parade, June 16, 1951. e_cl_0111.

Page 183 Senator Adlai Stevenson shaking hands with Sam Rayburn while campaigning with Lyndon Johnson in Fort Worth, October 1952. e_cl_0112.

Page 184 Voters and election workers at a voting precinct in Fort Worth, 1952. e_cl_0169.

Page 185 Thurgood Marshall giving a speech at the 1954 NAACP convention, Dallas, July 1954. e_cl_0004.

Page 186 U. N. Ambassador Ralph Bunche speaking at the NAACP convention, Dallas, July 1954. e_cl_0010.

Page 187 Ralph Bunche being interviewed at Love Field, Dallas, July 1954. With him are, from left: Dr. R. A. Ransom, C. W. Flint Jr., and Ollis Malloy. e_cl_0008.

Page 188 Dr. Martin Luther King greeting a woman at the Majestic Theater in downtown Fort Worth. The woman next to Dr. King is Mrs. Vada Felder, who had invited him to the city. e_cl_0259.

Page 189 With Dr. King at Love Field are, from left: Brother Kirby Holmes, Mrs. Vada Felder, singer Francine Reese Morrison, two unidentified people, Fannie Mae Williams, and Reverend Calvin Browning. e_cl_0001.

Page 190 Dr. King visiting Dr. Aurelia Harris' home in Fort Worth, with gospel artist Francine Morrison seated on Dr. King's left. At left is R. L. "Pie" Melton of The Fort Worth Mind. Dr. Harris is the second woman from right, seated on the edge of sofa, and the Reverend Ahnin H. Forbes on right, October 22, 1959. e_cl_0003.

Page 191 President John F. Kennedy and First Lady Jacqueline Kennedy departing Air Force One upon arrival at Carswell Air Force Base, Fort Worth, November 21, 1963. e_cl_0110.

Page 192 President Jimmy Carter at campaign rally at Fort Worth Stockyards, 1980. e_cl_0093.

Page 193 The Reverend Jesse Jackson, 1980. e_cl_0096.

Page 194 Hillary Clinton, c. 1986. e_cl_0283.

Page 195 George W. Bush at Mt. Olive Baptist Church in Arlington, with the church's pastor, Reverend N. L. Robinson, 1991. e_cl_0284.

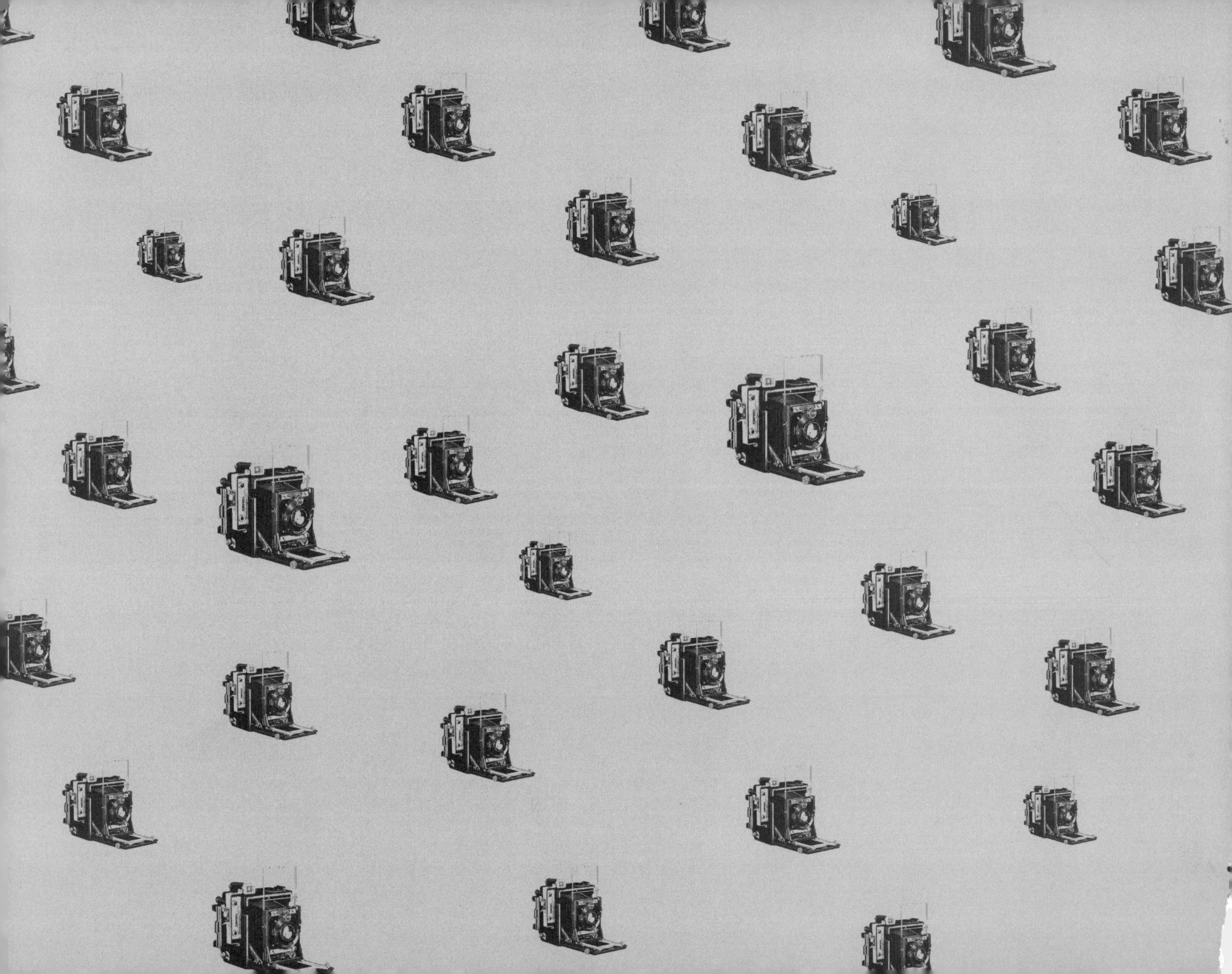